Dear Rabbi Mintz,

With thanks
For your friendship

ידידך

Pesach v. Kol

ArtScroll Series™

Rabbi Nosson Scherman / Rabbi Meir Zlotowitz
General Editors

by the author of
The Maggid Speaks, Around the Maggid's Table, In the Footsteps of the Maggid, Along the Maggid's Journey, Echoes of the Maggid, Reflections of the Maggid, In the Spirit of the Maggid, Traveling with the Maggid, Perspectives of the Maggid, and Bris Milah

Published by
Mesorah Publications, ltd

Rabbi Paysach J. Krohn

Enthralling Stories
of Inspiration and
Introspection

FIRST EDITION
First Impression ... November 2012

Published and Distributed by
MESORAH PUBLICATIONS, LTD.
4401 Second Avenue / Brooklyn, N.Y 11232

Distributed in Europe by
LEHMANNS
Unit E, Viking Business Park
Rolling Mill Road
Jarow, Tyne & Wear, NE32 3DP
England

Distributed in Australia and New Zealand
by **GOLDS WORLDS OF JUDAICA**
3-13 William Street
Balaclava, Melbourne 3183
Victoria, Australia

Distributed in Israel by
SIFRIATI / A. GITLER — BOOKS
6 Hayarkon Street
Bnei Brak 51127

Distributed in South Africa by
KOLLEL BOOKSHOP
Northfield Centre, 17 Northfield Avenue
Glenhazel 2192, Johannesburg, South Africa

ARTSCROLL SERIES™
IN THE SPLENDOR OF THE MAGGID
© Copyright 2012, by MESORAH PUBLICATIONS, Ltd.
4401 Second Avenue / Brooklyn, N.Y. 11232 / (718) 921-9000 / www.artscroll.com

---

ALL RIGHTS RESERVED
The text, prefatory and associated textual contents and introductions
— including the typographic layout, cover artwork and ornamental graphics —
have been designed, edited and revised as to content, form and style.

No part of this book may be reproduced
IN ANY FORM, PHOTOCOPYING, OR COMPUTER RETRIEVAL SYSTEMS
— even for personal use without written permission from
the copyright holder, Mesorah Publications Ltd.
except by a reviewer who wishes to quote brief passages
in connection with a review written for inclusion in magazines or newspapers.

THE RIGHTS OF THE COPYRIGHT HOLDER WILL BE STRICTLY ENFORCED.

ISBN 10: 1-4226-1323-2 / ISBN 13: 978-1-4226-1323-8

Typography by CompuScribe at ArtScroll Studios, Ltd.
Printed in the United States of America by Noble Book Press Corp.
Bound by Sefercraft, Quality Bookbinders, Ltd., Brooklyn N.Y. 11232

דוד קאהן　　　　　　　　　　　　　　　　ביהמ״ד גבול יעבץ
　　　　　　　　　　　　　　　　　　　　ברוקלין, נוא יארק

ב״ה

יקירי הרב ר' [...] שליט"א

לשמחה מה זו עושה...

הרצ"ב ותהלה לצ-ק - החיבור הלאחיני של מצוות
שאול, ומברך ותהלה בצדק. הלשון שאמרו בשמחות אמ, ב/לח
באמת שאמר מצוער עד ה' הבאים שיגיע לשמים וגבורית לאשר"ג
לא מצינו נאמרו בה שום דבר לשמחה שברי כל המשאול מבבר רבים
כך (שואל ובנו)... לשמחת תלקחת... ומס"פ ב כרנה לפתוח לפני דא ושלחו
בקא... לקלה לשמחת הבנצבת שרואו בן עולם ועני אלפים מצליחים הכא, וכלו
אורך שלאכות שמי וידעני שם הם מקשרים ליל, וידעת האסטוריה
שלמשה שוה לך?.

וכל חיין הם סמל איך שוואנות על ה' אולה שמועה לך מכאב
גדולות תקשואלא גם כתן הבגד הינן ונאת נתה הסס עליון גם כי
באחיני מקרב ב' בגביים שמך לו גם הבדר מובטחת אלך והיובלה
שכל עיין היום קנני שלום תקח תקנת את של עני של שמחת לסוצרת רבמי
לה פסק אתה לי עורא נותר עת לבל גבני שמחהת - אנא שר שלו

אוהבך הדורש השלמתך
ד׳ב קאהן
ח׳ מרחשון תשס"ג

Rabbi Shlomo Teitelbaum 85-30 124th Street Kew Gardens, NY 11415 (718) 847-9828	שמחה שלמה טייטלבוים קהל עדת יראים קיו גרדענס, נ.י. (718) 846-1571

בס"ד

ידידי הסופר וסיי"ן יגדלה את בריח אמרו"

מאתי ברכת לכבוד ידידי נפשי ידע מאוד
ונכבדי מופלא בית מדרשי הרב פאר יוסף
קרלבך שליט"א אשר כבר נעשיתי ז' שנה
ספרי המגיד התעלומים הנוראים שיש
והצלחה גדולה וכל מדת נעים ודעת מוכן
והוציא ספר שאין כמוהו לאצלה ארץ
בעבד וכן יוסיף להחיא לא שית לקחו
תאמינו שאמר דבר השם וקולו ברו
לברואים שליט בכתב הבעל עלאם הכרא
וכמו צדקת הרבים אלה יעשו לבריח
שי אברהם שלדין שאומר ישים ולשון דבר
צדקתם כן ינבה ד' ספרו לך השיני
ושאר ספרי להול אלה לגם הקדושים
ומתעסקים לא ספריו

ידי"נ מוקיר' באהבה בלב"ס

שלמה טייטלבוים

קהל נחלת יצחק ד'הומנא
CONGREGATION NACHLAS YITZCHOK
141-43 73RD AVENUE
KEW GARDENS, HILLS, N. Y. 11367

TEL. (718) 520-0115
FAX (718) 268-0186

NOACH ISAAC OELBAUM
RABBI
AUTHOR OF SEFORIM
MINCHAS CHEN

נח אייזיק אהלבוים
בעהמח"ס מנחת חן
רב ואב"ד דקהק נחלת יצחק
בקיו גארדענס הילס, נ.י.

[Handwritten Hebrew letter with rabbinical signature and official seal]

RABBI BINYOMIN EISENBERGER
1448 Fifty Sixth Street
Brooklyn, New York 11219

בנימין א. אייזענבערגער
רב דקהל היכל התפילה
ברוקלין, ניו יורק יצ"ו

בעזהשי"ת

מקום גדול הניחו מן השמים למע"כ ידי"ן הרב **פסח קראן שליט"א** להתגדר ולזכות את אחינו בנ"י בדרשותיו המעוררים ובספריו המעודדים - ושופכים מים טהורים וקרים על נפשות עייפות מאורך הגלות וטרדות הזמנים.

סיפר הרה"ק מרוזין זצ"ל, כי בעת שביקר את הרה"ק בעל אוהב ישראל מאפטא זצ"ל, אמר לו האוהב ישראל, שלפני ביאת המשיח יתגברו הנסיונות מאוד בענין אמונה, ויצטרכו רחמים מרובים שיוכלו להתחזק באמונת ה', ושאל הרוזינער, ומה יהיה העצה להנצל מנסיונות אלו? וע"ז השיבו: **"מען זאל רעדן פון צדיקים, אפי' פון אונז".**

אשריכם הרב פסח שליט"א שנפל בחלקכם לחזק אחב"י ובטוב טעם ודעת להכניס רוח חדשה ומרעננת בתוכינו, ע"י שהנכם גורמים – "מען זאל רעדן פון צדיקים" – וגם לרבות עובדות וסיפורים מ –צדקותיהם של אנשים מן השורה, שעליהם מאיר אור של "אפי' פון אונז" שאמר הרה"ק הנ"ל ברוב ענוותנותו.

יהי רצון שתזכו להמשיך להאיר לארץ ולדרים עליה, וגם ספר הנוכחי יזכה ל-**"בכל הארץ יצא קוום ובקצה תבל מליהם"**, להגדיל תורה ולהאדירה ולהרים קרן ישראל.

החותם באהבה ובכבוד הראוי

✍ Table of Contents

Author's Preface	13
Acknowledgments	15

Part A: Distinguished Sacred Deeds — 19

A Cup of Blessing	21
An End to a Means	23
To See and Remember	27
Commitments to a Covenant	29
Dressed for the Occasion	37
It Was Not Write	39
A Lesson for Life	41
Sick Leave	46
Tehillim Treasure	47
A Catskills Payback	49
First But Not Last	52
Frontline Vision	54
An Open-Hand Policy	55
Glee and Gaiety in Greece	57
A Song of Angels	61
Studies in Sensitivity	64
Of Impact and Inspiration	67
Heads Up	68
A Covenant for Eternity	71
A Day of Designation	75
Healing Process	78
In Close Proximity	79

A Commitment Beyond	81
A Stellar Cellar	83
Missing Sanctity	86

Part B: Gracious Traits and Character — 91

Noble Compassion	93
Standing Tall	99
Real Power	101
An Unlocked Secret	103
Wedding Gift	105
Bread of Survival	108
To Walk the Talk	111
The Point Was Love	114
Paid in Full	121
Character in Full Bloom	124
Warmth on a Winter Night	126
Perfect Fathers	128
Choice Selection	131
Bar Mitzvah Lessons	132
Acid Rain	136
Sacred Letters	139
Small Talk	142
Yielding Dividends	145
Courtesy in Chicago	147
Carry with Care	149
A Gift of Elevation	150

Part C: Precious Chinuch Gemstones — 153

The Talmud and the Talmid	155
Crowning Glory	159
From a Tear-Drenched Siddur	161
Etched in Stone	163
Criticism, Conclusions, and Culminations	168
Home Rule	171
Total Recall	173

Defining Moments	176
Returnees	179
Window Dressing	187
Holy Fire in Warsaw	189
Knowing an Angel	192
A Mother's Light	193
Windblown Jews	195
Waiting in Williamsburg	197
Sense and Sensitivity	199
Vision in Vilna	201

Part D: Divine Orchestrations — 205

World-Class Music	207
Of Monumental Significance	211
A Promise Fulfilled	213
Related After All	216
Minyan Mobility	218
A Life-giving Exchange	220
Overtime Benefits	224
It's All in the Names	226
Chedva – A Joy Remembered	230
Rescue Reciprocated	234
Plaque in Time	236
A Link in Time	239
Retrieved Items	241
Book Return	245
With Feeling	248
From Generation to Generation	250
The Show Must Go On	254

Part E: Reflections, Sense, and Wisdom — 259

Vines of Wine	261
Bombs Bursting in Air	262
Roots and Routes	263
Lifetime Revenge	265

Show Time	267
Driving Home a Point	269
Why Me?	270
Perfect Fit	272
Compassion Priorities	274
Medical Counsel	275
Clouds on the Horizon	277
Far Sighted	279
Life Chapters	280
Moving On	282
Winter Spring Summer Fall	283
It's Life of Course	285
A Light for Generations	286

Indices

Index of Personalities	291
Index of Topics	299
Index of Sources	313
Glossary	331

Author's Preface

אֲדֹנָ־י שְׂפָתַי תִּפְתָּח וּפִי יַגִּיד תְּהִלָּתֶךָ

It is with a deep sense of gratitude to Hashem that I present this eighth volume of stories in the Maggid Series. *Chazal* (*Shabbos* 104a) teach that the letter ח, the eighth letter in the Hebrew alphabet, connotes favor. They explain the sequence of the Hebrew letters to mean, אַלֵּף בִּינָה, *[If you] learn insight,* i.e., study Torah, גְּמוֹל דַּלִים, *aid the needy, [then]* ה׳ ו׳ (this combination represents the name of) *the Holy One Blessed is He* (see Rashi, *Succah* 45a), זָן אוֹתְךָ, *will sustain you* and וְחָן אוֹתְךָ, *favor you.*

It is my hope and prayer that the stories offered in this volume will find favor in your eyes and be as enlightening and inspirational to you as they were to me. I express my gratitude to Hashem for His favor in allowing me the opportunity to find and write these precious stories.

By Divine Orchestration this book is to be published right before Chanukah 5773/2012, when the number eight plays a prominent role. The single spiritually pure sealed flask of oil that was found in the *Beis HaMikdash* should normally have burned for one day, yet miraculously it lasted eight days. Why eight?

In the plain sense, it was because it would take eight days to produce new oil for the Menorah.

In a deeper sense, as explained by Maharal and others, the number eight symbolizes man's ability to transcend the limitations of physical existence. The number seven symbolize completeness: the days of a week, the seven heavens, the seven blessings at a wedding. The number eight symbolizes events beyond nature.

That was the inherent lesson of Chanukah. Though the Jews were heavily outnumbered by the Syrian-Greeks, they were victorious because when Hashem offers His merciful protection, the weak can overcome the strong, the few can defeat the many, and the wanton fall to the few who are diligent students of Torah. Rabbi Samson Raphael Hirsch suggests that eight symbolizes a new beginning, similar to the octave in music on the next level (*Vayikra* 9:1). It is my prayer, therefore, that the stories in this eighth book will help us transcend the mundane and aspire to higher levels of *Ahavas Hashem*, *Ahavas HaTorah*, and *Ahavas Yisrael*.

The Maggid Series began with the publication of *The Maggid Speaks* in 1985. It was the fruition of an idea I presented to the legendary Maggid of Jerusalem, Rabbi Sholom Mordechai HaKohen Schwadron (1912-1997). His stories were classic, their lessons were life-changing, and his delivery was enthralling. However, to reach thousands of English-speaking adults and children, I suggested that we write a book together and he readily agreed. Two and half years later, the first Maggid book was published.

Rav Sholom often downplayed his role in the stories, saying, "I am merely a tape recorder, retelling and repeating what I heard from others. It is the story or parable itself that has significant merit and value." Now as this book is to be published the following occurred to me:

When one lights the Chanukah menorah, the *shammes* kindles the wicks so they give light to the homes and hearts of our nation. The *shammes* then "steps aside" and lets the flames speak for themselves. In presenting these stories, I follow the example of the *Shammes*. I am privileged to "light the fire" and then let the message of the story bring light and guidance to people's lives.

Shammes, in Hebrew, is spelled שמש, which, interestingly can stand for שלום מרדכי שבדרן. Ever since I started writing these Maggid books, I have tried to follow his lead. Rav Sholom's effervescent personality and inspirational and fascinating *derashos* brought illumination, magnificence, and radiance to his listening audience. I hope and pray that with the written and spoken word, I will always follow IN THE SPLENDOR OF THE MAGGID.

Acknowledgments

פִּתְחוּ לִי שַׁעֲרֵי צֶדֶק אָבֹא בָם אוֹדֶה יָ־הּ
*Open up for me the gates of righteousness;
I will enter them and thank Hashem (Tehillim 118:19).*

The Sforno explains that the plural form of the word שַׁעֲרֵי (gates) indicates that there are two places where one must express gratitude: within the gates of the Beis Medrash and within the gates of the Bais HaKnesses — a shul. Perhaps the intent here is to teach that for every aspect of life, both spiritual and physical, one must express gratitude.

In the last *pasuk* of *Tehillim,* David HaMelech writes, כֹּל הַנְּשָׁמָה תְּהַלֵּל יָ-הּ הַלְלוּיָ-הּ, from which *Chazal* teach, עַל כָּל נְשִׁימָה וּנְשִׁימָה שֶׁאָדָם נוֹשֵׁם צָרִיךְ לְקַלֵּס לַבּוֹרֵא, *For every breath of life, one must praise his Creator (Bereishis Rabbah* 14:9). We should take nothing for granted, not even the seemingly routine act of breathing [as well as walking and talking]. Thus, as I pause to give thanks to those who have impacted my life, especially since the publication of the most recent Maggid book in 2008, *In the Spirit of the Maggid,* I cluster together those who have guided me *b'ruchnius,* those who have seen to it that I hear noteworthy stories, those who have given me incredible opportunities, those who have hosted my wife and myself in cities and countries throughout the Jewish world, and those who have tended to my physical welfare in times of need. I am grateful beyond words to each of these individuals. It is my continuous wish and prayer that our friendships endure for the rest of our lives.

Dr. Chaim Abbitan (Cedarhurst), Mr. and Mrs. Shoul Anisfeld (Toronto), Mr. and Mrs. David and Fiona Aronovitz (Johannesburg),

Rabbi Elazar Boruch Bald (Brooklyn), Rabbi Leibish Becker (Monsey), Mr. and Mrs. Ari and Simi BenMergui (Miami), Rabbi and Mrs. Ezra and Betty Berkowitz (Zurich), Mrs. Matti Berkowitz (Brooklyn), Dr. Eli and Mrs. Suzy Bio (Amsterdam), Mrs. Leah Dolinger (Ashdod), Mr. Sholom Ber Eber (Brooklyn), Ms. Adi Gedali (Washington Heights), Mr. Aaron Gestetner (Montreal), Mr. Tzvi Goldberg (Brooklyn), Mr. Chaim Boruch Halberstam (Brooklyn), Mr. Dov Harris (London), Mr. and Mrs. Alfred and Rachelle Homberger (London), Mr. Duddy Iczkovits (London), Mr. Haim Ishakis (Athens), Rabbi Shlomo Karpes (Johannesburg), Rabbi and Mrs. Shmuel and Miriam Katz (Amsterdam), Mr. Elly Kleinman (Brooklyn), Rabbi and Mrs. Chananya and Faige Kramer (Baltimore), Rabbi and Mrs. Eliezer and Baila Krohn (Passaic), Rabbi and Mrs. Avrohom and Genendel Krohn (Waterbury), Dr. Lewis Kurtz (Great Neck), Mrs. Leah Leshkowitz (Brooklyn), Mrs. Symie Liff (Jerusalem), Mr. Benny Marvin (Brooklyn), Mr. Mitch Mailman (Stamford), Mr. Mordy Mehlman (Brooklyn), Mr. Yaniv Meirov (Forest Hills), Rabbi Eli Munk *z"l* (Brooklyn), Mr. Imonuel Natanelov (Flushing), Mrs. Raizel Paperman (Paris), Rabbi Avrohom Nisson Perl (Brooklyn), Rabbi and Mrs. Ephraim and Elisheva Perlstein (Far Rockaway), Mr. and Mrs. Max and Sarah Perlstein (Brooklyn), Rabbi and Mrs. Shlomo Dovid and Chaviva Pfeiffer (Kew Gardens), Yoel Pfeiffer (Kew Gardens), Dr. Isaac Pinter (Brooklyn), Mr. and Mrs. Moshe and Jennifer Rose (Detroit), Mr. Michael Rothschild (Monsey), the Rowe family members, R' Dov, Yitzchok, Eli, A.J. (Queens and Jerusalem), Mr. and Mrs. Shea and Raylee Rubenstein (Brooklyn), Rabbi Yaakov Salomon (Brooklyn), Mr. Ari Scharf (Brooklyn), Mrs. Miriam Schoen (Jerusalem), Mr. and Mrs. Dovid and Sharon Schild (Bergenfield), Mrs. Miriam Schreiber (Chicago), Mrs. Leah Sekula (Monsey), Mrs. Gloria Silver (Toronto), Dr. Marc Silverman (Kew Garden Hills), Mr. Eli Slomovits (Lakewood), Mr. Marki Spitzer (Antwerp), Rabbi Mordechai Suchard (Monsey), Rabbi Mordechai Tropp (Elizabeth), Rabbi and Mrs. Mordechai Tussia (Mexico), Rabbi Zecharia Wallerstein (Brooklyn), Rabbi Boruch and Faygi Wasyng, (Antwerp), Mrs. Dini Weidberg (Toronto), Dr. Meir Wikler (Brooklyn), Mr. Greg Wolski (Queens), Mr. David Zitzser (Manhattan), and Rabbi Chaim Dovid Zweibel (Brooklyn).

For the sake of veracity, in these stories, I used the names of the participants unless they requested otherwise. If they preferred anonymity, I used pseudonyms, indicated by an asterisk.

Rav Dovid Cohen has been my rebbi and *moreh derech* for more than forty years. His guidance and brilliance, coupled with his love and concern for me, have formed a foundation on which I have been able to build for more than four decades. Almost all that I do has been filtered through his *Daas Torah*. May Hashem grant that he and his wonderful family know only *mazel, nachas,* and *berachah*.

Rabbi Yaakov Salomon is among the most talented and clever people I know. His concern for Klal Yisrael in his work for Aish and Inspire is an example for all of us. I treasure and welcome his counsel, as he understands life and people with a keen insight. I am honored and thankful for his friendship.

Rabbi Meir Zlotowitz has etched for himself a place in Jewish history as he, with Rabbi Nosson Scherman and Rabbi Sheah Brander and their incredible team at ArtScroll/Mesorah, opened the possibilities of learning and growth in Torah and *Yiras Shamayim* to hundreds of thousands of Jews throughout the world. Undoubtedly among the throngs around the English-speaking world who celebrated their completion of Shas this summer, there were thousands who could not have done it nor would have attempted it without ArtScroll's incredible translation and elucidation of Shas. To me personally, Rav Meir has been a mentor and close friend for decades. I can never thank him enough for the opportunities he has afforded me and for the limelight he has provided me with the publication of the Maggid books, the book on *bris milah*, and the DVDs about the Jewish communities that once flourished in the countries to which I have led tours.

Rabbi Nosson Scherman has shepherded this book from its very beginning. Patiently and meticulously, he took time from his demanding schedule to edit every word of this manuscript. If the sentences flow and the concepts are clear, it is his deft pen and broad scope of Torah and world knowledge that have made it so. His input has graced and enhanced these stories. It is an honor and a privilege to work in tandem with him.

Mrs. Frimy Eisner has a command of the English language like few I have ever met. Her precise and dexterous editing has graced this book. She choreographs a sentence with just the right word so that nimble expressions dance from the page. It is elevating to work with her.

Many thanks to Rabbi Moshe Rosenblum, who kindly reviewed and corrected all the Hebrew quotations in this volume.

I thank Eli Kroen for the *splendorific* cover; his talents continue to amaze me. I thank Mendy Herzberg for orchestrating the process of bringing this book from manuscript form to its publishing finale. I thank Mrs. Faygie Weinbaum, who proofread diligently with consummate skill and Mrs. Sury England for her expert pagination. I thank as well two of my granddaughters, Chaya Mindy Perlstein, and Nechama Rochel Krohn for proofreading the manuscript.

On Friday night we sing the following verse from *Aishes Chayil*: רַבּוֹת בָּנוֹת עָשׂוּ חָיִל וְאַתְּ עָלִית עַל כֻּלָּנָה, *Many daughters have amassed achievement, but you have surpassed them all* (Mishlei 31:29). The word וְאַתְּ, *and you*, which is comprised of א and ת, the first and last letters of the Hebrew alphabet, represents totality, from *aleph* to *tav*. The true *Aishes Chayil* is just that: a *complete* personality comprising many traits that enhance the lives of all around her. My wife Miriam is exactly that kind of personality. I am infinitely grateful to Hashem for granting me to have her as my partner in life. Whatever I have accomplished has been possible only because of her encouragement, her advice, and her carrying the burden of running an active home and wholesome family life — all with wisdom and good cheer.

I know that I and my contemporaries are links in the chain of *Mesorah* as we optimistically protect, preserve, and pass on our precious legacy to our children, grandchildren, and, we hope, great-grandchildren. May the stories of the people, both great and common, in this volume be an inspiration to all of us, today and tomorrow, to grow in our *Ahavas Hashem, Ahavas HaTorah*, and *Ahavas Yisrael* so that we merit seeing Mashiach in our time.

Paysach J. Krohn	פסח יוסף קראהן
October, 2012	חשון ח"י תשע"ג
Kew Gardens, New York	

Part A:
Distinguished Sacred Deeds

✥ A Cup of Blessing

Part of the beauty of being a *mohel* is that one is able to participate with a family at a most joyous moment in their lives. Every *bris* is special, but, as in every profession, some are more special than others.

In June 2012, I was asked to perform a *bris* for a family I was close to. Little did I know that it would become one of the most memorable I had ever had the *zechus* to do. A *bris* symbolizes the transmission of our *mesorah* to a new generation. At this *bris* it was much more than that. History, tragedy, triumph, and sentiment combined to make the moment moving and magical.

The story begins in a ghetto more than 60 years ago; it was told to me, before davening on the morning of the *bris*, by the infant's great-grandfather, Rabbi Yisroel Rosenfeld.

Yisroel was only 15 years old, but he viewed the future with a sense of foreboding. It was a few days before Shavuos in May 1944, and he and his family were trapped in the ghetto of Chust, Czechoslovakia, which was then occupied by Hungary. Rumors were rampant that the ghetto would soon be liquidated and everyone would be deported. The Jews knew that deportation meant at best a grueling survival or at worst a cruel death. They realized that it would be foolish to take along family treasures, for they would surely be confiscated.

All in the ghetto thought that they would be deported to a location somewhere in Hungary; no one knew that they would be sent to Auschwitz, in Poland. Late that evening, Yisroel took four precious family items to the family's wooden shed; it had an earthen

Distinguished Sacred Deeds / 21

floor because chickens were kept there. With his hands, he dug into the soft earth and buried the treasures. The shed was behind his grandmother's house, so he would remember where it was if he lived to come back.

The treasures included the pocket watch of his father, Reb Dovid, his mother's two silver candlesticks, the *atarah* of his father's tallis, and the most treasured family possession of all, the *becher* that the Satmar Rebbe, Rabbi Yoel Teitelbaum (1887-1979), gave his parents when he married them in Chust years before. Two days after the items were hidden, the ghetto was liquidated. Not a Jew remained in Chust.

Through tragedy, toil, and terror, Yisroel miraculously survived his year and a half in Auschwitz. Sadly, his parents did not. When the war was over, Yisroel was broken and frail, but still committed and focused. In honor of his parents he would build a life they would have wanted him to lead.

Once he and his compatriots were liberated, he was determined to return to Chust. After months of survival in DP camps, towns, and villages, he was finally on a train back "home."

He arrived in Chust hoping to relive the past. He went directly to his old home, but the occupants would not let him in. He was an "unwelcome interloper," and they refused even to answer his questions. They threatened to call the police. Quickly, he rushed over to the shed behind his grandmother's house.

The earth was much harder than he remembered. Slowly and carefully, he began digging with a piece of wood he found nearby, and eventually he found the items he had buried. The pocket watch, the candlesticks, the *atarah,* and the precious silver cup. It was bent out of shape from the trampling on the shallow ground that covered it, but he would eventually take it to a silversmith who would repair it.

Grasping his newly recovered treasures, Yisroel left the area as fast as he could. He did not want any confrontations with the anti-Semitic citizens of his hometown. Eventually he immigrated to America. There he married and settled in Denver, Colorado, where he became the first teacher at the newly opened Hillel Academy.

One of his first students was my wife Miriam, who was in his class for several years, since he always taught the highest grade. His influence, warmth, and scholarship were appreciated by hundreds of students who passed through his classes in his many years as a *mechanech*. I met him years later, when my wife and I were engaged, and my friendship with him and his family blossomed.

Decades later, I had the privilege of performing *brissen* in New York for a number of Rabbi Rosenfeld's grandsons. Now, in June 2012, he had come to New York to attend the *bris* of his first great-grandson, held in the White Shul in Far Rockaway, New York. He would be the *sandek* and I would be the *mohel*.

That morning, after he told me the story before Shacharis, he held the *becher* with pride as he said, "We have used this *becher* for every *bris* and wedding in our family, since I retrieved it. Today marks a milestone in our family. It is the first time that we are using this *becher* for a fifth-generation child. This child is my great-grandson and my parents used it first!" His warm smile portrayed pride and an everlasting gratitude to Hashem.

Normally I do not speak before a *bris*, but this one was different. I felt it would be inspirational to explain the significance of the cup we were about to use. "This *becher* symbolizes our Jewish nation," I said. "We may be trampled on for years, other nations may have given us up for dead, but at the end it is we as a nation who survive and outlive our adversaries. This *becher* is truly a כּוֹס שֶׁל בְּרָכָה, *a cup of blessing*."

I suggested that those who wished could come up after the *bris*, to drink some wine from this goblet of greatness. And indeed more than 20 people lined up afterward to taste and savor the sweetness of this sacred saga.

↜§ An End to a Means

The following story is personal, painful, and poignant. Though the initial events occurred more than a decade ago, not a day goes by that I don't think about it three times. It is my hope that this episode will affect you as it has me, and that you will remember it every day as well.

It was the morning of 9/11. I had performed a *bris* and was on my way home to put away my instruments and then head for the airport on the way to Toronto, where I was to speak that night. While I was driving, my wife called and said, "Did you hear what happened? A plane crashed into one of the Twin Towers, and the airports may be closed. Don't go to LaGuardia until you listen to the news and find out if flights are being canceled."

When I got home I turned on the radio just in time to hear the frantic frenzied newscast that a second plane had flown into the second of the towers, causing a huge fireball. Now both buildings were aflame. Airports across America were shut down, panic and fear spread across the country as news traveled with lightning speed that a third plane had crashed into the Pentagon outside Washington D.C., and a fourth plane had gone down in Pennsylvania. The course of American and world history would be changed forever.

Shocked at the tragedy, numbed by its scope, and horrified that it still might not be over, New York practically came to a halt. People tried to contact their loved ones to find out if they were safe as bridges were closed to vehicular traffic, trains were halted, and phone service was overloaded; no one had ever experienced anything like this in peacetime.

That afternoon Mrs. Rachel Reifer, the principal of Shevach Girls High School in Queens, called me. "I dismissed the girls early today, but they are coming back to school at 9 a.m. tomorrow," she said. "I am calling an assembly and I need you to come and give the girls a Torah *hashkofah* on what happened today."

Mrs. Reifer, originally from England, was new to Shevach. The Board of Directors, myself included, had hired her a year earlier, as we were impressed with her enthusiasm, broad range of knowledge, and ability to relate to students. I had spoken for the school many times, but this was overwhelming.

"Mrs. Reifer," I protested, "I'm as confused and frightened as anyone else. I can't make sense of what happened, and I have no idea how to interpret these events. Please get someone else."

She would not take no for an answer so I told her I would call various *talmidei chachamim*, I would look in *sefarim*, and if I could come up with something worth saying, I would call her back. A few hours later I consented.

The next morning, Mrs. Reifer, as the principal, opened the assembly. Staff and students waited anxiously for someone to define the moment, give strength and reassurance, and allay their terrible fears for the future. In just a few sentences, Mrs. Reifer did just that. She began, "In every *siddur*, following *Aleinu* are three sentences that are usually printed in a smaller typeface than the *Aleinu* itself. The words begin אַל תִּירָא מִפַּחַד פִּתְאֹם, וּמִשֹּׁאַת רְשָׁעִים כִּי תָבֹא, *Do not fear sudden terror or the calamity of the wicked when it comes* (Mishlei 3:25). [We then say to the nations of the world] עֻצוּ עֵצָה וְתֻפָר, דַּבְּרוּ דָבָר וְלֹא יָקוּם, כִּי עִמָּנוּ קֵל, *Plan a conspiracy and it will be annulled speak your piece and it shall not stand, because Hashem is with us*" (Yeshaya 8:10).

She explained, "As believing Jews we must never be afraid of sudden horrors that may befall us, especially when they are perpetrated by the nations of the world — because Hashem is with us. He will protect us. He will shield us."

I was so moved by those words that I decided that morning that I would try never to miss saying those three verses after *Aleinu*, every time I davened. Years went by and it was October 2006. On Chol HaMoed Succos, my precious mother, Mrs. Hindy Krohn, with whom I had a special bond (see Dedication in *Reflections of the Maggid*), passed away. She had been a widow for close to 40 years and even after I married, I never lived more than three blocks away from her (a credit to my wife). The *shivah*, which began after Succos (one does not sit *shivah* on Yom Tov), replicated the *shivah* for my father, Rabbi Avrohom Zelig Krohn, 40 years earlier, who passed away on Shemini Atzeres in October 1966. Then, too, we started sitting *shivah* immediately after Yom Tov and in a strange way, in 2006 it was almost as though we were sitting *shivah* for both of them simultaneously.

Distinguished Sacred Deeds / 25

The *shivah* ended on Motza'ei Shabbos. Shortly after Shabbos, R' Moshe Reifer, husband of Mrs. Rachel Reifer, called me. My first inclination was that it was a condolence call and that he hadn't realized that the *shivah* had ended. And indeed he was talking about a woman and death, but he was crying and I could not make out his words. I wondered, *Why is he crying about my mother? He didn't even know her.* And then as I listened more carefully I realized he wasn't talking about my mother — he was talking about his wife!

Tragically, the night before as Mrs. Reifer was crossing Route 59 in Monsey, she was hit by a car and was killed instantly. Mr. Reifer was calling to tell me about the funeral the next morning, and he asked me to spread the news in Queens.

The devastation felt by her family, friends, colleagues, and students at Shevach High School was inexpressible — such an accomplished woman cut down in the prime of her life, leaving a husband and children totally bereft.

Thirty days later, a *sheloshim* memorial service was held in her honor at the Yeshiva of Spring Valley. Close to a thousand people filled the auditorium. I told the audience what she had said on 9/11, and how it had affected me so that since then I had been saying that paragraph after *Aleinu* three times a day. I encouraged everyone to undertake the same thing as a merit for the *neshamah* of Rachel Perl bas Yitzchak.

However, despite the assurance and the encouragement I derived from the first two verses, the third one, a verse from *Yeshayah* (46:4) puzzled me. The word אֲנִי (I) appears five times in the same verse. What is Hashem telling us? I, I, I, I, I? וְעַד זִקְנָה אֲנִי הוּא, וְעַד שֵׂיבָה אֲנִי אֶסְבֹּל, אֲנִי עָשִׂיתִי וַאֲנִי אֶשָּׂא, וַאֲנִי אֶסְבֹּל וַאֲמַלֵּט, *Even till your seniority I remain unchanged [and will care for you], and even till your ripe old age I shall endure [therefore do not worry]; I created you and I shall bear you; I shall endure and rescue you.*

I think that for our generation of the iPod, iPhone, and iPad, there is a great lesson in that verse. Hashem is teaching us how one should behave in the selfish iGeneration. Not I *want*, I *need*, I *must*, but, as Hashem says, I *protect*, I *bear*, I *save*, I *rescue*, I *carry*.

We were brought into this world to take the talents granted us and use them to serve others. As Rabbi Yitzchak Volozhiner writes in his introduction to his father Rav Chaim Volozhiner's *sefer*, *Nefesh HaChaim*, "My father … would rebuke me when he saw that I did not become involved in the problems of others. This is what he told me, "This is what man is all about: לֹא לְעַצְמוֹ נִבְרָא, *You were not created for yourself.*"

In my *siddur* I have the words אֲנִי underlined. It is a daily reminder of what Hashem wants our focus to be. For this reason, I would encourage everyone to say the *al tira tefillah* three times a day, because it not only gives us *chizuk* in difficult times, כִּי עִמָּנוּ קֵל, *for Hashem is with us*, but it gives us direction toward what we should really be in a self-centered world. It is the essence of וְהָלַכְתָּ בִּדְרָכָיו, *and you shall follow in His ways* (Devarim 28:9).

> May it indeed be a *zechus* for the *neshamah* of Rachel Perl bas Yitzchak.

⇝§ To See and Remember

One of the most searingly tragic incidents that ever struck the New York Jewish community was the death of 9-year-old Leiby Kletzky, in the summer of 2011. Coming home from day camp, he apparently lost his way, was kidnapped, and, a few days later, was found no longer alive. While he was missing, thousands of Jews of all stripes searched for him in virtually every street, every building, every store, and every yard in Borough Park and nearby Kensington and Midwood. The missing child was all anyone talked about. He was all anyone thought about.

Meanwhile, not far from where Leiby lived, another 9-year-old boy, Zalmy,* had been acting rebelliously for months. He refused to put on his *tzitzis* and would go to yeshivah and day camp without them. No matter how much his parents pleaded, cajoled, and offered prizes, he refused to wear his *tzitzis*.

When he heard the news that a boy his age was missing and that everyone was searching frantically for him, Zalmy told his mother that he would resume wearing *tzitzis* as a merit for Leiby, so he would be found. For two days he wore his *tzitzis* — and then the tragic news spread: Leiby was no longer alive.

Zalmy's mother was quietly anxious. Would he go back to his rebellious ways and refuse to put on his *tzitzis*? She thought it would be better to wait and see and not to raise the issue. To her relief and joy, her son continued to put on his *tzitzis* every morning.

During the *shivah*, Zalmy's mother felt that she had to let the Kletzkys know that Leiby had been an impetus to the resumption of a mitzvah by Zalmy.

Thousands of people came to the Kletzkys to pay condolence calls. Security guards were set up at the door to keep the constant flow of people moving. The lines often extended down the stairwells to the front door of the apartment house because so many people came to show their concern and care for the family. Zalmy's mother waited in line and slowly made her way into the Kletzky apartment.

When she reached Mrs. Kletzky and her daughters, she told them how her Zalmy had been moved to change and wear his *tzitzis* again. Although she was sure the Kletzkys would not even remember her, as throngs of people were coming in and expressing words of comfort, Zalmy's mother was satisfied with having related how Zalmy had reacted to Leiby's disappearance.

After the *shivah*, however, R' Nachman Kletsky called Zalmy's mother and asked that she and her son come to his apartment. He said that his family had been very moved by Zalmy's sensitivity and wanted to meet him personally. When Zalmy and his mother arrived, R' Nachman greeted the child warmly and told him how grateful the Kletzky family was that he had performed such a special mitzvah in Leiby's *zechus*. He then gave Zalmy a pair of Leiby's *tzitzis*. "I know," said R' Nachman "that Leiby would be very happy to know that a young *tzaddik* like you is wearing his *tzitzis*."

R' Nachman bent over to kiss Zalmy on the forehead and said, "This kiss is not from me, it's from Leiby."

Can there be anything more tender?

How can a person take his severe personal pain and turn it into an act of memorable inspiration? Our people are great in triumph and in tragedy.

Zalmy's mother told me recently that every morning when her son puts on those *tzitzis* he says, "*Le'zecher nishmas Leiby.*"

~§ Commitments to a Covenant

The *Netziv*, Rabbi Naftoli Tzvi Yehudah Berlin (1816-1893), in his *Ha'amek Davar* (*Bamidbar* 15:41) writes that although every Jew is obligated to perform all the mitzvos, it is natural for people to develop an affinity for one or more particular mitzvos. Some excel in learning, others in *tefillah*, others in Shabbos, and still others in *chessed*.

Rabbi Yisroel Mitzman, originally from Ukraine and today a rebbi in Monsey, New York, has made it his life's endeavor to provide a proper *bris milah* for young men who immigrate to America from the former Soviet Union. From when he first taught at Beis Miriam–Bais Yaakov school in the Bronx and then at the Sinai Academy in Brooklyn and in Camp Shoroshim (for boys from the former Soviet Union), he has convinced dozens of boys to have a *bris*.

As a *mohel*, I am fascinated that someone who has no *mohelim* in his family should be so engaged in this mitzvah. When he was our Shabbos guest, I asked him about it. He told me this incredible story to explain his passion for *bris milah*.

His parents lived in the Kamenetz-Podolsk district in Ukraine, where a great yeshivah once existed. When Ukraine was still part of the Soviet Union, Jews were not free to practice their religion. Those who did so in spite of the danger risked losing their jobs, serving a jail sentence, or being sent to frigid exile in Siberia.

Yisroel's father was proud of his *Yiddishkeit* and was known to all as Avroom (for Avrohom). It was the only name he went by. Even gentiles knew him by that name. He always wore a head covering. At home it was a yarmulke and in public it was some type of hat. He played violin and, as part of a four-man band, barely eked out a living for his wife and children. The other musicians were gentiles. Together they performed at weddings, funerals, restaurants, and even at parties in the offices of the KGB, the secret police.

Avroom's closest friend was Itzak Hersch who held a secret *minyan* in his house. There was even a *shochet* who secretly slaughtered chickens for Jews in the neighborhood. When Yisroel was born after five girls, Avroom was dancing in the hospital, exclaiming, "I have a son, Hashem gave me a boy." When he came home he frolicked in his front yard, "Hashem gave me the mitzvah of *milah!*"

He could not contain himself. Daringly, he sent word to a *mohel* in Chernovitz, 60 miles away, to come and perform the *bris*. The *mohel*, who feared for his life every time he performed a *bris*, agreed to come only if the *bris* was kept as quiet as possible, without any fanfare whatsoever. Somehow, some of Avroom's relatives found out about it and informed the authorities, for fear of severe repercussions if it became known that they were aware of Avroom's "rebellious" actions. KGB officers warned Avroom that making the *bris* was against the law and he would be severely punished if he went through with the ceremony.

He said defiantly, "My grandfather did it to my father, my father did it to me, and I will do it to my son, regardless of what happens."

"Just try it," they responded and walked away.

Two days after the *bris*, KGB officers arrested Avroom and jailed him for four months. They intimidated him, beat him, and warned him that if he ever did this again he would be put away for life. He reflected, "It was Hashem Who said that a Jew must be circumcised. Could a KGB threat outweigh that?"

Thankfully, their next child was a girl, but two years later his wife, Yeedis (Yehudis), gave birth to twins, a boy and a girl. The authorities summoned Avroom to headquarters and warned,

"Don't be foolish enough to circumcise him. Do you know how many Jews died at Nazi hands because the Germans saw that they were circumcised? You yourself were in our army. You fought the Nazis for five years and were wounded. You were loyal to the Motherland. Why change now?"

Avroom took a deep breath and said, "What G-d does we cannot always understand, but He told us what we have to do and I will do it not matter what!" They shouted that if he transgressed their orders he would be sent to Siberia and would never see his family again.

Avroom bribed the hospital administrators to allow him to take the infants home earlier than the usual 10-day stay. He contacted the *mohel* in Chernovitz, asking him to come to Kamenetz-Podolsk, where he hid the *mohel* overnight. The next morning, the eighth day, the *bris* was performed clandestinely, not in Avroom's own home.

Once again his secular relatives turned him in. A few days later, officers stormed Avroom's home and dragged him to KGB headquarters. Enraged, they threw him into a cell and told him he would be sent to Siberia.

A few hours after the arrest, Yeedis Mitzman dressed her nine children and took them to KGB headquarters and asked to be taken to the commander. Surprisingly, she was ushered in at once. She walked directly to the startled commissar and addressed him before he could say a word. In a powerful voice she courageously said, "If you keep my husband here or send him to Siberia, there is no way I can raise my nine children alone. Here — you take them and care for them. They are your responsibility," and she stormed out!

The commissar was dumbfounded. He had no idea what to do with the children. He called after her, "*Granshdanka* (citizeness); please wait — don't go yet." Within minutes, as children do, the little ones began to run around the office, pulling at window shades, climbing over tables and chairs, and making a ruckus that confounded the officers who stood watching them helplessly. Mrs. Mitzman waited downstairs in the lobby, davening quietly as she waited to see what would happen to her children.

Fifteen minutes later the police chief entered the lobby with Avroom and his children in tow, the newborns held by older siblings. "Go home," he said to Mrs. Mitzman, "and take everyone here with you. We don't want them here." And then he added in a threatening voice, "And make sure you and your family are never seen here again!"

Rabbi Yisroel Mitzman smiled with pride as he finished the story. "My father and mother had such *mesiras nefesh* for the mitzvah of *milah*. That's why I am so passionate about it, as well.

"But I have one more story for you," he added with a smile. "I have been involved with many boys as they had their *bris milah* and I am always amazed at their courage and commitment. Don't forget, many of these boys were already in their teens and they were nevertheless anxious to have a *bris*. I have had many interesting experiences. But this story is my favorite."

I couldn't wait to hear it.

Avroom, Yeedis, and their nine children eventually immigrated to *Eretz Yisrael* where their son Yisroel became a serious *yeshivah bachur*. He studied in the Yeshiva Nesivos Olam. After his marriage, he joined the Sha'arei Emunah Kollel in Jerusalem. He studied *safrus* (*Sefer Torah* calligraphy), wrote *mezuzos*, and worked diligently with Rabbi Yitzchok Silber (1917-2003), the brilliant Russian *tzaddik* and mathematician, helping bring immigrants from the former Soviet Union closer to authentic Judaism.

In 1989, Rabbi Mitzman's father-in-law, who lived in New York, became very ill and wanted his daughter, Tzirel Liba, to come to America for a few months to tend to him. Rabbi Mitzman was not sure if he should accompany his wife or remain in Israel, as he was doing well in his personal Torah study and was accomplishing a great deal with the young people he mentored. He consulted Rabbi Aaron Leib Shteinman, with whom he had a close relationship. Rabbi Shteinman's advice illustrated the wisdom and insight of *Gedolei Torah*. "You too must go," he said, "because if you stay here, her father will be in constant fear that she will soon leave him to return to Israel, and this will hamper his recuperation."

Rabbi Mitzman was stunned. He could not see himself leaving his learning and his work with the youth, but Rabbi Shteinman reassured him, saying confidently, "Hashem will guide you."

While in New York, Rabbi Mitzman joined the Ohr Someyach Kollel in Monsey, but then was offered a teaching job at the Beis Miriam–Bais Yaakov School, which was the only Jewish school left in the Pelham Parkway section of the Bronx. Most of the school's 80 students were Americans, but 15 were immigrants from the former Soviet Union. Rabbi Mitzman accepted the position and became their teacher.

He stressed the beauty of mitzvah observance and Torah study, but that conflicted with what the parents of his students had in mind. Most of them were not observant and resented it when their children showed any interest in becoming religious. The parents sent them to the yeshivah because they were afraid for the safety of the children in the Bronx public schools, not because they wanted Orthodoxy.

Rabbi Mitzman told his boys that if they studied well and showed improvement in their mitzvah observance, he would put them on a special list — the list of those who would be privileged to have a *bris milah*. With this clever approach, any boy, even if he wanted a *bris*, would have to earn the right to be added to the exclusive list. One 10-year-old, Dmitri,* was very diligent and hoped that one day he would have a *bris*. Soon he was one of the first five "signed up" on the *bris* list.

That night his mother called Rabbi Mitzman and left an indignant message on his answering machine, "Maybe we can talk!" she said angrily.

Rabbi Mitzman called her back at once and was surprised at her vehemence. "Listen," she said. "I know what my son wants and needs. He does *not* want to have an operation and he does *not* need to be circumcised to be considered Jewish."

"You are so right," said Rabbi Mitzman cautiously. "He is Jewish even without a *bris milah*. But look at it this way. You left the Soviet

Distinguished Sacred Deeds / 33

Union because of religious persecution. Here in the United States we are free. You can be a Jew and be proud of it. Your son understands the pride of being Jewish. He has taken to mitzvah observance so beautifully. He loves Torah study and he knows that having a *bris* is a matter of Jewish identity. Please don't take this opportunity away from him."

The conversation continued and Dmitri's mother was getting nowhere with Rabbi Mitzman. What made matters worse was that she knew in her heart that he was right and that she did not have the proper words to debate him. "I am going to have my father speak to you," she said exasperatedly, and hung up.

The next day Boris Bershadsky* came to see Rabbi Mitzman. They sat down in a small office and Boris began, "My daughter tells me you want my grandson to have a *bris*. Dmitri is a little boy. Why are you forcing this on him? It's not right what you are doing to him."

Rabbi Mitzman explained that it was the boy who had volunteered to have himself circumcised. "Dmitri *wants* to be on that special list. He is proud to be a *Yid*," Rabbi Mitzman explained.

Rabbi Mitzman then changed the topic. "Tell me about yourself and your parents," he said softly.

Boris sat back in his chair and began reminiscing. "My father was named Avrohom," he began. "We lived in Minsk and everyone loved him. In those days, when I was very young, Shabbos in our home *was* Shabbos. It was a special day. I remember my mother lighting the candles on Friday night. She would cry when she did it."

Tears welled in Boris' eyes as he recalled his charmed youth. "I miss those days so much. I miss my parents. I miss my hometown. I miss the atmosphere we had in the house in those days." For 15 minutes he spoke about the years gone by, the eventual persecutions, and their escape. He was crying when he finished his soliloquy.

"Did your father see to it that you had a *bris*?" Rabbi Mitzman asked.

"*Vus mainst du* (what do you think)?" Boris blurted out. "Of course not! He was afraid to have it done and when I got older I joined the Communist Party and I did not want to have it done. It's strange — in Belarus I was called a Jew, and here I am called a Russian."

"Well," said Rabbi Mitzman, "there you had no choice but here you have a choice and you can be called a Jew again. Do you know that Avraham Avinu sits at the gateways of *Gehinnom* and stops anyone who had a *bris* from entering?" (See *Bereishis Rabbah* 48:8; see also *Along the Maggid's Journey*, p. 246.)

They continued to talk and suddenly Boris said, "You know what, I'll do it. I want to have a *bris*. My daughter will kill me if I tell her of my decision so *you'll* have to tell her about our conversation. But me and Dmitri, we'll do it together."

Rabbi Mitzman called Dmitri's mother and told her that he had met with her father and that he was a very special individual. "He feels close to your son and understands now what your son understands. He says they will both do it at the same time."

"What?" shrieked the mother. "I am going to send my husband after you. This is not communism. This is a free country. You can't force anyone to do anything."

"They both made their own decisions. I don't force anyone to do anything," Rabbi Mitzman said.

Two days later, Dmitri's father, Viktor Katzev,* stormed into Rabbi Mitzman's office and began ranting and raving, attacking Rabbi Mitzman's integrity, all the while not letting him get a word in edgewise. "What do you want from my family? How can you force anyone in this country to be Jewish? You are brainwashing my son." On and on he rambled but Rabbi Mitzman remained silent letting the verbal storm blow over. When Viktor finished, Rabbi Mitzman asked him softly, "You are a Jew and your father was a Jew. Do you know who the first Jew was?"

"I have no idea," Viktor said angrily, "but I know everything I have to know to be Jewish."

As they continued their conversation, Viktor began talking in softer tones. Rabbi Mitzman is a quiet gentle person; it is hard for anyone to be angry at him. He discussed Jewish history with Viktor, he told stories of people who showed extraordinary

Distinguished Sacred Deeds / 35

commitment to mitzvos and he continued with episodes of *Kiddush Hashem* in the concentration camps.

Then Rabbi Mitzman said, "You know the first Jew, Avraham Avinu, was called an *Ivri*, which means, *one who is on the other side*. You see, Avraham Avinu stood on one side of the world with *his* beliefs and values while everyone else in the world was on the other side with *their* beliefs and values. For over 3,000 years this beloved mitzvah of *bris milah* has been performed with joy, as part of the covenant that Jewish people have with Hashem. It is our sign of Jewish males. Throughout the ages fathers did this for their sons, who in turn did it for their sons. Why should you break the chain?"

Like his father-in-law a few days earlier, Viktor was placated by Rabbi Mitzman's calm demeanor and soothing words. "You're right. Dmitiri should have a *bris*, and so should I. *Both* of us will do it. But what am I going to do about my wife?" Viktor said, his face creased in a frown. "She can't see anything beyond the boy's pain. It's not that she hates mitzvos or religion, but she does not want him to suffer."

"You know," Viktor said before Rabbi Mitzman could even reply, "I have an idea. I will give my wife something she has wanted for the longest time. We will all have a *bris* on the same day and I will give her that special gift."

And so on a remarkable Tuesday morning, a mother, a son, a father, and a grandfather all came to the medical office where the world-renowned *mohel*, Rabbi Yitzchok Aaron Fischer of Monsey, would perform their circumcisions. There was tension and excitement in the waiting room as Rabbi Fischer asked, "So who wants to be first?"

Dmitri spoke up, "I am ready!" His mother gasped at his courage and determination. After his *bris* he was given his Hebrew name, Avrohom — after his great-grandfather from Minsk. The grandfather, Boris, was next, and then came the father, Viktor. They celebrated festively afterward with the wine and cake that Rabbi Mitzman brought, and Viktor handed his wife the pearl necklace she had dreamed of.

Each of the three patients lovingly embraced Rabbi Mitzman. As he watched them all go home together he shook his head in disbelief and uttered over and over, "*Baruch Hashem, Baruch Hashem,*" — or as they would say in Russian, *slava Bogou.*

↜ Dressed for the Occasion

On a recent trip to South Africa, Mr. Peter Fine of Cape Town told me this poignant story that happened in the Claremont Hebrew Congregation, where he davens. I am grateful to Rabbi Ivan Lerner, of suburban Washington, D.C., a well-known *kiruv* expert, lecturer, and author of booklets on family issues, who filled me in on the details. He was the rabbi of the Claremont Shul when the story took place. I thank as well Rabbi Matthew Liebenberg, the current Rav of the Claremont shul, and my great-niece Danya Ross for their help with the story.

When life became more difficult for Lithuanian Jews in the early 1900's, many of them sought to escape from pogroms and persecution and settle somewhere where they could rebuild their communities. Between 1860 and 1940, tens of thousands of Lithuanian Jews from cities and towns like Vilna, Kovno, Shavli, and Ponevezh found a safe haven 9,500 miles away in South Africa, mostly in Cape Town and Johannesburg. Until a large emigration in recent years, there were 85,000 Jews in South Africa; over 85 percent were of Lithuanian descent.

Johannesburg had such a strong Lithuanian presence that the Ponevezher Rav, Rabbi Yosef Shlomo Kahaneman (1886-1969), came there regularly to enlist support for his yeshivah in Israel. The yeshivah had its origins in the town of Ponevezh, located in northeastern Lithuania, so South Africa's Jews had a natural affinity for it. Thanks to the generosity of the Jews of Johannesburg, the Rav acquired an office building in their city, whose rentals helped fund his network of *Batei Avos* — schools and dormitories for orphaned children of the Holocaust and for children from broken homes.

In 1928 Aaron Wasserman, a short, delightful man who spoke no evil of anyone, immigrated with his wife to Cape Town, the southern tip of South Africa. When "Vossy" (as he was known to everyone, because he pronounced his last name "Vasserman") first arrived, he took menial jobs to eke out a living, but eventually he became the *shammes* (sexton) of the Claremont Shul. He served his community diligently and revered his rav, Rabbi Lerner, who showed him extreme sensitivity as, sadly, Vossy and his wife Evelyn had no children.

Vossy dispensed the *aliyos* every Shabbos, put away the *Siddurim* and *Chumashim*, prepared the Shabbos *Kiddush* (called a *Berachah* in South Africa), changed the *paroches* (curtain) on the *Aron Kodesh* for the *Yamim Tovim* and *Yamim Noraim* (High Holy Days), made sure people received their *lulavim* and *esrogim* in time for Succos, and served as *chazzan* when no one else was available. He was the Jewish "jack-of-all-trades" and everyone loved him. The shul was his life.

One year, a few days before Rosh Hashanah, Vossy came into the main sanctuary of the Claremont Shul to replace the *paroches* on the *Aron Kodesh* with the resplendent white one that was used from Rosh Hashanah till after Shemini Atzeres. Because he was short, he used a tall ladder to do the job properly. When the curtain was hung, he took out the *Sifrei Torah* to change their *mantlach* (covers) for the special white ones used for the *Yamim Noraim*. The *Sifrei Torah* in the Claremont shul were tall and stately, and it was not easy for Vossy to reach their tops to put on the new covers.

As Vossy toiled quietly, Rabbi Lerner walked into the sanctuary and saw him trying to cover the *Sifrei Torah*. Rabbi Lerner saw immediately that Vossy was struggling and so he walked over to try and help. Vossy raised his hands and said, "Rebbi, please let me do this alone. This is my special mitzvah."

"But we can do it together, and it will easier for you," protested Rabbi Lerner.

"No, no, Rebbi," Vossy replied. "I want to do it myself. Please let me explain.

"You see," he continued, "when we lived in Lita [Lithuania], my parents were so poor that they could only afford to buy each of the children one suit a year. I remember like yesterday," he said, with a soft, warm smile, "on the day that my father came home with a new suit for one of us, we all gathered around to watch as my mother ceremoniously put the new clothing on one of my siblings. It was a holiday for the whole family. The thrill and the excitement for all of us were very great.

"I have no children," Vossy went on. "These *Sifrei Torah* are my children. When I 'dress' them in their special Yom Tov 'clothing,' I am as happy as my mother was when she dressed her children. So Rebbi, please don't help me. I am as happy and as proud as my mother was."

It Was Not Write

Project Witness is a nonprofit educational resource center created and directed by Mrs. Ruth Lichtenstein, editor of the newspaper *Hamodia*. The center's function is to inform and instruct the public in understanding the Holocaust and to explore the faith of the survivors and the victims.

In May 2012, Project Witness sponsored an evening of lectures depicting the trials and tribulations of Jews under the domination of the Nazis. I discussed their heroic commitment to *yahadus*. I related the following story from *Dignity to Survive*, by Yona Emanuel.

Chana Goldschmidt was raised in France, and the only school she could attend was a public school. Religious Jews were granted special permission exempting them from writing on Shabbos. However, in winter when Shabbos came while school was still in session, Chana requested special permission not to write late on Friday afternoons. The teacher said, "I see that you are serious, and so I will allow you to pretend that you are writing, even though you are not."

Chana was content with that arrangement, but when she came home and told her father, Reb Yehoshua, what the teacher had said, he refused to let her go along with the plan. "You will be setting a bad example for the other Jewish children in the class. They will think you are writing even though you aren't, and they may write because of you."

From that moment on, the sanctity of Shabbos became a cornerstone of Chana's life.

Years later, she married into the Emanuel family and moved to Holland. In 1944, she and her family were ejected from their home and taken to the misery and torment that was the Bergen-Belsen concentration camp.

It was on Tishah B'Av of that year that all the inmates in the camp were collectively punished for the first time. There was no food for anyone, not for the elderly who were pale and frail, not for the children who were crying from hunger, nor for the adult men and women. Chana cooked a small bit of cereal without milk for her 4-year-old daughter, Batya. When the cereal was almost ready, two Jewish kapos (Jewish camp police) caught her violating the order not to prepare food. Chana was summoned for trial.

The trial was set for Friday night, Shabbos Nachamu. These mock trials usually took a long time, as there were lengthy speeches by the Jewish kapos, the witnesses, the defendant, the defendant's lawyer, and then, of course, the judge's ruling. Everyone at the trial was Jewish and all were inmates of Bergen-Belsen. The trials were a sham; everyone knew in advance what the verdict would be.

Surprisingly, Chana's trial was brief. The verdict was harsh: "No bread ration for two days!" Chana did not defend her "crime," nor did she allow her defense counsel to plead for a lesser punishment.

The family waited for her in the barracks and they were surprised when she returned rather quickly; they had expected the trial to stretch for hours. When they questioned her about the brevity of the trial and asked why she did not permit her defense counsel to plead for a lesser punishment, she replied with an unforgettable answer.

"Besides the Jewish judges, witnesses, and kapos, another Jewish man was there, recording every word of the protocol. Every word I would have said would have been written by that Jew on a Friday night. If I allowed my counsel to defend me, I would have caused that Jew to be *mechallel Shabbos* by writing about the case."

Then she finished with a flourish befitting a Shabbos queen. "It is better for me to be hungry for two days than to cause a Jew to write on Shabbos!"

> The English author Edward Bulwer-Lytton wrote, "The pen is mightier than the sword." To Chana Emanuel, the threat of Shabbos transgression by pen was mightier than the potential punishment that could be meted out by the sword.

~§ *A Lesson for Life*

When Yossi (Yosef Eliezer) Pressburger of Flatbush suddenly passed away in Detroit on a business trip in January 2011, his family and friends were stunned, since he had celebrated his 48th birthday only a few days earlier. His *chessed* was legendary and his work for worthy organzations was boundless. His sensitivity and refined peronality were reflected in his concern for the community and individuals.

As an example, one of his seven children told me of a man in his early 20's who once knocked on their front door while the family was eating their Shabbos meal. The visitor was welcomed in and ushered to the table, but no one knew who he was or why he had come.

"This is the fourth time I have come to your home, but I never had the courage to knock on your door before. Finally, today I did it. You won't believe this, but I am Dennis, your neighbor down the block from 15 years ago."

"What?" the older people at the table exclaimed. "How can you be Dennis? He was not religious and his parents moved out of the neighborhood when our block became very Orthodox."

"Well, I *am* that Dennis, and I came to tell you something, Mr. Pressburger. It was something that you did when I was a child that changed me."

Everyone remembered how Dennis had been made to feel uncomfortable because he didn't attend a yeshivah or wear a yarmulke. His was the only Jewish family on the block that drove on Shabbos. The neighborhood children had very little use for him.

"It was one Rosh Hashanah," he said, "and I realized years later that you were coming home to blow shofar for your wife. You saw me in the street, you knew I was not observant, but you invited me in to listen to the shofar. I agreed to go with you. The sounds of the shofar that day pierced my heart and I never forgot it. When I was older I decided to be like your family — and it was the shofar that got me started. So you are all correct, I am no longer Dennis, I am Dovid; actually, Dovid Leib."

> Such was the concern and *chessed* of Yossi Pressburger. Hundreds of people came during the *shivah*, but not many were able to sit and talk with the mourners for long as the rooms were very crowded.

One such woman who could not stay long took with her a lesson that would have dramatic repercussions — that very afternoon.

Mrs. Rachel Raber did not know Mr. and Mrs. Pressburger, but she knew Yossi's three sisters from Baltimore. The Pressburger home was teeming with people and there was no room for her to sit and get into a real conversation with any of the sisters. She stayed for a while, but since Yossi was known and loved by so many people, there was a constant flow of visitors and she realized she should make room for others. At one point, Mrs. Raber even wondered why she had come; her presence hardly seemed to matter — or so it seemed.

As she and others were about to leave, one of the sisters, Mrs. Dina Steinhardter said, "I would like you to leave with something about my brother. He never, ever missed an opportunity for *chessed*.

If there was something to be done he was there to do it, no questions asked. He took advantage of every chance to do a favor." She added one more thought, "If you are ever in a position to do a *chessed*, don't waver. Do it in my brother's *zechus*."

The women said, "*HaMakom yenacheim* … (May Hashem comfort …)" and left. Mrs. Raber got into her car and drove away. She had driven only a few blocks when she stopped at a red light on Avenue N and East 19th Street, the corner of Toras Emes Kamenitz Yeshivah. As she waited for the light to turn green, she noticed a woman sleeping in the driver's seat of a car parked at the corner. The car was parked a bit askew but Mrs. Raber attributed it to snow that had been piled up after a recent storm; people had shoveled their sidewalks and dumped the snow near the curb.

But there was something about how the woman was sleeping. Was it the way her head arched back on the headrest? Mrs. Raber sensed that something might be wrong, but there was no place where she could pull over to check. She reasoned that the woman might have dozed off as she waited to pick up her child from school. After all, she seemed to be a young mother who likely had a son in the yeshivah. It was close to dismissal time, so she was probably waiting for her child. But maybe not … something gnawed at Mrs. Raber.

She thought of what Mrs. Steinhardter had said about her brother Yossi: *He never missed an opportunity for chessed.* Mrs. Raber decided to call Hatzolah. *What's the worst that could happen?* she thought as she dialed the number on her cell phone, *I'll be mistaken and they'll think I was just nosy.*

"Please forgive me," she began apologetically to the dispatcher, "maybe I am wrong but there is a woman sleeping in a car on N and East 19th. It doesn't look right. Someone should check it out. Again, please forgive me if I'm wrong, but it might be serious."

The dispatcher thanked her for the call and said the EMTs would be there in moments. Mrs. Raber drove on and wondered what would happen. Twenty minutes later, her phone rang. "This is Hatzolah calling," the voice on the other end announced, "Did you call about 20 minutes ago about the lady on Ave N and East Nineteenth?

"Yes," answered the startled Mrs. Raber. "How is she?"

"It's a miracle you called," he said. "She was in diabetic shock and if she hadn't been attended to immediately, she could have died. You saved her life."

Diabetic shock (hypoglycemia) is a serious health risk for a diabetic. If it is not treated quickly, it can become a very serious condition that causes fainting. Diabetic shock can lead to a coma or even death.

Mrs. Raber was stunned. What a *zechus* that she had called Hatzolah! Her mind raced with frightening thoughts. What if she hadn't been there just at that moment? What if she had driven down another street? What if she hadn't had a suspicion that something was amiss? What if she hadn't made the call? What if she had rationalized that nothing was wrong, that it was just a mother waiting for her son? Hashem's orchestration of this life being saved was nothing short of miraculous. She was grateful that Hashem had allowed her to be His agent.

Before the dispatcher hung up, he said, "Remember, whenever you are in doubt, call! Don't have *rachmanus* (pity) on us. Have *rachmanus* on the person who may be in trouble."

Unquestionably a good thing for all of us to remember.

Four weeks later, Mrs. Raber received a call from the mother-in-law of the woman who had been unconscious in the car. "You don't know me," she started, "but I am calling you to thank you on behalf of our family for having made that call to Hatzolah. You actually saved two lives that afternoon, not just one."

"And how is that?" asked Mrs. Raber.

The woman replied, "My daughter-in-law is expecting, and had anything happened to her, the same would have happened to the baby."

Mrs. Raber cried from joy.

"We would like to buy you a gift, we just don't know how to show our thankfulness," said the grateful mother-in-law.

"No, thank you," replied Mrs. Raber. "I would not exchange this mitzvah for a gift."

A few months later a healthy little girl was born to this mother;

and yes, mother and baby are fine, *Baruch Hashem*.

Chazal (*Shabbos* 153a) teach that before Rav died, he said to his students, "אַחִים בְּהֶסְפֵּידָא דְהָתָם קָאִימְנָא, *Give me a warm eulogy for I will be standing there.*" *Eitz Yosef* explains Rav's directive. Throughout life, one's *neshamah* grows spiritually as mitzvos are done or as Torah is learned. When one passes away, that escalation stops. Thus, the *neshamah* remains *standing* at whatever level he has achieved.

However, if a person's memory continues to be an inspiration to others, inspiring them to perform mitzvos, then the soul of the deceased continues to grow spiritually, corresponding to the spiritual growth his example has brought about in others. Rav instructed his students to deliver warm eulogies so that others would learn from him; then his *neshamah* could continue to grow spiritually.

This also explains the Talmudic teaching (*Rosh Hashanah* 32b) that on Rosh Hashanah and Yom Kippur, סִפְרֵי חַיִּים וְסִפְרֵי מֵתִים פְּתוּחִין לְפָנָיו, *The books of life and the books of death are open before Him [Hashem]*. Most people understand this to mean that the books of life and death are open, and in them Hashem "records" who will live and who will die in the coming year. However, others understand it to mean that not only are the books of the living open during these days of judgment, but even the books of those who have passed on are also open. If their deeds and teachings are still inspiring people to do good deeds, they earn more spiritual merit in the World of Truth.

Yossi Pressburger is not here, but his influence lives on. Two lives were saved because his love of *chessed* inspired someone to make a call she otherwise might not have made.

May Yossi's memory continue to inspire others so that it becomes a threefold blessing: for his *neshamah*, for those inspired to do *chessed*, and for the beneficiaries of that *chessed*.

✥ Sick Leave

Rabbi Yaakov Bender, Menahel of Yeshiva Darchei Torah in Far Rockaway, New York, told me an illuminating story regarding *bikur cholim* (visiting the sick). When his father, Rabbi Dovid Bender (1912-1965), was a young man, he enjoyed a close relationship with Rabbi Shlomo Heiman (1892-1945), Rosh Yeshivah of Torah Vodaath. For four years they studied together daily in the Beis Medrash of Torah Vodaas as a *chavrusa* (study partnership). Later, when Rabbi Heiman's illness made it too difficult for him to come to the yeshivah, Rabbi Bender would go to his home in Williamsburg, and they would study there.

When Rabbi Heiman was hospitalized near the end of his life, Rabbi Bender was constantly at his bedside. One day the doctors told Rabbi Bender, "No one is to be allowed to visit the Rabbi. He is too weak. You must keep everyone out — and no exceptions."

Later that day, Rabbi Moshe Feinstein (1895-1986) came to visit Rabbi Heiman. Rabbi Bender was bewildered. On one hand, how does one refuse Reb Moshe permission to enter, especially since Reb Shlomo would certainly want to see the great Torah scholar? On the other hand, the doctors said that no one should be allowed in, as visitors could be harmful to the patient.

Rabbi Bender explained the severity of the situation to Rav Moshe and apologized profusely as he explained that doctors had given orders that no visitors should be allowed in.

Reb Moshe smiled and said, "If that is the case, then the mitzvah of *bikur cholim* today is *not* to visit. However, the mitzvah is comprised of two parts, the first is *visiting* the patient; the second is davening for the patient" (*Yoreh Deah* 335:4). Reb Moshe stood outside the hospital room, recited a *perek* (chapter) of *Tehillim,* and left.

No pressure, no complaints, just compliance — with the *Shulchan Aruch* and with the doctors.

This story brought to mind something that Rabbi Binyamin Moskovitz, Rosh Yeshivah of Yeshivah Medrash Shmuel of Jerusalem, told me. While compiling the DVD, *Sense and Sensitivity: The Essence of Bikur Cholim*, together with my son-in-law Chanaya Kramer of Kol-Rom Multimedia, I interviewed Rabbi Moskovitz about the importance of *bikur cholim* and he said, "Aside from everything else, *bikur cholim* affords us a rare opportunity — to daven in the presence of the *Shechinah* [Divine Presence]."

Indeed, *Chazal* teach that the *Shechinah* rests at the head of the *choleh* (ill person) (*Yoreh Deah* 335:3) "Thus," says Rabbi Moskovitz, "after I have completed praying for the *choleh*, I take advantage of this opportunity and pray, facing the head of the bed, for my own needs and challenges.

"After all," he added, "how many times in life are we able to daven so close to the *Shechinah*? One must take advantage of this incredible opportunity."

"You should advise others to do so," he told me.

And so I am doing just that!

~§ Tehillim Treasure

Rebbetzin Batsheva Esther Kanievsky of Bnei Brak, Israel, who passed away in Cheshvan 5772/November 2011, came from extraordinary spiritual stock. Her grandfather was the legendary Rabbi Arye Levin *zt"l* (1885-1969), the great *tzaddik* of Jerusalem, and her father was Rabbi Yosef Sholom Eliyashiv (1910-2012), the revered *posek hador* in Jerusalem. Her father-in-law was the *gadol hador*, the Steipler Gaon, Rabbi Yaakov Yisrael Kanievsky (1899-1985), and her husband was the *gadol hador* Rabbi Chaim Kanievsky, *shlita*.

Rebbetzin Kanievsky absorbed holiness and character traits from each of these great men and was a warm, loving, caring, concerned, wise mother and grandmother to the

Distinguished Sacred Deeds / 47

thousands of women who came to visit her in her modest apartment on Rechov Rashbam in Bnei Brak. She affectionately dispensed advice and guidance and gave encouragement and strength to the demoralized and downtrodden who reveled in her presence.

One day a modern-looking young Israeli woman came to the apartment. The woman, Riva, was accompanied by her mother, who spoke privately to Rebbetzin Kanievsky to explain the dire circumstances for which she needed help. Riva had become irreligious and now was engaged to a gentile she had met in college. Her parents were heartbroken and thought that if anyone could change their daughter's mind, it would be the Rebbetzin.

Try as the Rebbetzin would, however, there was no swaying the young woman. The Rebbetzin spoke to her about the sanctity of a Jewish family and the beauty of a Jewish home, but though the young woman listened attentively, her mind was made up. Inflexible though she was, she was nevertheless touched by Rebbetzin Kanievsky's warmth and wisdom. Even she could see that the Rebbetzin was holy and genuinely cared about her.

Their conversation was about to end when Riva said, "Rebbetzin, it has been an honor to meet you, but I cannot change my mind at this point. However, I am ready to accept one mitzvah — any mitzvah that you tell me — and I promise you I will try and observe it every day for the rest of my life."

The Rebbetzin was taken by surprise. What could she suggest? What mitzvah could she choose that Riva would not consider too difficult and might cause her to become more opposed to authentic Judaism? The Rebbetzin picked up her *Tehillim* that lay on the nearby table and said, "Recite one chapter of *Tehillim* each day; I don't think that would be too difficult for you."

The two women bid each other farewell and embraced warmly. As the young woman turned to leave, the Rebbetzin said, "Wait. Let us start today. Here, I have my *Tehillim*. Let's read a chapter together."

The Rebbetzin leafed through the pages of her worn and tear-stained *Tehillim*, settled on a page without even looking down, and said, "Let's begin!"

She had turned to the beginning of Chapter 43. They began reading together. שָׁפְטֵנִי אֱלֹקִים, *G-d, please judge me [and see that I am worthy of help against my enemies]*, וְרִיבָה רִיבִי, *and champion my cause.* The young woman and the Rebbetzin looked at each other in amazement. Her name was Riva! What were the chances that the chapter they started would have her name in it? The next words in the verse startled them, מִגּוֹי לֹא חָסִיד, *against a nation unkind.* The word גּוֹי also means *gentile*.

They read on, מֵאִישׁ מִרְמָה וְעַוְלָה תְפַלְּטֵנִי, *deliver me from a man of deceit and iniquity.*

The young woman fell on the Rebbetzin's shoulders, weeping. The message was so clear, the directive so straightforward. Only Hashem Himself could have orchestrated this. Riva and the Rebbetzin cried on each other's shoulders. When Riva looked up, she said, "I won't marry him."

And she didn't.

◈§ A Catskills Payback

It is the custom of Jews in time of need to go to *kivrei tzaddikim*, the gravesites of righteous people, to pray for their needs. The *Maharil* (cited in *Ba'er Heiteiv Orach Chaim* 581:17) writes that one must be careful not to direct his or her prayers to the *tzaddikim*; rather one prays only to Hashem, asking that we be helped in the merit of the *tzaddikim*.

Drashos HaRan (8) writes that those who have already perished [know what is happening in this world, and] can pray for our benefit. He notes that Kaleiv prostrated himself at the *Me'aras HaMachpelah* to pray that he be spared from the counsel of the spies (*Bamidbar* 13:22). (See also *Rashi, Bamidbar* 20:12 and 20:15 regarding the Jews in Egypt, and *Rashi, Bereishis* 48:7 regarding the Jews at *Kever Rachel*.)

In the 1950's and 1960's, a well-known hotel in the Fleischmanns, New York, Catskills Mountains area, was the Lederer Park House, owned by the Lederer family. Many rabbanim, roshei yeshivah, and *talmidei chachamim* would come there with their families for a summer vacation. Among those who vacationed there were Rabbi Moshe Feinstein (1895-1986); Rabbi Pinchus Hirschprung (1912-1998) of Montreal; Rabbi Aharon Kotler (1891-1962); the Blushever Rebbe, Rav Yisroel Spira (1889-1989); the Kopischnitzer Rebbe, Rabbi Avrohom Yehoshua Heschel (1888-1967), and the Satmar Rav, Rabbi Yoel Teitelbaum (1887-1979).

Reb Aharon did not wish to have his meals in the main dining room, preferring instead the quiet serenity of his own room. The Lederers had three sons who fought over the privilege of bringing Reb Aharon his meals. More often than not the honor fell to Sruli.* Rav Aharon came to like him and always thanked him profusely for his trouble.

Decades went by, the staff changed, and new sets of families came to vacation at the Park House. The glory days of Reb Aharon and his contemporaries became a faded memory ... except to the Lederer family. They always took pride and spoke of those magical summers and what a *zechus* it was for the family to host many of the *gedolim*. Mrs. Machi Spitzer, Sruli's older sister, always spoke with pride about how her brothers, specifically Sruli, served Reb Aharon faithfully.

Sruli was now married and had a daughter who was 27 and still searching to find a *shidduch*. Her two sisters were waiting for her to become engaged so they could start the *shidduch* process themselves. Mrs. Spitzer was visiting *Eretz Yisrael* with her older sister, Mrs. Dina Kupferstein and decided to go to the *kever* of Reb Aharon Kotler, who is buried on Har HaMenachos in Jerusalem, and pray that Sruli find a *shidduch* for his daughter. After all, Reb Aaron "owed him one."

They came to the cemetery one late afternoon, and the two women struggled to find the *kever*. Finally they saw one with the name Kotler. There were dozens and dozens of little stones atop the monument, testifying to the fact that many had visited there. Mrs. Spitzer said *Tehillim* and then started talking to Hashem in English. "*Ribono shel Olam,* You know how my brother served this great *gadol,* Reb Aharon. He always brought the meals on time and with happiness. Please ...."

She was interrupted by her sister, "Machi, you are standing at the wrong *kever*. This is Reb Shneur Kotler's (1918-1982) *kever*. Reb Aaron's *kever* is here."

Mrs. Spitzer stopped davening and walked sheepishly to Reb Aharon's *kever*. After saying *Tehillim* she started again, loudly, "*Ribono shel Olam,* you know how my brother Sruli served this great *gadol* Reb Aharon. He always brought the meals on time and he brought them with joy ...." Again she was interrupted.

"You know that Reb Aharon did not speak English," her sister said.

"I am not davening to Reb Aharon," Mrs. Spitzer replied. "I am davening to Hashem and He understands all languages."

She continued davening. "Hashem, just like Sruli brought the meals at the appropriate time and with joy to Reb Aharon, in Reb Aharon's *zechus* please bring joy to Sruli's daughter and bring her the right *zivug* (marriage partner) at the right time."

Mrs. Spitzer left the *kever* feeling fulfilled. She had come to *Eretz Yisrael* for a wedding, but had made a special trip to daven at Reb Aharon's *kever*. She knew in her heart it was the right thing to do.

Three months later, Sruli's daughter became a *kallah*! At the *vort*, Mrs. Spitzer asked her niece who the *shadchan* was. "Let me introduce them to you," the *kallah* said excitedly, "They are Rabbi Shragy Kotler and his wife. Reb Shragy is the son of Reb Shneur Kotler and the grandson of Reb Aharon."

Mrs. Machi Spitzer smiled to herself. *Yes,* she thought. *It all makes sense; for reasons they cannot imagine.*

As people began to put the incidents together, someone figured out that 27 years earlier, on the day the *kallah* was born, her father Sruli was serving Reb Aharon his meals when he got the call that his wife had just given birth to a baby girl, and Reb Aharon had given him a *berachah* on the wonderful news!

Distinguished Sacred Deeds

He probably blessed Sruli to merit bringing his new daughter to the *chuppah*. Who could know that Reb Aharon and his family would play such an active role?

That night the *chassan* had his own story to tell. Reb Shneur had a close-knit group in Lakewood for whom he gave a private *vaad* every week. The *talmidim* of the *vaad* became extremely close to the Rosh Yeshivah and had a close relationship with him. The *chassan* had been a member of that group and his brother felt that Reb Shneur could be an appropriate messenger in Heaven to help him find his *shidduch*! So when his brother went to *Eretz Yisrael*, the future *chassan* asked him to please daven at Reb Shneur's *kever* to help him find a *shidduch*.

> The *kallah's* aunt had davened at Rav Aharon's *kever*, the *chassan's* brother had davened at Rav Shneur's *kever*, and a short time later Rav Shneur's son, Rav Aharon's grandson, was the *shadchan*. *Tefillah* at *kivrei tzaddikim* works!

◆§ First But Not Last

Naftoli Baum,* a talmid in the Beis Medrash of the Mirrer Yeshiva of Brooklyn for a number of years, became engaged to Faygie Hiller.* He told the good news to his Rosh Yeshivah, Rabbi Shmuel Berenbaum (1920-2008). Reb Shmuel inquired about the *kallah's* family, and was happy to hear that her late grandfather was Rabbi Betzalel Tenenbaum, a friend of his from their days in Shanghai, where the Mir Yeshiva found refuge during World War II. Rabbi Tenenbaum had taught in Yeshiva Beis HaTalmud and had been the Rosh Yeshivah in Yeshivas Karlin Stolin in Brooklyn until he passed way.

Reb Shmuel said that he would be glad to be the *mesader kiddushin* at the wedding of his talmid and his friend's granddaughter, and the Hiller family relished the renewed connection. However, two days before the wedding, Reb Shmuel's son called the *chassan*, Naftoli, to say that the Rosh Yeshivah had contracted cellulitis and regretted that he was confined to bed and would not be able to attend the wedding.

Naftoli asked if he could visit the Rosh Yeshivah and was allowed in. Reb Shmuel gave him a very warm *berachah* and said "Don't worry; I will be at the *bris* of your *bechor.*"

Naftoli and Faygie were married, but for five years had no children. The couple spent much time, effort, and money in their attempt to bring a child into the world. There were complicated medical tests and procedures, and tense anticipation as days, weeks, and months went by without any positive results. They thought of going to *Eretz Yisrael* to pray at the *kivrei tzaddikim* (gravesites of the righteous), but it was not feasible as Faygie was under constant medical care.

In 1998 Naftoli won a trip to Israel to attend the Mirrer *Yarchei Kallah* in Jerusalem. He flew to Israel and learned all day. Although he had hoped to daven at the holy places, the learning schedule was so rigorous that there was no time. Nevertheless, he simply could not forgo the opportunity to daven at the *kever* of his Rosh Yeshivah, Reb Shmuel, who was buried in Sanhedria, only minutes away from the *Yarchei Kallah.*

Naftoli went to the *kever* and from the depths of his heart cried and called out, "Rosh Yeshivah, you, said you would be at my son's *bris*. I don't have a child yet. Please, Rebbi," he sobbed "for the sake of my wife and her grandfather, who was your *chaver*, please intercede in *Shamayim* that we be blessed with a child."

Naftoli left the cemetery buoyant, unburdened, and hopeful.

And within a year, the Baums became the parents of a little boy. Incredibly, the child was born on Rabbi Shmuel Berenbaum's *yahrzeit,* 28 Shevat, 5768. The baby was named Betzalel Shmuel after the two hallowed friends from Shanghai, Rabbi Betzalel Tenenbaum and Rabbi Shmuel Berenbaum.

A few days after the birth, Rabbi Usher Berenbaum, Reb Shmuel's son, said to Naftoli, "You know that you will have another child soon."

"I wish you were right," said Naftoli, "but do you know how hard it was for us even to have this child? I don't see how it can happen in the near future."

Distinguished Sacred Deeds

"My father was extremely careful with every word he uttered," said Rav Usher. "He said you would have a *bechor* (a firstborn), implying that there would be at least one other child after the first."

And sure enough, a little more than a year later, Mrs. Baum had a second son.

⌘ Frontline Vision

In 2006 Rabbi Shlomo Mandel, Rosh Yeshivah of Yeshiva and Mesivta of Brooklyn, attended a family bar mitzvah in Passaic, New Jersey. During Shabbos, an Orthodox young man accompanied by his children approached the Rosh Yeshivah and said, "Rabbi Mandel, I am honored to meet you. I want you to know that my children — and what I am today — is only due to your father."

Rabbi Mandel smiled. His late father, the beloved Rabbi Manis Mandel (1916-2006), had been the Menahel of the Yeshiva and Mesivta of Brooklyn for more than 60 years. Reb Shlomo assumed that the young man and/or his wife were probably former students and, like thousands of others, felt like children of the legendary Rabbi Mandel.

"What makes you say that?" Reb Shlomo asked, sure that he would hear the same type of response he had heard on dozens of occasions before. What he heard this time, however, was so startling and sagacious that he would include it among the stories he told when he eulogized his father.

In the late 1930's Rabbi Mandel founded an afternoon Talmud Torah on Meserole Street on the outskirts of Williamsburg, for Jewish public-school students. As a talmid of Rabbi Shraga Feivel Mendlowitz (1886-1948), Rabbi Mandel was imbued with a burning desire to spread knowledge of Torah and love for mitzvos to every Jewish child.

After Japan attacked America on December 7, 1941, thousands of young American boys were drafted; one of them was Nathan (Nosson) Lipman,* a student in Rabbi Mandel's Talmud Torah. Before Nathan left home to join the army, Rabbi Mandel called him into his office and said, "Nosson, I know it will be hard for you in the army to always get kosher food. I can't tell you not to eat what they serve, but this I will tell you. Make a commitment not to eat doubles — a second portion — of any food that you suspect is not kosher. It will be your way of remembering that you are a Jew."

"Throughout my father's years in the army," the young man continued proudly, "he never ate doubles of any food that may not have been kosher. When he was discharged, he was proud that he had maintained your father's standards of kashrus. He now felt more connected to Hashem.

"He figured if he could discipline himself in the army, he could do it at home, too. Slowly he began undertaking mitzvos, one by one, and eventually he became completely religious. He sent me to yeshivah and now," he said, pointing to his children, "look at me! I am in *chinuch* (Torah education) and look at my family. It's all because of your father, his caring, and his wisdom."

> *Talmidei chachamim* are called the עֵינֵי הָעֵדָה, *the eyes of the community* (see *Bamidbar* 15:24), for they have vision and perspective. Rabbi Manis Mandel *saw* to it that the young soldier should remain connected; he thereby caused the soldier's children and grandchildren to be *observant*.
>
> A double blessing, because he refrained from eating doubles.

∾§ *An Open-Hand Policy*

A number of years ago, I was asked to speak at the Agudath Israel Convention on the topic, *Problems and Possibilities in the Secular Workplace*. As a *mohel*, I do not consider myself as working in the secular workplace, so I interviewed more than 50 people — doctors, lawyers, businessmen, merchants, employers, employees, travel agents, therapists, and salesmen — to get a sense of their daily challenges.

It was an eye-opening experience. I learned about the challenges of honesty, anti-Semitism, immorality, and materialism that confront our people constantly. Of all the interviews, perhaps the most memorable was the one with Mrs. Shaindel Becker* of Borough Park. Her insight and the resolution of her problem were remarkable.

Mrs. Becker works with her husband in Lower Manhattan in their ladies' handbag business. Best Bags by Becker* is known throughout the industry for its integrity and the high quality of its merchandise.

Mrs. Becker was a "jack-of-all-trades" in the office. She served as secretary, bookkeeper, designer, and interior decorator of the company showroom.

Every morning she supervised the delivery of merchandise at the warehouse loading dock. The driver, Carlos Mantilla,* would back his truck up to the dock and unload boxes of ladies' bags. Workers stacked them; Mrs. Becker counted them and then signed the manifest. Carlos was a middle-aged family man who always had a smile and a kind word. Each day, after Mrs. Becker gave him the signed receipt, he would shake her hand and bid her good day.

She knew it wasn't proper to shake a man's hand but she never had the courage to say anything for fear Carlos would be insulted and it would harm their business relationship. To Carlos, the handshake was merely a courtesy.

One morning, Mrs. Becker was reciting *Ashrei* during *Shacharis*, saying every word slowly and carefully. She came to the most significant *pasuk*, where we are all required to concentrate on the translation: פּוֹתֵחַ אֶת יָדֶךָ, וּמַשְׂבִּיעַ לְכָל חַי רָצוֹן, *You [Hashem] open Your hand and satisfy the desire of every living creature* (*Tehillim* 145:16). This is our declaration that our livelihood is in Hashem's hands (see *Orach Chaim* 51:7 and *Mishnah Berurah* note 14). She knew it was the *pasuk* related to *parnassah* (livelihood).

She paused and thought about what she just said. She repeated it silently: פּוֹתֵחַ אֶת יָדֶךָ, וּמַשְׂבִּיעַ לְכָל חַי רָצוֹן.

Suddenly something occurred to her that she hadn't thought of before. *It's not about **my** opening **my** hand that brings us a livelihood. It's Hashem's hand that has to be opened. Whether or not I open my hand to Carlos is not what determines my parnassah. If Hashem opens His hand, we will have it regardless. That is all that matters.*

That morning, she checked the delivery and signed the manifest. Before she handed it to Carlos, she asked him if they could talk for a moment off to the side.

"Carlos," she said, "you are always very kind to everyone here. I've never been able to say this before, but please understand, it's nothing personal. In our religion, it's not proper for a woman to shake a man's hand. Please understand, I do appreciate your kindness and efficiency, but I can't shake your hand."

Taken by surprise, Carlos thought for a moment and then said respectfully. "I am sorry if I did something wrong. It won't happen again."

"It's not your fault," said Mrs. Becker. "How could you know?"

Indeed, it never happened again, and Carlos kept up his friendly, perfect service.

> In *Iggeres HaRamban*, the famous letter that the Ramban wrote to his son, he says, "וְכַאֲשֶׁר תָּקוּם מִן הַסֵּפֶר תְּחַפֵּשׂ בַּאֲשֶׁר לָמַדְתָּ אִם יֵשׁ בּוֹ דָבָר אֲשֶׁר תּוּכַל לְקַיְּמוֹ, *When you rise from [Torah] study, ponder carefully what you have learned; see what there is in it that you can put into practice.*" Who would imagine that one could do that when they concentrate on the words of *tefillah* as well?

◆§ Glee and Gaiety in Greece

During the summer of 2012, I had the wonderful opportunity to lead a group of 50 people on a journey to Greece. Guided by a wonderful Greek Jew, Haim Ischakis of Athens, we traveled to various cities that once had sizable Jewish communities. Though *Yiddishkeit* in these communities is just about nonexistent today, the shuls are maintained in their original magnificence.

The shuls in Volos, Trikala, Athens, Salonika (Thessaloniki), and Yannina (Ioannina) were astounding in their beauty. In the beautiful city of Yannina, where we stayed for Shabbos, I told the following story about a yearly celebration that used to take place there. It is part of the heritage of the city where 4,000 Jews lived at the start of the 20th century.

For centuries, many of the Jews in Yannina lived in the old fortified part of the city (or Kastro). Walking within its walls, one could only imagine how festive this celebratory day had been. The day was called *Purimopoulo* (pronounced Purim-oh-poo-lo) in Greek or *Purim Katan* (small Purim) in Hebrew. It was celebrated two days after *Tu B'Shvat*, on 17 Shevat.

The Jews in Yannina were known as Romaniote Jews. They were not descended from the tens of thousands of Sephardic Jews who came to Greece after their expulsion from Spain in 1492 and Portugal in 1497. Rather, the Romaniote Jews were descendants of Jewish slaves, whose parents had been taken from Jerusalem by the Roman general Titus, after the destruction of the Second *Beis HaMikdash*, and who later moved to Greece. Hence the term Romaniote.

Many of those Jews came to Yannina from Sicily, Italy. Sicilian Jews felt they had been miraculously spared from death in 1352, when they lived in the town of Syracuse, and thus they established a day of celebration. This tradition was carried on in Yannina. This is the story of the miracle.

From time to time, the king of Sicily, at the time King Louis of the House of Barcelona, would visit the Jewish community. The *chachamim* and the congregants of the synagogues would come out to greet him.

The royal court demanded that as a show of respect for the ruler, the *Sifrei Torah* of all the synagogues be carried as the people came out to welcome him. Sephardic *Sifrei Torah* are contained in tall round circular cases called *tikkim*. These circular cases, made of sterling silver or wood, are often covered with mantles of embroidered velvet. The cases are hinged in the back; when the Torah is placed on the *bimah*, the cases are opened wide, revealing the Torah portion to be read that day. These open *tikkim* are placed upright on the *bimah*, unlike Ashkenazic shuls where the Torah's mantle is removed and the Scroll is kept open and flat on the *bimah* when it is read from.

Though the *chachamim* in Sicily respected the king, they felt that it was inappropriate for the Torah Scrolls to be used for mundane matters. Therefore, when they knew the king was to visit, they would remove the Torah Scrolls from the *tikkim* and greet the monarch with the beautiful array of closed Torah cases. The procession was colorful and spectacular.

The removal of the Torah Scrolls was a closely guarded secret until one Jew of Syracuse, Hayyim Shami, became one of the king's ministers. He became an apostate, changed his name to Marcus, and betrayed his fellow Jews. He told the king that the Jews secretly despised him and the proof was that when they came to greet him, the *tikkim* were empty, proving that their words of admiration and loyalty were also empty and insincere.

The king refused to believe the accusation. Marcus said, "I can prove it. Go to the Jewish community and tell them to open the *tikkim*. You will see that they are empty!"

The king agreed to the plan and decided to come on a particular day. That day was 17 Shevat. The night before his arrival, the *shammash* in the main shul in Yannina, Ephraim Baruch, had a dream. In it a man of sagacious appearance came to him and told him that a plot would be perpetrated against the Jews of Sicily. The man said, "Tomorrow the king is coming to town. Go quickly to all twelve shuls and make sure the Torah Scrolls are in the *tikkim* so that when the king arrives and the *Sifrei Torah* are brought out, he will be able to see for himself that the Jews really respect him."

Ephraim Baruch hurried to the *chachamim* and *shamashim* of the other shuls and learned that, strangely enough, some of them had had the same dream. They quickly ensured that the Torah Scrolls

Distinguished Sacred Deeds / 59

were all in their *tikkim*, not saying anything to the community members. In the morning, they waited eagerly to see if their dream had been a true message.

Sure enough, by midmorning, the royal entourage made its way into Syracuse. Everyone rushed to the town square to greet the king. The monarch sent a messenger to the first *chacham* he saw who was carrying a *tik*.

"Open it," he demanded as the king watched carefully. To the king's relief the Torah Scroll was there in all its sanctity. The king bristled inwardly at Marcus's lie, but felt he should check the other *tikkim*.

One after the other, the *tikkim* were opened, and in each one the Torah Scroll was there. The king was furious and embarrassed that he had been deceived by Marcus. In a grand gesture, he proclaimed that his loyal Jews would not have to pay taxes for the next three years and that the fraudulent Marcus would be hanged.

The Jews of Sicily composed songs and held festivities in honor of being spared punishment. From then on, anyone with the family name Shami was not given the first name of Hayyim, the name of the apostate minister. The 17th day of Shevat became a day when people went to the shul in the morning and read from a specially written Hebrew *megillah* telling the story of this miraculous salvation.

The *megillah* is an ingenious composition, using words and phrases from *Megillas Esther* to embellish this remarkable story. For example, in describing the night that the *shammes* Ephraim Baruch had his dream, verse 9 reads, בַּלַּיְלָה הַהוּא נָדְדָה שְׁנַת אֶפְרַיִם בָּרוּךְ שַׁמָּשׁ הַקְּהִלָּה אֲשֶׁר בְּעִיר סָרָגוֹסָה, an obvious reference to the words of *Megillas Esther* 6:1: בַּלַּיְלָה הַהוּא נָדְדָה שְׁנַת הַמֶּלֶךְ, *That night, the king's sleep was disturbed.* Verse 14, describing the inauguration of an annual celebration to commemorate the events, states, עַל כֵּן קִיְּמוּ וְקִבְּלוּ הַיְּהוּדִים הַנִּמְצָאִים בְּעִיר סָרָגוֹסָה עֲלֵיהֶם וְעַל זַרְעָם ..., an obvious reference to the words in *Megillas Esther* 9:27, קִיְּמוּ וְקִבְּל [וְקִבְּלוּ] הַיְּהוּדִים עֲלֵיהֶם וְעַל זַרְעָם ..., *The Jews confirmed and undertook upon themselves and upon their posterity ....* In Sicily and later in Yannina, on this day visits were made from one family to another, gifts of food were exchanged similar to *shalach manos*, a festive meal was held in the evening, and many proprietors closed their stores for the day. The children danced and frolicked on the cobblestoned streets all day and night.

> May all Jews, wherever they are, be protected from their enemies from within and without, and may we all merit to see and celebrate the Final Redemption.

◈§ *A Song of Angels*

In 1971, Rabbi Dov Levy started a school for special children in Jerusalem. He had become painfully aware that there were few religious facilities for such children and he wanted his own son, Avrohom, who had Down syndrome, to be able to develop to his fullest potential under *frum* auspices.

The school was called Seeach Sod, an expression found in the Nusach Sefard *Kedushah*, which can be understood as "concealed conversation," alluding to the veiled potential that lies within every challenged child. (שִׂיחַ is also an acronym for שִׁקוּם יְלָדִים חֲרִיגִים, which means "rehabilitation for special children.") The school began with a small kindergarten class and has over the decades grown into a network of schools serving more than 650 special-needs children from throughout Israel. Seeach Sod today includes an early daycare center, preschools, an elementary and junior high school for girls, a Talmud Torah and yeshivah for boys, a vocational center, a community-based residential program, and respite center.

A few years ago, a noted music teacher, Chaim Sofer, was hired to give the boys voice lessons and teach them basic harmony. Eventually there were enough boys to form a choir, and soon the Pirchei Seeach Sod Choir began performing throughout Israel. The sight and sounds of special-needs children singing beautifully touched audiences deeply, and they responded with thunderous applause. At times the boys received standing ovations as people cheered with tears streaming down their faces.

In the spring of 2012, it occurred to Mrs. Yocheved Gottesman, International Director of Seeach Sod's public relations staff, that it would be marvelous if the boys could perform at one of the major celebrations that summer in Jerusalem to celebrate the Twelfth Siyum HaShas of Daf Yomi. It would give the boys a strong sense of self-esteem and provide Seeach Sod with a huge measure of public recognition.

When she contacted some of the coordinators of the events they did not seem interested, except for one group. The organizers of the major English Siyum HaShas considered the offer, but with one condition. Seeach Sod would have to place an ad in the event journal and pay stage rights and a vendor's fee, just as would all the other companies and institutions that would be recognized at the Siyum. The total came to thousands of dollars, which Seeach Sod did not have.

The organization's Chief Executive Officer vetoed the idea, explaining there were more pressing priorities for the use of their limited funds. The CEO did say that if Mrs. Gottesman could find a sponsor, it would indeed be wonderful to have the boys perform for such an esteemed audience. She knew she could not ask Seeach Sod's primary donors for contributions, for she had just appealed to them to help sponsor a summer camp. Her project was additionally hampered by the fact that most people would rather sponsor ongoing therapy for a special-needs child, dedicate a room in the respite center, or buy a wheelchair for the organization than sponsor a performance that would be forgotten when the event was over.

Mrs. Gottesman had to think of someone she had not approached before, someone who was sensitive to children with special needs, someone who had a caring heart. And then it occurred to her: the Wolf family in Brooklyn. They indeed were extraordinary people.

Close to 20 years earlier, they had adopted an infant and then found out that she was autistic. It made no difference to them. The loving attention they provided their precious daughter Bruchie was incredible. The time they gave her, the patience they had with her served as shining examples of parenting to all who knew them. Mrs. Gottesman, then a 16-year-old high school student in the Tomer

Devorah School for Girls in Borough Park, often came to the Wolf home as a volunteer to talk, play, and work with Bruchie. Over the years she spent countless hours in the Wolf home and came to know what astonishing people they were. However, that had been many years earlier. Now she was hoping that they would understand the impact this Siyum HaShas performance could have on the children.

Would they even remember her? Hesitatingly, she called Mr. Lazer Wolf. Indeed, he remembered her well, but explained that as noble as the cause was, his funds were tied up at the moment. His dear wife Goldie had recently passed away and he was having a *Sefer Torah* written in her honor, to be presented at the bungalow colony in upstate New York, where they spent their summers.

However, he did not reject the idea out of hand. He listened intently as Mrs. Gottesman explained the tremendous amount of self-esteem these boys would attain if they were able to perform at that venue. Mr. Wolf said again that money was tight at the moment, but he still wanted to think about it.

He told me recently that when he discussed the idea with some of his friends, one of them offered a fresh perspective. "Look how unique it would be," the friend said. "Here in America you would be honoring your wife by completing the writing of a *Sefer Torah*, which is *Torah She'biksav* (the Written Law), and in Israel they would be honoring her at an event that is celebrating the completion of *Torah She'baal Peh* (the Oral Law). There is a totality here that is not easily achieved anywhere else. And Goldie was a total personality in her *bein adam laMakom* and *bein adam lachaveiro*, so it would be fitting."

The idea was intriguing. A few days later, Mrs. Gottesman called again. Mr. Wolf asked about the choir and the program for the evening. He was stunned by what Mrs. Gottesman told him.

"It's the night of the seventeenth of Av," said Mrs. Gottesman. There was silence on the phone for a moment before Mr. Wolf spoke excitedly.

"I don't believe it — that's the night of my wife's first *yahrzeit!*" said Mr. Wolf. "And earlier that afternoon is when there is going to be the *Hachnasas Sefer Torah* at the bungalow colony!"

And so, incredibly, at the exact same moment, 1:15 in the afternoon in New York, while the *Hachnasas Sefer Torah* was taking place in Monticello, the Pirchei Seeach Sod choir was performing at 8:15 in the evening in Jerusalem, both honoring the late Goldie Wolf. The boys sang the lively song, *Tov L'hodos LaShem*, and thousands of the assembled danced, clapped, rejoiced, and sang with them. It was one of the highlights of the evening.

Recently the head of the Bituach Leumi (National Insurance Institute) visited Seeach Sod. After he had toured the facilities, he said, "In *Kedushah*, the words *seeach sod* precede the words *sarfei kodesh* (holy angels). I am not sure who the holy angels are here in Seeach Sod: the dedicated staff or the precious children."

> I would say that the answer is both. That's why I named the story as I did.

⇜§ Studies in Sensitivity

> *Chazal* (*Yevamos* 89a) teach that Jews are רַחֲמָנִים and גּוֹמְלֵי חֲסָדִים, *compassionate and benevolent*. The common characteristic of these traits is sensitivity to others. In this tender story, we witness a specific sensitivity that manifests itself numerous times. Interestingly, the story comes full circle.

For many years, Dr. Meir Wikler, an author and psychotherapist, had a *chavrusa* (study partner) with whom he finished numerous *mesechtos*. When his *chavrusa* moved to *Eretz Yisrael*, Dr. Wikler began searching for someone to take his place. After making inquiries in some *batei medrash* in his Borough Park neighborhood, he decided to place signs in the various shuls, asking if anyone was seeking a *chavrusa*.

At the Bais Meir Shul,* known for the many *minyanim* that took place there throughout the day, he asked the elderly rav, Rabbi Zisha Berger,* for permission to post a sign. The rav asked what the sign was about and Dr. Wikler explained that he was looking for a *chavrusa*.

"How about learning with me?" Rabbi Berger asked. "I am semi-retired and I would enjoy learning with you."

Dr. Wikler was surprised but thrilled that he could have the opportunity to learn with such a noted *talmid chacham*. "If you would be willing to learn with me," Dr. Wikler said happily, "I would be honored." He hadn't expected his search to end so abruptly and successfully.

Rabbi Berger was already in his high 70's, but his mind was sharp and his Torah knowledge was expansive. And indeed, it was a pleasure to learn with him. The two finished *mesechta Berachos*, but after two years Dr. Wikler began noticing that he had to say things more than once, and sometimes Rabbi Berger would forget what had been said just a few moments earlier. Soon Rabbi Berger was repeating himself and often found it difficult to pay attention to Dr. Wikler.

Sadly, the rabbi was suffering from the onset of dementia and was losing his sharpness and attentiveness. Dr. Wikler realized that he was really just learning alone. There was no feedback from Rabbi Berger and Dr. Wikler missed the advantages of the give-and-take of a good *chavrusa*. He wondered if he should continue his learning sessions with the rav.

He sought the counsel of one of his personal rebbeim, Rabbi Eliezer Ginsberg of Brooklyn. "Don't stop learning with him," advised Rabbi Ginsberg. "Not because you will gain anything from it but because of Rebbetzin Berger. When she sees and hears her husband in contact with a study partner, she is proud and is able to maintain a tie to the past, when he was still sharp and involved. You must continue for her sake."

And so Dr. Wikler continued the *seder* (study session) for a few more months, until Rabbi Berger could no longer come to shul. He was hospitalized for an illness and eventually the *seder* came to an end. Within a year, Rabbi Berger passed away.

Distinguished Sacred Deeds

Throngs of people came to be *menachem avel* the Berger family and spoke about the rav in his good years. When Dr. Wikler came to the home, one of the sons told him, "You will never know what your learning with our father did for our mother. She got such strength from seeing him go to shul, from being able to learn with you. She felt he had a purpose, a direction."

Dr. Wikler was startled, for that is exactly why Rabbi Ginsberg had told him to continue the *seder*. He was grateful for the advice and satisfied that he could be of service to the Rebbetzin. He told the family what Rabbi Ginsberg had advised and they were all touched by his sensitivity.

Two weeks later, he met an older son of Rabbi Berger, who had been sitting *shivah* in a different city. "I heard what you told my brother," he said, "so I must tell you something that they did not remember.

"Many years ago, when my father had just started in the rabbinate, a man in his shul was, *nebach,* in a car accident and was in a coma. He was in the hospital for a while but he eventually was taken home in his comatose state. My father went to visit him every single day and would spend time learning with him. We said to him, 'Why do you go? He probably doesn't even know you are there.' He replied, 'I go because it is a *chizuk* (a source of encouragement) for his wife. She sees and hears me learning with her husband and she feels he is accomplishing something. It gives her hope that perhaps one day he will be able to learn again as he used to before the accident.' "

And so, incredibly, the rav who had learned with someone else just to give *chizuk* to the man's wife, years later was learned with, for the exact same reason: to give *chizuk* to *his* wife.

מִי כְּעַמְּךָ יִשְׂרָאֵל, Who is like Your nation Israel?

❧ Of Impact and Inspiration

The email was only a few sentences, but the heartwarming story it told and the lesson it taught was astounding. The immediate ramifications were heartwarming; the possible consequences for future generations were awe-inspiring.

It behooves each of us to take this episode to heart. One never knows what others see and how others judge us.

In December 2011, Avi, the son of my dear friends Rabbi and Mrs. Michoel and Selina Rovinsky of St. Louis, married Lizzy Bentley of Indianapolis, Indiana. Lizzy's parents, Doctor Richard and Caryn Bentley, are wonderful people involved in their local Jewish community. Over the years they have befriended a wide gamut of Jews, not all of them yet committed to Orthodoxy.

The Bentley hospitality knows no bounds and their home is open to all Jews. The Bentleys attended their shul's Purim *seudah* in 2012, a few months after the wedding; among the invited guests were the Kranbergs,* from across town, whom the Bentleys had come to know through their communal involvement. The Kranbergs are growing in their observance and consider themselves traditional Jews. During the Purim *seudah*, the conversation turned to Avi and Lizzy's wedding, which everyone agreed had been splendid.

The next morning, Rabbi Rovinsky received the following email from his *mechutanim*, the Bentleys.

> *Have you had a chance to see the photos yet? Some great shots — very creative! B"H we continue to receive mazel tovs and nice comments on the chasunah! For example, at the shul Purim seudah tonight, a couple came up and told us they decided to send their kids away to Jewish high school just because of the ruach they saw from Avi and Lizzy's friends at the wedding! They realized their kids would probably not develop such friendships and Yiddishkeit in public school. B"H, isn't that amazing?!*
>
> *Regards,*
> *Rick*

Rav Avrohom Pam (1913-2001) once said that people are wrong to think that the primary *Kiddush Hashem* is when our behavior inspires gentiles to recognize the greatness of Hashem and our nation. "This is not so," exclaimed Rav Pam. "While it is certainly important that Jews act in a way that causes gentiles to think highly of us, the *pasuk* says, '... וְנִקְדַּשְׁתִּי בְּתוֹךְ בְּנֵי יִשְׂרָאֵל, I should be sanctified among the children of Israel' [Vayikra 22:32]. Jews inspiring Jews is what the ultimate *Kiddush Hashem* is all about."

> Imagine the responsibility of *yeshivah bachurim* and Bais Yaakov girls at weddings and other *simchos*. How can anyone drink excessively or dance wildly in a manner that could cause guests and house staff to judge Orthodox people negatively by how they behave at a wedding? The young men and women who danced that cold winter night of December exuded warmth that could bring about sacred generations until Mashiach. What a great *zechus* they had!

৺ৡ Heads Up

The Baal HaTanya, Rav Shneur Zalman of Liadi (1745-1812), was the founder of the Chabad movement, which has adherents worldwide. He authored the *Shulchan Aruch HaRav*, the *Tanya*, and *Siddur Torah Ohr*, compiled according to the *nusach* of the Arizal. Because of his growing number of followers, the anti-Semitic Russian authorities arrested him several times, confining him to a cell where only one chassid was permitted to visit him.

On one of those occasions, the Rebbe asked his devoted disciple to bring him his *tallis* and tefillin. The chassid was surprised. "Isn't the Rebbe afraid that the guards may harm him if they see him wearing his *tallis* and tefillin?"

"Don't worry," the Rebbe assured him. "Hashem will protect me and everything will be fine."

The chassid obeyed and brought the Rebbe his *tallis* and tefillin. The next morning the Rebbe prepared himself for Shacharis and donned his *tallis* and tefillin, with the chassid watching his Rebbe's every move. Soon the chassid heard the guard coming down the hallway. He was terrified, for he knew the guard was a terrible anti-Semite.

As the guard peered into the Rebbe's cell, he stopped in his tracks. He stared intently at the regal countenance of the Rebbe and watched him praying with intensity. He said nothing as he observed the manifestation of holiness in an exalted human being. After a few minutes he returned to his post outside the hallway. The chassid was astounded. He was completely amazed that the guard had allowed the Rebbe to daven without scolding him or threatening punishment.

The chassid went home, brought his *tallis* and tefillin to the prison, and the next morning donned them just as the Rebbe did. When the guard saw the chassid davening, he shouted furiously, "What do you think this is — a synagogue? Get rid of those religious articles — or else I'll throw you into your own cell!"

Frightened, the chassid quickly removed his *tallis* and tefillin and put them away. When the guard was gone, the chassid whispered to his Rebbe, "Why is it that when the guard saw the Rebbe in *tallis* and tefillin he did nothing, but when he saw me, he became furious and forced me to take them off?"

The Rebbe smiled and explained, "*Chazal* teach (*Menachos* 35b) that the verse, וְרָאוּ כָּל עַמֵּי הָאָרֶץ כִּי שֵׁם ה' נִקְרָא עָלֶיךָ וְיָרְאוּ מִמֶּךָּ, *Then all the people of the earth will see that the name of Hashem is proclaimed over you, and they will revere you* (*Devarim* 28:10), is a reference to the people of the world seeing Jews wearing their תְּפִלִּין שֶׁבָּרֹאשׁ, tefillin of the head."

The Rebbe continued, "*Chazal* could have said, אֵלּוּ תְּפִלִּין שֶׁעַל הָרֹאשׁ (*These are the tefillin* **on** *the head*), instead they said, אֵלּוּ תְּפִלִּין שֶׁבָּרֹאשׁ [which literally means, *These are the tefillin* **within** *the head*]. Why did they use that word? We wear tefillin *on* our heads, not *in* our heads."

The Rebbe's insight is beautiful. "When someone dons tefillin he must take what is written on the *parshios* of the *tefillin* and make it part of his mindset. Only those who make that commitment are revered when they wear their tefillin. But if one puts on tefillin without such a firm commitment, such a person has merely placed tefillin *on* his head, not *in* his head. Such an act does not evoke the same reaction."

In this light, I wish to share a powerful lesson that Rabbi Elchonon Wasserman (1875-1941) learned from his great teacher, the Chofetz Chaim (1838-1933), based on the first *parashah* of *Krias Shema*, which is inserted in tefillin.

The Chofetz Chaim's son-in-law, Rabbi Tzvi Hirsch Levinson, was the *mashgiach* (spiritual supervisor) in his father-in-law's yeshivah in Radin. He worked diligently to bring out the best in each *bachur* and spent his entire day in the *beis midrash*. After many years of working with the *bachurim*, he wished to devote more time to his own studies. He told the Chofetz Chaim that he wished to step back a bit from his responsibilities.

The Chofetz Chaim ruled that Reb Tzvi Hirsch should not leave the *beis midrash*, because the *talmidim* are the future of *Klal Yisrael*. The Chofetz Chaim explained his reasoning.

"Every day you recite in the *Shema*, וְאָהַבְתָּ אֵת ה' אֱלֹקֶיךָ, בְּכָל לְבָבְךָ, וּבְכָל נַפְשְׁךָ, וּבְכָל מְאֹדֶךָ, *You shall love Hashem with all your heart, with your entire soul, and with all your* מְאֹדֶךָ, *meodecha* (*Devarim* 6:5). Many people understand the word מְאֹדֶךָ as 'your resources, i.e., money.' However, when *you* say these words, you cannot possibly be thinking about money. First of all, you have no money and secondly, money does not mean anything to you. This verse is exclaiming an intent to sacrifice for Hashem something that is dear: לְבָבְךָ, *your heart*, נַפְשְׁךָ, *your soul*, but what are you thinking when you say the word מְאֹדֶךָ?

"The *Ramban* (ibid.) gives the answer," the Chofetz Chaim continued. "He simply translates the word מְאֹד as *very*. In other words, for the sake of Hashem, one must be ready to give up everything that is dear to him. The *Ramban* uses the words מְאֹד מְאֹד, *very, very*, to emphasize that one must be willing to give up even something that is *very* important to him."

Said the Chofetz Chaim, "What is the מְאֹד in your life? It's the study of Torah. To you there is nothing more important. And that's what you have to be willing to give up for what Hashem really wants, and that is that you continue developing the *bachurim* of the yeshivah and not only be focused on your own personal growth in learning."

In the spring of 1938, Rav Elchonon applied this lesson to himself. He had come to the United States to raise funds for his yeshivah in Baranovitch, which was in desperate financial straits. One evening he felt the desire to temporarily halt his fund-raising, in order to sit and learn. But he reconsidered. "My wanting to learn now is the work of the *Yetzer Hara*, all so that I should not raise funds for the yeshivah, which needs it so badly."

> Let us look into ourselves and see what is the *very* in our lives. Then, when we recite the *Krias Shema* with that commitment, we will be wearing tefillin *within* the head, not merely tefilllin *on* the head.

⇜§ *A Covenant for Eternity*

Having been a mohel *for more than 40 years,* Baruch Hashem, *I was fairly certain that there was not a* bris *story that I hadn't heard already. A* bris *in Bermuda? Been there. A* bris *in Puerto Rico? Done that. West Point? Been there; done that. So what place or situation could there be that*

Distinguished Sacred Deeds / 71

would be new to me? However, my dear friend and colleague, Rabbi Michoel Rovinsky of St. Louis, told me a story that is both inspiring and sad; it is unusual and certainly remarkable.

Rabbi Rovinsky is one of the finest, most capable, and charismatic *mohelim* I have ever met. He is known throughout the Midwest. Having been in involved in *kiruv* with various organizations, he ensures that every *bris*, especially those he does for the non-Orthodox families, is a moving *kiruv* experience. He explains the significance of the mitzvah and often follows up with the families to inspire them to give their child a religious education.

He is so adept that midwives and nurses in hospitals from Dallas to New Mexico, from Milwaukee to Utah recommend him even to their non-Jewish patients, because they know that his care and deftness are unsurpassed. They all know he is a rabbi, but it makes no difference; when it comes to a circumcision, they want Rabbi Mike. So it was no surprise when Reb Michoel received a call from a mother in Winchester, Kentucky, asking him to circumcise her newborn son. The Hagstroms* lived on a farm, away from towns and cities.

The mother told Rabbi Rovinsky that she would come home from the hospital on Tuesday and so he scheduled himself to drive to Winchester, arriving on Wednesday. Since the baby was not Jewish, the circumcision could be done on any day. The baby would then be four days old.

Two days later, Reb Michoel's wife Selina heard from cousins in *Eretz Yisrael* who were making a wedding. "We really want you at our *simchah*," they told her on the phone, "and we were able to get a very reasonable flight for you. We'll pay for your ticket. Would you please honor us and come?"

A free trip to *Eretz Yisrael*? And for a family *simchah*? It was a no-brainer. *Of course* she would come, but first Reb Michoel had to reschedule the Hagstrom circumcision in Winchester so that he could be home with his children. He called and told the Hagstroms that he would have delay his trip to Winchester by a week or so. They were fine with that. "It will give us time to settle in after the birth," said Mrs. Hagstrom — and Reb Michoel could not agree more.

Mrs. Rovinsky found the trip and wedding in Yerushalayim to be invigorating and thrilling. Two days after she returned to St. Louis, R' Michoel drove six hours to the serene and peaceful farm out in rural Kentucky.

As Reb Michoel was preparing to perform the circumcision, Mrs. Hagstrom said, "You are a rabbi, aren't you? In this box, I have something that seems to be Jewish. Would you know what it is?"

Reb Michoel opened the small black dust-covered box and was stunned to see a small *siddur* and a folded tallis. "Where did you get these?" he blurted. "These things are holy."

"I just took it from my grandfather's house. He died two weeks ago and we were going through his belongings," she said innocently.

"Your grandfather was Jewish?" Reb Michoel asked.

"I guess so," she answered matter-of-factly.

"Was his wife Jewish?" Reb Michoel was so emotional that he was almost screaming.

"I don't really know, but if it's important, we can find out by making some calls later," said Mrs. Hagstrom.

"No," said Rabbi Rovinsky. "This is something we must know right now, before I perform the circumcision. If your grandmother was Jewish, that means that your mother was Jewish and you are Jewish and the baby is Jewish. In that case, then what we are doing here today is not just a medical procedure. It's a holy *bris* — a covenant with G-d. And if so, this is a real cause for great celebration."

Half an hour later, after calls were made and questions were asked, it was determined without a doubt that the infant was a Jewish child. Hashem had seen to it that he was not circumcised before the eighth day. True, the *bris* would be done well after the eighth day, but it would be a kosher *bris* nonetheless.

Reb Michoel was beside himself with joy. He wanted to dance. There was no one else at the *bris* except for the parents and Rabbi Rovinsky, but he told them the *Shechinah* — Hashem's Presence — was surely there.

The six-hour drive back to St. Louis flew by quickly as R' Michoel continued to be amazed by the *Hashgachah Pratis* — his wife's trip to *Eretz Yisrael* that pushed off the circumcision and turned it into a *bris*, the timing of the grandfather's death, and Mrs. Hagstrom's curiosity about the contents of the box — all so that the child who was named Eliyahu would have a sacred *bris*.

A few days after he returned home, Reb Michoel filled out a beautiful *bris* certificate, which included the child's Hebrew name and Hebrew birthday. He had it laminated and sent it off with a thoughtful letter to the Hagstroms. He wished them *mazel* and *nachas* and said he hoped the child would grow to be a blessed Jew.

Two weeks later, Reb Michoel received an email that broke his heart.

> *Dear Rabbi Rovinsky,*
>
> *Your kind words and beautiful thoughts have given us much comfort in this difficult time. Your letter and certificate came in the mail just as we came home from burying our son Winston, whom you named Eliyahu. He died suddenly the other day from SIDS [Sudden Infant Death Syndrome], and we buried him on our farm in a quiet, serene place. You wrote that you hoped he would be a blessed Jew and we feel that he died just that way. Thank you for being who you are and for all you have done for us.*

Reb Michoel cried as he read and reread the email. Through tear-filled eyes he looked up the date that little Eliyahu had passed away. It was June 8, 2011, the first day of Shavuos, the *yahrzeit* of David HaMelech. *Chazal* teach (*Shabbos* 130a) that David HaMelech said that he was elated that he had had a *bris*, for there were times — when he was in the bathhouse — that his *bris* was the only mitzvah he had with him, for it was engraved on his body. Little Eliyahu, in a sense, was like David HaMelech: *bris milah* was the only mitzvah he had. In the *Olam Ha'emes*, Avraham Avinu would protect him. He had the sign of the holy covenant of Avraham, and that was eternal.

A Day of Designation

Mr. Yechiel Benzion (Benny) Fishoff is among the most beloved people I know. For more than six decades, he has served and supported a host of organizations throughout the Jewish world. His counsel has been sought and treasured by *Klal Yisrael's* greatest leaders. He has composed numerous *niggunim* and published *sefarim* containing rare letters of *Gedolim*. He is a warm and eloquent speaker and always has a kind word for everyone. Additionally, he is a diplomat par excellence, having settled countless personal, business, and organizational disputes. It is no wonder he is beloved by young and old alike.

On a flight back from Poland where he chaired an international Shabbos gathering of Gerrer chassidim, he shared a poignant story that culminated with an interesting *psak halachah* and an incredible orchestration of *Hashgachah Pratis* (Divine Providence).

With the outbreak of the war in 1939, the tremors of the impending Holocaust were felt throughout Europe, and many people sought visas to countries of refuge. The teenaged Benny Fishoff was able to escape from Poland to Vilna, where he enrolled in the transplanted Yeshivah Chachmei Lublin. During Chol HaMoed Pesach he received a tragic letter from his father R' Dov Berish. Benny's younger brother, Yaakov Yitzchok, had died on 25 Adar 2, but there was no information about how and where it happened. Benny wondered if he was supposed to sit *shivah*, since he learned the news a few weeks after it happened.

He went to the home of Rav Chaim Ozer Grodzinsky (1863-1940), the *Av Beis Din* of Vilna, who instructed him to begin sitting *shivah* immediately after Yom Tov (see *Yoreh Deah* 402:1). Benny followed the Rav's instructions and sat *shivah* for his brother when Yom Tov ended.

Eventually Benny made his way to Shanghai, China, with the Mir Yeshivah *bachurim*, where he remained with them in safety until after the war (see *Echoes of the Maggid,* p. 213). In 1947 Benny came to America, where he married and built his family. He had heard nothing about the whereabouts of his parents, but, knowing of the magnitude of the slaughter of Jews by the Nazis, he assumed his parents and siblings were among the *kedoshim*. He had no specific day to commemorate for the *yahrzeit* of his parents, three sisters, and two brothers, so he decided to keep 25 Adar, the day of his brother's *yahrzeit,* as the *yahrzeit* for his entire family.

From then on, on every year 25 Adar he said *Kaddish* for his parents and family, learned *Mishnayos* as a merit to their souls, and offered cake and liquor in shul so that people could recite blessings in the merit of his father, mother, sisters, and brothers.

In 1983, Benny decided to return to his hometown in Poland to see if there were any Jews remaining from the time his family had lived there. Poland was still under communist rule and Benny realized that he would not be able to travel as freely as he wished, nor would it be easy to solicit information, for people might suspect him of being an American spy.

In Poland he learned that a man named Benslovitch was the only Jew left in his hometown, Wloshchowa. As Mr. Fishoff walked the streets of Wloshchowa, he encountered an old woman who offered to take him to Benslovitch's home.

They took a taxi and as they were driving the woman suddenly pointed and called out, "There he is!"

Benny jumped out of the taxi, walked over to the man, and whispered, *"Dee redst Yiddish?* [Do you speak Yiddish?]"

The man recoiled. Instinctively he feared that the stranger might be a spy. "I am a *Yid,"* Benny whispered quickly. "You have nothing to worry about. My name is Fishoff. I used to live here," he said in Yiddish.

"Fishoff?" Benslovitch exclaimed. " *Dee keeks ois pinkt vee der tatteh!* [You look just like your father!] I remember your family. They were all taken on Erev Yom Kippur to Treblinka. Six thousand people were taken by train. My brother and I managed to escape, but your parents were killed. Your family's *yahrzeit* is Yom Kippur, because they were all gassed on that day!"

Benslovitch invited Mr. Fishoff to his house, where they discussed old times. Benny could not help but notice the trinkets and artifacts hanging on the wall. It was obvious that Benslovitch had intermarried and forsaken his Judaism.

Mr. Fishoff was in a quandary. For years he had been keeping 25 Adar as the family *yahrzeit* and now Benslovitch claimed with certainty that the actual *yahrzeit* was Yom Kippur. Was Benslovitch reliable?

When Mr. Fishoff came back to New York, he went to discuss the matter with the *Gadol Hador*, Rav Moshe Feinstein (1895-1986), with whom he had a close relationship. (Mr. Fishoff had sponsored publication of *Dibros Moshe* on *Chullin* and the *Igros Moshe* volume that includes *Even Ezer* 4 and *Choshen Mishpat* 2.) Rav Moshe listened attentively to the entire story and then asked, "Is that man who gave you the information a *shomer Torah u'mitzvos* [an observant Jew]?"

Benny did not wish to tell Rav Moshe what he had seen in Benslovitch's home. He shook his head, saying, "I'm not sure. I don't know."

Rav Moshe thought for a few moments and then said, "You have been keeping the *yahrzeit* for your family as the same day as your brother's *yahrzeit*. Continue keeping that day for your whole family."

"And what about what the fellow said, that he thinks the *yahrzeit* is Yom Kippur?" Mr. Fishoff asked.

"You can say a *Kaddish* on Yom Kippur for your father," Rav Moshe answered with a smile, "It can't hurt."

Years later, in August 1999, in memory of his parents, Mr. Benny Fishoff sponsored ArtScroll's Schottenstein Edition of Tractate *Kesubos*. Learning of *mesechta Kesubos* would soon be started as part of the Daf Yomi schedule that is kept by Daf Yomi participants throughout the world. Many thousands of Jews and hundreds of study groups opened the volume on the same day in accordance with the Daf Yomi schedule.

By Divine Orchestration the very first day of that new *Kesubos* cycle was 25 Adar 2, the exact day designated by Rav Moshe as the *yahrzeit* of Benny's parents and family, in whose memory the volume was dedicated.

~§ Healing Process

The eighth blessing of *Shemoneh Esrei* begins ,'רְפָאֵנוּ, ה, וְנֵרָפֵא, *Heal us, Hashem, and then we will be healed.* Numerous commentators note that the text of the *tefillah* could have read simply, 'רְפָאֵנוּ, ה, *Heal us, Hashem.* Why the added phrase, *and then we will be healed?*

Some explain that our prayer asks that Hashem should completely heal our ailments and illnesses so that they are gone forever. The intent of the words is thus, 'רְפָאֵנוּ, ה, *Heal us, Hashem,* in such a way that וְנֵרָפֵא, *we will be healed permanently,* not merely temporarily.

Others interpret the words to mean 'רְפָאֵנוּ, ה, *Heal us, Hashem* [from any ailments we may have]. וְנֵרָפֵא, *and protect us against future illness* (Tefillah L'David; see ArtScroll's *Shemoneh Esrei* by Rabbi Avrohom Chaim Feuer, p. 134).

Both interpretations are timely and meaningful. Regardless of how the words are understood, however, one thing remains constant: the onset of an illness, its duration, and one's recovery from it are all dependent on Hashem's will. A doctor is merely His agent in healing and recovery. No human being can decree or guarantee results.

In this remarkable episode told by Rabbi Dovid Gibber of Brooklyn, we witness a man taking matters into his own hands — with obvious Heavenly results.

For years Rabbi Gibber has davened in the Tarnapol shul in Kensington, Brooklyn. He knew that Mr. Aaron Zisel Weichbrod had not been well, but he didn't know many details. Rabbi Gibber noticed, though, that Mr. Weichbrod always davened with great intensity.

One day, Rabbi Gibber said to him, "I am inspired by the way you daven. It's nice to see people who take *tefillah* seriously."

"Thank you," replied Mr. Weichbrod. "But I want you to know that though *tefillah* is invaluable, when someone learns Torah, it is the most wonderful thing. It brings יְשׁוּעוֹת וְנֶחָמוֹת (salvation and consolations)."

Rabbi Gibber is a *maggid shiur* (Torah lecturer) (at that time he taught at the Chasan Sofer Mesivta), so he understands the value of Torah study. But it seemed to him that Mr. Weichbrod was referring to something more specific.

"What do you mean?" asked Rabbi Gibber.

"I have been suffering for a long time with colitis and ileitis," came the reply. "It got to the point where I needed constant iron transfusions because my blood count was low and I was losing so much blood. A few months ago, on a Shabbos morning, I was saying the verse, תּוֹרַת ה' תְּמִימָה מְשִׁיבַת נָפֶשׁ, *The Torah of Hashem is perfect, restoring the soul* (Tehillim 19:8). Suddenly it occurred to me that the Torah teaches us, כִּי הַדָּם הוּא הַנֶּפֶשׁ, *for the blood, it is the life* (Devarim 12:23). It dawned on me that perhaps, to improve my blood situation, I should increase the amount of Torah that I learn. Man's blood is called נֶפֶשׁ, *life*, and David HaMelech wrote that Torah restores the נֶפֶשׁ, so I decided to increase my daily learning time by five minutes a day. I started that 13 months ago, and *Baruch Hashem*, since then I have not needed a single iron or blood transfusion!"

> *Chazal* teach that Torah is considered סַם חַיִּים לְכָל גּוּפוֹ, *A medicine of life for the entire body* (Eruvin 54a). It is amazing that this medicine can be self-prescribed. (See *Orach Chaim* 61:3, *Mishnah Berurah* note 6.)

ᵉ§ *In Close Proximity*

Chazal teach that doing a favor for a deceased person is a great act of *chessed*, because the beneficiary will not be able to repay the favor (see *Rashi, Bereishis* 47:29). Therefore, such a favor is called a *chessed shel emes*, a true kindness. In this touching story told by Rabbi Yaakov Bender, the Rosh Yeshivah of Yeshiva Darchei Torah of Far Rockaway, Hashem's orchestration of events led to a *chessed* that was not only impressive, but magnificent.

Rabbi Simcha Wasserman (1900-1992) settled in Israel in the 1970's after more than two decades in Los Angeles, where he founded and headed Yeshiva Ohr Elchonon (see *Along the Maggid's Journey*, p. 61). In Jerusalem he joined Rabbi Moshe Mordechai Chodosh to reestablish Yeshiva Ohr Elchonon, and served as its co-Rosh Yeshivah till the end of his life.

While in Jerusalem he developed a very close friendship with the Knesset member Rabbi Shlomo Lorincz (1918-2009) who represented Agudas Yisrael. They were *chavrusas* (study partners) for many years.

Reb Simcha and his Rebbetzin purchased burial plots in Har HaMenuchos, near Givat Shaul, in western Jerusalem. They passed away within days of each other: Reb Simcha on 2 MarCheshvan 5753/1992 and his Rebbetzin just a few days after his *shivah*, on 12 MarCheshvan 5753 (see *Reflections of the Maggid*, p. 93).

Many years earlier, Rabbi Shlomo Lorincz had bought a plot on Har HaZeisim (Mount of Olives), which has been a burial place for Jews since Biblical times. Har HaZeisim is one of three scenic peaks located just east of the Old City of Jerusalem. However, after Rebbetzin Wasserman passed away, Rabbi Lorincz told his family that he wished to sell his plot on Har HaZeisim and buy one in Har HaMenuchos, next to Reb Simcha.

His reasoning was poignant and sensitive. "Reb Simcha and his Rebbetzin had no children," Rabbi Lorincz said to his family. "Who then will come to pray at his *kever*, especially on the day of his *yahrzeit*?"

Indeed, Rabbi Lorincz sold his plot on Har HaZeisim and purchased one very close to where Reb Simcha was buried. Seventeen years later, Rabbi Lorincz passed away on Rosh Chodesh Cheshvan. Because the custom is not to visit a cemetery on Rosh Chodesh, the Lorincz children would come to visit their father's gravesite on the day after the *yahrzeit*, 2 MarCheshvan, and then, to abide by their father's wishes, would pray at the grave of his friend, Reb Simcha, on the exact day of his *yahrzeit*, the second day of Cheshvan!

✦§ A Commitment Beyond

Throughout the days of *Selichos* up to the final moving *tefillah* of *Ne'ilah*, which concludes the *Asseres Yemei Teshuvah*, we cry out to Hashem, זְכוֹר בְּרִית אַבְרָהָם וַעֲקֵדַת יִצְחָק, *Remember the covenant of Abraham and the binding of Isaac*. The merit of that commitment to Hashem has often been a source of merit for *Klal Yisrael* throughout the ages. In times of peril, we beseech Hashem to protect us because of the enormous devotion and faithfulness of our great Patriarchs.

The following story is related by the Veitzener Rav, Rabbi Dov Berish Meisels (1902-1974), in the preface to his book of responsa, *Mekadshei Hashem*. It is an eloquent testimony to the incredible faith and loyalty of our people.

I n the slave-labor section of Auschwitz, the Nazis announced that 1600 boys would be rounded up. Anyone who was "too short" to perform slave labor would be sent to the gas chambers. After the *selektion*, it was found that only 200 were tall enough; 1400 were to be killed. The kapos (Jewish camp police) herded these children into an enclosed area where they were held for over 24 hours without food or water.

The kapos seized the boys on the first night of Rosh Hashanah. Many fathers tried to bribe the kapos with anything they had to set their sons free. Some of them had smuggled cigarettes, money, or diamonds into Auschwitz. Every father who tried to save his son from certain death knew well that another boy would be taken to be killed instead. The Nazis knew the exact number of the boys in the stockade, and if the count was short, the kapos would be held responsible and could be tortured or shot. If a kapo accepted a bribe to free one boy, he would seize another boy as a substitute.

On the first day of Rosh Hashanah, a father whose only child, a son, was in the stockade came to ask Rabbi Meisels a heartrending question. "My son has been taken to be killed. I have the money to ransom him, but if I do it, another boy will be taken in his place.

Distinguished Sacred Deeds / 81

May I save my son at the expense of someone else's life? Please, Rabbi, am I allowed to do it? I will obey, no matter what you tell me."

Rabbi Meisels trembled upon hearing the question. The father's sincerity was clear. Pained though he was at the plight of his son, he was haunted by the possibility that he could be the cause, albeit indirectly, of another boy losing his life. "This is a question of life and death," replied Rabbi Meisels, his voice quivering. "In the time of the *Beis HaMikdash* one needed the Sanhedrin to rule on this type of matter. Not only don't we have a Sanhedrin here, but I have no *sefarim* to look into nor do I have any other rabbanim here to consult with. I can't answer you."

The man would not accept this response. He needed clarity; he needed direction one way or the other. "Rebbe," he begged, "please give me a clear ruling while I still have the opportunity to save my only child."

Rabbi Meisels felt helpless. "Please," he said, almost crying himself, "don't pressure me. I don't have any *sefarim* here, I can't consult with anyone, I can't give you a ruling."

The man in quiet desperation said to Rabbi Meisels, " Rebbe, I see you cannot permit me to ransom my one and only child. So if the answer is no, then I accept this judgment from Hashem with love."

"Please, please, my dear *Yid*," Rabbi Meisels said, heartbroken, "I did not say that you cannot redeem your son, I just said that I am not the one to make the ruling. Do as you see fit, as though you didn't ask me."

"Rebbe," the brokenhearted but determined father said, "I did as the Torah requires. I asked a *shailah*. In other times you gave me clarity. Now you are not saying anything. That means that I may not redeem my beloved child."

"I did not say that," protested Rabbi Meisels. "I just said I can't rule on this here and now."

The father said. "If there was any way to permit me to ransom my son, you would tell me. Since you haven't said anything, I assume that the Torah does not allow me to do it. If that is what the Torah wants, I am prepared to let matters be as they are. I will not do anything to remove him from the group."

The father who sobbed softly did nothing — but in reality he did everything. On that Rosh Hashanah, the anniversary of the original *Akeidas Yitzchak* (see *Pesikta Rabbasi* 41), he prayed that Hashem accept his personal *akeidah* as He accepted the one from Avraham Avinu at Har HaMoriah. This father in Auschwitz approached the level of the first father of our people.

> This year, when we read about *Akeidas Yitzchak* on the second day of Rosh Hashanah, let us remember the loyal Jews through the ages, who brought their own *akeidah*.

✥ A Stellar Cellar

Lady Amélie Jakobovits, wife of Lord Immanuel Jakobovits (1921-1999), Chief Rabbi of the British Commonwealth, was a personality in her own right. The daughter of Rabbi Eliyahu Munk (1900-1981), a prominent rav in Ansbach, Bavaria, and Paris, France, Amelie was raised in a deeply religious home. Having escaped as a child with her family from the Nazi occupation of France, she was extremely sensitive to survivors and lived her adult life with a fierce determination to perpetuate the ideals of Torah and *Yahadus* to the coming generations.

Lady J, as she was fondly known, was a friend to all. She had the energy of many women. She was a dedicated wife as well as a doting mother, grandmother, and great-grandmother. She was an ardent writer, a spirited speaker, a dynamic fund-raiser, and a champion of many Jewish causes. She mixed as easily with royalty as she did with the humblest members of her community. I had the privilege to know her, as our families were close when she lived in New York, and I am honored to be friends with many of her descendants.

One Seder night she kept everyone spellbound as she told the following poignant story about a childhood friend named Gerty Guttman." In a sense it was a reflection of her own life: escape, heroism, and commitment. I am grateful to her sister, Mrs. Ruth

Distinguished Sacred Deeds / 83

Neuberger of Borough Park, and to my daughter-in-law, Mrs. Genendel Krohn of Waterbury, Connecticut, for sharing the story with me.

Gerty Guttman was born in 1928 in Nuremberg, Germany, where she and her siblings attended religious schools. As she grew older, it became increasingly perilous for Jews to remain in Germany. The family knew they would have to leave to remain alive — but how — and where?

One day in 1933, Nazi storm troopers marched into Nuremberg and ordered that all major buildings must fly the swastika flag by that evening. In 1936, when the situation became progressively worse, the Guttman family moved to Paris as Leopold Guttman obtained employment with distant relatives. Within a year, Leopold had been drafted into the army, leaving his wife and children to fend for themselves.

In the 1940's, when the Nazis began bombing Paris, Mrs. Minna Guttman and her children boarded the last train out of Paris. It was Erev Shavuos.

The mass of humanity on the train led to confusion, fear, and desperation. Children were separated from parents, men pushed their wives and children onto the train, and some people were even shoved off the train although they had already boarded. For months afterward, Jews and others trying to escape the bombardment and Nazi occupation would crowd onto trains bound for southern France, which had not yet been occupied.

Numerous times, Gerty was separated from her mother by the pushing and shoving at each station, but once the train began moving again, she managed to find her family.

Except for the one time she didn't. No matter how much she searched, she could not find her mother or siblings on the train. She decided to get off at the next station, hoping to find a familiar or at least a friendly face in a nearby village. She wandered from place to place, and one cold night she fell asleep in a forest. She awoke in fright several times and realized she could no longer exist this way. As dawn broke, she saw a lone farmhouse in the distance and decided to knock on the door.

A kind and courageous gentile farmer welcomed Gerty in. He assured her that he would protect her and told her that he was already hiding another girl. He said that Gerty could stay with the other girl in his cellar. Within a few days, two boys and another girl joined them, and for days none of them admitted to being Jewish.

Eventually all the children revealed that they were Jewish, though each was on a different level of religious observance. For now, though, it made no difference; they were happy to be alive and thankful they had shelter from the freezing winter. Two windows near the top of the room were their only source of light. Every day the farmer would lower a net laden with some food through the windows. He could not allow them to leave, for if they were seen by the Germans or their collaborators, the children and the farmer would all be killed.

The five children developed a closeness and a bond of friendship that would last for life. One morning one of them realized that the sun seemed to be getting brighter day by day. Soon afterward they could see blades of grass growing alongside the window frame. That meant that winter was over and spring was coming. And if indeed spring was on its way, what would they do about Pesach?

Regardless of their individual commitment to *Yiddishkeit*, they each had celebrated Sedarim in their families; how could they manage one here? The next morning they asked their host, the farmer, if he could give them some flour, a bottle of water, a newspaper, and a few matches. Somehow they would try to bake a matzah and eat it on the night they would designate as Pesach.

The farmer gave them the water, newspaper, and matches the next day, but it took a few days until he could provide flour. Provisions were very hard to come by and even the farmer had very little food. Eventually the five children were given their flour. It was a day of celebration.

One afternoon, they poured the water into the flour and kneaded the dough quickly as they tried to make it as flat as possible. One of the boys lit the newspaper and the others held the dough over the fire to bake it. They laughed at the weirdest-looking matzah any of them had ever seen. It may even have been *chametz*, but it was one of the holiest matzos they would ever eat.

As evening came, they spoke of their upcoming Seder. There would be no finery, no silver candlesticks, no wine, and no new tablecloth. But the boys exchanged clothes and the girls did the same so that everyone wore something "new" for the Seder. One of the boys remembered the *Kiddush* and one of the girls said the *Mah Nishtanah*. They sang the songs they remembered (probably *Dayeinu* was included) and spoke of the eternal hope of freedom that lies in the heart of every Jew. They ended their Seder by singing together whatever they remembered of the *Chad Gadya*.

> Did Hashem's *malachim* cry that night as they watched this scene from their Heavenly abode? I know that I cried as I typed the words describing this holy Seder.

Rebbetzin Jakobovits finished the story and said to her children and grandchildren, "May Jews never be in that situation again, but may we always strive to be as sincere and dedicated as those children were."

◈§ Missing Sanctity

The great *tzaddik*, the Ohr HaChaim HaKadosh, Rav Chaim Ben Attar, known for his Torah, Kabbalah, and sacred piety, lived a sad life. He passed away when he was only 47; he had no children with his first wife, Patzonia, and although he and his second wife, Esther, had several daughters he died a poor man in Yerushalayim.

Born in Morocco, he left there to settle in *Eretz Yisrael*, but was diverted and settled temporarily in Livorno, Italy, where he lived for several years. Ironically, this turned out to be one of the happiest periods of his life, as the Jews of Livorno supported him graciously. It was there that he wrote his classic commentary on Torah, *Ohr HaChaim*. He writes glowingly about the Livornese Jews in his introduction. "I found the people of Livorno to be *yechidei segulah* (exceptional individuals), who pursued the word of Hashem with diligence." He specifically thanks the affluent Irges, Carvaloui, and Bassan families who enthusiastically helped finance the publication of his works.

To me, the most remarkable story about him took place after he passed away. Although what happened then could most likely not happen in our times, the lesson is relevant to every Jew.

During his final illness, his wife Esther asked, "How can you leave me so destitute? We have no funds — how will I carry on after you're gone?"

The Ohr HaChaim told her, "A month after I die someone will come to buy my tefillin. You should charge him an exorbitant amount, which he will surely pay." Then he added. "You must make one stipulation. He must be extremely careful when he wears them to observe their holiness and sanctity. While wearing the tefillin, he should not be thinking of anything except for Torah and *tefillah*. And he must be careful not to talk *devarim beteilim* (idle chatter) while they are on his arm and head."

A few days later the great *tzaddik* passed away. And indeed, after a month a man from Constantinople, Turkey, came to the Ohr HaChaim's widow in Jerusalem and offered to buy the *tzaddik's* tefillin. The widow told the gentleman that she would indeed sell them to him but there were conditions: he would need to be extremely careful to maintain their extreme sanctity and not be involved with anything but Torah and *tefillah* while wearing them. He readily agreed, and then paid the very high price she requested.

The first morning that the man put on the tefillin, he felt as though he was in a higher sphere. His concentration on the *tefillah* was extraordinary. He felt elevated and inspired as he made a connection with his Creator as never before. His words flowed with ease and assurance as he poured out his heart in supplication and prayer.

Distinguished Sacred Deeds / 87

This went on for a few weeks; the man looked forward to putting on those tefillin every morning. Then one day he was confronted with a crisis. One of his employees came running toward him in shul and exclaimed in a panic-filled voice that he was needed desperately in his office. The man tried to shoo the worker away, indicating with his hand that he did not want to be bothered. However, the young worker, not understanding the sanctity that was required at the moment, insisted that he needed an answer to solve an urgent problem or else his employer would have to come to the office immediately.

Finally the man rationalized that it was better to answer the worker quickly and resume his davening rather than to leave the shul, which would mean a much longer break in his concentration. He answered the query as quickly as he could and resumed his davening — but it wasn't the same.

His concentration was gone; his mind wandered as he no longer felt the elevation he had felt before. He was devastated. At first, he thought this distressing condition would last only the rest of that morning, but when he donned the tefillin the next day, it was as though he was wearing a different pair. The aura was gone. He regretted having answered the young worker as morning after morning he tried to recapture the quality of his *tefillah* but he couldn't. He began to wonder if something was wrong with the tefillin.

One day after Shacharis, he went directly to the town's *sofer* (scribe) and asked him to check the tefillin. He told the *sofer* what had happened and watched anxiously as the *sofer* carefully opened the *battim* (the black boxes) to remove the *parshios* (the parchments within).

The *sofer* gasped in amazement. Wordlessly, he showed the parchment to the man, who nearly collapsed. The parchment was blank! The letters were all gone! The holiness that he had vowed to maintain had been compromised — and so the sacred letters of the Ohr HaChaim's tefillin had vanished.

> It is hardly imaginable that such a stark lesson would be delivered today. But the story is certainly relevant for each of

us who dons tefillin every morning. Tefillin require our attentiveness. Optimally, one should not speak while wearing tefillin; the least one can do is be careful to speak only about something that is relevant to mitzvah observance or to the enhancement of prayer.

And yes, texting is out of the question.

Part B:
Gracious Traits and Character

~§ Noble Compassion

There is a famous expression, "A picture is worth a thousand words." To me, one of those eloquent pictures is the stunning photograph of the US Airways plane, mostly submerged in the wintry waters of the Hudson River, with its crew and passengers standing precariously on the wings, waiting to be rescued by boats and ferries.

It happened on January 15, 2009, shortly after US Airways Flight 1549 took off from LaGuardia Airport in New York for Charlotte, Virginia. Its pilot was Chesley Burnett Sullenberger III, known to his friends in the airline industry as "Sully." There were more than 150 people on board.

The 2 p.m. takeoff was routine, but a minute-and-a-half into the flight, a flock of birds was sucked into the engines of the plane, causing them to stall. Captain Sullenberger radioed the control tower that there was an emergency, that he had no power and that he could not even make it back to LaGuardia. The next closest airport was in Teterboro, New Jersey, but he quickly calculated that it, too, was out of reach.

Below was Manhattan with millions of people. Sully had to crash-land somewhere. If he tried to land on a street or highway, he might kill not only everyone on board but many people on the ground, as well. In a split second he decided to land in the Hudson River. In an emergency landing on water, the nose of the plane must be up and the wings must be perfectly level. Just a few years earlier, the pilot of a large airliner had attempted such a landing but failed to land level in the water. A wing snapped off and the plane broke up; there was an explosion killing most of the passengers.

Sully announced calmly and firmly to crew and passengers, "Brace for impact." Spectacularly, he then landed the plane on the Hudson River as though he had water-landed hundreds of times. It was perfection personified. All 150 passengers and four crew members survived safely. Incredible!

A year later, on the anniversary of the experience, Captain Sullenberger was brought to the Hudson River to recount the event. Asked how he had had the courage, the incredible concentration, and the strength of character to accomplish his heroic feat, he answered that when he was in his early teens he had lost his father under tragic circumstances. His pain and loneliness were excruciating. He said that at that time he resolved to enhance or save lives whenever he could so that no one, if he could help it, would go through what he did.

Sully revealed that when he was gliding over the George Washington Bridge and had to make the snap decision of where to land, he thought of the hundreds of relatives and friends of the people on board who would experience the awful anguish he felt as a youth if he did not land the plane safely. That gave him the nearly superhuman determination to do the almost impossible.

> Sully will be lauded as long as he lives. It was his resolve to spare others the pain he felt as a teenager that gave him the strength to perform a historic feat in a nearly hopeless situation.

> Such noble compassion was displayed by two chassidic teenage girls from Williamsburg, Brooklyn, who wish to remain anonymous. Their act made them heroines, but only a chosen few know what they did.

It was Chol HaMoed Succos and the two sisters were paddleboating on the lake in Prospect Park. A father and his two little boys were in a boat near them. The boys were wearing life vests, but the father was not. Suddenly, a gust of wind blew off the yarmulke of the 4-year-old boy and it fell into the water. The child reached out to grab it and fell into the water himself.

The father instinctively jumped into the water to save his son. From where they were, the girls could not see either the father or the boy. Half a minute later (which seemed like an hour), the father bobbed above the surface with his coughing and choking son. He pushed his son over the side, back into the boat.

However, the father could not get into the boat. He was afraid that if he hoisted himself in by holding the side, he would tip the boat over and endanger his children. He didn't have a life vest and held on to the boat for dear life.

One of the girls immediately took out her cell phone and called 911 and Hatzolah. They paddled toward the boat. The father's face was pale and he was losing strength. He was probably freezing and afraid that he would drown. These girls had lost their own father a few years earlier in a car accident and were determined not to let the two little boys in the boat lose *their* father as well.

They quickly steered their boat alongside his, but realized they were not strong enough to lift him out of the water. Thus they positioned their boat in such a way that he was able to put one hand on their boat and keep his other hand on his children's boat to provide balance and impetus. With the strength he had left, he was able to hoist himself into the boat where his children were. He fell into the boat and lay listlessly on the bottom. The girls thought he had died.

After what seemed like an eternity, a helicopter and a police boat appeared. The police towed the man's boat to shore, where Hatzolah was waiting. Everyone was so busy that no one asked how the man had been rescued from the water. Only the two sisters knew; and no one else would have ever known what they did except that they told their mother that night. They were determined to spare those children the horrible grief they had suffered. They knew the pain and were resolved not to let others feel it.

Noble heroics because of noble intentions.

Gracious Traits and Character

Mrs. Sarah Rivkah Kohn, today married and a mother of children, lost her mother when she was 9 years old. She would come home from school believing that her mother would be there, but, sadly, she wasn't. Sarah Rivkah never forgot that longing for her mother's embrace and the accompanying emptiness she felt. That's why, years later, she and her husband Shmuli started a support group for children who have lost a parent. It's called, "LINKS: We're in it together."

Today, more than 600 orphans are members of LINKS. Shabbatons are held for the girls every year, there is a magazine where they can share their emotions and perspectives, and intermittent get-togethers are scheduled throughout the year so that the girls can verbalize their grief and ease their sorrow. A recent Shabbaton hosted girls from London, Los Angeles, Monroe, Williamsburg, Monsey, Lawrence, Chicago, and, of course, New York. The ambiance and good cheer as they related to each other was heartwarming; the awe in which they regard Sarah Rivkah is incredible.

She recognized their pain because she never forgot her own. She is another example of a noble deed because of noble sensitivities.

Because many of these children no longer have a parent who blesses them Friday night, every Erev Shabbos at approximately 1 o'clock both the boys and the girls receive a phone call with a recorded *berachah,* a two-minute inspirational thought on the *parashah*, and a particular good wish for that week. Any orphan, child or adult, can register to receive this *berachah* by calling 718-305-6080. The *berachah* is given by this writer, who lost his father at the age of 21.

> Through the experience of our own pain we can become more sensitive to others who are in pain. Is someone ill? Has someone lost a family member? Is a family suffering with a child at risk? Is there a child lagging behind in school because he needs special tutoring? Is someone challenged because of a physical or mental handicap? Are there those who need help finding their mate in life? Is a child of a single parent not being taken to outings like others in his

or her class? Does a single mother need help with her shopping because she has no one to watch her children at home? Everyone should react to such situations, especially those who can personally relate to them and can therefore reach into their own reservoirs of the strength that enabled them to overcome these challenges.

People who have gone through pain have a greater capacity to feel the pain of others. Perhaps we should look at ourselves not as having been merely targeted for tragedy, but rather as having been appointed to help others cope with suffering. Of course we would have preferred that our suffering had never happened, but once Hashem has brought it upon us, we can eventually elevate the experience by being His messenger of goodness and assistance.

Perhaps the person who has spared more people from tragedy than any other in our generation is a quiet, reserved gentleman who has suffered like few others. With superhuman determination, he rose from the depths of despair and sorrow to save thousands from sharing his fate. He is Rabbi Yosef Ekstein, of Brooklyn, founder of Dor Yeshorim, whom I had the honor to meet over a decade ago.

In the early 1960's, he was studying in Jerusalem and accepted a position as a kashrus supervisor in Argentina. Years earlier, his father Reb Kalman Eliezer had helped establish the Orthodox community in Buenos Aires, so his son, a young, energetic *talmid chacham*, was deemed by the community to be a wonderful choice for the position. In 1965, a year after he and his wife were married, they had their first child, Ben Zion. Their joy was boundless as they looked forward to building a family, but after a few months they began to notice that Ben Zion seemed to be weak; he had floppy muscle tone, couldn't swallow, and was having seizures.

As he grew older there were other problems, paralysis, mental retardation, and, finally, blindness. At 2 two, Bentzi was diagnosed with Tay-Sachs, a debilitating incurable genetic disease that leads to inevitable death, usually before the child even reaches his third birthday. The wait, the anticipated dread, and the final days of Bentzi's life were almost too much too bear. He passed away when he was 4, but that was only the beginning.

The tragedy repeated itself as the Eksteins had a second child, a sweet girl named Basya. She too started life doing all things normal babies do, was cooing, smiling, growing — and then she too began regressing. Soon it was confirmed that she too had Tay-Sachs. And so from the age of 8 months, the dreaded countdown began. A short while later, little Basya returned her soul to her Maker.

Their third child was healthy, but then they had two more children with Tay-Sachs. The Eksteins were crushed but not defeated. Reb Yosef constantly told his wife what he had heard from his father as a youngster. "You are a miracle child," his father told him more than once. "The building in which you were born, in Budapest, was bombed shortly after your birth. Your mother (Pessel) had to run with you from amid the rubble of the building to safety. Miraculously, you survived. You were destined for great things."

Reb Yosef was never sure what his father meant, but now, after four excruciating deaths over a period of 20 years and his family's move to Monroe, New York, he finally took action. He embarked on a project that would eventually spare countless people the heartache and the anguish that he and his wife experienced.

Though Reb Yosef had no background in medicine, biology, or genetics, he threw himself into researching the topic and soon he became an expert in the field. He attended lectures, read scholarly articles, and incredibly, without a formal medical education, designed a test that would determine if a couple was genetically compatible. After consulting with Torah authorities and medical personnel, he founded Dor Yeshorim, which screens young men and women to determine if their children would be born with Tay-Sachs. The organization began public screening in 1983. Though genetic compatibility testing was not popular in the beginning, Reb Yosef was not swayed by his critics and detractors. He forged ahead to the point where today close to 98 percent of Orthodox young men and women are tested by Dor Yeshorim.

Rabbi Ekstein created an international system that has eradicated the occurrence of Tay-Sachs and other recessive genetic illnesses common to Jews of Eastern European descent. Over the years, tens of thousands of young men and women have been tested. Dor Yeshorim has informed more than 1700 couples that they were not compatible, which meant that they had a one-in-four chance of having a child with Tay-Sachs. Dor Yeshorim has thus spared 3400 families (and their relatives and friends) from tragedies! The results are kept absolutely confidential.

> One can only imagine the *zechus* of Reb Yosef Ekstein and his colleagues at Dor Yeshorim. And by the way, ever since he started public screening, he and his wife have been blessed with five healthy children!
>
> Noble people with noble intentions; how fortunate we are to have them in our generation — and to learn from their example.
>
> Indeed, this is how Rav Samson Raphael Hirsch understands the words that Hashem said to Avraham Avinu: וֶהְיֵה בְּרָכָה, *And you shall be a blessing* (*Bereishis* 12:2). It is not that Avraham Avinu was told that he would become blessed but rather it was a directive that he should be a blessing to mankind by bringing happiness and inspiration. Thus it is a directive to *every* Jew to be a blessing to others. We can learn from people like Chesley Sullenberger, the two Williamsburg girls, Sarah Rivkah Kohn, and Rabbi Yosef Ekstein — and we would be wise to do so.

◈§ Standing Tall

When visitors would bid farewell to Rabbi Yosef Chaim Sonnenfeld (1848-1932), the Rav of Yerushalayim, he would always be sure to tell them, וּרְאֵה בְּטוּב יְרוּשָׁלָיִם, *And may you gaze upon the goodness of Jerusalem* (*Tehillim* 128:5). It was a gentle reminder that one should always see the positive aspects of the sacred city and its people. Knowing that all too often people focus on the negative, Rabbi Sonnenfeld counseled them to look for and say only good things.

This is the essence of the memorable phrase that the Rebbe Reb Elimelech of Lezhensk (1717-1787) wrote in his lengthy prayer, תְּפִלָּה קוֹדֶם הַתְּפִלָּה, *Prayer Before the Prayer*, which many recite before Shacharis every morning. It is a moving supplication to Hashem asking that we achieve closeness to Him and to mankind. It includes the plea, אַדְרַבָּה תֵּן בְּלִבֵּנוּ שֶׁנִּרְאֶה כָּל אֶחָד מַעֲלַת חֲבֵרֵינוּ וְלֹא חֶסְרוֹנָם, *To the contrary; place in our hearts the capacity to see the virtues of our friends and not their faults.*

Looking for the Good was indeed the topic of the Chofetz Chaim Heritage Foundation's international program for Tishah B'Av 5772/2012. After relating the aforementioned thoughts of Rabbi Yosef Chaim Sonnenfeld and the Rebbe Reb Elimelech, I told the following remarkable story that I first heard from Mrs. Shaindy Applebaum of Brooklyn.

Reader — be prepared; your attitude toward others may change forever.

In December 2004, Rabbi Eliezer Geldzahler, Rosh Yeshivah of Yeshivas Ohr Yisroel in Brooklyn, known for his inspirational effect on his many talmidim and his vibrancy in *Chassidus,* tragically passed away after he was in a terrible bus accident in Israel. His family, including his wife Baila and 13 children, friends, admirers, and *talmidim* were devastated by this horrific loss. All who knew his greatness in Torah and *ahavas Yisrael* grieved for weeks and months afterward.

Two years after his passing, Rabbi Geldzahler's daughter Chana Malka was driving on the Garden State Parkway in New Jersey. She stopped at a rest stop to get gas. A dwarf who worked at the station came to the car and started pumping gas. After inserting the nozzle securely, he began washing the car windows. He noticed a large picture of Rabbi Geldzahler on the back seat.

He stopped working and asked Chana Malka, "You know that man?"

Surprised at the question, Chana Malka answered, "Yes, he was my father."

"What do you mean *was*?" asked the dwarf, suddenly looking concerned.

She said slowly, "He lost his life in a bus accident two years ago."

The dwarf looked horrified and began to cry.

"You knew my father?" Chana Malka asked in amazement.

"I have been waiting for him for the last two years," the dwarf said. "You see, every day I come to work, hot or cold, rain or shine. People stop for gas all day long. No one ever looks at me. I know I look unusual and people are afraid of me. Even when they pay me they avoid eye contact.

"A few years ago, your father came for gas. He looked me straight in the eye, as no one ever did. 'You are an inspiration,' he said. 'You were born with a condition that some would consider a severe handicap, but you did not let yourself become a victim. You get up every morning, you come to work, and you earn an honest wage. You are a role model. I am the head of a large school in Brooklyn,' your father said, 'and today I will tell all the boys about you, for you are a shining example.'"

The dwarf looked up at Chana Malka and, shaking his head from side to side, said with tears in his eyes, "Your father made me feel special. He made me feel tall."

~§ Real Power

Another remarkable example of looking for the good in others involved a friend of mine. He owns Maximum Light and Power,* which builds power lines for electric utilities across America. More than 20 years ago, the company put in a bid to build seven miles of power lines in New England.

Only a few of the top construction companies had been invited to submit bids. The inviolable rule in their business is that a bid must include all expenses expected to be paid by the municipality. Nothing can be added after submission. Nathan Weiner,* an officer in the Estimating and Engineering Dept. of Maximum Light and Power, was assigned to calculate what the municipality should be charged to have the power lines installed. The competition for the lucrative contract was fierce.

Mr. Weiner formulated Maximum's bid after an intense analysis of the engineer's drawings, charts, and maps. His submitted bid was by far the lowest, and after a few hours of deliberation Maximum was awarded the contract.

Mr. Weiner was elated that his bid was successful, but he was puzzled by how his bid could have been more than two million dollars lower than that of his closest competitor. Something was not right. He went back to his office late at night to unravel the enigma.

Close to midnight, he realized that he had made a colossal error. Inadvertently, he had failed to include one part of the engineer's drawing in his calculations. That part represented one mile of the power lines — he had presented the cost of *six* miles of power lines, not seven! This could potentially be a loss of over two million dollars to his company! He was stunned and humiliated. He could not sleep all night.

The next morning he came into the office of my friend, Manny Poster,* and handed in his resignation. "What in the world is this?" exclaimed Manny, who is an extroverted, gregarious person.

Mr. Weiner, a grown man, started crying. "Mr. Poster, I did the dumbest thing I have ever done. I am resigning because due to my error you stand to lose over two million dollars. I presented the bid for six miles instead of seven."

"Now you listen to me," Manny said forcefully. "There is no way I will accept your resignation and you are and will always be my man in estimating and negotiations."

"But look at the loss I've caused you. How can the company afford this?" Mr. Weiner groaned. "How will I ever make this up to you?"

Manny sighed and said, "Nathan, look at it this way. You are now my most trusted estimator and negotiator — because I know without a doubt that you will never make this kind of mistake again. You will be so meticulous in your calculations from now on, that there is no one, and I repeat, *no one*, that I would trust more than you! Anyone can make a mistake, but you will never make this one again, so you are more than ever my man. Get back to your office and know I have full confidence in you."

Unbelievable as it may sound, a few months later Nathan Weiner was promoted to Vice President of Estimating and Engineering, a top position in one of the leading companies in the field. It happened because Manny Poster saw the good in what seemed to be a horrendous situation. Who would think to look at a two-million-dollar mistake as a stepping stone for future achievement? Only a positive, caring, considerate individual who is shrewd enough to see the good in everyone. That is *real* light and power. I am proud that Manny considers me a friend.

⋈§ An Unlocked Secret

Shlomo HaMelech writes, "דְּרָכֶיהָ דַרְכֵי נֹעַם, *The ways of [the Torah] are sweet*" (*Mishlei* 3:17). We should strive in our everyday behavior to live up to this credo. Our *Gedolei Torah* personify this characteristic in their daily lives, and this is one reason we are exhorted to be close to them, so that we can learn from their example.

Fishel Levner,* a talmid in the Gateshead Yeshivah Gedolah in England, was a sprightly boy whose comments always made others laugh. He was popular with both staff and students, as he was a *masmid* (diligent in his Torah studies), kind and generous, and quick with a quip.

After three years in the yeshivah, he decided to learn in *Eretz Yisruel*. His friends prepared a *seudas preidah* (farewell party) for him. There was much excitement and anticipation for the festive *seudah,* especially because everyone was looking forward to the unique speech that Fishel would surely give. The speech turned out to be more than anyone expected.

Rabbi Avrohom Gurwicz, the Rosh Yeshivah, spoke glowingly about Fishel's learning and spirit, and his comments were echoed by another rebbi and by Fishel's *chavrusa* — (study partner). Then it was Fishel's turn. He spoke about his years in the yeshivah, praised his rebbeim and friends, and then said the following.

"All of us know about the Rosh Yeshivah's greatness in Torah, but I would like to tell you about the Rosh Yeshivah's *middos.* This happened three days after I came into the yeshivah. I was playing around with friends and soon they started chasing me. I ran to the back of the *Beis Midrash* and into the *otzar* (the library). I locked the door so they could not enter. They banged on the door incessantly, but I just laughed, telling them I would never let them in, so they might as well give up. And indeed, after a few minutes they left.

"However, about 10 minutes later the knocking resumed. 'Who's there?' I called out.

" 'It's the Rosh Yeshivah,' came the reply. 'I need a sefer.'

" 'Oh, you can't fool me,' I said derisively. 'I know it's you chaps, so I'm not opening the door.'

"A minute later there was a knock again. 'It's the Rosh Yeshivah,' said the voice on the other side. 'I need a *sefer.*' Once again I didn't believe it.

" 'Don't try and fool me,' I said, 'I know it's you chaps.'

"There was silence on the other side of the door. A few seconds later, there was a softer knock and the voice said, 'It's the Rosh Yeshivah.'

"It then dawned on me that perhaps it really *was* the Rosh Yeshivah. I opened the door slowly, peeked out, and saw to my utter dismay it really was our Rosh Yeshivah! I was humiliated beyond belief. But before I could even say a word, the Rosh Yeshivah had bowed his head and covered his eyes with his hand so he wouldn't see me and I would not be embarrassed. He walked right past me into the *otzar.*

"I hurried out, astounded by the Rosh Yeshivah's sensitivity."

Fishel continued "Until this moment, the Rosh Yeshivah had no idea who that *bachur* was. Tonight I want to publicly ask the Rosh Yeshivah for *mechilah* and thank him for his great kindness and sensitivity. I know one thing for sure: had the Rosh Yeshivah seen me that day, I would have left the yeshivah that afternoon because of the humiliation. It was only the Rosh Yeshivah's great sensitivity that allowed me to stay here and have three wonderful years of learning."

Everyone had expected Fishel's speech to be memorable. They never anticipated how unforgettable it would really be.

❧ Wedding Gift

Chazal (*Taanis* 25b) teach that once there was no rain in *Eretz Yisrael* and there was a danger of famine. The community asked Rabbi Eliezer to pray for rain. He prayed — but the rain did not come. The people then went to Rabbi Akiva and beseeched him to pray. He composed the *tefillah Avinu Malkeinu (Our Father, our King)* and it rained.

Not surprisingly, people murmured that, obviously, Rabbi Akiva was a greater *tzaddik* than Rabbi Eliezer. Then, a Heavenly voice (*bas kol*) declared, "*It's not that one is greater than the other, but this one [Rabbi Akiva] is* מַעֲבִיר עַל מִדּוֹתָיו, *a forgiving person, and the other [Rabbi Eliezer] is not a forgiving person.*"

The *Mesillas Yesharim* (Chapter 19) teaches that when one does not have the kind of *middah* that Rabbi Akiva had, Hashem judges him strictly according to the letter of the law. Hence, when a person is forgiving, lenient, and yielding after being wronged, Hashem acts "measure for measure" and is forgiving, lenient, and yielding when the person does something wrong. Thus, the *tefillos* of people like Rabbi

Akiva are more likely to be answered. The *Mesillas Yesharim* concludes that when one does *chessed* (acts of kindness), Hashem in return grants him *chessed* as well.

In this incredible story that I first heard from Rabbi Moshe Chaim Byron, of Sanhedria Murchevet in Jerusalem, we witness the trait of a yielding personality, and its unbelievable aftermath.

In Jerusalem there is a wedding hall known as the Wolf Hall, run by the world-renowned *tzedakah* organization, Yad Eliezer. There are two banquet halls situated side by side within the building. Ulam Aleph is a bit a larger and more elaborate than Ulam Beit, but they are both relatively simple compared to some of the other wedding venues in the city.

In March 2009, two families called the caterer at the Wolf Hall on the same day to schedule weddings for the same evening. The Goldbergs* called earlier in the day and requested the larger hall, Ulam Aleph. The caterer agreed and the Goldbergs came in to sign a contract. A few hours later the Silverbergs* called to make a wedding there on the same evening, and they too wanted the larger hall. The caterer explained that regrettably Ulam Aleph was already taken, as the Goldbergs had signed a contract. Having no choice and needing the wedding the same night, the Silverbergs agreed to use Ulam Beit.

A few days later the Silverberg *kallah* called the Goldberg *kallah* and asked her if she would be willing to switch so that her family could use the larger room. "We are having family come from America and we are now expecting more people than we originally thought, so we could really use the extra space in Ulam Aleph."

"I have to discuss the matter with my parents," the Goldberg *kallah* said. They discussed it and after a few days the Goldberg *kallah* called back the Silverberg *kallah* to say, "I am really sorry. We too need the extra space so we can't give up the larger room."

"I understand," said the Silverberg *kallah* somewhat dejectedly but politely. "Your family did call first, so you are entitled to it."

Time went by and both families sent out invitations. On Shabbos *Parashas Vayeitzei* the Goldberg *kallah* was in shul listening attentively to *Kerias haTorah*. She remembered that Rashi explains how Rachel gave up her chance to marry Yaakov and gave her sister Leah the passwords and signals that she and Yaakov had made up so that her father Lavan could not deceive Yaakov. Rachel made an enormous sacrifice so that Leah would not be embarrassed (see *Bereishis* 29:25 and *Rashi*). The Goldberg *kallah* then thought, *Rachel, who gave up what was precious to her, is known as the "Mammeh Rachel," the quintessential mother of Klal Yisrael. Hundreds of thousands have gone to pray at Kever Rachel, but not everyone goes to pray at Leah's kever. And the Beis HaMikdash was located in Binyamin's portion of Eretz Yisrael and he was a descendant of Rachel.*

She thus decided right then that she would be like Rachel and be a *vatran* — and give up her right to the larger banquet hall. At home after davening, she discussed it with her parents. Her parents said, "This is your wedding. If you would rather take the smaller hall for yourself, it will be a bit more crowded. But if that's what you want, it is okay with us."

That Motza'ei Shabbos the Goldberg *kallah* called the Silverberg *kallah* and said, "I was thinking about it, and after having discussed it with my parents we decided that you and your family can have Ulam Aleph. We will manage in Ulam Beit. And the fact that the invitations are out is no problem because they don't mention the Ulam. They will just post signs at the entrance: Silverberg guests — Ulam Aleph; Goldberg guests — Ulam Beit.

The Silverberg *kallah* was overjoyed. Now her family would be seated more comfortably and there would be more dancing room. She thanked the Goldberg *kallah* profusely.

The night of the wedding, the caterer at Wolf Hall received a call from a wealthy man in New York. "I am marrying off my daughter tonight," he said, "and *Baruch Hashem* I am able to do it in a comfortable manner. I am so grateful to Hashem for all that He has provided for me and my family that I would like to sponsor a wedding in Yerushalayim on this same night. I know you have two wedding halls and that one is more modest than the other. Probably those in the smaller hall are more financially strapped; so I would like to pay for the entire wedding that is taking place in Ulam Beit."

And that is exactly what he did. He paid for the catering, the photographer, the flowers, and the music.

> The *Ribono Shel Olam* saw how the Goldberg *kallah*, a daughter in *Klal Yisrael*, acted, and He acted accordingly. Because of her overwhelming *chessed* and *vitur*, Hashem granted her great *chessed* as well. Exactly as the *Mesillas Yesharim* wrote.

◆§ Bread of Survival

The following story of *Hashgachah Pratis* (Divine Providence) is one of the most touching I have ever heard. I am grateful to Rabbi Michoel Levi, *Menahel* of Beis Yaakov D'Rav Meir of Brooklyn, for having shared it with me. He heard it from the brother of the protagonist, who wishes to remain anonymous.

For more than two years, Mrs. Rachel Hendelis* tended to her ailing mother in the hospital. She would sit by her mother's bedside for hours every day. Usually there was not much for her to do as her mother lay quietly asleep; however, Mrs. Hendelis felt it was important to be there in case of an emergency. Indeed, every so often a crisis arose and she was grateful to have been there.

After some time in the hospital, her mother passed away. Looking back at the ordeal of her mother's illness, Mrs. Hendelis thought that it would be a good idea if there were a volunteer system in which people would donate their time to take over a shift at the hospital, offering respite to family members. After some research she found the HILF (Yiddish: help) organization in the Williamsburg section of Brooklyn, New York, that offers that service — and more.

Aside from sending volunteers to hospitals to take over for family members at a patient's bedside and to call the family in case of an emergency, the wonderful people at HILF have designed a system whereby women cook meals for homebound elderly people, especially Holocaust survivors. The meals are cooked following impeccable kashrus standards, and drivers are assigned to pick up and deliver the food. Every woman has her "day," and she knows that by late afternoon the meals will be dutifully picked up and delivered. Mrs. Hendelis readily joined this volunteer group; her "day" was Tuesday. Indeed, every Tuesday she would rise early and cook for numerous people, including two elderly couples who were Holocaust survivors. By late afternoon, the designated driver would arrive, pick up the hot meals, and deliver them. The food was always most appreciated.

One morning Mrs. Hendelis received a call from the ladies at HILF. They asked if, just this once, she could cook for an elderly woman on Wednesday and deliver it herself. "Unfortunately," a woman in the office said kindly, "the usual cook and driver are not available. Could you do it? The woman lives near you."

"Of course," replied Mrs. Hendelis warmly. "I would do anything for HILF."

The next Monday, Mrs. Hendelis went shopping for special fruits and vegetables. She also made sure that the spices she had at home were neither too sharp nor bitter. On Tuesday she began cooking for her regulars and for the woman to whom she would deliver on Wednesday.

On Wednesday afternoon, as she drove to the recipient's home, she thought yet again at how wonderful and humble the people at HILF were. They did not hold public fund-raising functions; the organization was supported by just a few private people who raised the needed funds in a quiet dignified manner. She was proud to be a member of HILF.

When she rang the bell, a frail elderly woman came to the door and welcomed her. "I am from HILF," Mrs. Hendelis said proudly. "Today the usual driver could not be here and so I brought your meal myself."

The fragile woman looked up at Mrs. Hendelis and said softly, "Would you mind coming into my apartment for a few moments?"

"Surely," said Mrs. Hendelis. "Is there any other way I can help you?"

By now the two women were in the apartment's small dining room. The elderly woman's next words were startling and puzzling. "Do you mind if I look at your face?" she said, gazing intently at Mrs. Hendelis. Mrs. Hendelis was not sure if the elderly woman was completely rational.

"Please sit down," the woman said. "I seldom leave the house, so I don't get a chance anymore to speak to many people. Please stay for a few moments."

Mrs. Hendelis sat down and began to make small talk. All the while the woman stared at her intently. Suddenly she interrupted and said in a soft voice. "Are you Leah Sternberg's* daughter?"

Mrs. Hendelis was startled. "Yes, I am," she responded. "How did you know?"

The woman took Mrs. Hendelis's hand in hers and said with a pained smile, "You look just like her. I can never forget her."

She paused for a moment, not sure how to continue. Mrs. Hendelis noticed tears welling in the eyes of the woman sitting across from her. "Sixty-seven years ago your mother and I were in the Auschwitz/Birkenau concentration camp together. At one point your mother was so thin, she couldn't have weighed more than 80 pounds. We had been given our bread ration for the day, but your mother felt that she would faint if she could not get a little more to eat. She came over to me and asked for some of my bread. 'I won't make it otherwise. I am so weak,' she said. Of course, I gave her some bread."

The woman paused as she formulated what she wanted to say next. "Later she said to me, 'I don't know if we will ever get out of here alive. But if we do I promise you that one day I will pay you back.'"

The woman clutched Mrs. Hendelis's hand in hers and added, "Today she paid me back."

✒ To Walk the Talk

I often discuss the conflicts people have in their responsibilities to the community vis-a-vis the obligations they have to themselves and their family. *Chazal* note that צָרְכֵי עַמְּךָ יִשְׂרָאֵל מְרוּבִּין, *the needs of the Jewish nation are many* (Berachos 29b), and we all have a responsibility to help shoulder the burden. However, at times one wonders, at what cost in time and effort?

Rav Yitzchok Volozhiner writes in the introduction to his father's (Rav Chaim Volozhiner) classic work *Nefesh HaChaim*, "My father would rebuke me when he saw that I did not become involved with the anguish [and problems] of others. He constantly told me, 'This is the essence of man: לֹא לְעַצְמוֹ נִבְרָא, *he was not created for himself!* Rather [he was created] to help others in any way that is humanly possible."

Hashem did not bless us with talents or finances so that we should become rich and famous. He endowed us with His "gifts" so that we can benefit others. In this incredible story, we witness a rav extending himself in an extraordinary manner. I first heard the story in Detroit from the rav's son, Rabbi Shmuel Zimmerman. A few weeks later, the rav himself confirmed it and filled in the details.

In 1953, Rabbi Dr. Shraga Zev (Philip) Zimmerman (1928-2011) was an army chaplain in Camp (now Fort) Gordon, a huge facility outside Augusta, Georgia. This base in southeast America was known for its advanced military training for the United States Army Signal Corps. At the time, the United States was at war in Korea and the casualties were heavy. America lost more than 33,000 soldiers in that war. One Friday night as Rabbi Zimmerman was preparing his chapel for the Jewish servicemen who would come for services, a young soldier walked in carrying some letters. He seemed anxious and worried.

"Chaplain," he began. "I need a very big favor and I was wondering if there was any way you could help me."

"I will certainly try," replied Rabbi Zimmerman with a gentle smile. "First of all, *Shabbat Shalom*. Why don't you have a seat and we can talk."

The young man was too nervous to sit. He began in a frightened voice. "I need your help, Chaplain. I have three letters here. The first is an order notifying me that I am to be shipped overseas on Sunday morning to fight in Korea. Chaplain, I need a compassionate transfer," the young man pleaded desperately. "I am an only child to my elderly parents. We all survived the concentration camps — but now they are so frail and in such bad health! They would literally die if they knew that I was shipped out to Korea. The other two letters are from their cardiologists. The letters confirm their ill health and note how dangerous it would be to them if I go to Korea."

"We are in the middle of a war," Rabbi Zimmerman said, stating the obvious. "I don't know if I can do anything, but I will try."

Although it was Shabbos, Rabbi Zimmerman told me, Camp Gordon was surrounded by tall fences and he felt that he was permitted to carry the letters to the officer who might have the authority to countermand the transfer order. On Shabbos morning Rabbi Zimmerman rose early and walked six miles to the command post, where he hoped to speak to the commanding officer.

"Chaplain, what are you doing here so early?" said General James* as he greeted Rabbi Zimmerman.

"I have a great favor to ask you, sir," Rabbi Zimmerman replied.

He went on to explain the young serviceman's situation and his fear for his parents' lives, and requested that the orders be changed. He displayed the letters. General James had listened intently. He eyed the letters quickly and then firmly announced, "We are at war, Chaplain. There can be no reassignment and no transfer!" And then, to add emphasis to what he had just said, the general took hold of Rabbi Zimmerman's lapel. On it was pinned the official Jewish Chaplain insignia, depicting the *Aseres Hadibros* (the Ten Commandments). "You see these tablets," the Commander thundered. "They are made of stone. You know why they are made of stone? Because stones can't be broken. My orders are like stone —

they can't be broken. There will be no transfer and no reassignment."

Rabbi Zimmerman had considered that his request would be rejected, but he was stunned at the harsh and seemingly insensitive reaction. He thanked General James for his time, turned, and left the office. As he began his long six-mile walk back to where he was stationed, the general, who was standing at the door, called to him, "Chaplain, where's your jeep?"

"I have no jeep, sir," Rabbi Zimmerman replied.

"You have no jeep? How did you get here?" General James said with surprise.

"I walked, sir," Rabbi Zimmerman said as he turned back toward the general. "Today is our Sabbath, sir, and we are not permitted to drive a car. I wanted to help that serviceman and so I walked the six miles here this morning."

The general was astounded and asked incredulously, "You mean to tell me you walked six miles for the sake of that soldier and you're now going to walk six miles back?"

"That's correct, sir," Rabbi Zimmerman said firmly.

"Come back in here," the general ordered. Rabbi Zimmerman came back, wondering what he had in mind. "Get me Colonel Wright,*" the general barked into a phone on the wall.

Within two minutes, Colonel Wright, the second in command at the base, entered the office. James handed him the letter and said, "Colonel, I want this serviceman to be transferred at once to Governors Island in New York, with instructions that he must visit his elderly parents every night. Make sure my orders are carried out."

Rabbi Zimmerman was stunned. The turnaround had been so unexpected. He thanked both General James and Colonel Wright, shook their hands warmly, and began his long trek. The way back seemed faster.

> Remarkably, when the general realized the *mesiras nefesh*, the pure unmitigated commitment of Rabbi Zimmerman to another Jew, he was so moved that he shattered his self-proclaimed "stone" orders.

Gracious Traits and Character / 113

Rabbi Zimmerman, who came to be known throughout the Jewish community for his stewardship of the Freeda Vitamins business started by his grandfather, told me he never saw or heard from the serviceman again. Their relationship may have dissolved, but his example of *Kiddush Hashem* lives on forever.

The Point Was Love

The sudden passing in November 2011 of the beloved Rosh Yeshivah of Yeshivas Mir in Jerusalem, Rabbi Nosson Tzvi Finkel (1943-2011), brought forth an outpouring of stories depicting the love and concern he had for his thousands of talmidim.

The renowned Rabbi Chaim Kreiswirth (1918-2001), the Chief Rabbi of Antwerp, was once in Jerusalem and said that he planned to visit Rabbi Nosson Tzvi. His attendant was surprised. He said that since Rabbi Kreiswirth was 25 years older than Reb Nosson Tzvi, it was appropriate that Reb Nosson Tzvi should visit *him*.

Rav Kreiswirth replied, "Reb Nosson Tzvi has 3,000 talmidim; hence it is appropriate that I should go visit him."

When Reb Nosson Tzvi was told of this conversation he said, "It's not that I *have* 3,000 talmidim, it's that I *love* my 3,000 talmidim!" [Since then, the Mirrer Yeshivah has grown to 6,000.]

One of the talmidim who felt so loved was my nephew, Rabbi Yehudah Gutman of Denver, Colorado, who came to the Mir in 1990. He was in Reb Nosson Tzvi's night *chaburah* (select group of *bachurim*) before Reb Nosson Tzvi became Rosh Yeshivah, so their relationship was very close.

The following incident happened a year later, after Reb Nosson Tzvi became Rosh Yeshivah. It was a few days before Succos and Yehudah had purchased a beautiful *lulav*, which he kept near his bed in his dormitory. Over the years Yehudah had become an expert in the laws of the *arbaah minim* (four species used on Succos), because his father, my late brother-in-law Rabbi Yehoshua Gutman, was a primary source of *lulavim* and *esrogim* for Denver's Jewish community. Assisting his father, Yehudah had become an expert in the nuances and fine points of what constitutes a kosher and even an exquisite *lulav* or *esrog*. The *lulav* he purchased in Jerusalem was indeed beautiful.

The Shabbos before Succos, Yehudah went to visit cousins in Ashdod, but left his *lulav* in his room. That Shabbos, a guest of the yeshivah entered his room and saw the unoccupied bed. He asked Yehudah's roommate if he could sleep there. The roommate said, "I'm sure Yehudah wouldn't mind," so he granted the guest permission. When Yehudah returned on Sunday morning, not only was his bed not made but the *lulav* was on the floor under it, with its top split — which made it *pasul*! Yehudah was devastated.

Now, less than 48 hours before Yom Tov, most of the choice *lulavim* had already been sold; how could he possibly find another excellent *lulav*? He told Reb Nosson Tzvi about it and the Rosh Yeshivah told him not to worry. "I will have a choice of *lulavim* for you," the Rosh Yeshivah said. "I have many extras. People come here to give me a beauty and they are proud to think that the Rosh Yeshivah will use it. Come back later and you will have *lulavim* to choose from."

Yehudah went to the *Beis Medrash* to study and about an hour later, the Rosh Yeshivah's son, Reb Yitzchak, approached him and said, "Abba says you should come now. He has the *lulavim* for you."

Yehudah could not believe his good fortune. He went to the Rosh Yeshivah's home. In the dining room, five beautiful *lulavim* were set out on the table. "Take your pick," said the Rosh Yeshivah with a smile.

"One is nicer than the next," said Yehudah in amazement.

"Choose whichever you like. There's no need to rush," said the ever-patient Rosh Yeshivah.

Yehudah finally picked one and said, "How much do I owe Rebbi for this *lulav*?"

Gracious Traits and Character / 115

"What did you pay in the market for the other *lulav* you had?" asked Reb Nosson Tzvi.

"I paid 35 shekel for that one," came the reply.

"Good. Pay me 35 shekel."

"It would be an embarrassment to this *lulav* to pay only 35 shekel for it. It's worth 100 shekel for sure," protested Yehudah.

"Look," said the Rosh Yeshivah in mock seriousness. "I am the *moicher* (salesman) and you are the *lokeiach* (buyer). If you don't like the price, then you will have to leave without a *lulav*."

Yehudah smiled; he knew he had been outwitted. "Okay, I'll pay the 35."

As Yehudah paid and took the *lulav*, the Rosh Yeshivah said, "Oh, there is an additional fee."

Yehudah looked up in surprise. Reb Nosson Tzvi said, "You cannot have a *taineh* (complaint) against your roommate for what happened."

Yehudah chuckled and said, "Now this is getting expensive!"

The Rosh Yeshivah and his beloved talmid laughed together. Yehudah walked out with the *lulav* and never said another word about the incident to his roommate.

While leaving the house, Yehudah met R' Yitzchak, who told him the secret. Reb Nosson Tzvi had called a prominent seller of *lulavim* and *esrogim* and asked him to bring over a few of the best that he had left, for a beloved talmid!

Another nephew of mine, R' Dovid Rosen, today of Toronto, also experienced an act of tenderness by Reb Nosson Tzvi. Dovid had learned in the Mir for three years and then returned to America to learn in Beth Medrash Govoha in Lakewood. When he first came to the Mir, Dovid was in a special *chaburah* with Reb Nosson Tzvi and for a while learned privately with him. However, for the final year and a half that he was in the Mir, he had no direct connection to the Rosh Yeshivah.

About a year after Dovid returned to the States, there was an *asifah* (gathering) in Lakewood to honor Reb Nosson Tzvi. Over a thousand people attended, many of them coming primarily to personally say hello to the Rosh Yeshivah and receive his blessing and warm greeting. Dovid had never attended an *asifah* like this before and he felt the obligation to show his solidarity with Reb Nosson Tzvi and the yeshivah. He decided to make an appearance, give a small donation to the Mir, and leave.

The line to greet the Rosh Yeshivah seemed endless. Dovid stood patiently waiting, knowing how precious every word of the Rosh Yeshivah was to every former talmid. Suddenly he began to wonder, *Will the Rosh Yeshivah recognize me? There are thousands of talmidim in the Mir, and over the years hundreds have been in his chaburos and even learned privately with him. How could he possibly remember me?*

Maybe, he thought, he should just introduce himself the moment he meets the Rosh Yeshivah face-to-face to save him any embarrassment if he does not remember him. But that too could be embarrassing, for what if indeed the Rosh Yeshivah did remember him?

He decided he would extend his hand and wait for the Rosh Yeshivah to speak. Slowly but surely the line inched up. The Rosh Yeshivah was sitting in an armchair and as each talmid approached, he bent over Reb Nosson Tzvi to hear what he said, because his voice had become very soft and tired by that time.

Dovid was next in line. He was sweating in anticipation as he reverently bent down to the Rosh Yeshivah. Reb Nosson Tzvi lifted his right hand and softly placed it on Dovid's cheek, and with his radiant smile said with satisfaction, "My Dovid."

To this day, Dovid cries when he remembers that tender moment.

True love is expressed by the small things one does for another. My friend Rabbi Shea Ozer Halpern, a noted *askan* (community activist) in Manchester, England, gave a *hesped* (eulogy) on his beloved Rosh Yeshivah, Rabbi Nosson Tzvi, in which he accentuated numerous seemingly small but considerate acts of kindness and thoughtfulness that were an integral part of his life. The sum total adds up to an extraordinary personality.

One afternoon, Reb Nosson Tzvi made a *sheva berachos* in his home and invited Shea Ozer. It was a very hot day and Shea Ozer arrived late, while the meal was already in progress. Reb Nosson Tzvi noticed him and brought him a plateful of chicken and potatoes. Shea Ozer nodded his gratitude to the Rosh Yeshivah but said, "No, thank you."

Reb Nosson Tzvi took a knife and fork, cut a piece from the portion of chicken and ate it. Then, with a twinkle in his eye, he said to Shea Ozer, "The chicken is now *shirayim* (remnants of food left over by a prominent rabbi) and you are a chassid — so eat it!"

With his wit and charm, the Rosh Yeshivah made sure that his talmid would not leave hungry.

During the Pesach vacation, Reb Nosson Tzvi had planned to test new applicants to the yeshivah, but he was too weak to ask the questions, so he appointed a noted *talmid chacham* to do the testing while he sat by. He listened attentively to the give-and-take between the tester and the *bachur*. Based on what he saw and heard, Reb Nosson Tzvi decided whom to accept and whom not to.

During that period, there were about 300 applicants and the Rosh Yeshivah refused only 20. To one young man he said quietly, "Come back next *z'man* (semester). I want to test you again and accept you."

A member of the administration asked the Rosh Yeshivah why this boy was treated differently than the others who had been refused. The Rosh Yeshivah said, "The other boys said *Shalom Aleichem* to me but not to the *yungerman* who was testing them. This boy said *Shalom Aleichem* to both of us. He belongs in the Mir!" That sensitivity defines Reb Nosson Tzvi.

The following story was told to me by the father of the boy to whom it happened. He shared it with me at a Mirrer dinner in Brooklyn, and he was in tears as he told it. When I asked the son if I could repeat the story, he agreed, but asked me not to use his name.

Shmuel Kasner* stood in the office of the Lomdei Torah Yeshivah in Jerusalem, devastated. He had come from America to study there, and now they were telling him they had no room. "But one of your rebbeiim *farherred* (tested) me in America last summer and he accepted me," Shmuel protested.

"He was not the final authority on that," the registrar said. "And besides, we never heard from you that you were coming."

"But I faxed you all my information a few weeks ago," Shmuel said, exasperated. "It's got to be here in this office someplace. And I came all the way from Milwaukee.* How am I supposed to find a new yeshivah two days before the new *z'man*?"

Despite his pleading, Shmuel could not budge the registrar. Lomdei Torah's policy was that all the *bachurim* had to live in the yeshivah dormitory, and there were no beds available. Shmuel called his father, who made some calls, but to no avail.

Shmuel, a new mesivta graduate, was looking forward to learning in Jerusalem and now his carefully laid plans had fallen apart. He left Lomdei Torah dejectedly and went directly to the *dirah* (apartment) where his friend Yoni Kutner* lived with other *bachurim*.

Together they tried to apply at other yeshivos but none were willing to take in a boy right before the beginning of the *z'man*, especially since most were already filled to capacity. After two days that Shmuel spent roaming Jerusalem seeking a yeshivah, his father called and said that a prominent friend in New York had made an appointment for Shmuel with Reb Nosson Tzvi Finkel. The appointment was for 12:30 the next afternoon.

Shmuel was not excited about going to the Mir because he thought he would do better in a smaller yeshivah. He was only 18 years old and felt he would be one of the youngest in a yeshivah of

Gracious Traits and Character / 119

thousands. He was afraid he would get lost in the crowd. The thought was overwhelming.

Shmuel was nervous and jittery when he arrived at the Rosh Yeshivah's home. Reb Nosson Tzvi greeted him with a warm smile and said, "I've been waiting for you."

Shmuel smiled. The Rosh Yeshivah was waiting? For him? No one else in Jerusalem seemed to care whether he was there or not, and this Rosh Yeshivah was anticipating his visit? Already Shmuel breathed more easily. Reb Nosson Tzvi opened the Gemara on his table. He began talking in learning with Shmuel. He wasn't testing him and he wasn't challenging him; they were just having a conversation in the sweetness of Torah.

After a few moments, Reb Nosson Tzvi paused and said, "I know you've had a difficult time these last few days. Tell me what happened."

As Shmuel began detailing the events that led to his being refused admittance to Lomdei Torah, he saw Reb Nosson Tzvi's face contort in pain as he shared Shmuel's disappointment. Suddenly, Reb Nosson Tzvi said to Shmuel, "You know something? I cannot understand how Lomdei Torah could not accept a boy with your smile!"

Shmuel smiled shyly and said, "They never saw it!"

"Well, you can come to my yeshivah," the Rosh Yeshivah said to the no-longer-dejected boy. "And I will be your friend."

And he was — as Shmuel stayed and learned in the Mir (and at times privately with Reb Nosson Tzvi) for the next four years.

Rabbi Yitzchok Ezrachi once said to the *bachurim* in the Mir, "We are [as it says in the *Al HaNissim* prayer for Chanukah] גִּבּוֹרִים בְּיַד חַלָּשִׁים, *the strong in the hands of the weak.*" Indeed Reb Nosson Tzvi may have been physically weak and perilously frail but he was a tower of strength and inspiration for the love he showed to every talmid.

יְהִי זִכְרוֹ בָּרוּךְ, May his memory be blessed.

Paid in Full

Every Shabbos before Mussaf, we recite these reassuring words: וְכָל מִי שֶׁעוֹסְקִים בְּצָרְכֵי צִבּוּר בֶּאֱמוּנָה, הקב"ה יְשַׁלֵּם שְׂכָרָם, *... and all those who are involved faithfully in the needs of the community, may the Holy One, Blessed is He, pay their reward.* Those who work in the public sector know ruefully that at times compensation comes only from Hashem, for too often public service can be thankless, unappreciated, and often even a criticized endeavor.

A perfect case in point is the role of the tuition committee chairman of a Torah institution, who must not only delve into parents' financial situation, but also must uncomfortably negotiate with the parents about what they can or cannot afford to pay for their child's education, or what services they can provide to the school in lieu of payment.

Thankfully, there are noble people who accept this job graciously, and the Torah community is indebted to them.

In 1989, Avi Waldman,* an accountant in Golders Green, London, was chosen by fellow members to lead the tuition committee at the Chovevei Torah Boys School.* He was known for his integrity, fairness, and financial acumen. Everyone trusted him, but after a few months in his new position he became disenchanted. He appreciated the committee's trust, but he did not like confrontational conversations and he disliked challenging what he felt were inaccurate claims by some parents about their financial capabilities. Still, he made his calls and met with parents and donors because he knew it was in the best interests of the stability of Chovevei Torah.

The following story is one that Avi repeatedly tells with a blend of awe and disbelief.

It was one week before Pesach in 1990, and Chovevei Torah was trying to pay its staff on time so everyone would be able to make Yom Tov properly, without financial hardship. Avi called a parent

Gracious Traits and Character / 121

who had been negligent in his tuition payments. "I'm sorry to trouble you," he began softly, "but it's before Yom Tov and the rebbeim and teachers are entitled to their salaries. Is there any way you can pay us the 2000 pounds you owe us? We really need the money now."

The parent replied, "You are right. I am so sorry. I will take care of it right away."

Avi was relieved that the conversation had not become unpleasant. Avi waited all day for the person to show up. He didn't. He didn't even come on Erev Yom Tov. Weeks went by, Avi did not hear from the parent. Now it was almost Shavuos, so Avi called again.

"When we last spoke, before Pesach, you said you were going to take care of your tuition balance right away. It's almost Shavuos and I haven't heard from you."

"What are you talking about?" said the surprised parent. "I took care of it that afternoon!"

"What does that mean?" Avi asked incredulously. "I never got anything from you!"

"That same afternoon, after we spoke," said the parent, "I drove up to your home. I saw your son on a bike in front of the house and I asked him to give you the envelope with the 2,000 pounds I owed you."

"You gave it to my son? He never told me anything about it. I'll ask him if he remembers that you gave him the envelope."

Avi ended the call and approached his 8-year-old son, Tully. "Tully," he said gently, "Do you remember anyone giving you an envelope for me in front of the house, a few weeks ago, before Pesach?"

Tully looked up at his father and said. "No, Daddy, I would have given you anything that someone asked me to give you." Tully sensed something was serious and asked, "Did I do anything wrong, Daddy?"

"No, I don't think so," said Avi. "But try and think — did anyone give you an envelope while you were riding your bike before Pesach and tell you that it was for me?"

Tully insisted that he did not recall anyone giving him an envelope or anything else. Avi walked away thinking that this situation was ridiculous. Why would any responsible person give a child something of such value and not follow up to be sure it had reached the proper person?

He called the parent and explained that his son had no recollection of receiving any envelope six weeks earlier. "This is really a matter for a *Din Torah* (rabbinical adjudication)," said Avi to the parent. "You claim you delivered the money, I claim I never got it; I say it was irresponsible to give it to a child, you claim otherwise. I really don't want to take you to a *Beis Din* (rabbinical court), so first I will go to every home on our block and ask if anyone found an envelope with money in it."

The parent agreed that it was a fair thing to do. Avi went from house to house asking if anyone had found the envelope, but did not receive a positive response. Finally he came to one home and asked the gentleman who opened the door, "Did you by any chance find an envelope about six weeks ago …?"

"You mean an envelope with 2,000 pounds in it?" the gentleman interrupted.

Avi was startled! "How'd you know that?" he asked in disbelief

"Come in and let me explain," the gentleman said. Avi entered the home and the two men stood in the foyer, talking quietly. The gentleman began, "I know you won't believe this, but six weeks ago, right before Yom Tom, I was laid off. I was so humiliated I did not know how I would tell my wife. What made it worse was that I knew that we had little money to make Yom Tov. I was so worried. And then as I walked up to my door, I saw a white envelope on my lawn. It was unmarked, so I opened it — and in it was 2,000 pounds! I looked around and saw no one, so I had no idea how it got there. I figured this was *muhn min haShamayim*, a gift directly from Hashem. And to tell you the truth, that's the money we used to make Pesach. It was truly Heaven sent."

Avi told the man the background story of the envelope and the money. "Well, now that I know that money is *mammon hekdesh* (consecrated money), of course I will pay it back," the gentleman said. "I still don't have a job, so I can't pay it all back at one time. I promise I will pay it completely, but it will be in installments."

Avi was thrilled. He returned to his home and called the parent who had left the envelope. "You will never believe this …." He went on to tell the whole story of how a fellow on his block, who had just lost his job, found the money, and used it for his Pesach needs.

The parent thought for a moment and said, "Tell him that he can keep the money, he doesn't have to pay it back. I will pay you the 2000 pounds I owe you for tuition — and this time I will deliver it personally, directly to you."

And that afternoon he did!

> When Avi tells this story, he concludes by saying, "And this episode makes all the aggravation worthwhile."

‑§ Character in Full Bloom

> Through this heartrending story, we gain insight into the level of concern that great people have for others. I first heard this story in Jerusalem, before Succos of 2010; I found it so illuminating and inspiring that I used it in numerous lectures throughout Yom Tov. I am grateful to Reb Shmuli Sorotzkin of Lakewood, New Jersey, who first told it to me as we trekked through the hills, gardens, and valleys of *Ir David* (the City of David) in ancient Jerusalem.

In 1971, Rabbi Yisroel Sorotzkin, one of the youngest sons of the famed Lutzker Rav, Rabbi Zalman Sorotzkin (1881-1966), died at age 47 in Israel. Rav Yisroel was a renowned *talmid chacham*, a *dayan* (rabbinical judge) in Tel-Aviv, and a *maggid shiur* in the Lomza Yeshivah of Petach Tikvah. He left four children, among them, Michoel, who was 13 ½.

Reb Yisroel's older brother, Rabbi Boruch Sorotzkin (1917-1979), was one of the roshei yeshivah in the Telshe Yeshivah in Cleveland,

Ohio. Michoel's mother, Rebbetzin Chasidah Sorotzkin, felt it would be wise to send the boy to America so that he could be under the tutelage of his illustrious uncle, Reb Boruch. The Sorotzkin family was very close and she was sure that Reb Boruch would not only be a rebbi but also a "father figure" to the young orphan. Indeed Michoel studied in Telshe for several years, and became very beloved by Reb Boruch and his family. "Mickey," as he was known in Telshe, went on to learn in other yeshivos, but Reb Boruch and his family remained in constant contact with him.

In 1979, one of Reb Boruch's family members suggested a Cleveland girl as a *shidduch* for Mickey, and indeed they became engaged. The wedding was scheduled to be held in early summer.

The *kallah's* father, Reb Avrohom Freund, was very close to the Satmar Rav, Rabbi Yoel Teitelbaum (1887-1979), so Michoel went to Brooklyn to receive a *berachah* from the Rebbe. When the Rebbe was told the date of the wedding, he immediately said, "Why are you waiting so long? Make it earlier." No one made anything of the comment at the time; however a few months later, these words would haunt all who heard them.

At the time, Michoel's mother in Israel had been diagnosed with a life-threatening disease, but she planned to come to the United States to attend the wedding in Cleveland. On Sunday morning, one week before the wedding, Michoel called his mother to wish her a safe trip — but he was informed that she had just been rushed to the hospital. Sadly and unexpectedly, she passed away a few hours later.

Understandably there was great turmoil in the family on both sides of the Atlantic. Should Michoel go to the funeral? If he were to go to Israel for the funeral, the *shivah* (seven days of mourning) would not end until after the projected date of the wedding. Should the wedding be postponed? Should the funeral be delayed? Everyone had a different opinion, so it was decided to call Rabbi Moshe Feinstein (1895-1986) in New York and obtain his *psak* (religious ruling) and counsel. Reb Moshe advised that Michoel remain in Cleveland and not go to the funeral. He would therefore begin sitting *shivah* immediately and by the next Sunday morning the *shivah* would be over and he could get married that night as originally planned.

On the Friday of the *shivah,* Michoel called Reb Moshe to discuss the various halachos pertinent to a *chassan* being married immediately after *shivah.* Reb Moshe spent much time with Michoel going over every detail meticulously. He wished the *chassan* well and bid him a good Shabbos.

A few minutes later, Michoel was summoned to the phone as someone exclaimed, "Rabbi Moshe Feinstein is calling person-to-person." "Person-to-person" implied a sense of urgency. Michoel was frightened; what was so important that Reb Moshe was calling?

"I apologize," the *gadol hador* (the great Torah sage of the generation) began. "I am sorry for disturbing you," Reb Moshe continued. "There is one more thing I meant to tell you. There is a custom in America that the *chassan* buys the *kallah* a beautiful flower arrangement for the *Shabbos Kallah* [the Shabbos before the wedding]. Tomorrow will be the *Shabbos Kallah,* and all the *kallah's* friends will come to visit her. You, as an *avel,* may not buy a gift for her, and so her friends may wonder why she doesn't have flowers like every other *kallah.* Someone may make a hurtful comment. Therefore I would suggest that you have a friend buy flowers and present them to her before Shabbos in your name."

> Is this not extraordinary? The *gadol hador,* on Erev Shabbos, has nothing else on his mind than a *kallah* in Cleveland who might not have flowers? It is precisely such acts and concerns that constitute greatness. To a great man nothing is insignificant; to a great heart nothing is irrelevant. Oh, that we, too, would act in such ways.

✥ Warmth on a Winter Night

At a *vort* (engagement celebration), R' Moshe Lasker told the following story about an uncle of his, the great-grandfather of the *kallah,* that left me awed. It occurred in the East New York section of Brooklyn in the late 1950's. At that time, Rabbi Avrohom Pam (1913-2001) lived there; he gave a nightly *shiur* at the Young Israel of New Lots.

One night there was a major snowstorm and the streets of East New York were void of people. The wind howled, blowing the snow into drifts and making walking treacherous. Rav Pam nevertheless started putting on his rubber boots and his coat as he prepared to make his way to the shul to give the *shiur*.

"How can you go out on a night like this?" Rebbetzin Pam protested. "First of all, no one will even show up because of the weather, and second, it's dangerous for you to be outside on such a cold, stormy night."

Rav Pam understood her hesitation, but replied, "I have to go, because if even one person makes the effort to come, I have the responsibility to give the *shiur*."

The Rebbetzin knew that her husband would not be dissuaded. Rav Pam walked the 10 blocks to the shul gingerly and slowly, shielding his face from the bitter frost of the evening. He entered the shul not knowing what to expect. When he came to the room where he gave the *shiur*, he was astounded. Indeed, only one person had come. It was Mr. Ben-Zion Raphael Lasker — and he was not even one of the regular attendees. Of all people, Rav Pam certainly had not expected *him* to come out on a night like this.

Rav Pam greeted Mr. Lasker warmly and asked, "Why did you make such an effort on such a stormy night after a long day's work?"

Mr. Lasker smiled. "I knew that you would surely come, and I was afraid that no one else would show up. I felt that it would have been terrible for you to have walked out in this snowstorm for nothing — and so I came!"

> Two great people — with mutual sensitivity, caring, and dedication. May their memories be a blessing — as they are worthy of emulation.

Gracious Traits and Character

~§ Perfect Fathers

For more than a year, I worked with my son-in-law, Chananya Kramer, director of Kol-Rom Multimedia, to produce an all-encompassing DVD to educate people on the importance and proper manner of performing the mitzvah of *bikur cholim* (visiting the sick). The DVD is entitled *Sense and Sensitivity: The Essence of Bikur Cholim*.

As this project was developing, it occurred to me that we should expand it to include a segment directed exclusively to the *cholim* (those who are ill) — be they in a hospital, nursing facility, or homebound — with the intent to give them hope and encouragement. We sought rabbanim who had a personal connection to illness and who could therefore relate to *cholim* in a delicate way. What each of them recorded was masterful.

One particular story, told by Rabbi Raymond Beyda of the Syrian Sephardic community in Brooklyn, left me in tears and deeply moved. I hope I can transmit in words the poignancy of the story as he told it.

A few years ago Raymond's son Meir (Mickey), who is married and a father of children, contracted leukemia. Meir needed weeks of hospitalization, and his parents, Raymond and Jamie, became his primary caregivers. The treatments and medications Meir required produced horrific side effects. Weeks turned to months; when Meir was finally discharged, he moved into his parents' home so that he could have the most devoted caregivers at his side 24 hours a day. Meir's wife, Lillian, and their children visited him daily but because the senior Beydas had taken over the intense daily care of Meir, Lillian could tend to their children in as normal way as possible.

Meir's stay at home was short lived. His condition deteriorated as he grew weaker with each passing day and he returned to the hospital. Once again the stay extended for agonizing weeks. The back–and-forth from hospital to home and then to hospital again lingered for more than two years. One day the doctor came into the room and announced that Meir would have to undergo a battery of tests to see if an operation would be necessary.

Raymond and his wife were crestfallen. Their son was too weak; he had no strength to undergo a major operation. They voiced their apprehension to the doctor who said, "I understand your concern, but if the tests show that he requires the operation we will have no choice."

On the morning of the tests, Raymond and his wife were sitting alongside Meir's bed waiting anxiously for the transport personnel who would take Meir down to the first floor where the tests were to be administered. While everyone was waiting anxiously, one of Meir's doctors walked in. "Is everything okay?" asked Raymond.

"Yes," said the doctor. "I want to go down with Meir and be with him during the tests."

The Beydas were touched. The doctor did not have to do that. Most doctors would wait for the test results and then see the patient afterward Not this doctor; he wanted to accompany his patient and be there at this crucial point in time.

A few moments later the transport personnel came and wheeled Meir to the elevator as the doctor and the Beydas followed behind. They all went down together to the first floor. As they approached the testing area, the doctor told the Beydas to remain in the waiting room nearby.

"I'll be there with Meir," he said reassuringly.

The tests took close to an hour but the family would have to wait a full day to get results. The day seemed like a drawn-out winter month, but finally, as Raymond says, *"Baruch Hashem,* a thousand times over; the tests showed that he would not need the operation." The family breathed a collective sigh of relief.

Three weeks later this same doctor walked into Meir's room and addressed him and his parents. "I've come to bid you good-bye," he said softly. "You know I am a visiting doctor here and I have a rotation for which I must be at another hospital. But I want you to know that in the 10 years that I have been here, your son Meir has been among my favorite 10 patients. Maybe even in the top two."

Gracious Traits and Character / 129

Raymond smiled and proudly touched his son's arm softly. But he had to know more. "Doctor," he said, "why do you say that?"

The doctor, a resident who had come from India, smiled and said, "Remember a few weeks ago, when we were all downstairs, when Meir was waiting for those tests?"

"I'll never forget that day," said Raymond.

"I was standing next to your son as he was lying on the stretcher and I said to him, 'Meir, It's going to be good.'

"He looked up at me and said, 'Doctor, you have it all wrong. It is good, it's perfect.'

" 'Really?" I said, 'What do you mean?'

"Meir said to me, 'You know my father …'

" 'Of course I know your father,' I answered. 'He's sitting in the next room ….'

"'No, not that one,' said Meir, pointing to where you were sitting. 'I mean this one,' and he pointed Heavenward.

" 'Yes,' I said. 'I know about that stuff.'

" 'Well, you see," said Meir, 'my Father is perfect and everything that He does is perfect. That makes the condition I am in, perfect. Exactly the way it's supposed to be.' "

The doctor shook his head and said, "I don't know how a man that young got to be so astute and so smart. Your people who study the Torah — they have it right. In the short time that I've known Meir, he taught me more than all the other patients taught me in 10 years."

As the usually composed Raymond finished telling his story his eyes welled with tears. He addressed the *choleh* who would be listening and said, "Be confident that all that Hashem, our Father, does is perfect. Life is a roller-coaster with ups and downs, but that ride doesn't last forever. You can get better and with Hashem's help you will get better."

Rabbi Beyda wished all *cholim* a *refuah sheleimah* and we wish Meir ben Jackie (Yaffa) a complete healing as well.

❧ Choice Selection

Wherever I am, people stop to tell me their stories. At a *bris*, after a lecture, in an airport, outside a shul — I never know where the next story will come from.

Truthfully, I am very grateful to everyone. For I never know when I will hear a classic story that should be recorded and retold, one that will inspire many people. Although all the stories may have value, I write and tell only those stories that move and motivate me.

At a recent wedding in Antwerp, a guest from Montreal, Mr. Yehuda Grunberger, told me the following story over the din of the music and dancing. I was so taken by it that I typed it the next morning, on the flight back home.

Many years ago in Bnei Brak, Rabbi Chaim Kanievsky went to a store to purchase a *lulav*. The proprietor gave him a few to choose from. Reb Chaim picked one up, examined it carefully, shook his head, and then put it down. He picked up a second one, looked it over slowly, and that one too he put down. The third *lulav* met with his approval. He paid for it and left the store.

Someone who had been watching Reb Chaim in the store found it incredulous. He followed him outside and said to Reb Chaim's son-in-law, who had accompanied him, "I can't get over your father-in-law's *mazel* (good fortune). It takes me hours to find a good *lulav* and look how Hashem blessed him. In less than 10 minutes Reb Chaim found a *lulav* to his liking."

The son-in-law smiled and said to the gentleman, "Come, walk us home."

When they entered the apartment, the son-in-law took the man into a room and showed him that Reb Chaim had more than a dozen *lulavim* on a table! "You see," the son-in-law said, "Rav Chaim knows that people watch his every move. If he were to go into a store, examine a few *lulavim*, and leave without buying one, that owner would not be able to sell another *lulav*. People would assume that his merchandise is inferior. So no matter what store he goes into, my father-in-law buys at least one, so as not to hurt the storekeeper's reputation. If you add it all up," the son-in-law continued, "Reb Chaim probably spends more time than you do to pick the perfect *lulav*!"

What sensitivity! What understanding! What compassion!

ᴥ§ Bar Mitzvah Lessons

A good story needs a good ending. It can be surprising, whimsical, uplifting, or sometimes even sad. However, when a story has not only one ending and not even two — but *three* endings, and each comes as a bigger surprise than the one before, the story is truly worth retelling.

In this story, the overriding factor is Hashem's extraordinary orchestration of occurrences into a cohesive whole. The families involved are still incredulous as they recount the sequence of events over and over.

I am grateful to my son-in-law, Rabbi Ephraim Perlstein, who first told me this story.

The Gleibermans have been members of Rabbi Shimshon Sherer's very popular shul in Flatbush for more than 20 years. As the community grew, the number of *simchos* celebrated in the shul increased. A *bris*, a *Kiddush*, a bar mitzvah, an *aufruf*, a *sheva berachos* — these were almost weekly occurrences. Sometimes there would be a conflict; if a bar mitzvah and a *sheva berachos* were both to take place on the same Shabbos, which family would have the *simchah* hall? The system was that whoever called the *gabbai* first had priority. For years the system worked well.

In July 2008, Yossi and Estie Gleiberman began thinking about their son Binyomin's bar mitzvah, which was still two years away, in August 2010. Of course it was a bit early to be thinking of the event but the Gleibermans wanted to plan ahead. Binyomin would be in Camp Agudah during August, but his parents did not want the bar mitzvah *seudah* to take place there, as most of the family and friends would not be able to attend. And Binyomin's elderly grandfather, Reb Leibel Gleiberman, was not well; where could they find him a place in camp?

So with foresight, they reserved their shul's *simchah* hall for the first Shabbos after camp, early in September 2010, which would be the Shabbos before Rosh Hashanah. That would be the most convenient time for family and friends to come together, because the next few weeks would be the *Yamim Noraim*, followed by Succos, when most people prefer to be home.

Unbeknownst to the Gleibermans, the Braun family began thinking about *their* son's bar mitzvah, which was to be that same Shabbos in September 2010. R' Sheya Braun called the *gabbai* to reserve the date.

When the *gabbai* told Mr. Braun that the Shabbos was already reserved, he was surprised. Who else in the shul was planning so far ahead? The *gabbai* told him that the Gleibermans had already reserved that Shabbos months earlier.

"Do you think we could have both bar mitzvahs the same Shabbos?" Mr. Braun asked.

"It would be okay with me," he replied, "but you have to clear it with the Gleibermans."

Mr. Braun called Yossi, told him of the impending conflict, and suggested that perhaps they could share the Shabbos. Yossi was not happy with the idea, as he and his son Binyomin had prepared much of the *leining* of that week's *parashah* already. Yossi pictured the stifling crowd in shul, filled with two sets of relatives and friends, and did not like the mental image. Yossi said he would discuss it with his wife.

That evening, Yossi and Estie Gleiberman came to the reluctant conclusion that it simply could not work. There would be guests from both families who could not have *aliyos* because each family would have to be accommodated. Who would choose the *baal tefillah* for Shacharis? How much of the *parashah* would each boy *lein*?

Gracious Traits and Character / 133

How could they fit everyone into the *simchah* room? The problems were numerous and could become problematic. Mr. Gleiberman said, half in jest, "I guess that's what *Chazal* meant; שֶׁאֵין מְעָרְבִין שִׂמְחָה בְּשִׂמְחָה, *We do not intermingle one joyous occasion with another joyous occasion (Moed Kattan 8b)."*

Mr. Gleiberman called Mr. Braun the next morning and told him that as much as he would have liked it to work out, it just did not seem feasible. Things would just have to be left as is.

"I understand," said Sheya, "But maybe we could both go to Rabbi Sherer and figure out a way to work it out."

"I'll get back to you," said Yossi.

Yossi was concerned. He did not want to make an issue of this event. This was a *simchah* and he wanted to keep it that way. He knew that Rabbi Sherer, whom everyone loved, would be put into an uncomfortable position. Although Yossi felt that in all fairness the Shabbos before Rosh Hashanah belonged to him, he understood the Brauns' quandary.

That night, Yossi and Estie decided to yield that Shabbos to the Brauns. The Gleibermans would hold Binyomin's bar mitzvah in camp and make the best of it. They had no idea how they would do it, especially regarding finding a place for Yossi's father, but they hoped that with *siyata D'Shmaya* (Divine assistance), they would come up with a plan.

Of course, it also meant that Binyomin would have to learn a new *parashah*, but that was not an insurmountable problem. Peace in the shul was their priority and by yielding, the Gleibermans could defuse any resentment. They called the *gabbai* and told him of their decision.

The Brauns were extremely grateful.

A few weeks later, the Gleiberman's older son Eli, who had just come back from *Eretz Yisrael,* became engaged. People in shul were surprised. They had thought Eli would be home for a few weeks and then go off to learn in Lakewood, but soon after his arrival, a *shidduch* was proposed with the Jaroslawicz family, and within a month Eli and Avigayil Jaroslawicz were engaged.

The Gleibermans wondered whom the Jaroslawiczes had called for information about them and Eli. They had given the *shadchan* many people as references, but not one of them had been called.

At the *vort*, Yossi Gleiberman asked his new *mechutan*, Mendy Jaroslawicz, if he had checked with any of the references he had been given. The answer shocked Yossi.

"I called one person in your shul, my cousin, Sheya Braun. When he told me how you dealt with him, and how you yielded when you really didn't have to, that was good enough for us. We didn't have to check anything more."

Thus two *simchos* intertwined. Not the two bar mitzvahs, as was originally thought, but a bar mitzvah and an engagement interlocked by goodness and incredible *Hashgachah Pratis*, the relationship between the Jaroslawiczes and the Brauns.

But that was only the beginning. As the Gleibermans and the Jaroslawiczes became better acquainted, they shared their family history and the news of upcoming *simchos*. The Jaroslawiczes spend their summers in a bungalow colony near Camp Agudah and they offered the Gleibermans rooms there for the weekend of the bar mitzvah so that they could invite anyone they wanted. Binyomin *leined* beautifully and many relatives and friends were able to attend.

And if those two wondrous situations were not enough, a deeply significant event happened as a result of the bar mitzvah taking place in August: Yossi's father was able to attend. By September 2009 he had been admitted to the hospital; had the bar mitzvah taken place in September as the Gleibermans originally planned, he would not have been there.

Even Yossi would have been preoccupied with his father, who by September was in grave condition. Reb Leibel passed away two weeks later on Yom Kippur. Yossi's sadness was diminished a bit because of the *Hashgachah Pratis* that allowed his father to celebrate with the family just weeks earlier.

Yossi and Estie had been hoping for *siyata D'Shmaya* they got it in huge doses.

Gracious Traits and Character / 135

~§ Acid Rain

Two boys, Robby* and Joe, grew up together in Miami and attended the Hebrew Academy and Mesivta High School of Miami. They were friends all through their school years until their high school graduation in 1965. Joe went on to college and became a very successful lawyer, and Robby went to Telshe Yeshiva in Cleveland, where he became a *talmid chacham* and one of the primary talmidim of Rabbi Mordechai Gifter (1915-2001). In Telshe he was no longer known as Robby but rather as Reuvein, and today he is the well-known *posek*, writer, and leader, Rabbi Reuvein Graff,* living in Israel.

Rabbi Graff has published books, given countless *shiurim*, answered thousands of halachah and *hashkafah* questions via his website, and is a sought-after speaker. In 2005 he spoke in Brooklyn at the Agudah of Avenue L in Flatbush.

Mr. Mutty Smilow, who also grew up in Miami, hadn't seen Rabbi Graff in years and so he decided to call another Miami friend, Mr. Joe Weiss, who now lived in Brooklyn, and asked if he would like to join him in attending the *shiur*.

"That would be wonderful," said Mr. Weiss. "I haven't seen Robby in years and I would love to hear him."

Mr. Weiss had become a *talmid chacham* in his own right; he had finished Shas, dedicated a volume of ArtScroll's Schottenstein Edition of the Talmud, and is a contributing editor of ArtScroll's Schottenstein Edition of Talmud Yerushalmi. The two men came to the *shiur* and were amazed at the size of the crowd. It was standing room only and everyone was inspired by the wisdom and warmth of Rabbi Graff. Mr. Weiss and Mr. Smilow joined the line to say a few words to their old schoolmate, although they were not sure he would remember them. As they inched their way up to Rabbi Graff, they spoke about how great their old friend had become.

Rabbi Graff recognized Joe at once and called out, "Joe, it's so wonderful to see you after all these years." They chatted for a moment or two, and then Rabbi Graff whispered to Mr. Weiss,

"Would you mind waiting while I greet the people who are waiting for me? I must speak to you privately."

"Of course I'll wait," said Mr. Weiss, wondering what could be so important. He stepped to the side of the room and waited for the crowd to disperse. After a few minutes Rabbi Graff came over and began talking earnestly. "Joe, I can't tell you how happy I am to see you," he said. "I want you to know that for over 40 years, on every Yom Kippur I say an extra *'al cheit'* because of what I did to you."

Mr. Weiss was incredulous, "What are you talking about?"

"I can never forget what I did back when we were in school. Every year I've been asking Hashem to forgive me and every year I ask that I meet you somewhere so I can ask for *mechilah*."

"Really, Rabbi Graff," said Mr. Weiss, "I can't imagine what you are talking about."

"It goes back many, many years," Rabbi Graff said wistfully. "We were in chemistry class together, learning about hydrofluoric acid." (Hydrofluoric acid is extremely dangerous if it penetrates tissue and is equally hazardous if inhaled. It can cause serious burns.)

"You were an innocent kid then and after class I put some tape on a canister and wrote the word *acid* on it. I filled it with water and I called your name. When you turned around, I tossed the water in your face as a practical joke. You thought it was the acid. You screamed with fright and ran to wash it off, and everyone had a good laugh. You soon realized that it was only water but I have never forgiven myself for the anguish and embarrassment I caused you. Every year I ask the *Ribono shel Olam* for *mechilah* for my insensitivity. And now I've finally found you. Please forgive me for that mean-spirited prank."

Mr. Weiss was astounded. "I don't know what you are talking about," he said. "I don't recall such an incident. You must have me confused with someone else. It never happened to me and I don't recall such a thing happening in our class."

"But I'm positive it was you," insisted Rabbi Graff, "and so I am asking you for forgiveness."

"Of course I forgive you," said Mr. Weiss. "But I am telling you, you never did anything wrong to me."

"But just tell me you forgive me," pleaded Rabbi Graff.

"Yes," came the reply. "I forgive you wholeheartedly but I want to reassure you I have nothing to forgive you for."

That Shabbos Mr. Weiss's sister, Mrs. Tova Weiser and her husband Chaim, who live in West Orange, New Jersey, invited Mr. and Mrs. Ezra Goodman* for the Friday-night *seudah*. Ezra, a Miami native, had been a family friend of the Weisses for decades. Mrs. Weiser told Ezra, "You will never believe who my brother met the other night at a *shiur* in Brooklyn: Robby Graff, who is today Rabbi Reuvein Graff."

"Don't tell me about Rabbi Graff," snarled Ezra. "I have some of his *sefarim* but I have never opened them nor can I even look at his face on the dust jacket."

"What?" exclaimed Mrs. Weiser. "The man is such a *talmid chacham*, a leader in *Klal Yisrael*."

"Well, I can never forget what he did to your brother in chemistry class," Ezra said. "He threw water in Joe's face but Joe thought it was acid and he ran out of the class screaming in fright."

"You remember that it really happened?"

"Of course, I remember, I can still see it as it happened."

"Let me tell you what remorse is all about and then we'll see what you think of Rabbi Graff," said Mrs. Weiser. She then went on to tell him how for 40 years Rabbi Graff has been asking Hashem for forgiveness every Yom Kippur for that prank and how it has haunted him all this time. She recounted that Rabbi Graff had asked her brother for *mechilah*.

Ezra was dumbfounded. He had misjudged a man for decades. *I must call him,* Ezra thought. *Maybe I'm the one who should ask him for mechilah.*

> As Mr. Weiss recalls this story, he adds, "How careful one must be when playing a prank or doing something that is questionable! Look at the effect it had on Ezra Goodman. That act made him despise a *talmid chacham* for years.

Of course he was mistaken; Rabbi Graff felt remorse for over 40 years, but it certainly behooves us to be careful about our actions, for even bystanders and listeners can be affected by our mistakes."

When I first heard this story some years ago, I was hesitant to write it. After all, Rabbi Graff today is a noted Torah personality and perhaps it was not proper to publicize a childish prank. However I recently met him at a *kiruv* convention where we shared a podium. We discussed the story and I asked him about printing it.

"Of course you should print it," he said. "People make mistakes and it's important for everyone to know that. And if a mistake is made, one must ask forgiveness. It was a childish prank but it hurt someone, and I have no shame that I asked for *mechilah*. That was the right thing to do."

Although Rabbi Graff wanted me to use his real name, after consulting with others it was felt that it would not be right to expose him to ridicule for something he did as a teenager.

We are so blessed to have great people among us.

✥ Sacred Letters

One of the nicest things about being an author is that people everywhere — at a wedding, while traveling, or in the middle of a busy thoroughfare — seem eager to share a personal experience or pass on an inspirational or remarkable episode. I am grateful to all who share these events, for one never knows when a valuable nugget will be told that can be moving and motivating.

One morning as I was walking back from shul in Antwerp, Belgium, a chassidishe gentleman approached me and provided an unexpected jewel of a story. And like a pure jewel, the character trait displayed here is flawless. I had never met the man before, but he got right to the point. "I'm from Stamford Hill [London], and I've been hoping to meet you somewhere so I could tell you this great story. I'm only here for one day for a family wedding, but it must be *Hashgachah Pratis* (Divine Providence) that we met. Please don't use my name," he added emphatically, "I have no role in this story, but it happened to a neighbor I know well."

Reb Shaul Becker* was a well-known figure in Stamford Hill. He was a noted *talmid chacham*, a prosperous businessman, and a world-renowned antiques dealer. He collected old *sefarim*, rare manuscripts, unusual coins, and myriad items that collectors treasure.

One day a secular Jew entered Reb Shaul's office and offered to sell him three handwritten letters. "I am told," the potential seller said, "that these are rare letters from great rabbis and that they have significant value. I don't know who these people are, but I thought you, as a religious scholar, would know."

Reb Shaul examined the letters and was amazed. Indeed, they had been written by three *gedolei hador* (Torah giants) of the previous generation; Rabbi Boruch Ber Leibowitz (1864-1939), Rosh Yeshivah of Kaminetz; Rabbi Shimon Shkop (1860-1939), Rosh Yeshivah of Grodno; and Rabbi Isser Zalman Meltzer (1870-1953), Rosh Yeshivah of Slutzk. Reb Shaul was all too aware that there were people who stole antiques and then tried to sell them. He had no reason to believe that his visitor had stolen the letters, but it was possible that someone else had, and that the letters had been sold and resold until they had reached this dealer. The letters seemed genuine, but Reb Shaul had learned from experience not to jump to quick conclusions in the antiques business.

"I might be interested in these letters," said Reb Shaul. "Could you leave them with me for a day or two while I do some investigating?"

Reb Shaul's reputation was impeccable, so the dealer had no hesitation about leaving the letters with him. When the dealer had left,

Reb Shaul read the three letters carefully. They had all been written to Rabbi Chaim Shmuel Lopian, the brother of the legendary *tzaddik*, Rabbi Elya Lopian (1876-1970). Reb Chaim Shmuel Lopian had written *Ravcha D'Shmatissah*, a commentary on the classic *sefer*, *Shev Shmatissa*, by Rabbi Aryeh Leib, author of the *Ketzos HaChoshen*. The three roshei yeshivah had written these letters of approbation on Reb Chaim Shmuel's commentary.

The letters were indeed authentic, but who would ever have given up such precious letters? How could they have come onto the public market? Reb Shaul decided to call Reb Chaim Shmuel in Jerusalem to find the answer.

The next day, after much effort, Reb Shaul reached Reb Chaim Shmuel by phone. After introducing himself, he asked Reb Chaim Shmuel, "Did you recently have a burglary in your home?"

"No, *Baruch Hashem* not," came the reply. "But why do you ask?"

"I am holding in my hand three very precious letters written to you by the *gedolei olam* (world-renowned Torah giants), Reb Boruch Ber, Reb Shimon, and Reb Isser Zalman. They are *haskamos* to your *sefer*. How did they leave your possession?" asked Reb Shaul.

"You should be *gebentched* (blessed)," said Reb Chaim Shmuel gently. "I haven't possessed those letters in years. I had to marry off one of my children and I sold some of my possessions to raise money. I felt very honored when I received them, but I had no choice. I had to sell them."

The next morning Reb Shaul called the dealer and negotiated a price for the three letters. And that afternoon he went to the post office and mailed them special delivery to Reb Chaim Shmuel in Jerusalem!

> As a genuine Torah scholar Reb Shaul would have had great appreciation for these letters, but he did what he did because he is a precious jewel.
>
> Is there anyone out there who has other gems like this? If so, I'd love to hear about them — even if we meet in the street on a cold wintry day in Antwerp.

~§ Small Talk

Malka Lax of Szatmer-Cseke, Hungary, was all of four foot ten inches tall. Her husband Shlomo was six feet tall, but Malka was the giant in the family. She ran the family fabric shop; she tended their farm, oversaw the real estate, and provided for her immediate and extended family. Her honesty was impeccable and even gentiles, who normally shied away from doing business with Jews in the 1930's, felt comfortable in dealing with her.

Aside from her integrity, she had a kind word for everyone. People not only trusted her but looked forward to dealing with her, because she always made everyone feel special. She genuinely cared about every human being and they, in turn, cared about her. It was no wonder, therefore, that at the end of 1938, concerned gentile customers privately told her that they had information that Germany would eventually control Hungary and Jews would be imprisoned or exiled. They warned her about the anti-Semitic laws that were being enacted in Germany. "It's only a matter of time until they come here."

Intuitively she believed them and began making plans to leave the country with her seven children. Shlomo was already in America to see if his family would have a future there, but he was disappointed by the lack of *Yiddishkeit* and wanted to return to Hungary. She told her friends and family what she had heard about the Germans, but they scoffed and would not think of leaving their comfortable homes, businesses, and lifestyles. Malka knew that the cost of tickets for her and her seven children would be exorbitant. She tried to sell her properties, but there were no buyers. As she walked about dejectedly, she recalled the taunt that a gentile child had made to her son just the week before. "Drink milk from your cow while you can, because when the Germans come, *we* will own your cow!" Rumors were rampant that when the Germans came, Jewish property would be confiscated. Why would anyone want to pay for Jewish property now? Eventually it would be theirs for the taking.

The gentile mayor of Szatmer-Czeke, who had inside information that the Germans would soon occupy Hungary, called Malka to come to his office. He had often borrowed money from her to carry him over in difficult times, and now he wished to protect Malka's family. Behind closed doors, he made her a gracious offer. "I will build a room under part of my farm and camouflage it so that you and your family can stay until the war is over. I know it will be dirty and dark in there, but at least your lives will be saved."

Malka understood that the mayor would be risking his own life if he protected Jews, and she thanked him profusely for his generous offer. However, she said, "We cannot take a chance of remaining. I must find a way to leave the country with my family."

The mayor told her that it would be impossible for her to emigrate, but Malka was determined to find a solution. She had heard that an assimilated Jew, Mr. Lorinc, owned a bank in the county seat of Feher-Gyarmat. Though he had rejected his faith, Malka felt that if she offered him a good deal, she could persuade him to purchase her properties. And who could know —maybe at this perilous time he would help one of his own. It was her only chance. She traveled to Feher-Gyarmat with her heart in her throat and prayers on her lips.

The slight but determined Malka made her way to the business district in downtown Feher-Gyarmat and came to the Magyar Bank.* As she walked into the small lobby she was met by a clerk. "Where are you going? Do you have an appointment with anyone?"

"I have come to see the owner of the bank. I need a very important favor from him," she replied with confidence.

"Are you kidding?" the clerk said derisively. "The owner is a very nasty person. He does no favors for anyone. Does he even know you?"

"No, not yet," she said politely. "But I would like to get to know him. I am sure he can help me."

"I told you — he helps no one! He is stingy and selfish," the clerk retorted.

"Excuse me," said Malka to the clerk. "He is your boss, isn't he? You make a livelihood only because of him, is that not so? It seems to me your working conditions are quite fine here. How can you be so negative about a person you owe so much to? You should be praising him and be grateful to him."

Before the clerk could reply, a voice suddenly thundered from the floor above, "Send that woman right up to my office!" It was the owner himself, who had overheard the conversation through an open window in his office that overlooked the banking floor. The stunned, humiliated clerk sent the petite woman upstairs. Malka had no idea what to expect but she remained her courteous self. She greeted the owner pleasantly and he in turn acknowledged her presence with dignity.

After the two exchanged pleasantries, he asked her what she needed. When she told him of her plan to sell her holdings so that she could purchase tickets for herself and her children, he agreed almost immediately. "I heard your conversation," he said to her as he signed certain documents. "You are a special lady."

Malka left the bank exultant. Quickly she procured all the documents and visas she needed. She hastily arranged their departure and on Erev Pesach 1939, she and her children arrived at Ellis Island in New York, spared from horror and almost-certain death of the Holocaust. (Incredibly, Mr. Lorinc eventually sold the properties and gave the money to Malka's relatives, enabling them to survive the war in Hungary.)

It was her decency and sensitivity, unexpectedly overheard by Mr. Lorinc, that saved her life and the lives of her children. And what a life she had! She and her husband were blessed with more than 25 grandchildren and over 100 great-grandchildren, all of whom have remained loyal to the Torah. One of her daughters, Faigy, married Rabbi Moshe Yechiel (Murray I.) Friedman, founder of CounterForce, a guidance counseling service for yeshivah students, administered by Torah Umesorah. Rabbi Friedman's daughter, Mrs. Esther Rockove, wife of Rabbi Label Rockove, the Rav of Cong. Nachlas Avos in Richmond Hill, told me this story. Malka was her grandmother.

> It is said about Rav Yochanan ben Zakkai that no one ever greeted him first, even a gentile in the market, for he made sure always to offer the first greeting (*Berachos* 17a). Every human being is created *b'tzelem Elokim* (in the image of

Hashem). It behooves us then to be like Rav Yochanan ben Zakkai and treat everyone with dignity and respect. Malka Lax acted this way, so the irreligious banker, the gentile mayor, and the common folks in the Hungarian streets all tried to help her, thus smoothing the way for her family's salvation.

◆§ *Yielding Dividends*

Every Tuesday morning for three years, Rebbetzin Rus Attias of Bnei Brak accompanied Rebbetzin Batsheva Kanievsky, a"h, as she walked from the Lederman Shul in Bnei Brak to her home, after they davened Shacharis with the *hashkamah* (sunrise) *minyan*. At the *minyan*, many women would gather around the Rebbetzin to answer *amen* to her *Birchos Hashachar* (morning blessings) and then they would recite the blessings so that she and others would answer *amen*. After the davening women would come closer to receive her blessings and good wishes as she slowly walked home.

On the way she would relate inspirational stories that she had experienced with or heard about great *tzaddikim*, including her grandfather, Rabbi Aryeh Levine (1885-1969); her father, Rabbi Yosef Sholom Elyashiv (1910-2012); her father-in-law, the Steipler, Rabbi Yaakov Yisroel Kanievsky (1899-1985); and her husband, Reb Chaim.

Rebbetzin Attias kept notes on these stories and recently published them in *Shlishi B'ashmores*. She tells a story that I had heard years ago, but could not find a source until now. I was grateful to learn that the Rebbetzin herself had told it about her illustrious father, Rabbi Elyashiv.

In Bnei Brak, Zalman Langer* was to become bar mitzvah on Shabbos *Parashas Yisro*. For months he practiced the *leining* (Torah reading), and by the time his bar mitzvah week came, he knew it perfectly.

For that special Shabbos, his family gathered in his neighborhood and accompanied him to shul on Shabbos morning. When they entered the shul they were surprised to see a much larger crowd than usual. There were many people in shul that the Langers did not recognize. They soon learned that the gabbai had inadvertently told two different families that their bar mitzvah boy could *lein* the *parashah* that Shabbos.

A commotion began, but then Zalman asked his father to tell the *gabbai* that he would withdraw and let the other boy *lein*. Many in his family were surprised that he stepped down, but Zalman was firm. He would let the other boy *lein* and Zalman would be satisfied to have the *maftir aliyah* and *lein* the *haftarah*.

The next year, Zalman did *lein Parashas Yisro*, and he did it flawlessly. The same thing happened when he was 15 and 16; he *leined* his bar mitzvah *parashah* perfectly.

The following year, Zalman's mother became very seriously ill. She was hospitalized and the doctors gave her little chance for survival. The 17-year-old Zalman was at her bedside tending to her constantly.

In the same hospital, on a different floor, Rabbi Yosef Sholom Elyashiv was a patient. Rabbi Elyashiv asked that an exquisite *Sefer Torah* that was known to have a beautiful *ksav* (Torah calligraphy) be brought for the Shabbos *leining*. He also designated the *baal tefillah* for his *minyan*.

During *Shacharis*, someone realized that they had forgotten to arrange for a *baal korei*. Zalman, who knew that there would be a *minyan* in Rabbi Elyashiv's room, had come to join it, and when he heard that there was no *baal korei*, he offered to *lein*. "This is my bar mitzvah *parashah*," the young man said, "I can *lein* it."

Indeed, he *leined* so well that everyone, especially Rabbi Elyashiv, who was so particular about hearing every word enunciated with the proper *trop* (cantillation), was gratified. After the davening Rabbi Elyashiv asked who the young man was and why he was in the hospital.

Zalman was brought to the Rabbi, who asked him how he had become such a proficient *baal korei*. Zalman told the story of his bar mitzvah Shabbos. Rabbi Elyashiv then asked him why he was in the hospital. When Zalman told him about his mother and how doctors were giving up hope, Rav Elyashiv summoned his own doctor and asked him to personally examine Zalman's mother.

The doctor, a world-renowned specialist, saw Zalman's mother that afternoon and determined that she was receiving the wrong treatment and that her medications were exacerbating her condition. He prescribed a new course of treatment and the woman soon recovered.

Rebbetzin Kanievsky finished the story by saying, "Today that woman is alive and well, and it is all in the *zechus* (merit) of her son who yielded his *leining* to the other boy on the day of their bar mitzvahs."

❧ Courtesy in Chicago

This story is a treasure. The sensitivities displayed by the parties involved are worthy of emulation. I am grateful to Rabbi Dovid Zucker, the Rosh Kollel of the Chicago Community Kollel, for sharing the story with me. We were classmates in Torah Vodaath High School in Brooklyn, and he recently told me the story at our class reunion.

R' Yitzchok Cohen is a member of the Chicago Community Kollel where he came after six years in the Kollel of Beth Medrash Govoha in Lakewood.

On 26 Kislev 2011, R' Yitzchok had *yahrzeit* for his father, R' Shlomo Cohen. Customarily, on the Shabbos before one has a *yahrzeit*, one is called to the Torah for *Maftir* and is the *baal tefillah* for Mussaf. Thus, on the Shabbos before the *yahrzeit*, R' Yitzchok asked the *gabbai*, Reb Ephraim Hochberg, if he could be the *baal tefillah* for Mussaf.

This created a dilemma for the *gabbai*. Reb Pinchus Krystal, an older, highly respected member of the Chicago community, who was the Kollel's *baal Shacharis* on the *Yamim Noraim*, had *yahrzeit* on the Shabbos itself, for his father, Reb Binyamin Peretz. Rabbi Hochberg, the *gabbai*, assumed that Reb Pinchus had the priority for Mussaf. (See *Orach Chaim* 132, in *Biur Halachah*, where the Chofetz Chaim in his *Kuntros Mamar Kadishin* delineates the priorities.)

Rabbi Hochberg asked Rabbi Zucker what to do. Rabbi Zucker agreed that Reb Pinchus had priority since he had *yarhzeit* that day, but he suggested that the *gabbai* ask Reb Pinchus if he would forgo his right to the *amud* in favor of Reb Yitzchok, since he was a *kollel* fellow who had devoted himself exclusively to the study of Torah for many years.

Reb Pinchus acquiesced immediately. After davening, Reb Yitzchok thanked Reb Pinchus profusely.

"That is what my father would have wanted," said Reb Pinchus. "He loved *talmidei chachamim*, and you spend your entire day learning, so he would have wanted me to give preference to you."

Reb Yitzchok thought for a moment and said, "It's interesting. I think my father would have done the same thing. As a matter of fact, I will tell you a beautiful story about my father."

"My father liked to daven very slowly; he usually davened with the first *minyan* in Rabbi Chaim Weinfeld's shul in Brooklyn, *K'hal Toras Chaim*. However he never davened for the *amud*, because people at the first *minyan* had to go to work and would not appreciate his unhurried pace. When he had *yahrzeit*, and had to daven at the *amud*, he would daven at the second *minyan*, where the pace was more measured.

"On the third day of Chol HaMoed Pesach, when my father had *yahrzeit*, the davening took longer because of *Hallel* but the people did not mind his slow pace. Before the Torah reading, my father whispered to the *gabbai*, 'I am a *Kohen*.'

"The gabbai's face turned white. My father asked, 'Is there anything wrong?'

"'I did not know you were a *Kohen*,' said the *gabbai*. 'We have in shul a very old, frail man who has Parkinson's disease. He is our only *Kohen* who regularly attends this *minyan*. It takes him a full six minutes to walk from his seat to the *bimah* for the *aliyah*. [It took the gentleman a half-hour to walk the two and a half blocks from his home to the shul every morning.] If there is another *Kohen* in shul, we tell him right away, so he does not have to make that long trek to the *bimah*.'

"The *gabbai* continued. 'I did not know that you are a *Kohen* and so he automatically assumed he will get the first *aliyah*. He has started his walk already, and I feel bad to tell him that he should just turn around and struggle back to his seat. The first *aliyah* means a lot to him.'

"My father said immediately, 'Why, of course, if he started walking, let him come up. I give up my *aliyah*.'"

As Reb Yitzchok finished the story a thought suddenly came to him. "Could it be that the old man in the story may have been related to you? I believe his family name was also Krystal."

"My father indeed lived in Flatbush and he davened in Rabbi Weinfeld's shul," said Reb Pinchus. "That was him!"

Reb Yitzchok reflected aloud with awe, "So it was my father who gave his *aliyah* to your father. And now, years later, you repaid the favor by letting me have your Mussaf!"

Now that's remarkable!

Carry with Care

This may be the shortest story I have ever written in a Maggid book, but it is so precious.

As Mrs. Shoshanah Troppe and her nephew, Hershy Sputz, were carrying her wheelchair-bound mother up the stairs at a recent family wedding, she remembered something that her father, R' Zalman Gelernter, had told her when she was a child in the Crown Heights section of Brooklyn.

Mr. Gelernter was extremely caring to an elderly couple in a nearby nursing home. Their health had deteriorated and they needed constant help. Shoshanah once asked him why he went out of his way so much to help them so often. His answer stays with her until this day.

"Why did the Jews carry the broken *Luchos* with them in the *Aron*? They were broken — why didn't the people simply bury them?"

He answered his own question. "The Torah is teaching us that when *heilegeh* (holy) *Yidden* are broken, we do not discard them. Like the *Luchos*, the Jewish people 'carry' them with dignity, just as we did when they were whole."

How tender, how true, how instructive.

๛ੑ *A Gift of Elevation*

Chaya Munk, of Lakewood, knew as a child that she wanted to study in a seminary in Israel after high school. It wasn't merely growth in Torah and the atmosphere of the Holy Land that she was looking forward to; she would also finally meet her cousins, who were descendants of the great Rav of Yerushalayim, Rabbi Yosef Chaim Sonnenfeld (1848-1932).

Her cousins are sixth-generation Yerushalmis and they lived as did the Jews of previous generations. Their walk-up apartment in the Geulah section of Jerusalem was very modest; the living room served as the playroom and bedroom for three of their eleven children. Their washer and dryer were stacked atop of each other on the *mirpeset* (porch); the appliances were aged but functional. And yet, despite the lack of amenities, when Chaya first met them she was enamored. The Kaufman's were so pure, so in touch with Torah and *middos*! It made no difference that some of the chairs were broken, that they didn't match, or that the color in the curtains had faded. The warmth and the ambience in the home were inviting and Shabbos meals were sacred.

Chaya became very close to her relatives and their love for one another was mutual. One afternoon, Chaya invited 10-year-old Leah to go out with her. "I can take you wherever you like," said Chaya. "You make the choice."

Leah's eyes lit up. "I would love to go to a place with elevators and escalators. I was never on a long escalator."

"That's easy," said Chaya. "They have them at the Shefa Mall."

The two girls walked to Rechov Shamgar and entered the bustling mall. Little Leah's eyes darted back and forth as her eyes feasted on a colorful array of stores that sold clothes, food, housewares, and toys. Her smile and sparkling eyes reflected her joy. Up and down the escalators the two girls traveled and giggled. They used every elevator they could find and chatted delightedly, basking in their friendship.

"I would like to buy you something special," said Chaya. "What would you like?"

Leah's answer surprised and pained her. "I would like my own bar of chocolate. I love chocolate but I never get the chance to have it," she said wistfully.

Her answer underscored the poverty and the simplicity in which she lived. "Of course, Leah," Chaya said. "Let's go straight to the *makolet* (food store). I'm sure they have delicious chocolate."

They took one more escalator and went into the *makolet* teeming with people and foodstuffs. Chaya bought two bars of chocolate and said. "Let's share one before we go home, and the other you can keep for yourself."

Leah's smile was worth it all. They stopped in a small park, sat on a bench, and devoured the first bar, commenting on its richness and smooth flavor. Chaya was thrilled that Leah would have something special that she would treasure for a while until she ate it all. However, as they walked up the rickety stairs to the Kaufman apartment in Geulah, Leah turned to Chaya and said, "Chaya, could you please give my mother the bar of chocolate as a gift. I know she loves chocolate and she never gets to eat it."

Chaya stopped and looked at Leah. She thought, *This child is indeed a descendant of Rav Yosef Chaim Sonnenfeld.* Chaya had just learned in seminary about the *Yakirei Yerushalayim*, the treasured ones of Jerusalem. *This is how they were when they were young,* she thought, *how holy, how precious, how special!*

Gracious Traits and Character / 151

Part C:
Precious Chinuch Gemstones

☙ *The Talmud and the Talmid*

Taking in the sight of close to 95,000 Jews at MetLife Stadium during the Siyum HaShas on August 1, 2012 was awesome. Neither I nor anyone else in the stadium had ever witnessed that many Jews in one place, for one cause, all united in their desire to be moved and inspired to a greater love for Torah study.

Undoubtedly there were many, many reasons that people came to that awe-inspiring event: the gentleman from Norfolk, Virginia, who had finished Shas for the first time, the *maggid shiur* from Toronto who was celebrating the second time he had taught the entire cycle of Daf Yomi, the father from Mexico who wanted his young son to see so many Jews celebrating *Klal Yisrael's* Twelfth Siyum of Daf Yomi since its inception in 1923. And there was the following story, about a rebbi from Edmonton, Alberta, Canada, who had been inspired by a third grader.

A s I was sitting with my family, a man approached me and said, "Rabbi Krohn, this is such a great day for me. It's the achievement of a dream and the fulfillment of a promise. It's a great story, too; would you like to hear it? I know you like stories."

He was right. It is indeed a story worth knowing — and retelling.

In the autumn of 2001, Rabbi Akiva Serebrowski, fresh from the Mirrer Kollel in Jerusalem, began his teaching career as a rebbi in the Menorah Academy in Edmonton, Canada. He taught the combined third and fourth grades. For the first part of the year, he taught Chumash. His enthusiasm was contagious and his students responded accordingly. He was having an influence on parents as well, as they appreciated his total involvement in their sons' learning and general welfare.

As winter progressed, he readied the boys for the next step on the rung of learning: Mishnah. He spent an entire morning explaining the development of the Mishnah and its six orders, the Gemara, and the panorama of Talmud Bavli and Talmud Yerushalmi. The boys were awed at the breadth of the Torah and they were excited to begin learning Mishnah, which is the source of the entire Talmud, the Shas.

"As hard as it is to believe," Rabbi Serebrowski said, "there are actually people today and people who lived recently — *gedolim*, great people — who have mastered the entire Talmud, which is called Shas."

To the boys, that was staggering information. They gazed at their rebbi with awe. "I can bring you some pictures of these great men," he said thinking of his eight-by-ten photos of such *gedolim* as Rabbi Moshe Feinstein, Rabbi Yaakov Kamenetsky, Rabbi Shlomo Zalman Auerbach, Rabbi Chaim Kanievsky, and others. He had planned to hang these inspiring portraits on the classroom walls.

The class broke for recess, but Rabbi Serebrowski remained at his desk to grade papers. Two boys remained in the room, choosing not to go out into the cold Edmonton winter. Rabbi Serebrowski overheard what he at first thought was an amusing conversation. Simon Ratner* said to his friend, Josh Segal, "I don't think Rebbi knows the entire Shas, do you?"

"Of course he knows it," replied Josh, "He's a rebbi."

"But he's too young," protested Simon.

How innocent these children are! smiled Rabbi Serebrowski to himself. *Pure, holy neshamos.*

But suddenly the conversation took a turn that startled him. "Why don't we just go up and ask him?" said Josh.

Rabbi Serebrowski broke into a cold sweat. How could he tell them something that was not true? Of course he hadn't yet finished Shas. He had been learning intensely for many years in the yeshivah, but the entire Shas? He wasn't even close.

But if he told that to his students, they might be disappointed in him and it could make it harder for him to inspire the boys and their parents in the future. On the other hand, how could he lie? Rabbi Serebrowski remembered a story he had heard about Rabbi Yaakov Kamenetzky, who was known as the "Ish Emes," the man of impeccable truth.

As a student in Slabodka, Reb Yaakov once stayed with a local family over Pesach, because he could not go to his parents for Yom Tov. He was uncertain about the standard of kashrus in that household and tried to minimize what foods he would eat there. During Yom Tov, the hostess served a dish that Reb Yaakov preferred not to eat, but he didn't want to insult her. He told his hosts that he could see that the recipe included *gebrokts* (matzah crumbs or matzah flour), and that he did not eat *gebrokts* on Pesach. That solved the problem without embarrassing anyone. In actuality, Reb Yaakov had eaten *gebrokts* until that Pesach; however, he held that if one undertakes sincerely to do a mitzvah, it is as though he fulfilled the mitzvah from the moment he undertook it. Once he said that he does not eat *gebrokts*, he undertook it as a commitment that he kept for the rest of his life. (See *Sha'arei Teshuvah, Shaar Sheini, Haderech Shelishis.*[1])

Rabbi Serebrowski made a quick vow. "If Josh asks the question, I will start and complete the Daf Yomi, starting with the next cycle."

Josh walked up to the desk. "Rebbi," he asked. "Have you finished the entire Shas?"

Rabbi Serebrowski did not hesitate. The pure innocent sincerity on his talmid's face gave him the strength to answer and make the commitment at the same time. He smiled and nodded his head in the affirmative.

Josh was satisfied. He went back to Simon with pride. "I told you so," he said triumphantly.

A little more than three years later, Rabbi Serebrowski and his 5-year-old son Yehuda were sitting in his office at Menorah Academy watching the Eleventh Siyum HaShas on his computer

---

1. בֵּינָן שֶׁקִבְּלוּ עֲלֵיהֶם לַעֲשׂוֹת, מַעֲלֶה עֲלֵיהֶם הַכָּתוּב כְּאִלּוּ עָשׂוּ מִיָּד, *As soon as they have accepted upon themselves to perform it, it is as though they did it immediately.*

monitor. The building was eerily quiet. As he kept his eyes glued to the proceedings from New York, he remembered the commitment he had made when Josh asked the question. He realized with a jolt that his monumental task would begin the next morning.

He turned to his son and said softly, "Yehuda, in seven and a half years we are, *bli neder* (without a promise), going to celebrate the Siyum HaShas with all those people in New York." The little boy nodded proudly.

Over the next few years, the Serebrowskis moved from Edmonton to Toronto, where Rabbi Serebrowski became the general studies principal at Yeshivas Bnei Tzion of Bobov. To augment his income, he sometimes worked as a realtor. Along with the taxing hours of work came more family responsibilities as his family grew. But he kept at his Daf Yomi.

There were times that he actually arose at 4:30 a.m. to learn the *daf* before attending the 6:15 *minyan*. At other times he went to sleep after midnight in order to learn the *daf* for that day. Years of toil and commitment went by, but Rabbi Serebrowski's diligence never waned. Over the years he maintained a connection with Josh, who was then studying in Ohr Someyach in Israel. As the twelfth cycle of Daf Yomi was coming to an end, it occurred to him that he should celebrate the great occasion with his former talmid.

He called Josh's mother in Edmonton and told her that he was planning to purchase prime tickets for the Siyum HaShas at MetLife Stadium and would like to obtain one for Josh as well. She was so touched that she said she would bring Josh back from Israel for the occasion.

As the rebbi and talmid traveled to the stadium with two of the rebbi's sons, Rabbi Serebowski's reminded Josh what had transpired more than 10 years earlier in Edmonton. Josh had no recollection of it. Rabbi Serebrowski said, "Josh, that conversation you had with Simon years ago was a life-changing experience for me. I can never thank you enough. You put me on a pedestal and I simply could not fall from it."

At the Siyum, when the last page of the last tractate was completed, the rebbi and his children — those he raised and the one he molded — held hands and danced rapturously. Josh was riveted throughout the evening, absorbing the monumental *Kiddush Hashem* that was taking place before him.

After the event, Rabbi Serebrowski and Josh traveled to the great yeshivah Beth Medrash Govoha in Lakewood, where, during the next two days, they learned the first two *blatt* of *Berachos*. Afterward Rabbi Serebrowski drove Josh to Newark Airport where he boarded a plane back to *Eretz Yisrael*.

> This is only one story out of the countless others that brought people to the great Siyum HaShas of August 2012. In the Heavenly spheres Rabbi Meir Shapiro, the originator of the Daf Yomi idea 89 years earlier, was surely smiling. He had spoken of the unity in *Klal Yisrael* that would be accomplished by everyone learning the same *daf*. But who would have imagined that a third grader would be reunited with his rebbi 10 years after he posed a simple question!
>
> Perhaps we should ask that question of ourselves: "Have you finished the entire Shas?"

✥ Crowning Glory

> In the summer of 2004, I led a group of 120 people on a tour through Jewish Lithuania and Poland. Prior to the trip, I visited with Rabbi Avrohom Ausband, Rosh Yeshivah of the Yeshiva of the Telshe Alumni in Riverdale, New York, who said, "If you are going to Lublin, let me share with you a fascinating insight that I heard personally from Rabbi Pinchus Hirschprung (1912-1998)."

Rabbi Hirschprung was one of the primary talmidim of Rabbi Meir Shapiro (1887-1934), founder of the great Yeshivas Chachmei Lublin. In 1941, Rabbi Hirschprung was able to escape from Europe to Canada on the last boat to leave before the attack on Pearl Harbor. He eventually became Chief Rabbi of Montreal, a position he held from 1969 until his passing in January 1998.

Rabbi Meir Shapiro once attested to the fact that even as a youth Rabbi Hirschprung already knew over 2200 *blatt* of Gemara by heart! After the passing of Rav Meir Shapiro, Rabbi Hirschprung would test students who applied for admission to Chachmei Lublin. There were few in his generation who knew the entire Shas by heart, verbatim, as did Rabbi Hirschprung.

In 1923 at the first Knessia Gedolah of Agudas Yisrael in Vienna Rabbi Shapiro first proposed the Daf Yomi program. Rabbi Hirschprung told Rabbi Ausband that although it was his rebbi, Rabbi Meir Shapiro, who originated the idea of the Daf Yomi, it was actually the Imrei Emes, Rav Avrohom Mordechai Alter of Gur (1866-1948), who was the driving force in it becoming accepted throughout the world.

On Rosh Hashanah of 1923, just a few months after Rabbi Meir's Shapiro's dramatic proposal, thousands gathered in the Gerrer Beis Medrash to be with their Rebbe for Yom Tov. Prior to the start of Maariv, the Imrei Emes announced, "Tonight we shall start *mesechta Berachos* and learn a *daf* a day as was proposed by Rabbi Meir Shapiro."

The assembled rushed to secure their Gemaras, and with excitement and fervor began the first *daf* in Shas. The enthusiasm in Ger was the engine that pulled the locomotive of Daf Yomi.

Rabbi Hirschprung then added a fascinating incident that few people are aware of. During the *Aseres Yemei Teshuvah* (Ten Days of Repentance from Rosh Hashanah until Yom Kippur) of that year, Rabbi Meir Shapiro received a letter from his sister that described a poignant dream that she had the first night of Rosh Hashanah: Her mother was walking in *Gan Eden,* adorned by a majestic crown. She wrote that she wondered why she had that dream.

A while later, Rabbi Ausband heard the following story and put things together. When R' Meir was a little boy, his mother hired a special *melamed* to learn with him every day. She was so proud of his accomplishments that when he started learning Gemara she made a *seudah* for the local rabbis to commemorate the event. One day, the Shapiros moved to another area that was too far for the *melamed* to travel. Meir's mother arranged for a new *melamed* to learn with Meir starting from the first day when they moved in.

On moving day, the truckers brought the Shapiros' belongings to their new residence and the family settled in, but the *melamed* was nowhere to be found. There had been some confusion and the *melamed* did not know that he had to start on that day. As nightfall came and Mrs. Shapiro realized that the *melamed* would not be coming, she sat down and cried. The young Meir asked, "Momma, why are you crying?"

"A day of learning that is lost can never be made up," she replied.

He would never forget her answer. It penetrated his essence and was a credo he would live with the rest of his life. Rabbi Ausband felt this was the seed that implanted the importance of daily learning in the fertile mind of this young genius, Meir Shapiro.

Rabbi Ausband suggested, "It was Rabbi Meir Shapiro's mother's tears that were the first penetrating impression in his mind that every single day of learning is critical. It was from that seed that Daf Yomi blossomed. His mother deserved to be adorned with the royal crown of Torah. And that's perhaps why Rabbi Meir Shapiro's sister had the dream on that first night of Rosh Hashanah."

܀§ *From a Tear-Drenched Siddur*

Shlomo HaMelech writes, חַכְמוֹת נָשִׁים בָּנְתָה בֵיתָהּ, *The wise among women, each builds her house* (*Mishlei* 14:1). There can be no more apt description of the heroine of this story, for her astuteness and perceptiveness saved generations. We can only marvel at her ingenuity.

It was 1939 and Mrs. Esther Bernfeld realized that if her son Mayer (Miguel), in his mid-20's, were to remain with her in Topolcany (pronounced Topol'chany), Czechoslovakia, his life —

spiritual and physical — would be in danger. The Nazis were storming through one European country after another, targeting Jews for persecution and worse, and the Czechoslovakian Army was drafting as many young men as they could, so it was only a matter of time before Mayer would be taken from his home and perhaps never be heard from again.

There were few countries to which Jews could escape. America, Canada, and England were not admitting Jewish immigrants, claiming that their immigration quotas had long been filled. There were, however, five South American countries that were still issuing visas: Paraguay, Bolivia, Brazil, Chile, and Uruguay. Which would be best for her son? Where could he most likely be able to remain a religiously committed Jew?

As she pondered the dilemma, an imaginative idea came to mind. Her tear-drenched *siddur* was published by Shulsinger Brothers in New York. Mrs. Bernfeld wrote a heartfelt letter to the head of the company, conveying her concern for her son. She wrote "Which of these five South American countries is your busiest customer? To whom do you sell the most *Chumashim, siddurim,* and other *sefarim*?"

Her reasoning was obvious. Religiously committed Jews bought *Chumashim* and *siddurim,* so the biggest customer had the most dedicated Jews.

She waited anxiously for the reply. The letter came in a few weeks. The answer was the Hebrew bookstore in Montevideo, Uruguay. She immediately applied for a visa and sent her beloved Mayer to Montevideo, more than 7,000 miles from home. She gave him the address of the Jewish bookstore and told him to go directly there.

With the help of the store owner, Mayer established himself and eventually married. His children and grandchildren are all committed to the highest standards of *Yiddishkeit.* I remember when his son Yoel (Ervin) came to Yeshiva Torah Vodaath in the late 1950's, with other boys from Uruguay. Today R' Yoel, who told me the story, lives in Montreal with *his* children and grandchildren. His grandmother, Mrs. Esther Bernfeld, with her foresight and astuteness, was the catalyst to preserve four generations of *ehrliche Yidden* in her family.

Chazal teach, בִּשְׂכַר נָשִׁים צִדְקָנִיּוֹת שֶׁהָיוּ בְּאוֹתוֹ הַדּוֹר נִגְאֲלוּ יִשְׂרָאֵל מִמִּצְרַיִם, *In the merit of the righteous women who were in that generation, Israel was redeemed from Egypt* (*Sotah* 11b and *Bamidbar Rabbah* 3:6). May we merit having more women like Mrs. Esther Bernfeld in *Klal Yisrael* so that we may merit the ultimate Redemption.

◆§ Etched in Stone

Recently, my sister, Mrs. Yitty Gutman of Lakewood, New Jersey, called to tell me that yet another former talmid of her late husband, Rabbi Yehoshua Gutman, had named his newborn son after him. "This is already the eighth talmid who has named a child after Yehoshua," my sister said proudly. And then, with her voice breaking, she tearfully added, "They really loved him."

How true. My brother-in-law was a rebbi and then a principal in Yeshiva Toras Chaim of Denver, Colorado for more than 30 years. His talmidim revered him, his colleagues admired him, and his friends adored him. He had the easiest laugh, he was a remarkable *talmid chacham*, an incredible *baal korei*, and to top it off, he was knowledgeable in a myriad of fields. He could discuss any topic from *Chumash* to chemistry, from *Tanach* to trigonometry, from *psak halachah* to political science. Aside from everything else, he was a great *chavrusa* (learning partner). We studied together for years as *bachurim* in Mesivta Torah Vodaath before he went to learn in Lakewood. Eventually I introduced him to my sister and he became my brother-in-law.

Reb Yehoshua, as he was known, or Leo as he was called growing up in Washington Heights, was a genius in *chinuch* (Torah education). *Mechanchim* across the country consulted with him about controlling a class, inspiring a student, or convincing reluctant parents to let their children grow in Torah and mitzvos.

Reb Yehoshua once sat all night at the bedside of a talmid who had had two wisdom teeth pulled earlier that afternoon. In this way, if the boy awoke in pain at any time, Yehoshua could give him his medicine immediately. The talmid did indeed wake up at 2 a.m. He was startled to see his rebbi sitting and learning by the light of a small lamp, ready to help him immediately.

In the early 1970's, before ArtScroll existed, Reb Yehoshua wrote a translation and explanation of the entire *Viduy* of Yom Kippur, listing common *aveiros* that may have been transgressed throughout the year, so that his talmidim could refer to it on Yom Kippur.

Reb Yehoshua sent a boy out of class for being disruptive. He placed a chair outside the classroom so the boy could still listen to the *shiur* and Reb Yehoshua even responded to the boy's question during the *shiur*. That talmid and the entire class got the message. Disruptions will be punished, but Torah learning should not suffer.

When he had a Sephardic boy in his class, he wrote a special halachah test for him, according to the Bais Yosef, whose rulings are followed by Sephardim.

When he was principal, one of the high school boys cut class and went to my sister's home. She was the "mother away from home" for many of the out-of-towners; she understood that the boy was homesick and needed a break. So they baked cookies together.

A while later, Reb Yehoshua came home and noticed the boy placing the cookie pan into the oven. He asked the boy if he was feeling well, and when the boy's answer was yes, Reb Yehoshua went on doing what he had come home to do.

The next day Rabbi Gutman called the boy into his office. "I noticed in the attendance book that you missed classes yesterday. Is everything all right? Did you have permission to leave?"

The boy was shocked and said, "Rebbi, you saw me yesterday in your house and you didn't ask me anything about missing class. Why are you asking me about that today?"

Rav Yehoshua's reply was classic. "When you are in my home, it's like being in a foreign embassy. You are in a safe haven. My home is not the yeshivah. If a boy needs a place to be, he is always welcome. But that was in my home. Today I talk to you as the principal, and it's my job to teach you responsibility and accountability. That's why I am asking you today the questions that I did not ask yesterday."

> A year after Reb Yehoshua passed away; a *Sefer Torah* was dedicated in his honor by his family, friends, and talmidim. At the dedication, I related numerous incidents that his former talmidim had shared with me depicting his wisdom and insight as he motivated and inspired students. This story is my favorite.

Yeshiva Toras Chaim in Denver has the distinct advantage of being located less than half an hour from the breathtaking Rocky Mountains. On a clear day, one can see the snow-capped mountains in the distance. The majestic panorama beckons those near and far to come close to be embraced by its beauty.

Every year the Yeshiva hosts a *Shabbaton* for boys in Torah day schools from the Midwest to the West Coast. Boys from Dallas, Houston, Minneapolis, Phoenix, San Diego, Los Angeles, and even Mexico spend three days in the mountains with the staff and students of Toras Chaim. They snow tube, water-slide, mountain-climb, and barbeque. The hope is that the boys will be enthused by their experiences and will come to Toras Chaim for high school.

Precious Chinuch Gemstones / 165

In 1984, a seventh grader came to the *Shabbaton* from a day school in Mexico.* He had long hair, wore jeans and a T-shirt, and did not stop talking from the moment the plane landed in Denver. He went by his Spanish name, Pancho* (his Hebrew name was Pinchus), but by Friday night the other boys had nicknamed him "Mouth" because his worked nonstop. Pancho's father was not thrilled that his son might continue his religious studies in high school, but reluctantly he had allowed him go on the *Shabbaton*. Pancho's mother, though, was more positive about his opportunities. No one thought he would come back for the next year's *Shabbaton* when he was in eighth grade, but he did. And it was then, on a mountain in Vail, Colorado, that Rav Yehoshua became convinced that he could mold this child into a true *ben Torah*.

He encouraged the boy to ask his parents to send in an application. Pancho's father was not thrilled with the idea, but after many phone conversations with Rav Yehoshua, he reluctantly permitted his son to enroll in Toras Chaim.

Pancho got off the plane and arrived in the yeshivah dormitory with the same long hair he had had at the *Shabbaton*. Rav Yehoshua greeted him warmly and told him, "From today on you are Pinchus, a future *ben Torah*." With that began a rebbi-talmid relationship that lasted for decades. At the start there were turbulent times as Reb Yehoshua slowly and painstakingly guided the modern Mexican *bachur* in the yeshivah ways of dress, speech, and behavior.

Pinchus was brilliant, absorbing and retaining all that he learned, especially during the two years in the 10th and 11th grades, when Reb Yehoshua was his rebbi, but the transition to a refined *yeshivah bachur* was a long, slow process.

The turning point came in the 11th grade. Pinchus began to come to class wearing a necklace. It wasn't blatantly obvious, but Reb Yehoshua noticed it under Pinchus' open-collared shirt. Reb Yehoshua let two days pass without a comment. On the third day he asked Pinchus to stay after class.

After everyone left, Reb Yehoshua said to him, "I have a special gift for you."

Pinchus eyes widened: a present in the middle of the year? For no special reason? Reb Yehoshua took a small jewelry box from his pocket and gave it to Pinchus. Pinchus wasn't sure whether he should open it. "Go ahead," said Reb Yehoshua, "it's especially for you."

Pinchus unwrapped it and his mouth dropped open. Was his rebbi serious? On a piece of black suede fabric was one earring. "I figured it would match the necklace," said Reb Yehoshua with a half-smile.

Pinchus went back to his dormitory room and looked at himself in the mirror. He took off the necklace and never put it on again. He placed the earring in its box and put it in his pocket. He carried it with him for the next 20 years! He never went anywhere, including his wedding, without it. This was his eternal tie to his beloved rebbi, who had subtly delivered his message with a smile and sensitivity. It symbolized everything *chinuch* was meant to be.

Pinchus went on to learn in *Eretz Yisrael* and studied in a *kollel*. Today he is married with children. His youngest son is named Yehoshua Noach. Pinchus is a rebbi in a prominent yeshivah, perpetuating the lessons he learned from his great mentor. Three years ago, when my brother-in-law suddenly passed away two days before Yom Kippur, all who knew him were devastated.

A few months afterward, Pinchus approached Reb Yehoshua's son and asked if he would do him a favor. "I am a *Kohen*," Pinchus said. "I am not allowed to visit a cemetery. There is a *minhag* that when one visits a gravesite he places a stone on the headstone. I would love to add a stone to your father's *matzeivah*, but I have something different. I want to return something he gave me years ago. "

And so a few days later, my nephew Avrohom Gutman placed a little box with an earring on top of his father's *matzeivah*. Surely people who saw it afterward walked away puzzled. They could not know that this was a symbol of love etched in stone.

Precious Chinuch Gemstones

✥ Criticism, Conclusions, and Culminations

On a recent Project Mesorah trip to Poland that Rabbi Aubrey Hersch of London and I led, we spent a great deal of time talking to our group about the wisdom and insights of *gedolim*. We spoke of the compassion of the Rebbe Reb Elimelech, the insights of the Chozeh of Lublin, the foresight of Rav Meir Shapiro, the sensitivity of the Netziv, and the benevolence of Rav Chaim Soloveitchik.

One morning a member of the group, R' Yussi Seif of Lawrence, New York, and I were discussing the inherent wisdom of *gedolim*, specifically, their mode of criticism and their manner of motivation. He told me that years ago he had held a prominent managerial position with the mammoth conglomerate General Foods. He said that all managers were required to attend a sensitivity training course to learn how to effectively criticize their employees.

He explained. "Suppose I wanted to tell a speaker that I did not approve or agree with something he said. If I were to tell him straightforwardly, 'What you said is ridiculous, I don't agree with your premise, you've made a mistake,' the speaker would assuredly be offended and most likely not take the matter seriously. However, if I told him, 'The point you made about children was wonderful and the thing you said about teachers was fascinating; however, the thought you expressed about homework was something that I think has to be reconsidered,' it would more likely be palatable and the speaker would very likely rethink the matter."

Yussi continued, "They taught us, that it's a two-for-one ratio. Give two compliments for every criticism and you can be effective."

I was delighted to hear his insight because just a few weeks earlier, I had heard the following story from Rabbi Heshy Pincus, who heard it in a *shmuess* given by Rabbi Nosson Wachtfogel (1910-1998), the Mashgiach in Beth Medrash Govoha in Lakewood. Reb Nosson was a *talmid* of the legendary Mashgiach of Yeshivas Mir in Belarus, Rabbi Yeruchem Levovitz (1873-1936), under whom he studied for seven years. Reb Yeruchem had a profound influence on Reb Nosson and throughout his 55 years as Mashgiach in Lakewood, he often cited the teachings and personal behavior of his revered mentor.

Rav Nosson was discussing the important character trait of tenacity and persistence. He said that especially in the month of Elul and throughout the subsequent days of the *Aseres Yemei Teshuvah* (the Ten Days of Repentance between Rosh Hashanah and Yom Kippur), we resolve to improve in our *bein adam laMakom* (man-to-G-d relationship) and *bein adam lachaveiro* (person-to-person relationship). Though our intentions are surely good, as time progresses from Elul to Yom Kippur, we often fall short of our intended mark.

R av Nosson then told this story to illustrate this thought. In the city of Mir there was a young teenager who heard that a *minyan* had to be formed on Shabbos morning in Rav Yeruchem's home because he was ill and too infirm to come to shul. The boy volunteered to *lein* (read) the *sidrah* (the Torah portion of the week).

Shabbos came and the boy, by far the youngest person in this impromptu *minyan, leined* flawlessly until *chamishi* (the fifth *aliyah*). From *chamishi* until *shishi* (the sixth *aliyah*) he made a few mistakes. From *shishi* to *shevi'i* he made even more, and from *shevi'i* until the end of the *sidrah* he had to be corrected very frequently. It was embarrassing.

Afterward, Rav Yeruchem, with a luminous insight into a famous Talmudic teaching (see *Avos* 5:20), spoke to the boy. "My son, you fulfilled the teaching רָץ כַּצְּבִי, *run like a deer*, perfectly; you volunteered to *lein* as soon as you heard there was a need. You fulfilled as well perfectly the teaching גִּבּוֹר כָּאֲרִי, *be strong as a lion*, for you displayed the courage to *lein* in the presence of people who were much wiser and older than you are. However, you fell short in implementing the teaching of עַז כַּנָּמֵר, *be bold as a leopard*, for you did not complete what you started with the same proficiency."

The boy was both abashed and appeased. He was well aware that his performance had been lacking, and he had humiliated himself by *leining* so poorly in front of such an august audience. Rav Yeruchem knew just how to make the boy feel better while still admonishing him gently to be more prepared before undertaking such an assignment.

> I told this story to Mr. Seif, who shook his head in amazement. "That is the essence of *Gedolei Torah*. They don't need courses in sensitivity training. Their knowledge is ingrained and comes naturally to them by virtue of the Torah they have learned. In order to make his point, Rav Yeruchem first gave two compliments by interpreting the Mishnah in a unique manner and only then gently offered his constructive criticism."

Perhaps this concept can be deduced as well from the phrase in *Midrash Tanchuma Eikev* 6: הַמַּתְחִיל בְּמִצְוָה יְהֵא גּוֹמֵר אֶת כּוּלָהּ, *One who starts a mitzvah should fulfill it in its entirety*. Not only should the mitzvah be performed in totality but it should be done with the same enthusiasm, passion, and competence from beginning to end.

The Satmar Rebbe, Rabbi Yoel Teitelbaum (1887-1979), expounded on this topic with homiletic interpretations of both a verse in *Chumash* and an expression in the Shabbos Mussaf prayers.

The Torah writes תָּמִיד עֵינֵי ה' אֱלֹקֶיךָ בָּהּ מֵרֵשִׁית הַשָּׁנָה וְעַד אַחֲרִית שָׁנָה, *The eyes of Hashem, your G-d, are always upon it [Eretz Yisrael] from the beginning of the year to year's end* (Devarim 11:12). The Rebbe asked why the word *year* is spelled with the definite article ה, *the*, הַשָּׁנָה, **the** *year*, the first time it is used in the verse, but the second time it is written without a ה, simply שָׁנָה, *a year*.

"The answer is," said the Rebbe, "that often מֵרֵשִׁית הַשָּׁנָה, at the beginning of a new year, people say *this* will be **the** year that I improve, this will be the *year* that I progress. However, as the days and months pass, a person falls back into his regular habits and behavior, and at אַחֲרִית שָׁנָה, the end of the year, he realizes that the year has reverted back to being like every other year; it was just a שָׁנָה, an ordinary year.

"However, if we want Mashiach to come, we must make sure that at the end of the year, we are still observing mitzvos and acting in accordance with the Torah just as we did at the beginning of the year. That is alluded to in the Mussaf prayer (in *Kedushah, Nusach Sfard*), הֵן גָּאַלְתִּי אֶתְכֶם אַחֲרִית כְּרֵאשִׁית, *behold I have redeemed you in later times as in earlier times*. [The Rebbe focused on the expression אַחֲרִית, saying that it alluded to the above verse in *Devarim*. Hashem will redeem us when the end of our year is consistent with our resolution at its beginning.]

Hence, just as Reb Yeruchem taught, it's not only the beginning that counts: one must try to follow through to the very end. That's what Rabbi Nosson Wachtfogel was teaching about the period from Elul to Yom Kippur.

◆§ *Home Rule*

Chazal teach that we should act like Hashem: מַה הוּא חַנּוּן וְרַחוּם אַף אַתָּה הֱיֵה חַנּוּן וְרַחוּם, *Just as He is gracious and compassionate, so should you be gracious and compassionate* (*Shabbos* 133b). In this touching story that I heard from Rav Aryeh Ginzberg of Cedarhurst, New York, we see the wisdom and delicate sensitivity of one of the *gedolei hador* of the last generation.

Yoel Hendler* of Bayit Vegan, Jerusalem, was the only child of his elderly mother. He lost his father as a young child and his mother never remarried. He always studied in local yeshivos so that he would not have to dorm, thereby never leaving his mother alone at night. He was a devoted son and tended to his mother in every way he could.

When the time came for Yoel to think of marriage, he decided that he would marry only a young woman who agreed that his mother could live with them. He was determined not to abandon his mother for the sake of his personal happiness. Understandably, Yoel found it hard to convince a girl's parents to even consider him as a potential mate for their daughter. The few times that he did meet a young woman who was unaware of this precondition, the *shidduch* fell apart the moment she found out that she would have to share her new home with a mother-in-law.

Yoel's rosh yeshivah had tried to talk him out of his plan but it was to no avail. "It is simply not fair to any *kallah* to make such a demand," the rosh yeshivah explained. "Marriage is an adjustment in itself. Adding an aged mother-in-law to the picture is unfair and unreasonable." However, the more he tried to reason with Yoel, the more obstinate Yoel became.

"She has been a father and a mother to me," Yoel responded. "I am her whole life. How can I abandon her, especially at her age?"

The rosh yeshivah knew that Yoel was an exceptionally kind and considerate individual who wanted to do the right thing, but he felt that the young man was misguided. The rosh yeshivah decided to take Yoel to see Rav Shlomo Zalman Auerbach (1910-1995), whose wisdom and *Ahavas Yisrael* were unparalleled. "Let's go to Rav Shlomo Zalman," the rosh yeshivah suggested. "He could surely advise you."

Yoel consented, as he, like everyone else, knew that the rav would surely take every aspect of the situation into consideration.

Yoel and his rosh yeshivah made an appointment and, with great anticipation, arrived at Rav Shlomo Zalman's home in the Shaarei Chessed neighborhood. Rav Shlomo Zalman listened to the point of view of both the rosh yeshivah and Yoel, thought for a minute or two, and finally announced, "I agree with this fine young *ben Torah*." He turned to Yoel and said, "You should only marry someone who agrees to have your mother live with you," and then with his warm smile Rav Shlomo Zalman added, "And I give you a *berachah* [blessing] that you should find such a girl very soon!"

The rosh yeshivah was stunned. He simply found it hard to believe that Rav Shlomo Zalman would sanction such an unreasonable demand. However, this was the *gadol hador* speaking, and so the rosh yeshivah accepted the decision.

Incredibly, within three months Yoel found his *"basherteh"* (his intended partner) and they became engaged. Yoel informed Rav Shlomo Zalman of the great news and the rav blessed the new *chassan* and *kallah* that they build a *bayis ne'eman b'Yisrael*, a home in *Klal Yisrael*, loyal [to Hashem].

The day after the wedding, Rav Shlomo Zalman called the *chassan* and said, "Now is the time for you to find a suitable residence for your mother." The *chassan* was startled; hadn't Rav Shlomo Zalman told him to marry only a girl who would agree to his mother moving in with them? Rav Shlomo Zalman continued, "Let me explain. Your intentions are very noble. However, your way is not the normal way for a young couple to begin their lives. You are of such fine character and so loyal to your mother that you had to find someone on your elevated level. That's why I told you to marry only someone who would agree to this condition. *Baruch Hashem*, you have found your partner. You will both go to visit your mother often and make her feel that she not only still has her son, but she also has a new daughter. Now go and build your home with your wife, and may Hashem bless you both."

And that is exactly what they did!

✥ Total Recall

Rabbi Moshe Weinberger of Brooklyn, New York, was surprised to hear the voice of a former *talmid* on the phone. "It's so good to hear from you, Meir," said Rabbi Weinberger. "We haven't spoken in ages." Meir Friedland, who had been Rabbi Weinberger's talmid in Mesivta Bais Shraga in Monsey 10 years earlier, was now married and living with his wife and young family in Belle Harbor, New York.

"Rebbi, I am making a *siyum* on all six volumes of the *Mishnah Berurah* and I would be honored if you would attend," said Meir.

"Mazel tov, that's *gevaldik*, that's wonderful! I am so proud!" exclaimed the effervescent Rabbi Weinberger. "It's so kind of you to remember me and invite me, but why me, of all people?"

"Well, Rebbi, it's only because of you that this whole thing happened," said Meir.

"Me?" laughed Rabbi Weinberger, "How so?"

"I don't know if you remember this," began Meir, "but many years ago when I was in your class in Beis Shraga you announced that you were giving a test on the *Mishnah Berurah* that we had learned. And then you said, 'And I expect every boy to get 100 on the test.'

"Some in the class laughed, and one boy said, 'That never happens, how can everyone get 100?'

"What you said to that boy is something that I never forgot. You said, 'Boys, if you get an 80 on a Gemara test, it means you know the material fairly well but there is room for improvement. But if you get an 80 in *Mishnah Berurah,* that deals with *halachah*, that means that you are doing things wrong 20 percent of the time. That's not acceptable.'

"That always stayed with me and when I went to learn in Mir in Yerushalayim years later, I started a serious *seder* in *Mishnah Berurah*. It has taken me all these years, but I finally completed it and the inspiration came from you."

> This heartwarming story illustrates the influence a rebbi or morah can have with a well-phrased expression of wisdom and encouragement. Quite often, a student retains words that the teacher has long forgotten saying. Thus, teachers in whatever capacity must choose their words carefully, for once they are uttered they have a life all their own. Rabbi Weinberger's one expression brought about endless hours of learning and adherence to mitzvos.
>
> The story brought to mind a whimsical incident that began when I was a freshman in Yeshiva Torah Vodaath High School.

It was PTA night and my mother was speaking with my English Literature teacher, Mr. Hyman Ozer. He was our favorite teacher; we even made him a surprise birthday party. As they were talking, he said, "Mrs. Krohn, your son is a wonderful writer, but he'll never write a book."

My mother was taken aback by the comment. Not that she was expecting me ever to write a book, but she wondered what prompted that remark. "Why do you say that?" she asked.

"He's too religious," Mr. Ozer said, "nobody will read what he writes."

My mother came home and told me what Mr. Ozer said — and I never forgot it. Thirty years later, when I was married with children *The Maggid Speaks* was published by ArtScroll and I went looking for Mr. Ozer. I asked many high school friends if he was still alive, if he was still teaching, and if so, where.

My friend Mitchell Mann, who was working in the public school system and was familiar with Jewish teachers throughout the city and the suburbs, told me that indeed Mr. Ozer was alive and well and that he was the head of the English Department in a Jewish high school in Long Island. I found the school's phone number and called him.

"Mr. Ozer, It's nice to talk to you," I began. "Do you recall that you taught in Yeshiva Torah Vodaath 30 years ago?"

"Of course I remember," he said, "I have wonderful memories of that school."

I told him that I was his former student and had a gift to give him, and I wondered if I could visit him at his school.

"You have a gift for me?" he asked. "Why, that is so kind. Yes, of course you can come. I am here every afternoon," he said with excitement. I told him I could be there the next day.

When I arrived at his office, I noticed that he had hardly changed. Though graying at the temples he was as dapper and handsome as he was when he first taught us. After recalling old times I said, "You were always our favorite teacher," and I showed him our graduation yearbook, *The Scroll*, in which he had been invited to write a letter to the graduates. Then I said, "Mr. Ozer, I don't expect you to remember this, but on PTA night during my freshman year, you told my mother that although you thought I was a good writer, I would never write a book. Well," I continued as I took out the freshly printed book, "I have a gift for you. I just wrote a book of Jewish short stories and I have autographed it for you."

"Why, that's wonderful. Thank you" he said, "I am very proud."

He leafed through the pages, nodded and smiled with approval, and said, "Come with me."

He put his arm around me and escorted me into one of his classrooms. The teacher and class all turned their attention to Mr. Ozer. "Boys, I want to introduce you to a former student of mine," he said with pride. "He just wrote a book and I taught him how to write!"

From that moment on we began a close friendship that has lasted until this day. I was the guest speaker at his retirement dinner and my mother was in the audience. Of course I told this story, and everyone, including Mr. Ozer, laughed.

> The lesson, though, is no laughing matter. A respected teacher made a comment and a student remembered it for 30 years! It is imperative for every teacher to remember that both benevolent and hurtful words can stay with a child forever. Teachers' words can build or break a personality. Construction and destruction are in their hands. They should choose their words carefully — for they are crafting the building blocks of the future.

~§ *Defining Moments*

In his collection of biographies, *Giants of Jewry*, Rabbi Aaron Surasky relates an incident in the Chofetz Chaim's youth that had lifelong ramifications. The Chofetz Chaim, Rabbi Yisrael Meir Kagan (1838-1933), was orphaned at the age of 11 when his father, Reb Aryeh Leib, passed away when he was only 47.

Reb Aryeh Leib was a tutor in Vilna, and because there was nothing more that the local hometown *melamdim* in Zhetl could teach Yisrael Meir, Reb Aryeh Leib would take the boy with him to Vilna, where he taught him and engaged others to learn with him. After Reb Aryeh Leib passed away and there were no funds for private tutoring, Yisrael Meir stayed in Vilna and studied with boys much older than he.

At the time, *maskilim* (secularists) tried to lure bright young Torah students to the study of mathematics, science, and Western culture. Such *maskilim* were rampant in the *batei midrashim* of Lithuania. Tragically, many potentially great Torah scholars were swayed by their promises of a brighter and more prosperous future.

One *maskil*, Adam Hakohen Levenson, set his eyes on young Yisrael Meir, and day after day hounded him to leave his Torah studies. Yisrael Meir became frightened as he realized that Adam Hakohen was having an effect on him. His resistance was weakening. He tried to avoid Adam Hakohen, but to no avail. The persistent *maskil* was in and around the *beis midrash* every day. Yisrael Meir then made a difficult but determined decision. He would stop coming to the *beis midrash*!

He left Vilna and remained hidden until he heard that Adam Hakohen had left town to pursue boys in other areas. During those days, Yisrael Meir accomplished less in his Torah studies than he would have had he remained in Vilna, but he would cite the Talmudic teaching, יֵשׁ קוֹנֶה עוֹלָמוֹ בְּשָׁעָה אֶחָת, *One can acquire his portion in the World to Come in one moment* (*Avodah Zarah* 10b). The Chofetz Chaim said, "The decision I made at that moment, as difficult as it was at the time, saved my future. I knew in my heart that I could not fend him off, so I had to leave even the holiest of places." Yisrael Meir eventually returned to the *beis midrash* and became the great Chofetz Chaim.

> In this light, a story I heard from Rabbi Nosson Muller, the *menahel* of Yeshiva Toras Emes Kamenitz in Brooklyn, depicts the significance of a principled decision made with determination. Though not nearly as momentous as the Chofetz Chaim's decision, it teaches us the difference in one's legacy that a timely decision can make.

On an evening in February 1998, a 23-year-old *bachur*, Chaim Schonbrun, was learning in the *beis midrash* of Beth Medrash Govoha in Lakewood. Everything was going well as he and his *chavrusa* were debating a point. Suddenly Chaim clutched his chest, fell forward, and collapsed. *Bachurim* ran to assist him and an ambulance was called immediately. However, despite Hatzolah's quick response, it was too late. Chaim had passed away.

Shock and dismay spread throughout the Lakewood community. This had never happened in the *beis midrash* before, and its meaning and portent stymied everyone. Family, friends, and fellow talmidim attended Chaim's funeral with a sense of overwhelming sadness. The Novominsker Rebbe, Rabbi Yaakov Perlow; Rabbi Elya Ber Wachtfogel, Rosh Yeshivah of the Yeshivah of South Fallsburg; and some of the Roshei Yeshiva in Lakewood offered heartbreaking eulogies. The young man had been plucked from this world with a startling suddenness. The tears shed and the words spoken about Chaim were heartrending. New stringencies were accepted regarding the respect one should accord a *beis midrash*. Friends in the yeshivah decided that as a merit for Chaim's *neshamah*, they would complete the study of the entire Shas by the end of the *sheloshim* (30-day mourning period).

Those who eulogized Chaim spoke of him as a *kadosh*, a holy person who died while studying Hashem's Torah. He was a sacred soul who perished doing Hashem's will.

Rabbi Muller told me this story and added a personal note. "I knew this young man. We lived in the same neighborhood. Let me share with you something only a few people know. Earlier that evening, Chaim and his friends gathered at a restaurant in Deal, New Jersey for a *seudas preidah*, a farewell gathering for a friend who was leaving to learn in *Eretz Yisrael*.

"The young men, all *bnei Torah*, wished their friend well and spoke of the value of learning in *Eretz Yisrael*. The ambiance was pleasant, the food was tasty, and the good cheer emanating from close friends was tangible. Suddenly Chaim glanced at his watch and realized that it was only 20 minutes to night *seder* [evening learning session]. He looked up and announced, 'I've had a wonderful time but I must get back to *seder*.'

"One of his friends said firmly, 'But we have not even been served dessert yet,' implying that his leaving would be impolite.

"'I'm sorry,' Chaim said. 'Seder begins in 20 minutes and my *chavrusa* will be waiting for me. Here, use my credit card, but I must leave.'

"Some of the friends were surprised that Chaim would leave so abruptly. However Chaim's mind was made up. He wished everyone well, and left the restaurant. He came to *seder* on time and starting learning with his *chavrusa* almost immediately. Within half an hour he was gone.

"Imagine," exclaimed Rabbi Muller, "if he had stayed in the restaurant and perished there, he would always be known as the *yeshivah bachur* who died in a restaurant! However, because he decided when he did to do what he did, he will now always be remembered as the holy student who died in the sanctity of a *beis midrash*, over his Gemara. He remains forever in our minds as a holy and revered soul."

> There comes a time in life when we need courage and strength to overcome external pressures. Great people draw from their reservoir of resolve and make a commitment that molds their life and their legacy. May we each be blessed with that internal power to make the right decisions at the proper time.

⊷§ Returnees

The prophet Malachi declares that prior to the great day of Mashiach's coming, Eliyahu HaNavi will inspire the hearts of children and parents to repent: וְהֵשִׁיב לֵב אָבוֹת עַל בָּנִים וְלֵב בָּנִים עַל אֲבוֹתָם, *And he [Eliyahu] will turn back [to G-d] the hearts of fathers with [their] sons and the hearts of sons with their fathers* (Malachi 3:24). Rashi comments that the process will start with the children's genuine sincerity, which will, in turn, inspire their parents. Though we have not yet merited the coming of Eliyahu to herald Mashiach's arrival, we know that throughout the world young men and women who had no previous connection to authentic Torah Judaism have changed their lives and displayed remarkable commitment to Torah and mitzvos. Often they even influence their parents to adopt the Torah way of life.

In Israel today, there is a movement called Shuvu (Return), which was pioneered by Rabbi Avrohom Pam (1913-2001), the Rosh Yeshivah of Torah Vodaas in Brooklyn. In the first 20 years since its inception in 1991, Shuvu established 67 schools throughout the country, educating more than 15,000 boys and girls from the former Soviet Union. I was asked to speak in Miami on Shuvu's behalf and, in preparation, I interviewed Mrs. Brocha Weinberger, Shuvu's Educational Director. She told me countless extraordinary accounts of children's commitment. Here are four of those stories. I am sure you will be as inspired by them as I was.

Lior Shifrin, an 8-year-old boy in the Shuvu school in Acco, listened transfixed as his teacher, Mrs. Rachel Linder, told her class the story of Chanukah. These Russian immigrant children were not accustomed to seeing their fathers light a Chanukah menorah every year. Many of them had never even heard of the festival.

Mrs. Linder detailed the numerous mitzvos that the Syrian-Greeks forbade the Jews to perform, such as *bris milah* and keeping Shabbos. "It was just like under the Communists," she said, "where it was forbidden to perform a *bris milah* and most Jews had no choice but to work on Shabbos."

After Chanukah, the school had a two-day vacation. When school resumed, Lior was absent. This did not seem unusual; many children were home with colds, and some may not yet have returned from visiting far-off relatives. However, when three days went by and Lior did not appear in class, Mrs. Linder was concerned.

She asked Lior's classmates where he might be but they had no idea. *Were Lior's parents upset that the school was too religious? Had they transferred him to a public school?* The thought of losing Lior as a student alarmed Mrs. Linder, for he was a child with great potential. After school that afternoon, she called Lior's mother to inquire about him.

"It's your fault," exclaimed Lior's mother to Mrs. Linder. "He is not in school because of you!"

Mrs. Linder quickly tried to recall if she had scolded or embarrassed Lior in any way that would cause him to want to stay away from her class. "My fault?" she asked cautiously.

"Yes," was the firm reply. "You taught him that the Syrian-Greeks were like the Russians and did not allow infant boys to have their *bris milah*. When he insisted that we tell him what a *bris milah* meant, he inquired if he had ever had a *bris*. When we told him that he hadn't, he absolutely insisted that he would not return to school until he had one. We had no choice but to arrange for a *mohel* to perform a *bris* on Lior. He came out of the hospital this morning and will be back in school tomorrow."

> Is this child not remarkable? Eight years old!
> Lior continued his studies and eventually attended Yeshivah Ashrei Ish in Bayit Vegan. Years later, for Simchas Torah, his yeshivah hosted 10 boys from the Shuvu Bat Yam School. At one of the Yom Tov meals, Lior told this story about himself. The boys were surprised to learn that Lior had once been a Shuvu boy with a background as limited as their own. They came away from that Yom Tov with a new role model to follow.
> Good choice.

Soccer is the sport of choice for schoolboys in Israel. Most have never heard of baseball; few, if any, know anything about football; and many, but not all, learn to play basketball. Soccer, however, is everyone's passion and they play with an intensity that borders on obsession.

Rafi Dayan of the Shuvu school in Kfar Saba was known throughout his school for the ferociousness with which he played soccer. No one wanted to be in his way when he chased after a ball, and few would try to steal a ball from him as he maneuvered down the field. One afternoon as he ran to shoot a goal, he stumbled and fell backward.

Instinctively he put out his hands to brace his fall, but when he landed he twisted his right wrist and at once felt excruciating pain. He lay on the ground motionless as his gym teacher, Gadi, and his team members gathered around him. He winced in pain, but did not cry. Gadi felt Rafi's wrist gingerly and though it hurt when it was gently squeezed and pressed, Rafi merely grimaced in anguish but did not shed a tear. "Big boys don't cry," was his mantra.

Gadi knew that the injury was serious and he took Rafi to the emergency room in the local hospital. After performing a preliminary examination and reading the X-rays, the doctor said that the wrist was indeed broken and that it required setting in a cast. The cast would cover Rafi's wrist, his hand, and most of the length of his fingers. As the cast was being set and Rafi saw that it indeed covered his fingers, he began to cry.

The doctor and Gadi were surprised. Rafi had been stoic until then. He had been calm and collected, but now he had suddenly succumbed to tears. "Is it too painful?" asked the doctor.

"No," answered Rafi, "it's not too painful."

"So why are you crying?" the doctor asked puzzled. "You seemed so strong up to now."

Rafi's reply stunned both his teacher and the doctor. "My parents are not religious. They hate whenever I do anything that might be a mitzvah. They get angry if I want to wear *tzitzis*, they don't allow me to go to shul on Shabbos, and they won't throw out the non-kosher food we have in our home. There is just one mitzvah that I can do at home without their knowing it, and I do it every morning. I wash my hands and recite the *berachah* '*Al Netilas Yadaim.*' Now with this cast, I won't even be able to do that!"

Tears welled in the doctor's eyes as he realized this was a child with the heart of an adult. "I have seen children cry before," the doctor said to Gadi, "but this is the first time that I was moved to tears myself."

At Rafi's follow-up visit, the doctor related to Rafi's father, Meir Dayan, what had transpired when the wrist was first set. Meir, a non-religious Jew from Kiryat Ono but still proud that he believed in G-d, was visibly moved. He felt a lump in his throat as he tried not to cry.

The next morning he observed the delight that Rafi had in being able to perform even part of the *Netilas Yadaim* mitzvah, carefully pouring water onto his fingertips. When the cast was finally removed, Meir and his wife, Ilana, were astounded at Rafi's genuine joy at being able to perform the mitzvah in totality. Though they had been content in their very limited practice of Judaism, they now realized that there must be more to it than they understood. They enrolled in a Shuvu class for parents and soon they too were washing their hands for *Netilas Yadaim* and, with a new sense of excitement and understanding, began performing other mitzvos with Rafi and his younger sister Tziporah.

> Rafi and Tziporah were eventually able to leave the Shuvu system and enroll in regular Torah schools. Today their parents stand behind them with pride and honor as the children are no longer afraid to perform mitzvos at home.

In 1995 the Grinskys emigrated from Russia, leaving their elderly parents behind. They settled in Dimona, a secular Israeli town in the Negev, where they absorbed the culture of the area, devoid of any connection to *Yiddishkeit*. Nevertheless, they enrolled their daughter Esther, named after a great-grandmother, in a Shuvu school, due to its high educational standards.

As Esther grew, she took a liking to the school's Torah studies and decided to become a *shomeres Shabbos* (Sabbath observer). This was difficult for her, as her parents often took family trips on Shabbos, but she somehow managed to avoid participating, saying she had to study with friends or help others with their homework. The Grinskys took pride in Esther's study habits and told everyone they had a "scholar" in the making. One day Mr. Ivan Grinsky announced that his mother was coming to Israel for a visit to see her children and grandchildren, some of whom she had never met. The house was filled with joy and anticipation as "Babushka," whom everyone adored and cherished, was arriving after 15 years of separation.

Of course, the entire Grinsky family and even some of the cousins all planned to go to the airport to greet the special guest. Esther did not have a second thought about it. Regardless of her busy school schedule, she would put everything aside and travel with her parents to greet her grandmother. The day after her father's excited announcement, it occurred to Esther to ask what day her grandmother was arriving. Her jaw dropped when she heard the answer. "On Saturday morning," replied her father. She turned away before she might say something that would upset her parents, but she *knew* that she would not go to the airport by car on Shabbos. But how would she accomplish this?

As the day approached, she realized she would simply tell her parents the truth. That Shabbos morning as everyone was getting into the car, she told her father, "I am so sorry but I can't go."

"What!" her father shouted. "How dare you not come along to see Babushka? How dare you insult my mother! And why can't you come?" he bellowed.

"I love you, Papa," she said softly, "and I love Babushka as well. But I love Hashem and I love His Shabbos. I can't violate the Shabbos by riding in a car. I will wait at home by the door for Babushka, but I can't go the airport."

Regardless of her parents' frustration and arguments, Esther held her ground. It was getting late and the family had to leave. With fury and anger they sped off to Ben-Gurion Airport, convinced more than ever that this religion was not reasonable.

A few hours later the family returned home, and Esther was waiting at the door. She greeted her grandmother warmly with hugs and kisses. "Esther," said Babushka with obvious delight,

"You are even more beautiful than your pictures!" And they embraced again.

Later that afternoon, the grandmother sat down next to Esther and said softly. "My dear, why didn't you come to greet me at the airport? Were you too busy? I was looking for you."

"Babushka," Esther replied, "please understand. I have become a *shomeres Shabbos*. I don't ride in a car on Shabbos. I would have loved to come to see you but I could not do so because today is Shabbos. Please forgive me."

Esther's grandmother reached out to kiss her grandchild. She embraced her for a few moments not saying a word. Finally she said, "Esther, you have given me a gift that I never expected. When I was a little girl, my mother and grandmother would tell me about Shabbos and how they observed it in their youth. I came here to be reunited with my children and grandchildren; I never thought I would also be reunited with my parents and grandparents."

To me, the most inspiring time of the year to be in *Eretz Yisrael* is Succos and the days leading up to the Yom Tov. The electric excitement in the air as people prepare for the upcoming festival is tangible. The intense searching for the appropriate *Arba'ah Minim* (Four Species), the colorful array of *succah* decorations that adorn the vendors' stalls throughout the Meah Shearim and Geulah sections of Yerushalayim, the constant blaring of Jewish music, all add to the anticipation of the arrival of the Yom Tov.

The *succahs* themselves — on rooftops and porches, in alleyways and private backyards, in courtyards and small parking lots — are a sight to behold. Some are made of wood, others of fabric and draperies, and still others of hardened plastic. The following episode is about a unique private *succah* that may have been as holy as any built that year.

Yael Suchachova attended a Shuvu school in Nazeret Ilit in the northern part of Israel. Her Russian immigrant parents were not interested in religion, but like many other nonreligious parents, sent her to the local Shuvu school because of its high scholastic standards. A few days before Succos, in the year 2000, Yael asked her parents if they would build a *succah* for the family but they refused, claiming that it was too much of a bother. Besides, the neighbors would surely complain about the "monstrosity."

However, Yael wanted a *succah*. Her teacher had described eating in the *succah* as a joyful, festive occasion and the child did not want to be left out. And so she decorated her bedroom as a *succah*! She hung from her ceiling the colorful paper chains they had made in class. She neatly placed pictures of great rabbis on the walls of her room and suspended streamers from one wall to the other. She even hung plastic fruits from the ceiling: apples, pears, and lemons that looked like *esrogim*. The room looked spectacular.

Over Yom Tov she invited her classmates, her friends, and her grandmother to come and eat a meal with her. They sang the Succos songs she learned in school, spoke about the meaning of the *Arba'ah Minim*, and invited the *Ushpizin* (the special sacred Succos guests) to come and join.

> One can easily imagine that Hashem's holy angels visited Yael's *succah*.

Every year when the second graders of the Shuvu school in Natanya are ready to receive their *siddurim*, a special event is tendered in their honor. They travel by bus, with their parents and teachers, to the Great Synagogue in central Jerusalem, for an elaborate ceremony. The children are dressed in their finest clothes and are brought onto a stage, together with their parents. Mrs. Brocha Weinberger leads the ceremonies. She first explains to everyone the significance of prayer and then announces with flair, "I am now returning these *siddurim* to all of you precious children. In years gone by your ancestors used *siddurim* like these. For 70 years there was a break in their observance. Now once again you are resuming their tradition."

She directs everyone to turn to a particular page in the *siddur*. The children and parents then recite together, "*Shema Yisrael, Hashem Elokeinu Hashem Echad.*" The teachers who watch it every year are brought to tears. The guests and friends attending stand in awe and applaud.

> Throughout the world, *Klal Yisrael* has started taking steps in returning to Hashem. May He send us Eliyahu to guide us in completing this journey, which will end with the coming of Mashiach. May it be in our time.

✥ Window Dressing

In 1974, when the family of Rabbi Yitzchok "Itzikel" Fuchs, a noted Vizhnitzer chassid, was sitting *shivah* for him in Boro Park, they were visited by hundreds of people who had been affected by Reb Itzikel throughout his long, productive, and colorful life. Born in Sighet, Romania, he grew to become a remarkable *talmid chacham* who knew the entire Mishnayos by heart! He was an *askan* (communal activist) and the head of the Agudath Israel organization in Sighet.

In 1944, when German soldiers occupied Sighet, Reb Itzikel was fortunate to be away the day deportations began. He did not return to his hometown and immediately went into hiding. Throughout the war he was hidden by various gentile benefactors in Budapest. He cut off his beard and changed his clothes as he assumed a new identity.

After the war, Reb Itzikel went back to Sighet, where he immediately began helping despondent survivors leave for Israel or America. Much of his work was clandestine and illegal, but he knew there was no future for Jews in Romania. Government officials found out what he was doing and he was arrested and sentenced to 25 years in prison! It was only through the herculean efforts of the Skulener Rebbe, Rabbi Eliezer Zushia Portugal (1898-1982), and the Vizhnitzer Rebbe, Rabbi Chaim Meir Hager (1881-1972), that Reb Itzikel was released after "only" seven years.

> Now, during the *shivah,* family members of those he had saved came to pay their respects and laud his efforts. Dozens and dozens of people shared incidents of Reb Itzikel's *chessed,* both on communal and private levels. However, Jews who had been in jail with him in Romania told a story that stunned everyone and brought to the fore the incredible personality of Reb Itzikel. None of his children or grandchildren had ever heard it before.

In his cell, Reb Itzikel would murmur to himself as he constantly reviewed the *Shishah Sidrei Mishnah* from memory. One day he had an idea. He took a bar of soap and smeared it all over the window in his cell. When the window was clouded with the white residue, he took a sharp implement and scratched out the words of an entire *mishnah* on the window pane. When a fellow Jew would be incarcerated in his cell Reb Itzikel would teach him the *mishnah* over and over until he knew it by heart. He did this with numerous Jewish prisoners, and when they had memorized the *mishnah,* he would scratch another *mishnah* onto the soaped-up window. In this way he taught dozens of *mishnayos* to prisoners who had no *sefarim* from which to learn.

> This story was repeated numerous times after the *shivah* by children and grandchildren and it became a family legend. Years later, Rabbi Mordechai Gifter (1916-2001), the Rosh Yeshivah of Telshe, visited a former talmid of his, Reb Shlomo Chaimovits, to raise money for the yeshivah. Reb Shlomo's wife, Raizey, is a granddaughter of Reb Itzikel and had a beautiful portrait of him displayed in the living room.

The picture of Reb Itzikel, with his sparkling eyes and radiant smile, revealed a man who enjoyed life and was resplendent with *ahavas Yisrael*. Rav Gifter paused to look at the portrait and said to his talmid, "Tell me about this man. He has radiance about him." Reb Shlomo told the story about the *mishnayos* on the window. Rav Gifter thought for a moment and remarked, as only he could, "I always knew that soap could cleanse a body, I never realized it could cleanse a soul!"

✥ Holy Fire in Warsaw

At a lecture given for the benefit of Agudah's *Neshei Cares* organization in May 2011, the well-known principal and *mechaneches* Rebbetzin Ruthy Assaf told this remarkable story. Shortly afterward, as I was preparing for a trip to Poland with 57 yeshivah high school students from the Project Mesorah Program, I called her to hear the precise details so that I could tell this story at the last remaining section of the wall of the Warsaw Ghetto. This noteworthy story is historical, educational, and, most of all, inspirational.

Rav Kalonymus Kalman Shapira (1889-1943), a descendant of the Mezeritcher Maggid, Rav Dov Ber (1704?-1772), was appointed as the Rebbe of Piaseczno (pronounced Pe'ahzetzneh) in 1909, at the age of 20. He established the Yeshivah Da'as Moshe, which became one of the largest chassidic yeshivos in Warsaw between the wars. He wrote *Chovas HaTalmidim* and *Takanas HaAvreichim*. After Germany invaded Poland, Rabbi Shapira was interned with many of his chassidim in the Warsaw Ghetto. The Torah discourses he gave during that tragic period were collected after the war and published as *Aish Kodesh*. This is the story of those discourses.

Throughout his life the Rebbe focused on children's Torah education. He fought the secularization of Jewish life and felt strongly that only with positive, joyous educational methods could Jewish youth be inspired to love and observe Torah and mitzvos. In the ghetto he established a *mamlachah* (kingdom), where children even as young as 5 were welcomed so that they would daven, learn, and even dance with him.

As the vicious Nazi noose strangled the Jews of Poland, the Rebbe realized that soon he too would be sent to death, since the ghetto was being liquidated. He placed his writings into a canister and buried it, hoping that someday someone would find his lectures. Rabbi Shapira was sent to the Trawniki slave labor camp near Lublin, where he eventually died.

After the war, a young boy was playing in the ghetto area. While digging in the ground, he found the canister. The boy had no use for it, but he surmised that it might have some value. He approached an American soldier and offered it to him for an American dollar. The soldier bought it and opened it immediately. He surmised that the script was Hebrew and so he took it to the Jewish chaplain, Rabbi Zvi Hollander, who gladly accepted it.

When Rabbi Hollander emptied the canister, he was startled to read it contents. The opening page stated, "When you find this, there may be no Jews left in Poland, no Jews left even in Europe, and no Jews left in the world. But in Jerusalem there will be Jews, for Jerusalem cannot live without Jews. Please go to the first Jew you see in Jerusalem and ask him to print this, and I swear that whoever prints this and reads from it — I will pray for them at the *Kissei HaKavod* [Throne of Hashem's Glory]."

Rabbi Hollander soon realized that these were the writings of the great Piaseczno Rebbe. Wherever he traveled he tried to find relatives of the Rebbe but was unsuccessful. In America, Europe, and Israel he could not locate even one relative. Eventually the writings were printed as *Aish Kodesh*, but Rabbi Hollander's search continued.

One day, in Tel Aviv, Rabbi Hollander was walking along the Yarkon, the largest coastal river in Israel, when he noticed an elderly hunched-over man sweeping the street. The man's deep-set eyes and wrinkled face testified to a lifetime of hardship. Since he was wearing a cap, Rabbi Hollander assumed he was religious. *"Sholom aleichem, ah Yid,"* Rabbi Hollander greeted him.

The man looked up, surprised that anyone would stop to talk to him. He answered in a Polish Yiddish accent, "*Shoolem alychem.*"

Rabbi Hollander asked the gentleman if he came from Poland. The man nodded and said that he did. Rabbi Hollander asked where in Poland he came from and was startled to hear the man say, "Piaseczno."

"Did you know Reb Kalonymus Kalman?" asked Rabbi Hollander hopefully.

"Of course I knew him, I was with him as a child in the Warsaw Ghetto," the man said with a sense of pride.

Rabbi Hollander could not believe his good fortune. For years he had been searching for a connection to the *Aish Kodesh* and now he had finally found one. 'Tell me what it was like to be with him," Rabbi Hollander demanded excitedly.

"When he danced with us, it was like we were dancing with *malachim* [angels]. When he davened with us, it was like we were davening with *malachim*. When he learned with us, he would say, 'Open your hearts to Hashem.' When he davened with us, he would say the same thing — 'Open your hearts to Hashem,' and even when he danced with us he would say, 'Open your hearts to Hashem.'"

"But tell me a teaching of his," Rabbi Hollander insisted. "Tell me something you learned from him."

"After all these years, you expect me to remember something?" the man protested. "And after everything I went through, the most difficult times in Auschwitz, you expect me to remember anything?"

"Look," Rabbi Hollander said, in almost a pleading voice, "Your Rebbe was so great, he must have taught you so many things, I am sure you must remember one thing. Please."

The man closed his eyes, was quiet for a moment as his mind scrolled back to his early youth. He remembered something that had become a staple in his life. "The Rebbe used to say," he began slowly, "'*De gresta zach vus a Yid ken tin, is tzu tin a Yid a toivah [The greatest thing a Jew can do is to do another Jew a favor].*' That always stayed with me," he continued. "You think you can't do favors in

Auschwitz? If a man was crying, I would put my arm around him and try to comfort him; if a man was in pain, I would sit and listen to him. If someone needed a piece of bread, I would try to get it for him."

He continued, "And here in the streets of Tel Aviv, even a street cleaner like me can find favors to do. People need a smile, people need a listener, and people need someone who cares. That's what the Rebbe taught us."

Rabbi Hollander thanked the man profusely and wished him well. He told him he hoped to come back and meet him again someday. However, for now he finally had found a connection to the *Aish Kodesh*.

Six months later Rabbi Hollander came back to Israel and made it his business to travel to the Yarkon. He looked for the man but he was no longer there. He inquired of passersby but they did not know his whereabouts. Like so many of his Polish compatriots, the man was probably in the *Olam HaEmes*, but he had enhanced his Rebbe's legacy by teaching a value that will always inspire.

⇜§ Knowing an Angel

My dear friend Rabbi Boruch Levin of Detroit was a longtime talmid of Rabbi Elya Svei (1924-2009), Rosh Yeshivah of the Philadelphia Yeshiva. In a memoir, Rabbi Levin recalled a very significant, highly relevant insight of Rav Elya's. *Chazal* (*Chagigah* 15b) teach אִם דּוֹמֶה הָרַב לְמַלְאַךְ ה' צְבָקוֹת, יְבַקְשׁוּ תוֹרָה מִפִּיהוּ, *If the teacher resembles an angel of Hashem, Master of Legions, then people should seek Torah instruction from him*. Rav Elya asked, "Has any of us ever seen an angel? Would we even recognize one if we saw one? How then can this determine our decision from whom to seek Torah?"

His answer is classic. The *Zohar* (*Hashmatos* to Vol. 1, note 61, see also *Ramban, Bereishis* 1:11 and 2:8) teaches that every blade of grass has an angel that protects it and calls out to it, "גְּדַל, *Grow*."

Therefore, if one has a teacher who, like an angel, constantly prods him to grow, develop, and flourish, that teacher is indeed one from who to seek Torah. The transmission of genuine Torah is not merely an exercise in conveying facts or in enhancing the understanding of texts. It is much more. It is the teacher's ability to inspire growth; it is the teacher challenging and inspiring the student to develop and advance in his *Ahavas Hashem and Ahavas Yisrael*.

◆§ *A Mother's Light*

Aviel Michoel Livian was known for his *hasmadah* (diligence) in learning and his punctiliousness in mitzvah observance, At his bar mitzvah, Rabbi Moshe Weinberger, of *Aish Kodesh* in Woodmere, New York, addressed Aviel's parents, Yehoshua and Rivka, whom he had taught at Ezra Academy in Queens, when they and their families were becoming *baalei teshuvah*. The rabbi related this story.

Many years ago in the early 1950's, a group of *yeshivah bachurim* came to the Tchebiner Rav, Rabbi Dov Berish Weidenfeld (1879-1965), in Jerusalem, to talk in learning. The rav discussed a *sugya* (topic) and posed a difficult question.

The *bachurim* were stumped! They tried to think of an answer but no one would dare venture a response to this Torah giant unless he was sure it was correct. A tall *bachur* in the back said he would like to answer the question. The *bachur* was Rav Moshe Sternbuch, who today is known as one of the *gedolei Torah* in Israel.

When the Tchebiner Rav heard his answer, the rav shook his head and said firmly, "This is not your own answer."

The *bachurim* were taken aback by this seemingly strong statement. The Tchebiner Rav smiled and said, "Your answer is so good and so extraordinary that it is not possible that, at your age, you could have thought of it on your own. Rather, the answer most likely comes from your mother — from her prayers, her tears in crying to Hashem that her son be a *talmid chacham!*"

What Rabbi Weinberger was implying was obvious. True, Aviel was an extraordinary child, but he had become so because of the great sincerity and prayers of his parents, Rivka and Yehoshua, whom Rabbi Weinberger saw over the years develop into exceptional people.

Later that evening my son-in-law, Rabbi Shlomo Dovid Pfeiffer, told me an incident involving Rivka Livian as a teenager. Attending Ezra Academy, she became so inspired about Shabbos that she decided to light one candle every Friday night.

One Friday afternoon, while Rivka's mother was preparing for Shabbos, she asked Rivka to watch a younger sibling. Rivka played with the child and then fell asleep. She woke up after Shabbos had started. She was devastated! She would not be able to light her Shabbos candle! She walked into the dining room, saw her mother, and began crying. "Momma, I can't light my Shabbos candle! I feel terrible because I overslept!"

Suddenly, one of her mother's candles fell out of its holder and landed alongside Rivka's short candlestick, with its unlit candle still standing in its holder. The flame of the taller candle leaned against the wick of the smaller one and lit it! Both candles remained lit.

In this light, what Rabbi Weinberger said is noteworthy. In *Tanach*, Aviel was the father of Kish, who was the father of Shaul HaMelech (see *I Shmuel* 9:1,2). *Radak* points out that in *I Divrei HaYamim* (8:33), Shaul's grandfather's name was not only Aviel, it was also Ner (lamp).

The *Talmud Yerushalmi* (*Sheviis* 3:7) explains that while Kish's father's real name was indeed Aviel, he was also given the name Ner, because it was his practice to light lamps in dark streets, so that people could be helped by their light. In the merit of his good deed, he was rewarded that his grandson became king.

It is remarkable that Shaul HaMelech's grandfather, Aviel, had an additional name, Ner. The bar mitzvah boy Aviel Livian became who he is because of his mother's prayers. The incident with the *ner* was an early indicator of her sincerity. Hence in the time of *Tanach* and in our time, the names Aviel and Ner are a perfect match.

≈§ Windblown Jews

In *When The Siyum Calls,* a CD produced by R' Yerachmiel Begun in honor of the Twelfth Siyum HaShas in August 2012, Rabbi Noach Isaac Oelbaum, the Rav of Nachlas Yitzchok of Kew Garden Hills, New York, cited a remarkable insight of the Ridvaz, Rabbi Yaakov Dovid Wilovsky (1854-1913).

> The Ridvaz had been the Rav in Slutzk, Lithuania. He came to America in 1900 to raise funds for the publication of his monumental commentary, *Ridvaz* on the Talmud Yerushalmi. He visited Rabbi Yaakov Joseph, Chief Rabbi of New York, and found the great *gaon* and *tzaddik* to be despondent as a result of his unsuccessful attempts to regulate the kosher-meat industry in New York. Attacked by the non-religious Yiddish press and harassed by people who were profiteering by lowering the standards of kashrus, Rabbi Joseph's health was broken. The Ridvaz spent five months in America, during which he visited almost every major Jewish-populated center in the country before returning to Europe.
>
> In 1903 he immigrated to America and settled in Chicago, where he was appointed rav of numerous shuls. The Agudas HaRabbanim gave him the honorary title, "Zekan HaRabbanim of America." In the Windy City, the Ridvaz set out to enforce stringent kashrus standards among the slaughterhouses and butchers. Despite his heroic efforts, he was resisted at every turn, even suffering death threats. Discouraged, he eventually moved to *Eretz Yisrael,* where he opened a yeshivah in Tzfas.

Rabbi Oelbaum said that nowadays Torah study is no longer a *luxury*; it has become a *necessity* to protect us from the moral degradation of the world around us. He cited the Ridvaz, who spoke in the famous Pike Street Shul on New York's Lower East Side, "Shlomo HaMelech writes, כִּי נֵר מִצְוָה וְתוֹרָה אוֹר, *For a commandment is a candle and Torah is a fire* (*Mishlei* 6:23). Hundreds of years ago there were unlearned communities that maintained their intense Jewishness because they were filled with Jews known as *Mitzvah Yidden*. They scrupulously observed Shabbos, kashrus, and *tefillah*, but they were not *talmidei chachamim*. They *respected* Torah scholars but they themselves were not learned.

"A mitzvah is like a lit candle in a closed room. So long as there is no open door or window, the candle can remain comfortably lit. But once the wind can enter, the candle will be snuffed out.

"These *Mitzvah Yidden* remained secure because they were isolated from secular influence. However, once the winds of secularism, immorality, and materialism blew in, the *ner mitzvah*, the candle-power of the mitzvah, was extinguished. A small flame cannot survive a strong wind.

"But if, Heaven forbid, a house is on fire and a strong wind comes, the result is the opposite. The wind fans the fire, and makes it even bigger and more widespread.

"It is the same with Torah. When one studies Torah diligently and finds himself surrounded by fierce winds that challenge the holiness of his *neshamah*, the intense flame of Torah protects him and gives him strength to combat those alien winds. It even fans the flames and generates more study of Torah, as the holiness of Torah resists its enemies."

After citing the Ridvaz, Rabbi Oelbaum added, "If this was true in the early 1900's, how much more so is it today — a century later!"

Today, when we are subject to the biting winds of materialism, secularism, and immorality, we must combat them with dedication to more Torah study. The reason it was so important for many tens of thousands of loyal Jews to celebrate the Twelfth Siyum HaShas of Daf Yomi was to foster in us and in our children a desire for more Torah learning, in order for us to become closer to Hashem and to strengthen our resistance to the ill winds that threaten our survival as loyal Jews.

⊷§ Waiting in Williamsburg

He was only 15 when his father passed away in 1966; the sadness in the house was palpable. He had numerous older and a few younger siblings. His mother, a woman of stature, was overcome with grief. I remember being there during the *shivah* and hearing his younger brothers, not yet bar mitzvah, saying *Kaddish*. To hear such young children say *Kaddish* was heartbreaking.

He lived in the Williamsburg section of Brooklyn and in the morning would often walk to Yeshiva Torah Vodaath on Wilson Street, where one *minyan* started after another. Because he was already bar mitzvah, he wanted to daven "for the *amud*" every day as a *zechus* for his father, but he would often have to wait his turn. Since this shul was a gathering place for *aveilim* (mourners) who wanted the *amud*, a *gabbai* would carefully make sure that no one took the *amud* out of turn.

One morning, he was next in line. He waited patiently for the *minyan* to finish so he could lead the next one. Suddenly he looked up and noticed that the great Ponevezher Rav, Rabbi Yosef Kahaneman (1886-1969), had entered. The boy hurried to greet the legendary rosh yeshivah. "*Shalom aleichem,*" he said, "Can I do anything to help the Rav?" he asked.

"I have *yahrzeit* today," the Rav replied, "and I was looking for a place where I could daven for the *amud.*"

"Okay, I will try to arrange it," the boy said enthusiastically.

He told the *gabbai* that the great Ponevezher Rav was here and that he had *yahrzeit* and would like to daven for the *amud.*

"He will have to wait his turn," the *gabbai* said firmly.

"You know who he is?" the boy said, incredulous that anyone would treat the Rav with anything less than awe and respect.

"I don't care who he is," the *gabbai* insisted. "We have a system here."

"Yes," said the boy, "but it's my turn next and I would like to give my *amud* to the Rav."

"No such thing," said the *gabbai*. "If you give up your turn it goes to the one who is next after you! You can't give it away."

Precious Chinuch Gemstones / 197

The boy pleaded and begged; soon other men were trying to convince the *gabbai* that this was a special case and that an exemption should be made. The *gabbai* finally relented.

The boy davened with that *minyan* and said *Kaddish* in the back of the shul quietly so that the Rav would not realize that he had actually given up his turn. Nevertheless, the Rav realized that the boy was an orphan saying *Kaddish* and had arranged for the Rav to have the *amud*. The Rav thanked the boy profusely.

The boy asked the Rav if there was anything else he could do for him. The Rav said that he wanted to visit the Satmar Rebbe, Rabbi Yoel Teitelbaum (1887-1979). Did the boy know where he lived?

"Yes, of course I know," the boy said eagerly. "I will take you there."

As the boy came out of the Torah Vodaath building, he saw my uncle, Reb Moshe Ackerman, who was known to drive *gedolim* wherever they had to go. He asked my uncle if he would take the Ponevezher Rav to the Satmar Rebbe. Reb Moshe readily agreed and took the Rav and the boy to the Rebbe's home on Bedford Avenue. The Ponevezher Rav was admitted almost immediately and the boy accompanied him. As he observed their shared smiles and warmth, the boy marveled at how these two Torah giants reveled in each other's company. It is more than 50 years later, but the boy still talks about the radiance in the room that day.

When the two *tzaddikim* parted ways, the boy asked the Ponevezher again if he could do anything for him.

"Yes," the Rav said, "I have to go to Borough Park. Do you know where I can get a taxi?"

The boy said, "Don't worry, Rebbi, I will get one for you."

He ran a block to Lee Avenue where taxis were more apt to be found and within two minutes he flagged down a cab. He sat in the cab and directed the driver to where the Ponevezher Rov was waiting. The boy stayed in the cab but the Rav protested, "Please, you do not have to come with me all the way to Borough Park. I appreciate so much what you have already done for me."

"I'll stay in the taxi for just a few blocks," the boy said, "I'll get out near my house."

As the taxi turned into the service road toward the highway, the boy asked the driver to stop so he could get out. As he was about to leave, the Ponevezher said, "You have been so kind to me, I would like to bless you. I am a *Kohen*, you know."

The boy looked at the Rav and said sincerely, "Rebbi, bless my mother. My father passed away a few weeks ago and it is very hard for her."

The Rav realized for the first time that this boy had become an orphan very recently. The Rav embraced him and cried, hugging him and kissing his forehead. Finally he spoke. "I bless your mother that she should have strength and courage. I bless her that she should have *nachas* from all her children." He went on with warm wishes for the mother and family. And then he said, "And I bless you, that you become a great *talmid chacham* and a leader in *Klal Yisrael*."

The blessings of the great Ponevezher Rav came to fruition. That boy was Rabbi Yaakov Bender, Rosh Yeshivah and Dean of the Yeshiva Darchei Torah in Far Rockaway, New York. His father was Rabbi Dovid Bender, *menahel* of Yeshiva Torah Vodaath in Brooklyn, and his mother was Rebbetzin Basya Bender, of the Bais Yaakov High School and Seminary.

The priestly blessing became a reality and thousands today are better because of it.

◈§ Sense and Sensitivity

Rabbi Emanuel Feldman, for decades the noted rav of the Atlanta community, writes, "No Jew was ever attracted to a life of Torah by anger and the casting of stones." He relates an interesting story about a religious father and his young son, who were in the lobby of a Tel Aviv apartment building on Shabbos. The boy noticed a Jew walking into an elevator and said to his father, "The man going into the elevator — is he a *goy* (gentile)?"

The father said softly, "No, he is a Jew, but he forgot that it is Shabbos."

The man left the elevator and approached the father. "I heard your son's question and was curious how you would answer him. I thank you for being so considerate. From now on, in your honor, I will take the stairs on Shabbat."

Dignity and respect beget results.

We can never be sensitive enough. The following incident told by Rabbi Yisroel Reisman, the Rav of the Agudas Yisrael of Madison/Brooklyn brings the message home.

A family in Rabbi Reisman's shul was hosting a *seudah* for their son's bar mitzvah, and a number of less religious relatives had come to join the Shabbos celebration. Rabbi Reisman knew one of the guests from years before, and they reminisced about the "old times."

As Rabbi Reisman began walking downstairs to the *Kiddush*, he invited the guest to join him, using the common Yiddish expression, "Come, *mach a berachah*," literally, *recite a blessing*.

The man took umbrage, looked at Rabbi Reisman resentfully, and walked away. Rabbi Reisman didn't know what he had said wrong, but the man was clearly upset. Throughout the *Kiddush* and later that afternoon, Rabbi Reisman noticed that the gentleman seemed disturbed, so he approached him. "You seem distressed. Did I offend you in any way?" asked Rabbi Reisman.

"Yes, I am offended," said the man indignantly. "You think that just because I am not as religious as you are that I don't make a *berachah* before I eat. What nerve you have, telling me that I should make a *berachah* — I always make *berachos*!"

"It's only a colloquialism," protested Rabbi Reisman. "It's just a warm way of inviting someone to grab a bite or have something to eat."

Nothing that Rabbi Reisman said could pacify the individual. He was convinced that the Rabbi has been "talking down" to him.

Less-observant and non-observant people are extremely sensitive as to how they are viewed and spoken about by observant people. That makes it very important to exercise caution and sensitivity.

❧ Vision in Vilna

In the summer of 2003, I took my first trip to Lithuania, leading a group of 120 people to the yeshivos of yesteryear. The trip included the hallowed cities of Ponevezh, Telshe, Kovna, Kelm, and Slabodka where I would discuss the *Gedolei Torah* who had lived there and the yeshivos that they had built there. However, the first city we were to visit was perhaps the most daunting: Vilna. How can anyone possibly describe the greatness of the Vilna Gaon (1720-1797)? As his sons, Reb Avrohom and Reb Yehuda Leib, wrote about him near the end of their introduction to their father's commentary on the *Shulchan Aruch*, "One cannot evaluate the vastness of his wisdom, [nor can one] reach the limits of his understanding, [nor can one] convey the perfection of his holiness."

Yet we were there to grow from his legendary greatness and wisdom, and so, to the best of my abilities, I tried to relate a few stories and insights that revealed his astute approach to matters.

An incident that illustrates the Gaon's astuteness occurred when two men conspired to get a third man in trouble with the law. The two claimed that this fellow had committed a crime and their testimony seemed foolproof. No matter what questions the *beis din* asked, their answers were exactly alike as they claimed to have seen the man commit the crime.

In their hearts, the judges had a strong feeling that these two were lying, but there was no tripping them up on their testimony.

The case was brought before the Gaon. He listened to the description of the testimony and declared "They are liars!"

The judges were stunned. How could the Gaon be so sure?

The Gaon explained. "The Mishnah in *Sanhedrin* (40a) states [that after the two witnesses have given their testimony, the judges must decide] אִם נִמְצְאוּ דִבְרֵיהֶם מְכֻוָּנִין, *if the words [of the witnesses] concur*. The Mishnah is teaching that the witnesses' words [which surely differ in some respects] must be weighed, considered, and evaluated. If the facts correspond, even though they express them differently, they are believed. But if the accounts of two witnesses are exactly alike, word for word, there is nothing to consider, nothing to evaluate; they are telling a story they have contrived meticulously. Hence they are fraudulent witnesses."

The judges went back and interrogated the men more fiercely and found them indeed to be lying.

The Gaon had ingenious ways of understanding verses in Torah and *Tanach* through the *trop* (cantillation) with which the words are chanted in shul. At his gravesite I related this example.

Megillas Esther details how King Achashveirosh sought a new queen. The Gaon notes that the gentile contestants could not wait to appear before the king with the hope of being chosen as his queen, whereas Esther dreaded having to appear before him, for she feared that she might be chosen. In describing these scenarios the *Megillah* (2:12) writes: וּבְהַגִּיעַ תֹּר נַעֲרָה וְנַעֲרָה לָבוֹא אֶל הַמֶּלֶךְ אֲחַשְׁוֵרוֹשׁ, *Now when each girl's turn arrived to come to King Achashveirosh ....* The *trop* above the words נַעֲרָה וְנַעֲרָה, "*each girl,*" is *kadma v'azlah,* which in Aramaic means, "*get up and go,*" describing their enthusiasm and excitement. However, in the verse (2:15) that describes Esther's turn, the *trop* is *munach,* which means, "*remain still and hesitate.*" That *trop* appears five times (under the words וּבְהַגִּיעַ, אֶסְתֵּר, אֲבִיחַיִל, דֹּד, לָבוֹא)! This symbolizes Esther's reluctance to come before the king. The modest Esther had no yearning to live with the decadent and depraved Achashveirosh.

Many people have their favorite *"vort"* from the Gaon. A *vort* (lit., a word) is a short, pithy Torah thought that is clever and often astounding. When one hears a *vort* from the Gaon, one pauses in awe at how he derived this thought from a phrase or expression that tens of thousands have seen and heard before — but not the way he saw and heard it. One particular *vort* I related to our group was the Gaon's interpretation of the famous Talmudic teaching, אִם אֵין קֶמַח, אֵין תּוֹרָה, *If there is no flour there is no Torah* (Pirkei Avos 3:21). Conventionally this is understood to mean that one needs physical sustenance in order to continue his Torah studies. The Gaon perceived an additional message. The word קֶמַח means fine sifted flour. The Gaon explained, "If one does not sift the Torah he has learned by breaking down every point until he has determined that every aspect of this Torah thought is 'fine' and true, he lacks the essence of Torah knowledge."

Years ago, when my son Eliezer, who is left-handed, became bar mitzvah, I wrote a pamphlet, *Yad Eliezer*, that dealt with the *halachos* and *minhagim* pertinent to one who is left-handed. The pamphlet includes ritual things we all must do with either our right hand or left hand and those rituals that left-handers do differently than right-handers. (The pamphlet is available free to anyone who calls or writes me for it.[1]) It was during the research for that project that I came across this story about the Gaon.

The *Torah Temimah* writes (*Bamidbar* 6:23 note 130), "I heard from reliable sources that the Vilna Gaon blessed the great Torah scholar, Rabbi Yechezkel Landau, who became a Vilna *dayan*, under

---
1. Phone 718.846.6900 or email krohnmohel@brisquest.com.

his wedding canopy. The Gaon placed [only] one hand on Reb Yechezkel's head during the blessing. When the Gaon was asked about this he said, "Only *Kohanim* in the *Beis HaMikdash* bless with two hands."

I told our group that Rabbi Chaim Kanievsky in his *Kuntros Ish Itair* (note 43) writes, "The *Sefer Ohr Tzaddikim* (29) cites the *Arizal* who states that one should bless his children Friday night with his right hand. Rav Chaim adds, "This is no different for a right- or left-handed person."

It would seem from this that the proper way to bless children Friday night according to the Gaon and R' Chaim Kanievsky is with one hand, the right one.

> We left Vilna, inspired, wiser, thankful, but saddened. Vilna is no longer the vibrant Torah center it was. There is barely a semblance of religious Jewish life to remind one that Vilna was once called the Yerushalayim of Lita. The bastions of Torah have moved elsewhere. Perhaps this is why the Torah was given in the desert: to symbolize that Torah has no permanent home until the coming of Mashiach.

Part D:
Divine Orchestrations

꧄ World-Class Music

In 2009 I had the opportunity to spend a Shabbos in Detroit where I spoke for Rabbi Eli Yelen's Congregation Yagdil Torah and the Bais Yaakov Convention. On Friday night, as Rabbi Yelen and I walked to the convention, he told me a story that left me breathless. I have told the story countless times and seen both men and women gasp and weep as the story roars to its climactic conclusion. This is one of those rare stories that can literally change a person forever.

Rabbi Moshe Plutchok is a rebbi in Yeshivah Derech Chaim in Brooklyn. Every summer the yeshivah travels up to the Catskills to a camp in Greenfield Park where they have a *Kollel Mechanchim*, a *beis medrash* where many young men gather to learn and where they are joined by numerous *mechanchim* (teachers) from various other camps in the area. The sound of Torah emanating from this *beis medrash* is constant and thunderous.

In the early summer a number of years ago, Rabbi Plutchok and many of his colleagues and students arrived at the camp. On the second day of the season, he noticed a middle-aged newcomer. He appeared to be a businessman, probably vacationing at a nearby bungalow colony, but his intensity of study was extraordinary. He rarely looked up from his Gemara and when he had a difficulty with a passage, he did not hesitate to ask others who were much younger than he.

One day Rabbi Plutchok approached this well-dressed gentleman. "I've been watching you for a few days now," began Rabbi Plutchok, "and I am fascinated. I'm very impressed by your *hasmadah* [diligence in study], and I marvel at how you don't hesitate to ask when you need some clarification."

The man looked up and said words that stunned Rabbi Plutchok. "You don't know me," the man said, hesitatingly. "But the ArtScroll Gemara is carrying me." Rabbi Plutchok looked puzzled. The man continued, "I am very sick. I have liver cancer. If I were to think about how sick I really am, I would not be able to make it through the day. I come here to get away from my reality. I never had the opportunity to learn in a yeshivah when I was young. But now that ArtScroll has translated the Gemara into English, I can make a connection to my legacy. I can understand what Hashem wants from us."

Rabbi Plutchok was overwhelmed. "Sir," he said. "I would like to be your friend. I want to help you in any way I can. If you have any questions about what you are learning, don't look for someone to ask. Just ask me, and if I don't know the answer, I'll find out from someone else. Please feel free to come over to me whenever you need to."

The gentleman thanked Rabbi Plutchok profusely and the two became very close friends. The day before the season ended, Rabbi Plutchok came to the *beis medrash* in the morning and noticed that his friend was not there. He wondered if perhaps something had happened. But as he looked around the room, he saw the man sitting at the back of the *beis medrash*. His shoulders drooped and he looked pale and dejected.

Rabbi Plutchok rushed over to him. "Are you okay? You look a little pale this morning."

The man answered slowly, "My illness is progressing. And lately I've been thinking, 'What difference does it make if I learn? Who cares?' When all of you fellows learn, that is special. You are all *talmidei chachamim*. Do you think I understand everything, even in the ArtScroll Gemara? I understand a good part of it but not all. And it's the same when you or anyone else explains something to me. I understand most of it but not all, so what difference does it make if I learn? Who cares?"

Rabbi Plutchok told me that it was a miracle that he had heard the following story just the night before on a Jewish radio station. Thus, he was able to tell the following to the forlorn gentleman.

Many years ago, the greatest symphony conductor in the world was an Italian maestro, Arturo Toscanini. He died in 1957 at the age of 89. He was known for his intensity, his perfectionism, his ear for orchestral detail, and his photographic memory. An accomplished writer was working on a biography of the maestro, and often came to interview him.

One afternoon the biographer called Toscanini and asked for permission to visit the following night. Toscanini said, "Not tomorrow night." The writer asked again, but Toscanini insisted, "Tomorrow night I am doing something special and I can't have any interruptions."

"What are you doing that's so special?" asked the biographer.

"There will be a concert in Europe and I plan to listen to it on the radio. I led the orchestra last year and would like to hear how the conductor there leads it this year. I don't want any distractions, in order to concentrate on the music."

"But, sir," protested the biographer, "I would be honored to sit silently and discuss the concert with you after it's over. I promise I won't say a word during the concert. I will sit on the other side of the room and not utter a sound."

"You promise you won't say a thing?" asked Toscanini.

"Not one word," assured the biographer.

Toscanini relented and allowed the writer to visit during the broadcast of the concert performance.

The next night, at a quarter to 8, the writer came to Toscanini's home. At 8 o'clock the concert began. Together they listened for a full hour. As Toscanini switched off the radio, the biographer approached him and asked, "Wasn't that magnificent?"

"No, it wasn't," said Toscanini sternly. "There were supposed to be 120 musicians, among them 15 violinists but only 14 were there!"

The biographer was incredulous. *That's ridiculous*, he thought. *How could Toscanini possibly know from a radio broadcast that one violinist was missing?* He didn't dare question the great maestro, who was known for his temper. However, he had to find out for himself if it was true.

Divine Orchestrations / 209

The next morning he called the music director of that orchestra and said, "I am an American news correspondent. Please tell me how many musicians were supposed to be at that concert last night and how many actually showed up."

The director replied. "There were supposed to be 120 musicians, but one of the violinists called in sick. We had 14 instead of 15."

The biographer could not believe his ears! How in the world could Toscanini have known that? That night he returned to Toscanini's home and said to the maestro, "I owe you an apology. Last night when you told me there were only 14 violinists at the concert, I was sure you were just guessing. But I called the music director today and he confirmed what you said. How could you have possibly known?"

Toscanini paused for a moment and then said with authority, "There is a great difference between you and me. You are part of the audience; to you everything sounds great. But I am the conductor! And a conductor must know every sound that comes forth from the orchestra. When I heard the performance and realized that some notes were not coming forth, I knew without a question that one violinist was missing!"

Rabbi Plutchok concluded the story and then said to the ailing man, "Maybe to me it makes no difference that you are learning, but to the Conductor of the World Symphony, Who knows every line of music that can come forth, Who knows every line of Torah that can be learned and every line of *tefillah* that can be prayed — to Him it makes a difference!"

The man was so taken by these words that he embraced Rabbi Plutchok and said, "How can I ever thank you?"

The next day they parted ways. The following winter Rabbi Plutchok met the man's son and asked, "How is your father?"

The young man said sadly, "Rabbi Plutchok, my father passed away. However, I want you to know that after he came home from the bungalow colony, every time he opened his Gemara, he paused for a moment and said, 'I am performing for the Conductor of the World Symphony.'"

We are all musicians in Hashem's Symphony Orchestra. In any orchestra, the drummer cannot play the cello, the cellist cannot play the flute, and the flutist cannot play the violin. Each must play his instrument to the best of his ability.

Everyone of us is different, and everyone must perform his spiritual music with the talents, mindset, and personality he/she was given. No two people *are* alike and no two people should *try* to be alike. We must each be the best that we can be. Our focus must always be to perform on the highest level of our capability for the Conductor of the World Symphony.

✥ Of Monumental Significance

The *Midrash* counsels: לְעוֹלָם יִבְדּוֹק אָדָם בְּשֵׁמוֹת לִקְרוֹא לִבְנוֹ הָרָאוּי לִהְיוֹת צַדִּיק כִּי לִפְעָמִים הַשֵּׁם גּוֹרֵם טוֹב אוֹ גּוֹרֵם רָע, *One should always choose for his child a name that denotes righteousness, because sometimes the name itself can be an influence for good or an influence for evil (Tanchuma Ha'azinu 7).*

The Arizal, Rabbi Yitzchok Luria (1534-1572), writes that when parents choose a name for their child, they are endowed with a *Ruach HaKodesh* (a sacred Heavenly Spirit) that guides them to the appropriate choice. The name they choose is not coincidental; rather, they are steered to a particular name by Divine guidance (*Sefer HaGilgulim*, Chap. 59; see also *Sefer Taamei HaMinhagim* p. 397 in *Kuntros HaAcharon*, note 929).[1]

In this remarkable story we become privy to such Divine guidance.

Moshe David and Chanie Levy already had many children and had chosen the names of their children carefully, either using the name of a great *tzaddik* (for example, Avigdor after Rabbi

---

1. See also *In The Spirit of The Maggid*, p. 267, from the *Noam Elimelech* (*Bamidbar*), regarding the importance of name selection and the connection of *neshamos* between the child receiving the name and the person he is being named after.

Avigdor Miller [1908-2001] or Shraga Feivel after Rabbi Shraga Feivel Mendelowitz [1886-1948]) or a name that was lyrical and significant, such as Shira Brachah (a song of blessing) or Aryeh Simchah (lion of happiness; a reference to the lion found in the first words in *Shulchan Aruch, Orach Chaim* 1:1, יִתְגַּבֵּר כָּאֲרִי לַעֲמוֹד בַּבּוֹקֶר לַעֲבוֹדַת בּוֹרְאוֹ, *One should arise like a lion [in the morning] for service of the Creator*).

> Rabbi Moshe Feinstein encourages everyone to name children after righteous people, be they from previous generations or even living people, especially when there is no specific reason to use a particular name. (See *Igros Moshe, Orach Chaim*, Vol. 4:66.)

Their new child was expected in a month and the Levys had decided that if the baby was a girl they would name her Tirtzah, for two reasons. First, Tirtzah means *acceptable* or *pleasing*, and second, Tirtzah was one of the five righteous daughters of Zelaphchad (*Bamidbar* 26:33), who loved *Eretz Yisrael* (see *Bava Basra* 119b).

Two weeks before the birth, Moshe David's grandmother, Sarah, passed away, and the family was sure that if the newborn were to be a girl, she would be named after her great-grandmother.

Moshe David and Chanie understood how much the name Sarah would mean to his mother, but there was an additional element to be considered as well. Moshe David and Chanie were *baalei teshuvah* and were hesitant to name their children after relatives who had not been Torah observant. Thus they preferred to use a name that would have a positive influence on the child. On the other hand, the name Tirtzah would have no meaning to their family and would deeply disappoint Moshe David's mother. The Levys needed a plan.

> As a *mohel*, I have seen numerous families ripped asunder when it comes to choosing a name for a newborn. My feeling is that any relatives — including the baby's grandparents — should *never* state a preference for a name unless they are asked. A couple old enough to have a child is old enough to name the child. No one should interfere.

The child was due to be born near the *yahrzeit* of the legendary Sarah Schenirer (26 Adar I), the founder of the Bais Yaakov movement. Perhaps if they had to use the name Sarah they would have in mind that she be named after that great woman. And indeed, a few weeks later their daughter was born, and the Levys named her Sarah Tirtzah. Everyone was happy and Moshe David's mother was particularly moved.

A year later, one of the Levy girls, Shira Brachah, who attends the Bais Rochel School in Monsey, New York, was learning about Sarah Schenirer and the Bais Yaakov movement. The school principal, Mrs. Rifkah Pollack, told the students of Sarah Schenirer's history and her commitment to girls' education. Near the end of the lesson, Mrs. Pollack mentioned that Sarah Schenirer had passed away in 1935, corresponding to the Hebrew year 5695, which in Hebrew is written תרצ"ה.[1] Shira Brachah realized immediately that this spells Tirtzah; there was indeed a connection between Sarah and Tirtzah!

She ran home that evening and told her mother about her incredible discovery. Mother and daughter sought out a picture of the *matzeivah* (monument; headstone) of Sarah Schenirer, and indeed תרצ"ה appears on it.

Incredibly, the names the Levys had chosen were indeed bound by history. In His infinite wisdom, Hashem had influenced them to use names that would forever be linked to the matriarch of the Bais Yaakov movement. May little Sarah Tirtzah grow to be as influential in girls' Torah education as her namesake.

✑§ *A Promise Fulfilled*

On a Shabbos in December 1995, two days before Chanukah, Rabbi Gidon and Mrs. Peninah Nitsun of St. Louis, Missouri, had their fifth child, a boy. The timing of the birth was occasion for

---

1. The letters תרצ"ו have a numeric value of 695; the first 5000 years (five millennia) are represented by the letter ה (numeric value: 5); thus the year 5695 is written תרצה ׳ה.

great joy, as the Shabbos *bris* would combine four festive occurrences: the *bris*, Shabbos, Chanukah, and Rosh Chodesh. Adding to the festivities was the fact that Rabbi Nitsun is a *mohel*, and he would be performing the *bris* on his own son.

When naming their first four children, the Nitsuns had used names from *Tanach*. Their first son's *bris* was on Shavuos; he was named David after David HaMelech whose *yahrzeit* is on Shavuos. Their daughter Devorah was named after the prophetess (see *Shoftim* 4:4); their daughter Yocheved, who was born during the week of *Parashas Shemos,* is named after the mother of Moshe (see *Rashi, Shemos* 1:15); and their daughter Michal was named after the wife of David HaMelech (see *I Shmuel* 18:20).

For their new son, they considered Yehudah and Binyamin, both of whom are prominently mentioned in the week's *parashah* (*Mikeitz),* with Yehudah also being the name of Yehudah Maccabee, a hero of the Chanukah miracle. However, Mrs. Nitsun wanted to commemorate the special Shabbos with a name that would allude to the three mitzvos that the Syrian-Greeks had banned in ancient times, but that their family would now be fulfilling at the *simchah*: *bris milah*, Shabbos, and Rosh Chodesh.

Cleverly, she took the initial letters of the three mitzvos: ש from שבת, the מ from מילה, and the ח from חנוכה, and came up with the name שמחה, Simchah (joy). She added the name מאיר, Meir (shining light), symbolizing Chanukah. These two names were also the name of the great *gaon* Rabbi Meir Simchah of Dvinsk (1843-1926), author of the classic works *Ohr Some'ach* on the *Rambam* and *Meshech Chochmah* on *Chumash*.

The *bris* was celebrated with great joy as Rabbi Nitsun was the *mohel*, and his father-in-law, Rabbi Joseph Goldberg, a noted *mohel* from Brooklyn, New York, served as *sandek* for the first time. Rabbi Goldberg had performed thousands of *brissen*, including on his sons, grandsons, and great-grandsons.

It was an unforgettable moment of holiness and happiness to be cherished in the family forever.

Seven years later, Mrs. Penina Nitsun visited Baltimore and spent Shabbos with her younger cousin Uri Goffin and his family, whom she hadn't seen since her wedding. Throughout Shabbos the Nitsuns and Goffins caught up on each other's doings and exchanged the latest family information and tidbits.

"What are the names of your children?" Uri asked at one point.

When she mentioned that her fifth child was Meir Simchah, Uri asked, "Was that because of the story with Zaidy?"

Mrs. Nitsun was taken aback. "What do you mean?" she replied, startled.

The story Uri told was heartwarming and incredible. Mrs. Nitsun subsequently checked the facts with other family members and learned that it indeed happened just as Uri told it.

Mrs. Nitsun's great-grandfather, Rav Yisroel Avrohom Abba Krieger (1880-1931), was a close talmid of Reb Meir Simchah. Born in Shpeishuk, a small village near Kovno, Lithuania, he traveled to Jerusalem after his bar mitzvah and learned in the *beis medrash* of Rabbi Yehoshua Leib Diskin (1818-1898). In 1890 Rabbi Krieger returned to Europe and settled in Dvinsk, where he became a close talmid of Reb Meir Simchah.

Rabbi Krieger later served as rav in three cities: Koshedari, Lithuania; Frankfurt-am-Main, Germany; and Boston, Massachusetts. He authored numerous *sefarim,* including *China D'chaye, Lirtzonchem Tizbachu,* and the posthumously published *Taanugei Yisrael.* Sadly, his rebbi, Reb Meir Simchah, left no living descendants, as his only daughter died childless in his lifetime. Before Rav Krieger left Europe, he visited Reb Meir Simchah, and assured him that he would keep his name, Meir Simchah, in the family.

Rav Krieger passed away young, at 51, and many of his descendants named their children after him. Add to that the fact that many in the family named their children after relatives who perished in the Holocaust, so the name Meir Simchah was never used.

Meir Simchah Nitsun is the only one in the family of Rabbi Krieger who carries the exact name of the great Torah sage of Dvinsk. And until he was 7 years old, his parents had no idea that they had fulfilled a promise of their great ancestor.

~§ Related After All

Mrs. Lori Palatnik is one of the most remarkable women in today's *kiruv* world. A *baalas teshuvah* herself, she has inspired thousands of women in her two decades of writing, speaking, and teaching, primarily for Aish HaTorah and now also for her new Jewish Women's Renaissance Project. Her articles on Aish.com are read by thousands. Her contagious enthusiasm and her stories and insights have caused the Jewish roots of countless women to blossom.

She recently shared this story with me.

For 13 years Mrs. Palatnik and her husband, Reb Yaakov, directed Aish HaTorah in Toronto. Reb Yaakov founded the Village Shul in Toronto's Forest Hill neighborhood; the shul today has over 200 members. The Palatniks host many guests every Shabbos. At one meal, they and their guests played "Jewish geography" while discussing family origins. By the end of the meal it seemed that everyone knew at least one person in someone else's extended family. One of the guests, Alan Werner,* turned to Mrs. Palatnik and said, "Did you say that your maiden name was Selcer? I believe I know a religious relative of yours here in town."

Mrs. Palatnik smiled. "You must be mistaken. Not only do I not have any religious cousins but most have intermarried."

Mr. Werner was persistent. "I met someone who told me that he had relatives named Selcer; he is a religious gentleman who lives in the Thornhill section. His name is Jack Samuels."

Mrs. Palatnik was sure that it was impossible for Jack Samuels to be her cousin, because she had often asked her father about their past. She had researched her family roots and found no evidence of such a relative.

A few weeks later, Mr. Werner was at the Samuelses' home for Shabbos. "I go to a rabbi's house on the other side of town," he said to Mr. Samuels, "and I think that his wife may be your cousin."

Mr. Samuels shook his head. "If you are going to a rabbi's house for Shabbos, his wife is certainly not my cousin. As far as I know, I am the only one in my family who ever became religious."

However, Mr. Werner, a *baal teshuvah* himself, was persistent. He understood the emptiness a *baal teshuvah* may feel if he has no connection to his relatives. Discovering even a distant cousin was uplifting. He invited the Palatniks and the Samuelses to join him for dinner at a restaurant. "It's on me," said Mr. Werner graciously. "I'll be thrilled to watch you sort out this matter."

Incredibly, when the couples met, it did not take long for them to realize that indeed they shared the same great-grandmother! Everyone was delighted.

As they continued talking, Mr. Samuels told the following astonishing story.

Their great-grandmother had lived in the small Polish town of Ivansk. Ivansk had no yeshivos, nor was there one in the neighboring towns or villages. The townsfolk hired a *melamed*, a private tutor, to teach their children Torah, but poverty in the area was great, and often the people could not raise the *melamed's* meager salary. He threatened to leave, because he had a family to support. He said he would have to look elsewhere for his livelihood. Although she, too, found the burden of contributing to the *melamed's* salary overwhelming, the great-grandmother was heartbroken at the thought that her children would no longer study Torah. She tried to persuade the *melamed* to stay, but he said that he had no choice.

He packed his belongings, hired a driver, loaded his possessions onto the wagon, and prepared to leave. The townsfolk watched sadly as he said his good-byes. The driver was about to snap the reins to start the horse on its way when suddenly people began to scream. A woman had lain down directly in front of the horse, and with screams and tears she exclaimed, "If my sons cannot be taught Torah, I have no reason to live. Let me be trampled to death. I cannot bear the thought of my sons not studying Hashem's holy Torah."

That woman was their great-grandmother.

The people of Ivansk were shocked. They tried to reason with her but she would not budge. A crowd gathered and within minutes everyone agreed that somehow, some way, they would help her pay for the *melamed*. Even the *melamed* was overwhelmed at such self-sacrifice. He slowly stepped down from the wagon and announced that he would stay.

Rabbi and Mrs. Palatnik sat stunned. Tears rolled down Lori's face as she tried to picture her ancestor's incredible *mesiras nefesh* for Torah study. Jack said that when he was in the process of becoming a *baal teshuvah* he told his rabbi the story and the rabbi commented, "It is in the merit of that *tzadekes* that you came back to Torah and mitzvos."

That night Lori called her irreligious father and asked him if he had ever heard the story. "Yes," he replied, "I remember hearing it as a child."

"But you never told it to me," Lori said, almost crying. "Why didn't you ever tell it to me?" she sobbed.

"I didn't think it was that important," he said innocently.

Lori asked him if he knew any other stories about his grandmother. He said that he really didn't. And then nonchalantly he added, "You were named after her, Leba Rachel."

And that explains it all, doesn't it?

✍ Minyan Mobility

Ever since he was a young man, Reb Avrohom Pinter of Brooklyn made sure to always daven with a *minyan*. This wonderful trait continued into his adult years. Regardless of where he had to be, on business, vacation, or a family *simchah*, he always mapped out the three-times-a-day *minyan* availability before he went anywhere.

For more than 50 years, Rabbi Pinter was involved in Torah education, serving as principal in such schools as Yeshiva of Chofetz Chaim in Manhattan, Yeshiva Zichron Eliezer in Brooklyn, and Yeshiva of Eastern Parkway, to name a few. In 1997, Rabbi Pinter began feeling excruciating pain in his foot. His walking was hampered and he was diagnosed with a severe case of arthritis.

Though he lives only two blocks from the famous Veretzky (Landau) Shul on Avenue L in Brooklyn, it took him more than 20 minutes to walk to the *minyanim* there. Davening at Landau's was very convenient, as *minyanim* are going on constantly, from 5:55 a.m. to 1 a.m., throughout the day and night, but getting to a *minyan* for Rabbi Pinter was a slow, painful ordeal. Nevertheless, he was there three times a day.

Doctors finally decided that surgery was the only way to alleviate the pain. Reluctantly Rabbi Pinter agreed, but he feared that for weeks or months afterward he might not be able to get to a *minyan*, as he would not be able to walk even with a cane or walker. Even a wheelchair was not a practical solution, for people were not always available to push him there.

He looked into the feasibility of renting a motorized scooter, but the cost was exorbitant. Rabbi Pinter called Bikur Cholim societies, *g'machs* (free loan societies), and people in the health professions to ascertain if anyone knew where he could borrow a motorized scooter, but no one could help him.

Finally he called the Bikur Cholim of Borough Park and a kind woman, Mrs. Dinah Brodsky,* explained that though they did not have a scooter, she would call him if one became available. It was only a few days before his surgery and Rabbi Pinter was deeply disappointed and saddened that he would miss the opportunity to attend his daily *minyanim*.

Fifteen minutes later, he received a call from Mrs. Brodsky. "You won't believe this," she said excitedly. "I don't ever remember such a thing happening and certainly not with a motorized scooter!"

She explained that a widow from Coney Island* had just called to say she had a motorized scooter that had not been used in two years; she was wondering if the Bikur Cholim of Borough Park needed one. She explained that two and a half years earlier, her husband had suffered a serious leg injury and had great trouble walking. He bought a motorized scooter so that he could attend his shul's *minyan*. The shul directors had assured him that they would build a ramp, because going up the steps on the scooter would be impossible. The shul ran out of funds before the ramp was built, but the administrators promised to do it eventually. Shortly afterward, her husband died.

For two years the scooter sat unused in her garage and she was not sure what to do with it. "However," Mrs. Brodsky said, "last night her husband came to her in a dream and said, 'We purchased the wheelchair so that I could get to a *minyan*. I never got to use it. Maybe it can help someone else to get to a *minyan*. It would be a merit to my soul.'"

The dream was over in a moment, but the woman was shaken. She decided to call Jewish organizations to see if they knew of someone who could use it. Her first call was to the Bikur Cholim of Borough Park — and it came just minutes after Mrs. Brodsky had spoken to Rabbi Pinter.

Rabbi Pinter was thrilled with the news and asked the people of Rodeph Chessed to pick up the scooter for him. Members of Chaverim in Flatbush filled the tires with air, replaced the battery, and got the scooter working properly. Rabbi Pinter used it for 12 weeks after the operation, until he was able to walk on his own. Today a handicapped neighbor in his building uses it every day to get to shul.

> A dream became a reality — for individuals in Brooklyn and for a soul in the World of Truth.
>
> *Chazal* teach that there are great benefits when one davens with a *minyan* (see *Taanis* 8a), for when one davens with a *minyan* it is considered an עֵת רָצוֹן, *favorable time* (*Berachos* 8a). Understandably, in a favorable time, one's *tefillos* are more apt to be answered. Rabbi Pinter can attest to that.

~§ *A Life-giving Exchange*

Chaim Farber* of Passaic was surprised to get a call from his brother Sholom in Israel asking for money for a needy neighbor. "I'm really sorry, but I don't have anything substantial to give you, I wish that I could but I just can't," Chaim said regretfully.

"Look, I know you can't afford to give me much," said Sholom, "but there is this wonderful fellow in our neighborhood [Ramat Beis Shemesh], and he is a real *tzaddik*. Both he and his wife are very sick. He is confined to a wheelchair, she is on chemotherapy; they are marrying off a daughter and they just don't have any money. Maybe you can go around to the shuls in town and see what you can raise?"

Chaim trusted his brother. If Sholom said that the fellow was a *tzaddik* and that he and his wife needed the money desperately, that was surely the case. "Look," said Chaim, "I have never raised money before and besides, I am embarrassed to go fund-raising, but I will try."

"It's a tremendous mitzvah," Sholom reassured him. "They are truly special people and they deserve help."

Chaim typed a simple, straightforward letter that began, "Dear Fellow Mispallelim in Passaic." In the short letter, he told of the needs of this couple, who, he said, were very *ehrlich* (sincere) and explained that they needed money for *hachnasas kallah*. He signed it and gave his phone number so he could be reached if people wanted to donate. He wrote that in a few days he would come and collect any money people wanted to give him.

He hung copies of the letter on shul bulletin boards throughout Passaic. For a week no one called him and Chaim wondered if anyone had even bothered to read the letter. He then went to the shuls and asked people if they wanted to contribute. Surprisingly, quite a few had read the letter and said they had been waiting for him to come to collect.

Two days later, Chaim took a call from Asher Feldman,* who had seen the letter in Rabbi Aaron Cohen's shul, Kol Yeshurun. Asher was somewhat suspicious of such solicitations; he had encountered some dubious collectors and learned that it's wise to investigate. "Do you know this case personally?" Asher asked.

'I don't," replied Chaim honestly. "But my brother in Ramat Beit Shemesh knows the people well. He speaks very highly of them and I trust him implicitly."

Divine Orchestrations / 221

After a brief conversation, Asher said he would mail a check and, indeed, two days later Chaim received a check for $2,000. He was flabbergasted. He could not believe that his simple unprofessional letter had inspired someone to give that amount of money. He thanked Asher profusely and called his brother to tell him about this check and the other money he had collected.

Three months later, Asher received a call from Rabbi Shmuel Kalter* in Denver. They had met a few days earlier at a fund-raising seminar given by Asher. In the Jewish organizational world, Asher is known for his brilliant methods of fund-raising and has become a popular lecturer on the topic. Rabbi Kalter had attended a recent seminar in Stamford, Connecticut and was so impressed that he bought CDs of the entire series of Asher's lectures.

"I was listening to one of your lectures," Rabbi Kalter said, "and you mentioned someone in Israel who inspired you to become a *baal teshuvah* more than 20 years ago. You spoke so glowingly about him, but then you said you had lost contact with him and had no idea where he is. I know that person and I can give you his contact information."

"You know Shlomo Presser*?" Asher exclaimed with excitement and disbelief. "How do you know him and where is he today? You won't believe this," continued Asher, "but I have had him on my 'to do' list for months to try and track him down. And just today, I kid you not, just today, I deleted the line that said 'reconnect with Shlomo Presser,' because I gave up and thought that ever finding him was hopeless. I can't believe the *Hashgachah Pratis* (Divine Providence) that you should have heard the one lecture in which I mention him and that you know him."

"Shlomo was a talmid here in Denver [Yeshiva Toras Chaim] for many years," said Rabbi Kalter. "He eventually moved to Israel and is living in Ramat Beit Shemesh."

"What is he doing today? How is he?" asked Asher.

The reply took his breath away. "Both he and his wife are not well these days," Rabbi Kalter said sadly. "Their daughter just got married and they are still struggling to pay for the wedding."

This is impossible, thought Asher. *Just the other day I gave $2,000 for a family in Ramat Beit Shemesh to marry off a daughter and now I hear this. Could this be the family I donated to?*

And then it struck him; it surely had to be the same person! Sholom Farber, who had initiated the collection, was born in Denver and Rabbi Kalter, now on the phone, was also a Denverite. The pieces of the global puzzle were moving together. Indeed, after a short conversation it became obvious that, incredibly and unknowingly, Asher had given money for the one who had brought him to *teshuvah* years ago!

> When Asher told me the story, he said, "I never give that amount of money, certainly not for a cause that is publicized by a letter on a shul bulletin board! I can't understand why I did what I did. But I felt compelled to do it."
>
> Perhaps this is the answer. *Chazal* (*Megillah* 3a) bring the verse, וְרָאִיתִי אֲנִי דָנִיֵּאל לְבַדִּי אֶת הַמַּרְאָה וְהָאֲנָשִׁים אֲשֶׁר הָיוּ עִמִּי לֹא רָאוּ אֶת הַמַּרְאָה אֲבָל חֲרָדָה גְדֹלָה נָפְלָה עֲלֵיהֶם וַיִּבְרְחוּ בְּהֵחָבֵא, *I, Daniel, alone saw the vision, and the people [Chaggai, Zechariah, and Malachi] who were with me did not see the vision; yet a great fear fell upon them, and they fled into hiding* (Daniel 10:7). *Chazal* ask, If they did not see the vision, why were they frightened?
>
> The Sages explain, אַף עַל גַּב דְּאִינְהוּ לֹא חָזוּ מַזְּלַיְיהוּ חָזוּ Even though *they did not see the vision, their mazel* [representative angels] *saw it.* Every person is designated an angel that represents him in heaven. That is what is meant by a person's "*mazel.*"
>
> Asher didn't know what had compelled him to respond to a very unprofessional plea for *tzedakah*. Perhaps it was his *mazel* that saw and understood that this plea was especially for him.
>
> Asher reconnected with Shlomo, and this time it was Asher who became the inspirational guide. He encouraged Shlomo to go through with the operation he desperately needed, but was afraid to undergo. Not only that, Asher

Divine Orchestrations / 223

helped subsidize the lifesaving operation and thereby gave continued physical life to the one who had given him spiritual life.

∞§ Overtime Benefits

Moshe Mannies had been out of a job for a few months. For years he had been a successful salesman, but with employers cutting back on payrolls due to the recession, Moshe was laid off and was looking for work. Two weeks before Rosh Hashanah in 2007, he was hired by the manager of The Hat Box, a men's clothing and accessories store in Flatbush.

Understandably, during these two weeks the store was teeming with customers. On Erev Rosh Hashanah, Moshe was hoping to leave by 2 p.m. to prepare for Yom Tov. At 1:50 he told the manager that he would be leaving soon.

"Please stay," the manager said, "I'm sure we'll have many last-minute customers and I'll need your help."

Moshe was not happy about it, but he wasn't going to argue. After all, this was a new job and he didn't want to upset his boss. He decided to stay until 2:30, but then he would have to leave. At 2:20, a young couple, both in their mid-20's, walked in to buy shirts, ties, and cufflinks.

As Moshe was showing the young man various shirts in his size, the customer suddenly said, "Excuse me, but aren't you Mr. Mannies?"

"Yes, I am," answered the surprised Moshe. "Do we know each other?"

The young man bent over the counter and whispered, "Can we go off to the side to talk privately for a minute?"

"Of course."

The young man asked his wife to wait as he went to a corner of the store with Moshe. "Mr. Mannies," the young man said, "remember, about 10 years ago, you went around to the bungalow colonies selling watches, costume jewelry, CD players, and other such things?"

"Yes," said Moshe, taken aback that this young man knew that. For years, he had been peddling merchandise in the mountains.

"I was a teenager, I was out of yeshivah, and you hired me to drive around with you and help you," the young man explained. He wiped his brow as he continued hesitantly, "I stole from you that summer, but you never knew it. I took things and sold them on my own. I was a kid in a bad crowd and I wanted money. I was sorry afterward, but I was never able to pay you back and I had no idea where you were. But now it's just a few hours before Rosh Hashanah. I'm so glad I met you. I want to pay you back today."

Moshe knew that he had had a vanload of items that summer, but had never taken inventory and so he had no idea that anything was missing. Frankly, he did not recognize this fellow.

"I don't expect you to remember me," the young man offered, seeing Moshe's uncomprehending stare. "I looked much different then, and I was only with you for a few weeks."

Moshe smiled and said, "You're a *tzaddik*. Hashem should *bentch* you and your wife."

"I don't really know how much I took," the young man said, on the verge of tears. "So if I give you too little, please be *moichel* me and if I give you too much I certainly am *moichel* you."

The young man asked Moshe to remain in the store and told him he would be back in 10 minutes. He quickly paid for his purchases and left the store hurriedly with his wife. Moshe was in a daze. If hadn't stayed the extra half-hour as the manager wanted, this young man would not have had the opportunity for *teshuvah*. He thought of the *Chazal*, בְּדֶרֶךְ שֶׁאָדָם רוֹצֶה לֵילֵךְ בָּהּ מוֹלִיכִין אוֹתוֹ, *In the way a man wishes to go, they [Hashem's angels] lead him* (*Makkos* 10b, see *Maharsha*).

Moshe busied himself with other customers but could not get his mind off this young man. A short while later, the couple returned, beaming. The man handed Moshe a wad of 20-dollar bills. Moshe thanked him profusely and put the money into a manila envelope to count later. As the young couple turned to leave, Moshe said to the woman, "You married a very noble man. You are very lucky. Have only *mazel, berachah,* and a wonderful year."

Moshe went off to the side and counted the bills. There were 50 of them! He had just received a thousand dollars he hadn't counted on. Since he had been out of work for months, he really needed the money. This was going to be a beautiful Yom Tov season!

> How many of us have made mistakes in our youth? We may have hurt others with painful words, we may have embarrassed others with foolish acts of inconsideration, we may have caused financial loss by dishonest dealings and deception. It's never too late to make amends and never too late to ask forgiveness. This young man wisely seized an opportunity; let's make sure we seize ours should it ever come.

∽§ It's All in the Names

In this delightful story we once again witness the *Ruach HaKodesh*, Divine Wisdom, that Hashem bestows on individuals when they are choosing names for their children. I was told this story by Rabbi Eliyahu Steger, a noted *mechanech* from Yeshivas Chaim Berlin in Brooklyn. It happened in his family.

In 1977 the Stegers had a baby boy who was born on עֲשָׂרָה בְּטֵבֵת, *Asarah B'Teves,* the 10th day of Teves. The Stegers had decided to name him after Mrs. Steger's late grandfather Yosef Baruch, the father of Mrs. Steger's father, Rav Avrohom Jacobovitch of Toronto. They were sure that Rabbi Jacobovitch would be happy that the new infant was being named for his father. They were wrong.

Rabbi Jacobovitch is an ardent Breslover chassid. The Breslov dynasty began with Rav Nachman of Breslov (1772-1810), a great-grandson of the Baal Shem Tov. Rav Nachman's foremost disciple was Reb Nosson Sternhartz, who recorded Rav Nachman's teachings, most prominently *Likutei Maharan*. When the Stegers called Rabbi Jacobovitch to say that they were going to name the baby after his father, he said, "The *yahrzeit* of Reb Nosson is coming up, so I would prefer if you named the child Nosson."

The Stegers were amazed. Wouldn't someone want a grandson named after his father? The Stegers discussed the matter and decided to use all three names. They named the baby נָתָן יַעֲקֹב בָּרוּךְ, Nosson Yaakov Baruch.

Shortly after the *bris*, Reb Chaim Sheinfeld, an uncle of Rabbi Steger, known for his acumen in *gematrios* (numerical value of Hebrew words and letters) told Rabbi Steger something startling. "The *gematria* of the name Nosson (500) Yosef (156) Baruch (228) ben (52) Eliyahu (52) [= 988] is equal to the date of his birthday, *Asarah* (575) *B'Teves* (413) = 988."

You could add it up!

Interestingly, as countless others have done, the Stegers named their child after two people. As a *mohel*, I am often asked if this is a good practice, since the infant does not have the exact name of either of the people for whom he was supposedly named.

In 1980, Rabbi and Mrs. Avigdor Slatus of Savannah, Georgia, wished to name their newborn son Yoel Levi. Yoel would be after the Satmar Rebbe, Rabbi Yoel Teitelbaum (1887-1979), who had advised and encouraged Mrs. Slatus's grandfather, R' Moshe Stern, to move to Chicago, where he prospered and became a noted philanthropist. Levi would be after her uncle, who had perished in the Holocaust. Rabbi Slatus was advised by friends to consult with the Puppa Rav, Rabbi Yosef Greenwald, in New York, for he was known to understand the Kabbalistic nuances of given names. The Rav told the Slatuses that they should not use that combination of names because "the *neshamos* [souls] don't pair up." When Mrs. Slatus asked for some clarification of the matter, the Rav replied, "The last letter of Yoel is the same as the first letter of Levi, and so, when the names are pronounced together, the second ל is swallowed."

Rabbi and Mrs. Slatus suggested that they could reverse the names and use Levi Yoel, but the Rav pointed out that there too, the last letter of Levi (the letter י) is the same as the first letter of Yoel, so the same problem existed. The parents accepted his counsel and chose a different name. Interestingly, the Rav had no issue with the fact that they would name their child after two people.

> Noteworthy is the fact that three very great chassidic leaders had the sort of names to which the Puppa Rav objected. The Berditchiver Rebbe was Rabbi Levi Yitzchok (1740-1809); the *Imrei Emes*, the third Gerrer Rebbe, was Rabbi Avrohom Mordechai Alter (1886-1948); and the recent Vizhnitzer Rebbe was Rabbi Chaim Meir Hager (1887-1972). In all three cases, the last letter of the first name is the same as the first letter of the second name. Obviously, there are different views regarding names, and each person should consult his rav, rebbe, or rosh yeshivah before deciding conclusively what name or names to use for their child.
>
> In Rabbi Avrohom Horowitz's *Orchos Rabbeinu* (Vol. 1, pages 249-250), a compendium of laws and customs of the Steipler Gaon, Rav Yaakov Yisroel Kanievsky (1899-1985), a story is told about a young man who wanted to name his newborn son after the Mashgiach of the Ponevezh Yeshivah, Rav Yechezkel (Chatzkel) Levenstein (1895-1974). However, his father-in-law wanted the child to be named after his own deceased father, Moshe. The young man sought the counsel of the Steipler, who told him that the Chazon Ish, Rabbi Avrohom Yeshaya Karelitz (1878-1953), held unequivocally that if a child is given two names after two people, the name becomes a new entity and it is not considered as though the child was named after either person.

The Steipler therefore suggested that for the sake of peace in the family, the young man use the name Moshe and with Hashem's help in the future he would have another son and name him Yechezkel.

The Stegers in Brooklyn had come to a mutual understanding by giving all three names, which was amenable to both the grandfather and the young couple. Indeed, the name of their child, Nosson Yaakov Baruch ben Eliyahu, is the exact numerical equivalent of the words בְּרִיתִי שָׁלוֹם, *My covenant of Peace* (622 + 376 = 998), an expression used in the prayers of the *bris* and an allusion to the peaceful resolution that had come about at the *bris* of their child.

In *Sefer HaBris* by Rabbi Moshe Bunim Pirutinsky, a lengthy essay entitled *Kuntros Krias Shem* (p. 303) covers a wide gamut of issues regarding Jewish names. He cites *Kol Hator*, by a disciple and relative of the Vilna Gaon (1720-1797), Rabbi Hillel of Shklov, who writes that the Gaon claimed that every person's Hebrew name is sacred, and reflects the essence of his soul. He adds that names are not chosen randomly; there is Divine assistance given to parents as they choose their child's name. Hence, every name is alluded to somewhere in the Torah or in the words of *Chazal*, and sometimes in both.

In light of this statement, something remarkable happened to me in 2006, when I went to be *menachem avel* Mrs. Shira Zolty of Brooklyn, whose late father had been a *mohel*.

We had been discussing the topic of *bris milah* when her husband, Reb Yosef, asked me if I knew all the *Baal HaTurim's* on *bris milah*. I said, "I am a *mohel* and I wrote a book for ArtScroll entitled *Bris Milah*. I think I quoted all of them."

"Well, how about this one?" he asked, pointing to a commentary on the fourth verse in the Torah (*Bereishis* 1:4). "The verse states, וַיַּרְא אֱלֹקִים אֶת הָאוֹר כִּי טוֹב, *G-d saw the light that it was good*. The *Baal Haturim* writes that the final letters of the four words, אֶת הָאוֹר כִּי טוֹב are ברית." I was startled and a bit embarrassed; how could I not have known that *Baal Haturim*, which appears right at the beginning of the Torah! I admitted that I hadn't seen it before.

"I am not finished yet," Reb Yosef said with a smile. "The *gematria* of the words, אֶת הָאוֹר כִּי טוֹב, *the light that it was good*, equals your name, פסח יוסף קראהן, Paysach Yosef Krohn [401 + 212 + 30 + 17 = 660; 148 + 156 + 356= 660]."

May I only live to fulfill that implication.

◆§ Chedva – A Joy Remembered

There is a custom not to name newborns after people who have passed away young, since it may be a רִיעַ מַזְלֵיהּ, a bad omen for the child. (Rabbi Yaakov Kamenetzky held that the year of demarcation was 60).

However, Rabbi Moshe Feinstein writes (*Igros Moshe, Yoreh Deah* 2:122) that if someone was married, had children, and died a natural death, it is not a bad omen to name after him or her regardless of age of death, for that person lived productively and fulfilled his or her purpose in life. Reb Moshe notes that such great *tzaddikim* as Shlomo HaMelech and Shmuel HaNavi died at 52, and Chizkiyahu died at 54, yet those names are used without hesitation.

It seems, then, from Reb Moshe that if a person was killed or perished accidentally, one should add a name or change the spelling of the name by either adding or subtracting a letter of the name so that it is not exactly the same as the name of the deceased person. For example, giving the name גדליה, Gedalyah, instead of גדליהו, Gedalyahu, or vice versa. Even if the change of a letter would not change the pronunciation, Reb Moshe writes that such a change is sufficient. For example, the spelling of the name Akiva, עקיבא (with an א) could be changed to עקיבה (with a ה).

Presumably the same would apply to the names אהרן without a ו to אהרון with a ו, and דבורה with a ו to דברה without a ו. Even though the names are essentially the same, Reb Moshe felt that a change in the spelling was enough to prevent the רִיעַ מַזְלֵיהּ. He stipulates, though, that after adding or subtracting a letter, the name must still be a recognized name.

This was the dilemma facing Rabbi and Mrs. Yisrael Kleinman of Borough Park, as they pondered what name to give their daughter born in the winter of 1995.

A number of years before, Mrs. Shaindy Kleinman, a noted *mechaneches* in Brooklyn, had met a remarkable young woman, Chedva Silberfarb, who was known throughout Israel for her passionate speeches and eloquent talks about *Shemiras HaLashon*, the importance of proper speech. Chedva was beloved by women of all ages, for she was brilliant, warm, and ardent about her topic. She implored women from all walks of life to be careful in their speech and to foster *Ahavas Yisrael*.

In 1987 she was diagnosed with lung cancer and suddenly her message took on a desperate, compelling import. "Do it as a *zechus* for me," she implored her listeners throughout Israel. "Improve your manner of speech. I have a husband and children, I want to see them grow and I want to share in their *simchos*."

She cried and everyone cried with her. Many undertook upon themselves not to speak ill of others, others committed themselves not to speak *lashon hara* during specific hours of the day. They called it "Chedva's hour"; eventually it would be known as the program of *machsom l'fi*, sealing the mouth (see *Tehillim* 39:2).

In 1988 she came to New York for treatment. And though she was weak, she began lecturing in schools and community gatherings about *Shemiras HaLashon*. As in Israel, girls and women here were enamored by her fervent message. During this period, many people in America got to know her well, Mrs. Shaindy Kleinman and I among them.

Chedva and her husband Reb Yankel were kind enough to accept an invitation to spend Shabbos in my home. When they arrived, she showed my wife and me pictures of their adorable young children. It was heartbreaking because we knew how perilous her prognosis was. Her oldest, Luzer'keh, was only 4 years old. Chanaleh and Henoch were even younger.

In Brooklyn, Mrs. Kleinman attended a number of Chedva's lectures, including one in the Belz Bnos Yerushalayim School for Girls. Afterward, Mrs. Kleinman organized a gathering for Chedva in Williamsburg, which was attended by 500 women. It wasn't only Chedva's message that was imperative to Mrs. Kleinman; she wanted to garner as many *zechusim* as she could for the great young woman.

Reb Yankel and Chedva were able to return to Israel for a while to be with their family, but they returned to New York for further treatments. Tragically, on 13 Kislev in 1989, her sacred soul returned to Heaven. Women throughout the Jewish world wept openly as eulogies and memorials were tendered for this great woman who was only 27 when she passed away.

(Someone said that the Chofetz Chaim passed away at 93, according to one version; some say 95. Add Chedva's 27 years and it equals a lifetime of 120 years devoted to *Shemiras HaLashon*.)

Reb Yankel spoke at the *hespid* in Borough Park; he asked that 13 Kislev be designated as a *Yom Shemiras HaLashon* in Chedva's memory. And so, the next year Mrs. Kleinman arranged a Friday-night *kinnus* on Chedva's *yahrzeit*. More than 1,000 women attended! Year after year, Mrs. Kleinman arranged a Friday-night *kinnus* on the week of Chedva's *yahrzeit*; this event has been going on for 22 years. The crowds that come year after year are astounding. It could be the coldest or rainiest night of the winter, there is always an incredible turnout in the Bais Yaakov Hall to commemorate Chedva's life and message.

In the winter of 1995, the sixth year of the *kinnus*, Mrs. Kleinman was expecting her seventh child. As she hung the posters for the event, Mrs. Kleinman thought that if the child were a girl, she would want to name her Chedva. She felt that her husband would not approve because Chedva had passed away so young.

Rabbi Kleinman understood how much the name would mean to his wife but the fact that Chedva had died young, and his conviction that surely members of her family had already given the name, made him feel less compelled to comply with his wife's wishes.

Citing a source that he might rely on to use the name, he said to his wife, "In *Parashas Vayigash* (*Bereishis* 45:28), where Yaakov expresses his great joy when he learns that his beloved son Yosef is still alive, Rashi writes that Yaakov said, רַב לִי שִׂמְחָה וְחֶדְוָה, *There is much joy and gladness for me*. Therefore, if the baby is born during *Parashas Vayigash*, I would feel comfortable using the name."

Mrs. Kleinman smiled, "That's four weeks away. I don't think the baby will wait that long."

The date of the *kinnus* was approaching and Mrs. Kleinman worked diligently to make sure all would go smoothly. The chairs were set up, the custodian would be there, the speaker was confirmed, and the lighting was set. And then, a few hours before Shabbos *Parashas Vayeitzei*, Mrs. Kleinman was admitted to Maimonides Hospital to deliver her baby. She would miss the *kinnus* but it would be a night to remember.

On Friday night Rabbi Kleinman, who davens *Nusach Sefard*, recited *Ke'gavna* (the Kabbalistic entreaty said before *Borchu*). This week the words struck him as never before, בְּדֵין שֵׁירוּתָא דִּצְלוֹתָא לְבָרְכָא לָהּ בְּחֶדְוָה, *Then their prayers begin by blessing her* [the Shabbos] *with joy* .... He stared at the words, לְבָרְכָא לָהּ בְּחֶדְוָה, *blessing her with joy* .... That was remarkable. Chedva was there!

Later, after singing *Shalom Aleichem*, but before he recited *Kiddush*, he sang the words he had sung a thousand times before. This time they jumped out at him: אַתְקִינוּ סְעוּדָתָא דִּמְהֵימְנוּתָא שְׁלֵימָתָא חֶדְוָתָא דְּמַלְכָּא קַדִּישָׁא, *Prepare the feast of perfect faith, the joy of the Holy King* .... Once again he stopped and paused and gazed at the words חֶדְוָתָא דְּמַלְכָּא קַדִּישָׁא, *the joy of the Holy King*. Chedva was there — again!

Later that night, as the *kinnus* was in progress a few blocks away, Rabbi Kleinman told his wife that he now acquiesced: they should name the child Chedva Malka — Malka for the Shabbos Queen.

Mrs. Kleinman's joy knew no bounds. The birth, the timing, the Kabbalistic words of *Tefillah*, the name: Hashem's orchestration was spectacular, just as Chedva deserved.

> May Chedva Malka be as great as, and even greater than, her namesake.

~§ Rescue Reciprocated

It was horrific beyond words. One early evening in the summer of 2009, R' Zalman Fenster* was pulling into his driveway in Lakewood, New Jersey, something that he had done countless times before — but this time his neighbor's 3-year-old daughter, Shiffy Miller,* was sitting on the curb adjacent to the driveway. He didn't see her. His two-ton SUV drove over both of Shiffy thighs, crushing her femur bones.

Zalman heard her screams. He jumped out of his car and immediately saw the horrible injury. The little child lay motionless. He instantly called Hatzolah, tearfully describing what had happened. He couldn't stop crying as he said all the *Tehillim* he knew by heart.

Quick response time to get the child to the hospital was imperative. Every passing second felt like an hour. But in less than a minute, Shmuel Fein,* a veteran member of Hatzolah, drove down the block in his ambulance, lights flashing, and siren blaring, causing a crowd to gather. Shmuel and his partner, Eli Fogel,* raced out of the ambulance, wheeled out a stretcher, and together gently placed the comatose Shiffy on the cushioned mattress. Tenderly but swiftly, they lifted her into the ambulance. Eli sat with Shiffy, davening that she would survive as Shmuel sped thru the Lakewood streets and highways. They arrived at Jersey Shore Hospital within 20 minutes. Shmuel had radioed ahead to the emergency room, so a unit of medical personnel was waiting for their arrival.

Shiffy was placed into an induced coma as she underwent countless medical procedures. She was eventually put into a body cast that she would wear for six months!

That night, Shmuel, the driver of the ambulance, who had stayed in the hospital for more than an hour into the evening, found it hard to sleep. Though he was an experienced paramedic, the accident had unnerved him.

He thought back to the reason he had become a Hatzolah member in the first place. He, too, had been in a terrible automobile accident; it happened when he was 8 years old. It was 45 years ago, even before Hatzolah was founded. He was living in the East Flatbush section of Brooklyn, not far from Beth-El Hospital, which today is called Brookdale Hospital. He was on the way home from yeshivah when suddenly a pickup truck sped around the corner and hit him. He was propelled through the air and landed with a thud. Onlookers screamed and within seconds a crowd gathered as people prayed and raced around, trying to get help.

Just moments before the accident, a woman living on the block had come out to meet her own child coming from yeshivah. She saw the accident occur and ran toward Shmuel. He was bleeding profusely. She rushed to the corner of East 91st Street and Avenue A, into the office of Dr. Martin Merlis, a well-known general practitioner and pediatrician in the area.

"Come right now!" she shouted, "A boy on the block was hit by a car and we must get him to the hospital!"

Dr. Merlis was stitching a patient's cut. "Doctor," the woman cried, "You must stop what you are doing! This could be life or death!"

Dr. Merlis followed the woman to the child who was lying in the street. Someone went to tell Shmuel's parents. An ambulance was called and Dr. Merlis accompanied Shmuel to Beth-El Hospital, where they treated him and saved his life.

Now, at night, so many years later, a sudden thought crossed his mind. That woman who ran for Dr. Merlis to save him — her family name was also Miller, just like Shiffy's, the girl he had rushed to the hospital earlier. It couldn't be, could it? Was it a coincidence that the last names were the same? It was too late that night to investigate.

However, the next morning he made some calls and he realized the extraordinary Divine orchestration of events. Shiffy, the girl he had helped save by responding so quickly, was the granddaughter of the woman who helped save *his* life when she had responded quickly more than four decades earlier. He had saved the granddaughter of the woman who had saved him! He had paid back a noble deed and he hadn't even realized it.

> Today, three years later, Shiffy is walking without a limp and no one would even know that she had been the victim of a terrible accident. Her father told me that Divine Providence played a role even in the precision of the way the accident happened. The tire that rolled over Shiffy's thighs was the exact width of the space between her knee and her hip. Had the tire run over her even a half inch to either side, her hip or knee would have been crushed. The femur is one of the strongest bones in the body and thus her healing was much quicker and her recovery was complete.

ᛞ *Plaque in Time*

When Shlomo Elberg* of Milwaukee, Wisconsin,* was 4 years old, he was diagnosed with Marfan, a syndrome that may interfere with the development and function of the heart, eyes, blood vessels, and bone structure.

During his childhood, Shlomo's condition did not worsen, nor did it adversely affect his interaction with family or friends. Throughout his teenage years, however, his back and spine became quite painful and it seemed that he might eventually need back surgery.

By the time he was 17, he was in constant pain. His parents, R' Asher* and Penina,* were on a brief vacation in Israel and visited several rabbanim and *mekubalim* to ask for *berachos* for Shlomo. Rabbi Yaakov Hillel, the renowned Sephardic rav, advised them to have their mezuzos checked, especially the one on Shlomo's door.

Upon returning to Milwaukee, the Elbergs immediately had their mezuzos examined. They were stunned when the *sofer* told them that Shlomo's mezuzah had a flaw in the phrase, וְהִשְׁתַּחֲוִיתֶם לָהֶם, *and bow down to them* (*Devarim* 11:15). It seemed to them and to the *sofer* to be an indication of a flaw in someone's back or spine, which are affected when one bows.

Now there was no question in their minds that Shlomo would need surgery. The next Shabbos, a rav from Moshav David U'Shmuel,* in northern Israel, Rabbi Yigal Nafti,* came to address the Milwaukee community. His *divrei Torah* were fascinating and his personality was captivating.

On Motza'ei Shabbos, he went from house to house with a local rabbi to raise money for a *Sefer Torah* in his community. He was offering dedications of entire *Chumashim*, an individual *parashah*, or a complete topic found throughout the Torah (for example, the verses of *shiluach hakan, milah, the birchos Yaakov, the Shirah*, and so on).

The Elbergs decided to dedicate the entire *Parashas Vayeira*, which begins with Hashem's visit to Avraham Avinu, who needed healing from his *bris milah*. They hoped that Hashem would "visit" Shlomo as well and grant him a complete recovery.

A few weeks later, the doctors informed the Elbergs that the best hospital for Shlomo's surgery was the Ernie Banks Back and Spine Medical Center* in downtown Chicago, about 90 miles from Milwaukee. Because of the delicate nature of the surgery, world-renowned experts in Chicago were consulted and they recommended Doctor Fenton Santo.* The surgery was scheduled for six months later, on Erev Shavuos.

Understandably, there was anxiety as the day of the surgery approached. The night before the surgery, Shlomo's parents checked into a downtown Chicago hotel two blocks from the Banks Medical Center. Surgery was scheduled for 11 a.m. the next morning.

The Elbergs discussed their plans for the next morning. "Asher," Mrs. Elberg asked, "where are you davening tomorrow morning?"

"Well, I want to be with you and Shlomo as much as I can, so I figured I would daven in the hospital," he replied.

"Oh, no," cried Mrs. Elberg. "The day of our Shlomo's surgery, you must daven with a *minyan*. And besides, tomorrow is Thursday and there is *Krias HaTorah*. I don't want you to miss that, not on such an important day! We need all the *zechusim* we can get," she said firmly.

"Then I'll have to daven in a *vasikin* (sunrise) *minyan*," said Asher. "There is one in West Rodgers Park, about 20 minutes from here. I'll order a taxi now, because it's very early in the morning."

"Please do it," his wife pleaded. "It's worth the extra effort."

The next morning, R' Asher was up early for his cab ride to West Rodgers Park. So there would be no delay in returning, he paid the driver to wait for him and take him back immediately after davening. He davened with extra *kavannah* that morning and even asked the *gabbai* if he could have an *aliyah* as an extra *zechus* for his son. The *Mi Shebeirach* for a *choleh* after the *aliyah* brought tears to R' Asher's eyes.

As he turned away from the *bimah* to go back to his seat, he was stunned to see Rabbi Yigal Nafti. Before R' Asher could say a word, Rabbi Nafti said, "I can't believe I'm seeing you here. I have a present for you and was coming to visit you in Milwaukee after Shavuos to give it to you."

From his attaché case he took a beautiful plaque attesting that the Elberg family had dedicated *Parashas Vayeira* in the new *Sefer Torah* of Moshav David U'Shmuel. The plaque read, in part, "וַיֵּרָא אֵלָיו ה׳, *Hashem appeared to him* (*Bereishis* 18:1), to which *Rashi* says, וּבָא הַקּבָּ"ה וְשָׁאַל בִּשְׁלוֹמוֹ. *And HaKadosh Baruch Hu came and inquired about his welfare.*"

The unexpected visit from Rabbi Nafti — with the plaque to commemorate Hashem's *bikur cholim* visit to Avraham Avinu — gave R' Asher a sudden, wonderful feeling that the surgery would *b'ezras Hashem* be successful.

And it was!

On the way to the hospital, R' Asher, who came to this *minyan* only on the advice of his wife, called her and told her about the unexpected meeting and how he felt it was Hashem's signal that the surgery would go well. He said he was fortunate to have married her. She agreed.

~§ A Link in Time

Rabbi Sidney Glenner of Chicago, Illinois, is a well-known *askan* for national and international Jewish causes. On a recent trip to Greece, he told me this personal, poignant story.

The morning had been a glorious one in the Glenner family. Two weeks earlier, twin boys had been born to Rabbi Glenner's son and daughter-in-law, Daniel and Chayale. Both babies had various issues and their *brissen* had to be delayed. The older one gained weight nicely, so that morning the *bris* was held in Congregation Poalei Tzedek on Albion Avenue, where Rabbi Michael Small was *Mara D'asra*.

That afternoon Rabbi Glenner went to visit his elderly father, R' David. "Sidney, what brings you here?" asked Mr. Glenner. "I just saw you this morning at the *bris*. Is everything okay?"

The Glenners are known for their strong work ethic, and it was unusual for Sidney to leave the office during working hours. "Yes, Dad, everything is fine. I came to personally wish you a happy birthday."

R' David Glenner had turned 93 that day!

"That's very nice of you," said Mr. Glenner, who really did not think that it was necessary for Sidney to take time off from work for such a personal reason. Sidney's mother, Frieda, however, was thrilled that her son had come by, and she offered to make him a little lunch. He readily accepted and the three of them had a nice chat about the morning's *bris* and when the second baby would be ready to have his *bris*.

Sidney went back to work, happy to have spent time with his parents on this special day. That night, as he was getting ready for bed, he noticed that it was already 11:45. He decided to phone his father, who was a night owl and would not be disturbed or frightened by a late-night call.

"Hi, Dad," Sidney began. "You know, it's almost midnight and October 23rd is almost over, so I just wanted to be the last one to wish you happy birthday." He chuckled at his own witticism.

His father remained silent for a moment and then said seriously, "Sidney, you have always been a good son. I love you."

Sidney was taken aback. That was not how his father talked. He didn't usually verbalize the extreme love that he had for his family. From the way he treated them, they all knew he loved them, but this warm expression of emotion was unusual. Choked up, Sidney said, "Thanks, Dad, I love you too."

He hung up with thought and reflection. It felt so good to hear those words, even from a 93-year-old father who was already a great-grandfather many times over. He fleetingly thought that he should be saying them to his own children and grandchildren much more often.

At 3:30 that night, Rabbi Glenner took a frantic call from his mother, telling him that his father was in respiratory distress. Sidney rushed to his parents' home, but after he arrived he could only stand by helplessly as the Chicago Fire Department EMTs tried to revive his father. They did not succeed.

The last words that he had heard from his father were the most precious of all.

> How often do we say those words to our children and grandchildren? They crave it; they need it, at any age.
>
> And, yes, a week later the second of the twins was strong enough for his *bris* and was named after R' Avrohom David Glenner.

✥ Retrieved Items

We all have read and heard surprising stories how tefillin were lost and eventually found. The lost tefillin in this story were retrieved six and a half years after they were lost — an unusually long time. Interestingly, they were lost on the day after they were examined by a *sofer* (scribe), and were found just a few weeks before they were due for another examination; as the *Shulchan Aruch* writes (O.C. 39:10), tefillin should be checked twice in seven years.

What is remarkable about this story is how the seemingly unrelated events and individuals became intertwined, including a Mexican who harbored the tefillin for years and an Israeli who brought them back to their owner. So let us read how Hashem orchestrated a Mexican, an Israeli, and a Borough Park rabbi to collaborate in retrieving more than a lost pair of tefillin.

Mrs. Chava Ganberg* had not had an easy life. Shortly after her son Avrohom Zev's* bar mitzvah, she was separated from her husband and left to raise him and his siblings alone. Sadly, there was rancor and bitterness because of the separation and subsequent divorce, and the children were negatively affected. Avrohom Zev soon responded only to his new nickname, A.Z., and he became rebellious in other ways, as well.

During that time of turmoil, Mrs. Ganberg was looking for *zechusim*, and so when a man from Israel said he was collecting funds for a night *kollel*, where young men learned from 11 p.m. until Shacharis, she decided to give him a generous check in the hope that the "night" of her life — the dark aspects of her existence — would eventually see the dawn — the light heralding the end of her heartache.

In Chabad, bar mitzvah boys are given two pairs of tefillin, a pair of Rashi's tefillin and a pair of Rabbeinu Tam's tefillin.[1] The Rashi

---

1. The primary difference between Rashi's tefillin and Rabbeinu Tam's tefillin is the order in which the *parashios* are inserted in the *battim*. According to Rashi, the *parashah*

pair is used during Shacharis; the Rabbeinu Tam pair is donned afterward as the wearer repeats the *parashios* of *Krias Shema*.

As part of his rebelliousness, A.Z. stopped wearing the two pairs of tefillin he had been given by his grandfather. His mother was devastated.

Six months after she made the donation to the night *kollel*, the same man returned and said that as a token of appreciation, he had a gift for her son: a *klaf* (a parchment) with *Parashas Ketores*[1] written on it, and with her son's name, Avrohom Zev Ganberg, in Torah calligraphy, at the bottom of the parchment.

The Zohar (*Vayakheil*) says that on the day one recites *Parashas Ketores*, he will be protected from evil and not come to any harm.

Mrs. Ganberg wanted to keep this *klaf* in a holy place and so she placed it in her son's tefillin *beitel* (bag), hoping that one day he would resume wearing them.

Years went by. A.Z. hit rock bottom and began making his way back to *Yiddishkeit*. Slowly he became more attentive to mitzvos and resumed donning the tefillin that his grandfather had told him were written by a prominent *sofer* in Israel.

Avrohom Zev found a steady job. He was careful never to leave his tefillin unattended, whether in his office, shul, or car. One day, in Borough Park, he left his car for a few minutes to run into a vendor's office to discuss a business deal. When he came out he was stunned to see that his car had been broken into. Shattered glass from the rear window lay in the street and was strewn over the backseat. His attaché case, with the two pairs of tefillin inside, was missing! Avrohom Zev was heartbroken. He had finally started donning his tefillin — and now they were gone! He didn't know how he would tell his mother, who always told him how her father had made special arrangements to have these costly pairs of tefillin written in Israel. After making a police report and searching garbage bins in the Borough Park area, Avrohom Zev had no choice but to tell her. That night, alone, she cried.

---

of *Shema Yisrael* precedes the one of *V'hayah im shamoa*, whereas in Rabbeinu Tam tefillin, the *parashah* of *V'hayah im shamoa* precedes the *parashah* of *Shema Yisrael*.

1. See *Shemos* 30:34-36, 7, 8; *Kereisos* 6a, and *Tur O.C.* 132.

For years there was no word on the tefillin. Avrohom Zev bought new tefillin, but always wore them with a feeling of emptiness.

Four years later, in a factory in downtown Brooklyn, the Israeli plant manager of Levana's Leather Line,* Boaz Shomron,* went into a back room to daven Shacharis, as he had missed the *minyan* that morning. He thought he was alone, but suddenly he heard a voice behind him. It was Julio Chavez,* a Mexican factory worker.

"Nice straps," said Julio. "Is that what you do with them? I have a pair of those at home but I had no idea what they were for. I just knew they were Jewish things."

"You have a pair like these in your home? What are you doing with them? What do you need them for?" said Boaz, horrified that tefillin should be in a gentile's home. "I'll buy them from you," he added.

"I found them a few years ago in a garbage dump in a fancy velvet bag, I figured they must be something special if they were in such a nice bag. I know my history," said Julio. "Many Spanish people are really Jewish, but their ancestors couldn't show it because they were afraid of the Inquisition. A lot of people found out about their Jewishness years later. Maybe one day I'll find out that I am really Jewish and I'll need them, so I'm not selling them."

Boaz was impressed with Julio's knowledge of the *conversos* (it is inappropriate to call those Jews Marranos, for that is the word for pig in Spanish). Boaz was highly doubtful that Julio would ever find out he was Jewish. "I'll give you 50 dollars for them," said Boaz.

"No way," said Julio, sensing that he had an item of value. "Three hundred dollars or nothing."

"Julio, they mean nothing to you," said Boaz. "What about 100?"

"They may mean nothing to me," said Julio, "but they obviously mean something to you. How about 200?"

They could not reach an agreement, so Julio kept the tefillin. A year later, the Levana company was downsizing. Julio was laid off and given two weeks' notice. He bid good bye to Boaz and the two thought they would never see each other again. However, two

Divine Orchestrations / 243

years later Julio called Boaz. Julio had been looking for work for some time and needed money. "You still want to buy those Jewish boxes and straps?" he asked.

Boaz jumped at the opportunity. "I'll give you a hundred dollars for them," he said. "You know that I have a pair of those already, so I don't really need them, but if you still have the velvet bag they came in, I will give you 150 for the whole package."

"I need the money," said Julio, "but I want 200."

Boaz was not to be out-bargained. He said, "If you give me the tefillin and the case by tonight, you'll get 150. If you wait till tomorrow, then you'll only get 50."

Julio traveled from the Bronx to Brooklyn that afternoon. He delivered the tefillin and collected 150 dollars.

The next morning Boaz went to his shul in Borough Park and showed Rabbi Shaye Kohler* what he had purchased. "A Mexican who worked for me had these for years," said Boaz. "There are only initials, Aleph, Zayin, Gimel, on the outside of the tefillin bag, so I have no idea who they might belong to. What shall I do with them?" Boaz asked.

Rabbi Kohler and Boaz looked through the tefillin bag and found the *klaf* with the name Avrohom Zev Ganberg on it. "I know a *sofer* named Ganberg," said Rabbi Kohler. "He writes beautifully; perhaps these are the tefillin he wrote for his son and that's why the *klaf* has his name on it."

"I think I have your son's tefillin," Rabbi Kohler said excitedly when he reached Reb Shraga Feivel Ganberg. "Is your son's name Avrohom Zev?"

"No, that's not my son, but I have a nephew by that name. Maybe the tefillin are his. His were actually written by a prominent *sofer* in Israel."

Rabbi Kohler asked for the Ganbergs' phone number and called to ask if Avrohom Zev had lost his tefillin. Mrs. Ganberg and Avrohom Zev were ecstatic that after all these years the tefillin had been found and, according to Rabbi Kohler, were in good condition. Avrohom Zev said he would drive over immediately to retrieve them.

Rabbi Kohler made sure that Boaz was there when he returned the tefillin and the three of them marveled at how a chain of seemingly unrelated individuals had brought the tefillin back to their owner: the Mexican who found them and stored them, the Israeli who brought his tallis and tefillin to the office, and the rabbi who happened to know a *sofer* with the same last name as the young man who lost the tefillin.

There is more to the story. Rabbi Kohler was so impressed with the young man that he suggested a *shidduch* for him. Avrohom Zev rejected the idea. However, *Chazal* teach (*Kiddushin* 2b), that it is customary for a man to pursue a woman for marriage, just as a man searches for something he lost. Rashi explains (ibid.) that Adam HaRishon "lost" the rib from which Hashem created his wife. Thus every man, so to speak, is trying to retrieve his lost rib.

A year later, the same young lady was suggested to Avrohom Zev, and he remembered that Rabbi Kohler had once mentioned her to him. This time he pursued the *shidduch* and a few months later they were married. Remarkably, Rabbi Kohler had a hand in retrieving two "lost" items for Avrohom Zev.

> Avrohom Zev, his mother, and, of course, his wife couldn't be happier.

⇜ Book Return

In 1937, Rabbi Naftoli Carlebach, a noted *talmid chacham* who had studied in the yeshivos of Telshe and Mir, returned to his native Germany to become an instructor at the Wurzburg Teachers Seminary. Shortly after his return, Rabbi Carlebach began filing papers for permission to immigrate to America, since the Nazi party was increasingly spewing hatred against the Jews throughout the country.

On the nights of November 9 and 10, 1938, a brutal series of co-ordinated attacks throughout Germany left 91 Jews killed, 30,000 arrested, and countless Jewish shuls, homes, schools, and hospitals ransacked and burned. The German beasts burned over a thousand synagogues and demolished more than 7,000 businesses. The operation became known as Kristallnacht (the Night of Broken Glass). The Wurzburg Teachers Seminary, especially its library, was badly damaged.

The morning after Kristallnacht, Rabbi Carlebach came to the seminary and was stunned at the destruction he saw. He had already decided to leave Germany and had come to the school to bid farewell to the head of the seminary, Dr. Jacob Stoll.

Rabbi Carlebach entered the office and saw that Dr. Stoll was crestfallen. "I have decided that the time has come to leave the country," Rabbi Carlebach said. "I will go while I still can."

"Yes, you are fortunate," said Dr. Stoll, shaking in head in disbelief at what had happened the night before. "You had the wisdom to obtain your papers in time. Go to the library. You will see there is one corner where, by the grace of G-d, nothing was touched. There are two *Sifrei Torah* there and numerous shelves of *sefarim* are still intact. Take them with you to America so that they will be saved."

"I would love to," said Rabbi Carlebach, "but I don't know how much room I will have after I pack my family's belongings. But let me see what I can do."

Indeed, two *Sifrei Torah* were untouched, alongside numerous neat shelves of *sefarim* that had been donated by the family of the late rabbi of Hochberg. The *sefarim* dated from the mid 1800's. In 1931 the Jewish school of Hochberg, which had six classes, had been transferred to Wurzburg and incorporated into the Teachers Seminary. The merged institutions were housed in a new building. Years earlier, when the childless rabbi of Hochberg passed away, his nephew and niece donated his *sefarim* to the school; thus they were now part of the Teachers Seminary library.

Rabbi Carlebach took the two *Sifrei Torah* to the United States but had room for only about 10 *sefarim*. He became the rav of the Chambersburg Jewish community, in South Central Pennsylvania, 14 miles north of Maryland. There, and later in Detroit, he and his wife raised exceptional children, one of whom is Rabbi Binyamin

Carlebach, a rosh yeshivah in the Mirrer Yeshiva in Jerusalem, and brother-in-law and associate of the late Rabbi Nosson Tzvi Finkel (1943-2011). Eventually Reb Naftoli and his wife moved to Israel, where he was a *chavrusa* for many years with his neighbor Rabbi Simcha Wasserman (1900-1992) in the Mattersdorf neighborhood of Jerusalem.

The Carlebachs had many children and grandchildren, and he and his wife remained close to them all. In 1994, when their granddaughter Esther in New York was of marriageable age, Rabbi Carlebach wrote to ask whom the family was considering. When he heard that one of the prospective young men was Yehoshua Ottensoser, his interest was piqued. Rav Lazer Ottensoser of Hochberg was the man who had donated the *sefarim* that eventually made their way to the Wurzburg Teachers Seminary! And Rabbi Carlebach was the one who had preserved some of them!

With wit, he wrote a letter to his granddaughter, "Tell the young man Ottensoser, that if he becomes my grandson, he can have his ancestor's *sefarim* back!"

And that is exactly what happened. Shortly after R' Yehoshua and Esther were married in 1994, they traveled to *Eretz Yisrael*, where Rabbi and Mrs. Naftoli Carlebach presented the *sefarim* to the young couple during a festive evening at their home.

The *sefarim* included some of the rare remaining printed volumes of Rabbi Alexander Sender of Zholkov (1660-1737), author of the *Tevuos Shor*; and the writings of Rav Isaac ben Moshe Arama (1420-1494), author of *Akeidas Yitzchak*.

> Interestingly, when R' Yehoshua researched his distant relative Rabbi Lazer Ottensoser, he found that there was a Lazarus Ottensoser Foundation, directed by the Teachers Seminary in Wurzburg. Once the school was disbanded, Dr. Stoll sent the foundation's funds to prominent German rabbanim in Israel: Rav Gedalye Eisman, Rav Boruch Kunstadt, Rabbi Yonah Mertzbach, and Rav Michel Schlesinger. They were founding a yeshivah — and today it is the world-renowned Yeshiva Kol Torah in Bayit Vegan.

∾§ With Feeling

In June of 2011, Reb Abish Brodt of Brooklyn, Rabbi Menachem Nissel of Israel, and I led a group of 57 American *yeshivah bachurim* on a five-day trip to Poland, under the auspices of Project Mesorah, which is dedicated to giving yeshivah high school boys an appreciation of pre-war European Jewish history. We learned in the former *beis medrash* of Rav Meir Shapiro's Yeshivah Chachmei Lublin, davened at the *kever* of the Rebbe Reb Elimelech in Lizhensk, danced in the *beis medrash* of the *Chiddushei HaRim* in Ger, and walked through the horrifying barracks and crematoria of the concentration camps of Auschwitz and Majdanek.

In each place, Rabbi Nissel would provide the *bachurim* with its historic background, I would share relevant stories and inspirational insights, and R' Abish would lead us in song with his powerful, melodious voice. His choice of *niggun* was always appropriate to the occasion, and each song added depth and sensitivity to the trip. For example, at the *kever* of the Rebbe Reb Elimelech, Reb Abish sang *Aderabbah*, the song with lyrics from the *tefillah* that Reb Elimelech composed, אַדְרַבָּה, תֵּן בְּלִבֵּנוּ שֶׁנִּרְאֶה כָּל אֶחָד מַעֲלַת חֲבֵרֵינוּ וְלֹא חֶסְרוֹנָם, *To the contrary, guide us so that we see every virtue of our friends and not their shortcomings*. In the gas chambers of Majdanek, Reb Abish sang and cried the piercing melody of הַבֵּט מִשָּׁמַיִם וּרְאֵה כִּי הָיִינוּ לַעַג וָקֶלֶס בַּגּוֹיִם, *Look from heaven and perceive that we have become an object of scorn and derision among the nations*. And outside the cemetery where the *Chiddushei HaRim* and the *Sfas Emes* are buried, he led us in singing, שָׁמְרָה נַפְשִׁי כִּי חָסִיד אָנִי, *Guard my soul, for I am a devout man* (*Tehillim* 86:2). It was exhilarating to be in his presence.

While on the bus to Cracow, Reb Abish told me a fascinating story about his name, referring to an old custom in *Klal Yisrael*. The *Shelah* teaches that it is a source of merit to recite a Scriptural verse symbolizing one's name before beginning the יְהִיוּ לְרָצוֹן at the end of *Shemoneh Esrei*. The verse should contain the person's name, or else begin and end with the first and last letters of the name. This, writes the *Shelah*, is so that one will not forget his or her name on the day of Heavenly judgment in the World To Come. (See *Taamei HaMinhagim* no. 90; also *Kuntros Acharon*, ibid.)

Additionally, on the words וְתוּשִׁיָּה יִרְאֶה שְׁמֶךָ, *and the [man of] wisdom recognizes Your [Hashem's] Name* (*Michah* 6:9), *Rashi* writes, "From here we know that someone who says a verse every day that begins and ends with the letters that his name begins and ends with, the Torah will protect him from *Gehennom*."

For years, R' Abish had been searching for a verse that began with an א and ended with a ש as does his name, אביש, but to no avail. The *siddurim* that catalogued names and their corresponding verses listed many names that began with א, such as Avrohom, Aaron, Avigdor, Eliyahu, and Eliezer, etc. However, no *siddur* he had seen and no individual he spoke to could suggest an appropriate Scriptural verse.

> Interestingly I could not find a verse to suggest to my son Avrohom to use for his middle name, זעליג, Zelig. I thus recommended that he use the verse, זְמִרוֹת הָיוּ לִי חֻקֶּיךָ בְּבֵית מְגוּרָי, *Your statutes were music to me, in my dwelling place* (*Tehillim* 119:54), which begins with a ז and has a ג in the last word of the verse. Rabbi Dovid Cohen felt this was acceptable, since the main reason for this custom is that one remembers his Hebrew name; in this manner, one also makes a reference to his Hebrew name. Rabbi Yitzchak Dvoritz of Israel told me that Rav Zelik Reuvain Bengis (1864-1953), the Chief Rabbi of the Eidah HaChareidis of Jerusalem, spelled his name זעליק, Zelik, with a ק at the end; he therefore used the verse, זָרַח בַּחֹשֶׁךְ אוֹר לַיְשָׁרִים חַנּוּן וְרַחוּם וְצַדִּיק, *Even in darkness a light shines for the upright; He is compassionate, merciful, and righteous* (*Tehillim* 112:4), which begins with a ז and ends with a ק.

As the years went by, Reb Abish became world renowned, singing for rebbes and roshei yeshivah, performing at weddings and conventions, and even producing cassettes and eventually CDs. In 1985, Rabbi Shmuel Brazil, then studying at Yeshivah Sh'or

Yoshuv in Far Rockaway, composed numerous *niggunim* that became music staples in Jewish homes. He asked Reb Abish if they could collaborate on a music cassette. Abish readily agreed. They decided to call the album *Regesh*, literally, *Feeling*, and indeed, many of the songs were slow, hauntingly beautiful selections. The album sold more than any of his earlier cassettes, and *Regesh* became a household word.

A few months after the album was released, Reb Abish came upon a new Belzer *siddur*, *Avodas Hashem*. Still looking for an appropriate *pasuk* for his name, he opened the *siddur* to see if there was a page of names with their corresponding *pesukim*. The name Abish was there! (See page 872 in the *siddur*.) The *pasuk* was אֲשֶׁר יַחְדָּו נַמְתִּיק סוֹד בְּבֵית אֱלֹהִים נְהַלֵּךְ בְּרָגֶשׁ, *With whom together we would share sweet counsel, in the House of G-d we would walk with feelings of awe* (*Tehillim* 55:15).

Incredibly, the most popular album that he ever made, *Regesh*, was there in his *pasuk* all along.

◈§ From Generation to Generation

> Every morning we recite the blessing, הַמֵּכִין מִצְעֲדֵי גָבֶר, *[Hashem] prepares the steps of man*. Sometimes we find ourselves in places we did not expect to be. Surprisingly, something remarkable happens — and then we understand why Hashem brought us to there to begin with.
>
> In this story we witness the opposite. Someone was supposed to be someplace, but never arrived there. And that turned out to be *Hashgachah Pratis* (Divine Providence).

In November 1999, Rabbi Yaakov Mendelson and his wife Rashi were to be honored by their shul, Congregation Bikur Cholim, in Bridgeport, Connecticut, for their 10 years of service to the community. Friends and relatives from near and far would attend this gala event and Rabbi Mendelson wanted a guest speaker who would inspire the guests with both content and eloquence. He called his friend Rabbi Benzion Twerski of Milwaukee, who blends the worlds of chassidus and psychology. The son of the widely acclaimed Hornosteipler Rebbe and Rebbetzin, Rabbi Michel and Rebbetzin Faige Twerski of Milwaukee, Rav Benzion is a descendant of a long dynasty of chassidic rabbis. He was happy to oblige.

Rabbi Twerski was scheduled to take an early flight on Sunday morning and land at Newark's Liberty International Airport, where David Mendelson, the rabbi's brother, who was flying in from Montreal at around the same time, would meet him and drive him to Bridgeport.

On the designated day, David's plane landed in Newark but Rabbi Twerski was nowhere to be found! David went to the arrival gate and then to the baggage area, but there was no Rabbi Twerski.

Concerned, David called Rabbi Mendelson, who in turn called Rabbi Twerski. At the time Rabbi Twerski was sitting comfortably in his Milwaukee office, giving his regular Sunday morning *Chumash* lecture for women. He never answers the phone during a *shiur* but the ringing was incessant. After a while of listening to the continuous ringing, Rabbi Twerski thought perhaps there was an emergency, so he answered the phone.

"Rabbi Twerski, are you okay? Where are you?" Rabbi Mendelson sounded frantic.

"I'm giving my *Chumash shiur*, as usual. Is something wrong?" Rabbi Twerski asked.

"My brother is in Newark waiting for you! You mean you didn't take this morning's flight?" asked an exasperated, incredulous Rabbi Mendelson. "The dinner is tonight!"

Rabbi Twerski felt his stomach drop. "Tonight? I have it on my calendar for *next* Sunday!"

"No, it's today, tonight." said the stunned Rabbi Mendelson. "Can't you somehow get on a plane and make it here in time?" Rabbi Mendelson pleaded.

Rabbi Twerski had a full day of important visits and meetings that would be nearly impossible to cancel, including a hospital visit to a dying cancer patient.

Divine Orchestrations

"Look," said Rabbi Twerski, thinking quickly. "I won't leave you high and dry. I'm so sorry for my error. It's not like me to mix up an appointment, but I will get someone to replace me, don't worry. I'll get back to you as soon as possible."

"Who can replace *you*?" asked Rabbi Mendelson, feeling desperate. His carefully planned dinner would be missing a main component. He had been looking forward to an evening of joy and elevation for his family and congregants and now he realized there was bound to be disappointment and disillusionment.

He tried again to persuade Rabbi Twerski to attend. "Is there no way you can get here? Maybe you could travel through Chicago [a 90-minute car ride from Milwaukee but from where there are many more flights to New York]?"

"I won't let you down," Rabbi Twerski assured Rabbi Mendelson. "Just give me some time."

Rabbi Twerski apologized to the class and finished his *shiur*, then immediately punched in a phone number. His first call was to his esteemed uncle, Rabbi Aaron Twerski. Professor Twerski is a noted *talmid chacham*, a scion of the Chernobyl, Sanz, Bobov, and Hornosteipel dynasties; the former dean of Hofstra Law School, and the author of five books and over 70 scholarly law articles. He is also the twin of Reb Benzion's father, so Reb Benzion felt he could ask him for a big favor, and he was undoubtedly an exceptional choice to be the guest speaker. The only question was if he could do it.

After explaining his problem, Reb Benzion pleaded, "Please, Uncle Aaron, can you go to Bridgeport tonight to speak at that dinner? I am so embarrassed by my mistake and I need someone whom the crowd will really enjoy. You are the one!"

"I don't have anything to say," Rabbi Aaron Twerski said humbly. "As much as I would like to help you, I am really not the one. There is not much time to prepare."

"Uncle Aaron," Reb Benzion said, "no matter what you say, it will be wonderful. You have so much to give an audience, much more than I could ever give them. They would be fortunate to have you come."

Finally Rabbi Twerski, knowing the difficult predicament his nephew was in, consented to "pinch-hit."

"I can't thank you enough," Rav Benzion said. "I know it's a big *tircha* (bother) for you, but I'm really grateful for your kindness."

Rav Benzion called Rabbi Mendelson, who was relieved but still concerned at how he would explain the change of program to his dinner guests.

That evening an incredible thing happened; it was not only that Rabbi Twerski gave a resounding speech that was the highlight of the evening. Rabbi Mendelson was thrilled and the audience was inspired. The most important part of the evening was a conversation that Rabbi. Twerski had with a young man.

During the dinner, a *kiruv* professional in his early 30's, Rabbi Ezra Lachman,* approached Rabbi Twerski. "Can I have a private word with you?" he asked softly. For decades people have sought out the Twerskis for counsel and advice, so why would tonight be different? Indeed, people flock to Rabbi Twerski naturally, as he is wise and inspires confidence.

"We have no children," Rabbi Lachman said sadly. "My wife and I have tried everything medically but nothing has helped. Can you give us advice? Can you give us a *berachah* (blessing)?"

Rabbi Twerski smiled and said, "If you are in *kiruv*, then you certainly deserve a *berachah*. Besides, it is *Hashgachah Pratis* that you should ask me this question tonight. Just yesterday I learned something that I had never heard before. It was told to me in the name of the *Sar Shalom*, Prince of Peace, the first Belzer Rebbe, Rav Sholom Rokeach (1779-1855).

"Someone said, in the name of the *Sar Shalom*, that if one wants to have children, one should have special concentration when reciting the words in *Shemoneh Esrei*, in *Modim*, מָגֵן יִשְׁעֵנוּ, אַתָּה הוּא לְדוֹר וָדוֹר, נוֹדֶה לְךָ וּנְסַפֵּר תְּהִלָּתֶךָ, *Shield of our salvation are You from generation to generation. We shall thank You and relate Your praises.*

"The Rebbe said it does not mean merely that Hashem's protection continues throughout the generations but also that Hashem helps humanity by providing couples with children so that there will be generations and generations who will praise and laud His Name."

Divine Orchestrations / 253

Rabbi Twerski explained. "There are two ways to say this phrase. One way is מָגֵן יִשְׁעֵנוּ, אַתָּה הוּא לְדוֹר וָדוֹר, *Shield of our salvation are You from generation to generation.* That way we emphasize that Hashem protects from one generation to the next. The other way is to say, לְדוֹר וָדוֹר, נוֹדֶה לְּךָ וּנְסַפֵּר תְּהִלָּתֶךָ, *From generation to generation we shall thank You and relate Your praises.* This implies that we are praying for future generations [more children] who will be able to praise and laud Hashem.

"The next time you daven *Shemoneh Esrei*, have in mind your plight in life as you say this words, לְדוֹר וָדוֹר נְסַפֵּר תְּהִלָּתֶךָ, *from generation to generation we shall thank You and relate Your praises.* The Rebbe said that Hashem would help those who pray this way!"

Rabbi Lachman thanked Rabbi Twerski profusely for his words and assured him that he and his wife would heed his words.

Almost one year to the day later, Rabbi Yaakov Mendelson called Rabbi Aaron Twerski and said, "Do you remember that you came and pinch-hit for your nephew at last year's dinner? Well, today there is much to celebrate. I just returned from the *bris* of the son of that young man who sought your advice at the dinner."

Rabbi Mendelson then called Rabbi Benzion Twerski to share the good news with him as well.

> The *Ribono Shel Olam's* ways are incredible. He wanted Rabbi Benzion Twerski to have a share in the great *simchah* and so he had him deliver the messenger by not being able to deliver his own message.

⋆§ The Show Must Go On

On Tuesday, July 31, 2012, an urgent meeting took place in the Manhattan headquarters of Agudath Israel. The people responsible for planning and organizing the Siyum HaShas had to make a monumental decision. Over 90,000 people were expected to come to MetLife Stadium in New Jersey to celebrate the completion of the twelfth cycle of Daf Yomi. People were coming from all over America and even overseas. Thousands of children were being bussed in from summer camps. It would be a gala, historic event. But it was raining and the forecast was for showers and thunderstorms all day and evening Wednesday. Should the siyum be postponed to Thursday? Rearranging and changing their plans would be almost impossible for the thousands who were coming. But a siyum in an open-air stadium in the rain?

They consulted with weather experts and then, with apprehension in their hearts and prayers on their lips, the committee made the decision that the Twelfth Siyum HaShas would take place as planned. In fairness to the attendees, the Agudah ordered 25,000 ponchos to be distributed if people had to be protected from the rain. Wednesday morning started with the sun shining, but by 11 o'clock the rains started. As the afternoon progressed, the rains at times were torrential; highways were closed, flights were delayed, and the roads were clogged with traffic delays.

As the afternoon moved on and people began filtering into the stadium, it was still raining. People huddled in raincoats or ponchos, under umbrellas or the covered areas of the stadium. Looking up at the gray, forbidding sky, one could not help but wonder if the Agudah had made the right decision.

In the late afternoon, a meteorologist from the Weather Department showed Rabbi Shlomo Gertzulin the computer screen displaying an aerial weather map that showed thunderstorms within miles of all sides of the stadium. However, he said, the winds were blowing to the north and thus it would not rain over the stadium. At a few minutes before 7 p.m., the sun broke through the clouds and there was no rain at all. Remarkably, it did not rain again until after midnight that evening.

The night was almost magical. People were ecstatic and the excitement was tangible. It was perhaps the largest *Kiddush Hashem* ever to take place on American soil. Not only was the program uplifting in every way, but it seemed miraculous that it was apparently raining everywhere but at the stadium.

(Additionally, as everyone was filing out of the stadium a guard stood with a pad and a pen, making a mark every few seconds. When a passing rabbi asked what he was doing, he replied, "In all my years here, I have never received so many kind comments and thank-you's. I am marking off every time someone thanks me, for these people are the true giants of this stadium [alluding to the professional sports team, the New York Giants, who play there throughout the football season]."

(Mr. Ron VanDeVeen, Senior Vice President, Events and Guest Experiences at MetLife Stadium, wrote Rabbi Gertzulin, "There is no question that, in our collective years in the industry, we have not seen an event such as this one and it was our sincere pleasure to host it.")

The next morning I wondered: Why the rain? If Hashem wanted the "show" to go on without a hitch, why did He send the downpour and then the clearing? Why couldn't it be one of those days without a cloud in the sky?

After a while I remembered a story told to me by Rav Sholom Schwadron (1912-1997), the Maggid of Jerusalem. In 1948, when the Jordanians were bombing the city of Jerusalem, Jews raced to shelters for protection.

One morning, bombs and shells were falling in the Batei Ungarin section. People hurried to a local shelter, fearing for their lives. As they huddled together, there was a huge explosion as a bomb hit a gas tank. A ball of fire erupted, burning everything in its path. The flames were heading for the crowded shelter when suddenly, a second bomb fell on a nearby water tank, causing a huge gush of water to pour out right in the track of the fireball. Within moments the fire was out, and soon after, the people were able to leave the shelter.

The miraculous event was all anyone talked about. Someone asked the Brisker Rav, Rav Velvel Soloveitchik (1886-1959), "If Hashem was going to save the people in the shelter anyway, why did He orchestrate matters so that the shell hit the gas tank, causing a fire, and then another shell hit the water tank, putting out the fire? He could have just left things the way they were — no fire, no water tank — and the people would have been safe in the shelter."

The Rav answered, "It was the *Ribono Shel Olam's* way to let us know how much He loves us. Had they simply been safe in the shelter, with no bombs falling near them, they would come out after the 'all-clear' siren and would not have realized His great *chessed* and love for them. Now they know."

And that is how I view the torrential rains and then their cessation just before the program. It was a way to show *Klal Yisrael* that Hashem wanted us to be incredibly inspired by His boundless *chessed* and love for us.

> The next Siyum HaShas celebration for the completion of the thirteenth cycle of Daf Yomi will take place during the winter, in January 2020. May we all live to see what Hashem has in store for us on that day.

Part E:
Reflections, Sense, and Wisdom

✥ Vines of Wine

Chazal encourage us to marry our sons to the daughters of *talmidei chachamim* and to marry our daughters to *talmidei chachamim*. Doing so *"Is like [putting together] grapes of a vine with grapes of another vine, which is beautiful and acceptable"* (*Pesachim* 49a).

I often wondered why *Chazal* compare the union of a *chassan* and *kallah* from families of Torah scholars to the intermingling of grapevines. What not compare them to pretty cherry blossoms, beautiful apple orchards, gleaming orange groves, or sparkling tomato patches?

At the wedding of my dear friends, Rabbi Shaye and Shani Greenwald, the *chassan's* uncle, Rabbi Eli Greenwald of Brooklyn, New York, provided an astute answer.

Although every fruit or vegetable has a *berachah* expressing its origin — either from a tree or from the ground — the juice of that fruit or vegetable has an "inferior" *berachah*. For example, on eating an apple one recites the *berachah* בּוֹרֵא פְּרִי הָעֵץ, *Who creates the fruit of the tree*; however, on apple juice, one makes the *berachah* שֶׁהַכֹּל נִהְיֶה בִּדְבָרוֹ, *through whose word everything came to be*. The הָעֵץ blessing is more prominent than the שֶׁהַכֹּל blessing because it is specific, while the שֶׁהַכֹּל blessing is used for everything from meat and fish to water (see *Chayei Adam*, *Klal* 57:2). It is the same with the tomato and its "offspring," tomato juice. When eating a tomato one recites בּוֹרֵא פְּרִי הָאֲדָמָה, *Who creates the fruit of the ground*; however, when drinking tomato juice one recites only the שֶׁהַכֹּל blessing.

The only exceptions to this rule are grapes and grape juice or wine. When eating grapes one recites בּוֹרֵא פְּרִי הָעֵץ, but when

Reflections, Sense, and Wisdom / 261

drinking grape juice or wine, one recites a more prominent *berachah*, בּוֹרֵא פְּרִי הַגֶּפֶן, *Who creates the fruit of the vine.*

This, said Rabbi Greenwald, may be what *Chazal* imply when they compare the union of families of Torah scholars to grapes of a vine with the grapes of another vine. In praising the union, we express the hope that the children, the products of the marriage, will be even more prominent than their parents — just as the blessing on wine is more prominent than the blessing on the grapes.

> May this precious blessing come to fruition for all married couples.

⋇§ Bombs Bursting in Air

Chazal exhort us, דַּע מַה שֶּׁתָּשִׁיב לְאֶפִּיקוֹרוֹס, *Know what to answer a nonbeliever* (*Avos* 2:19). This knowledge is necessary not only to refute a nonbeliever; we need answers for ourselves, because an unanswered question may leave us with doubts and uncertainties about basic articles of faith. It behooves us, therefore, to gain authentic Torah insights and perspectives from the wise people of our generation. The following story, told by Rabbi Pinchos Lipschutz, editor of the *Yated Ne'eman*, is a case in point.

Rabbi Shlomo Wolbe (1914-2005), the renowned Mashgiach in Yeshivah Be'er Yaakov, gave a *shmuess* (spiritual discourse) a few weeks after the Yom Kippur War, to bring out the point of the "pintele *Yid*," the core of *emunah* (belief in Hashem) that lies deep within the heart of every Jew.

During the war an Israeli navy ship was attacked by an Egyptian warship. The ship was sinking and all on board knew that their lives were in danger. They acted frantically to save as many sailors as possible; even the nonreligious men were yelling, "*Shema Yisrael.*" They reached into the depths of their hearts as they prayed to Hashem in their moment of dire need.

A *bachur* listening to the *shmuess* asked a startling question. "Those sailors who were saved from death, who found Hashem in their moment of terror — did they put on *tefillin* the next morning?"

Even Rav Wolbe was taken aback by the question. He paused for a moment and answered with a sagacious insight. "You recently experienced Yom Kippur," he said, challenging the lad who posed the question. "You were a changed person, you were serious and introspective. Then at the end of the day, you shouted, '*Hashem Hu HaElokim*' seven times. But what happened the next day? How did you act and daven on the eleventh of Tishrei? Were you the same as you were at *Ne'ilah*?

"Maybe not — but that doesn't mean that your Yom Kippur was not genuine. It simply means that you have to connect experiences and grow from them. That is our challenge in life."

> We may find it easy to ridicule and demean those who are not on our level of faith. Too often we are smug and secure in our belief that we are as committed as we ought to be. This may be far from the truth. We need to be close to wise people in order to know what level we are really at and what we must do to develop and grow.

৵ Roots and Routes

> Sometimes a simple insight carries a profound message. The power of the message is reinforced because its truth is so glaringly obvious that one retains it for life.

Many years ago, in the town of Gateshead in the northern part of England, a youngster took a walk in a park with his *melamed*. The autumn trees were beautiful in their foliage, but some of the colorful leaves were strewn along the ground beside the park benches. "You see those leaves?" the *melamed* said. "They think they're free; they feel they can fly anywhere because they are no longer attached to the tree. In reality though, they will soon wither and die — because they are disconnected from their source.

"However, the leaves that are connected to the trees — *they* still have life. They can grow and flourish because they are connected to their source." Then the *melamed* added, "That's what Shlomo HaMelech meant when he wrote, 'עֵץ חַיִּים הִיא לַמַּחֲזִיקִים בָּהּ, *It is a tree of life for those who grasp it*' (*Mishlei* 3:18)."

The *melamed* continued. "In your life you will meet people who feel that if they are disconnected from Torah they are free, unencumbered by any restrictions or held back by any constraints; they can do what they please, when they please. But this is not so. Quite the contrary. People not connected to Torah are enslaved by their passions and controlled by their desires; and they are bound to die a spiritual death.

"On the other hand, the Torah that is our עֵץ חַיִּים, 'tree of life,' nourishes our souls and guides our emotions so that we can control what we do and when we do it." (See *Koheles* 3:1.)

The little boy told me that the *melamed's* message inspires him till this day. That little boy grew up to be HaRav Mattisyahu Salomon, *shlita*, Mashgiach of Beth Medrash Govoha in Lakewood.

> It seems to me that this same concept is taught in the *mishnah*, שֶׁאֵין לְךָ בֶּן חוֹרִין אֶלָּא מִי שֶׁעוֹסֵק בְּתַלְמוּד תּוֹרָה, *You can have no freer man than one who engages in Torah study* (*Avos* 6:2). Those involved in Torah study learn to command their whims and desires. They are not enslaved by their cravings or controlled by their desires.

Is the Torah Jew constrained or liberated? Rabbi Yehoshua Bienenfeld, today of Israel (formerly of St. Louis), answers this question using the metaphor of a violin.

The four strings of a violin must be drawn tightly over the fingerboard down to the tailpiece. If even one of the strings is too loose, the violinist will not be able to produce beautiful music.

Conversely, if one of the strings is too taut, it could snap and no music could be produced from that string. A precise degree of tautness is needed for the violin to produce its best sounds. Indeed, the strings are constrained, but that constraint is for the benefit of the violinist and his listeners.

> It is the same with each of us. We come into this world to "play spiritual music." The commandments of the Torah, like the tension applied to a violin's strings, may at times seem confining, but they are what enable our lives to be meaningful, in harmony with Hashem's will.
>
> Thus, being connected to our Source, which is Hashem and His Torah, not only allows us to blossom and flourish like the leaves on a tree, but also gives us the opportunity to strike the perfect chord, balanced between channeled direction and untamed freedom.
>
> May we all merit to see the flowering and development of our children and grandchildren.

∽§ Lifetime Revenge

The pain and trauma of Holocaust survivors never ends. As years go, by the anguish of what happened during the war years may fade into the recesses of their memory, but at any moment, a surprise comment or unanticipated occurrence can bring back the sorrow and the agony. Life goes on, but to the survivor every breath of life is significant and the survival of our nation is proof of the tenacity of Jewish people. A life's lesson was taught by one such survivor. I thank my friend R' Aaron Shmulowitz for sharing it with me.

In the summer of 2009, a *bris* in the Rotberg family took place in Brooklyn, New York; it was attended by Rabbi Hillel David. The infant's great-grandfather, Reb Yehuda Friedman, was a Holocaust survivor, and his joy at the *bris* was boundless.

Before the *bris*, Rabbi David approached him and said, "*Mazel tov!* This must be a very special occasion for you. After going through all that you did during the war, to live to this day is surely cause for great joy."

"You are so right," replied Mr. Friedman. "There were times in the concentration camps when I did not think I would survive. Who even had thoughts of getting married, becoming a father, then a grandfather, and eventually a great-grandfather? Indeed, it is an extraordinary *simchah*."

"Let me share with you a memory that I have from my youth," said Rabbi David. "When I was growing up, I heard of a fellow, Rabbi Boruch Berkowitz, who lived in Williamsburg. On Friday nights he would attend every *Shalom Zachar* he could. He would go from house to house, and sometimes even walk up 16 floors in an apartment building, just to extend a *mazel tov* to the family celebrating the birth of their new son. On some Friday nights, he attended 10 separate *Shalom Zachars*!

"When people asked him why he did this week after week, he would reply, 'This is my revenge on Hitler. I am a survivor. Hitler and the Nazis sought to wipe all Jews from the earth. Every new Jewish child undoes what Hitler and the Nazis tried to do. The growth of *Klal Yisrael* is our revenge, and I love to witness it.'"

A few days after the Rotberg *bris*, the great-grandfather, Mr. Friedman, called his grandson, who davens in Rabbi David's shul, and said, "Please give your Rav this message from me. This morning during davening a thought occurred to me that would have never crossed my mind if not for his comment about the fellow going to all the *Shalom Zachars* in Williamsburg.

"In the *Hallelukahs* [*Tehillim* 145-150, which are a part of Shacharis], there is the following verse. רוֹמְמוֹת קֵל בִּגְרוֹנָם וְחֶרֶב פִּיפִיּוֹת בְּיָדָם, *The lofty praises of G-d are in their throats, and a double-edged sword is in their hand* (*Tehillim* 149:6). This alludes to the double-edged knife that is used by a *mohel* during a *bris*. The next words in the verse are remarkable: לַעֲשׂוֹת נְקָמָה בַּגּוֹיִם, *to execute vengeance among the nations* [*who seek our demise*]."

David HaMelech in his infinite wisdom alluded to the fact that every infant's *bris* is retribution against those who wished to annihilate us. Indeed the birth and growth of our children is our greatest rebuttal to all who wished to eradicate us.

King David foresaw the future and the future lives on.

Show Time

In 1961, Rabbi Chaim Nussbaum and Rabbi Moshe Bobrowsky founded the Bais Yaakov High School of Toronto and engaged Rabbi Shlomo Freifeld (1925-1990) of New York to be its principal. Rabbi Friefeld, a *talmid* of Rabbi Yitzchok Hutner of Mesivta Chaim Berlin, was a dynamic, charismatic, brilliant *talmid chacham* who could converse with any Jew regardless of age, gender, or religious commitment. He was well versed in Torah and his worldly knowledge was broad. He was an ideal role model and teacher, and a perfect man for the job.

Although Toronto was a blossoming Orthodox community at the time, its suburbs were not. For example, Hamilton, Ontario, only 42 miles from Toronto, had a Jewish community center and an afternoon Talmud Torah for youngsters run by Rabbi Yosef Vilensky (son-in-law of Rabbi Elya Lopian), yet the students and parent body were mostly Reform and Conservative Jews. Rabbi Vilensky's teachers were Orthodox Torontonians, but they were not representative of the majority of Jews in Hamilton.

Rabbi Vilensky organized a fund-raising dinner for the Talmud Torah and invited Rabbi Freifeld to be the guest speaker. Although he knew that most of the dinner's attendees were not Orthodox, Rabbi Vilenslky was confident that Rabbi Freifeld would connect with everyone.

On the evening of the dinner Rabbi Freifeld made his way to the hall where the dinner was to be held. As the rabbi was about to enter the building, the doorman, stopped him, saying, "Excuse me, but you will have to come back tomorrow. There is no outside fund-raising here tonight."

Rabbi Freifeld understood that it was his long Lithuanian-style *kapatteh* (frock coat) and very wide upturned hat that had caused the doorman to think that the rabbi was a *meshulach* (a charity collector). Rabbi Freifeld said with a smile and a twinkle in his eye, "I hope you allow me in, I am the guest speaker."

The red-faced doorman apologized and ushered him in. Rabbi Freifeld was a tall, imposing man who exuded pride and confidence. He could feel the stares of the crowd, who rarely saw anyone like him. When he was introduced to speak, he could feel an anxious nervousness in the audience who surely thought that this bearded gentleman could not speak cultured English. They were expecting a flood of heavily accented words in fractured English, befitting a newly arrived foreigner.

To their surprise Rabbi Freifeld began to extol the beauty of Judaism with a powerful, robust eloquence that enraptured the audience. As he spoke of our legacy of Torah and the importance of our Jewish heritage, the attendees soon realized they were in the presence of greatness.

Then he stunned them! "I would like to share with you a story from the theater district in Manhattan," he said with a confident smile. The audience was flabbergasted! This man knew about the theater district in Manhattan? Could such a man be so cosmopolitan? They leaned forward attentively.

Rabbi Freifeld told them about a very wealthy tourist who came to New York from mid-America. He was among the most prominent people in his community and everyone knew that he loved to see Broadway musicals and plays. He assured his friends that while he was in New York he would get tickets to see what was then the most popular musical of all time, *South Pacific*.

"Do you have tickets?" they asked, as everyone knew that the seats had been sold out for months.

"Don't worry," he assured everyone, "I will get tickets, you'll see." He had no doubt that his wallet was big enough to get whatever he wanted.

He was wrong. There were no tickets to be had. He would be in the big city for five days, and with each passing day he became more frustrated. It was bad enough that he could not see the show — but what would he say back home to the neighbors to whom he had boasted?

On the last evening of his trip, he waited outside the theater and as the audience exited he asked people to give him a ticket stub and the playbill (printed program) of the evening. He had no trouble obtaining these useless items.

When he returned home, people asked him if he had seen the musical. Unwilling to lie outright, he showed them the stub and playbill and said, "Here. See for yourself. Here are the stub and the playbill."

Rabbi Freifeld waited for the audience to stop laughing, and then he thundered, "Many of you here in this room are like that gentleman. You have the *stub* of authentic Judaism, but you have not seen the real show!"

He then spoke about the richness of Torah study, the beauty of mitzvos, and the sanctity of the Jewish home. The stage was his, and he performed impeccably.

The audience stood up as one and gave Rabbi Freifeld a standing ovation.

His speech got rave reviews.

⋆§ Driving Home a Point

> In this powerful, pithy episode, a car almost went off the road — but at least the driver was straightened out.

Several years ago, my brother Rabbi Kolman Krohn was in a taxi in Yerushalayim. The driver was not wearing a yarmulke and he seemed angry and bitter. He barely grunted hello to my brother, who was obviously an observant Jew.

There was a stony silence in the taxi as the driver wound through the narrow side streets at breakneck speed. Finally my brother broke the silence and said in Hebrew, "*Anuchnu achim* (we are brothers)."

The incensed driver responded angrily, "*Anachnu lo achim* (we are not brothers). *Atah dati v'ani lo dati* (You are religious and I am not religious)!"

My brother turned to the driver and said softly, "My rebbi taught me that those who are *dati* (religious) and those who are not *dati* are brothers."

The driver looked sideways at my brother and asked disdainfully, "Who was your rebbi?"

My brother replied delicately "Adolph Hitler."

The driver whirled to face my brother as his mouth dropped open. He actually lost control of the car for an instant as it swerved toward a parked car, before he regained control. For a long moment he was quiet. Then he pulled over and stopped the car. He turned to my brother and said, "You are one in a million."

"No," my brother replied, taking the driver's hand. "We are *two* in a million, because *anachnu achim* (we are brothers)."

> Why must we wait for the killers and the anti-Semites of the world to teach us that we, all Jews regardless of religious commitment, are brothers and sisters? Of course we have differences — and great differences at that — but our goal must be to minimize those differences from within ourselves and not wait until we are all treated as despised equals from without.
>
> *Chazal* (*Midrash Tanchuma, Netzavim* 1) teach, שֶׁאֵין יִשְׂרָאֵל נִגְאָלִין עַד שֶׁיִּהְיוּ בַּאֲגוּדָה אֶחָת, *The Jewish people won't be redeemed by Mashiach till we are all one group.* That should be our priority.

✑ Why Me?

The following poignant story is a lesson in *emunah* (faith) in the most difficult times. It is painful to read but important to understand. It was told by Rabbi Yaakov Bender, Rosh

Yeshivah of Yeshiva Darchei Torah in Far Rockaway, at a PTA gathering in his school.

In the summer of 2011, Mrs. Soroh Krigsman and her husband R' Saadia, of Flatbush, realized that her illness was progressing at an inexorable pace. The prognosis was not good. The terrible illness had been diagnosed five and a half years earlier. It had been in remission but had now returned more virulently than before. The Krigsmans discussed whether to tell their children about their mother's serious condition.

They decided to tell their three married children, but to wait until summer camp was over before telling the three younger boys. "Let them have as pleasant a summer season as they can," reasoned Soroh. "There will be time to tell them after camp."

When the boys came home after the summer, they went directly to the hospital to visit their mother. She was weak and pale. Tears welled in the eyes of her youngest, Heshy.* His mother was even more frail than when he had last seen her, two months earlier. He suddenly realized that there was a good chance that his mother would not win her battle. He looked up at her, burst into uncontrollable sobs, and said, "Mommy, why you? Why you?"

Mrs. Krigsman held her son in her arms and waited for him to calm down. She wiped his tears gently, gave him a tissue, and then with the strength of the great women in *Klal Yisrael* said softly to Heshy and the other young children, "When I became engaged at 19 and others in my high school who had graduated long before me were still for looking for their *shidduch,* I did not ask, 'Why me?' When we had children right away and some of my friends who were married longer were struggling to have children, I did not ask, 'Why me?' And when we had *parnassah* (a livelihood), and others on the block were struggling to make ends meet, I did not ask, 'Why me?' And when we had *nachas* from all of you and others did not have what I had, I never asked, 'Why me?'

"You see, children, I have never asked *HaKadosh Baruch Hu,* 'Why me?' for the happy times, and so I don't think it's proper at this time to ask, 'Why me?'"

Heshy and his brothers were saddened but wiser.

A few months later this saintly woman, who fought the illness till her last minute, returned her soul to her Maker.

Her incredible approach to life may give us an insight to a question that puzzled me. When we bless our daughters Friday night we say, "יְשִׂמֵךְ אֱלֹקִים כְּשָׂרָה רִבְקָה רָחֵל וְלֵאָה, *May G-d make you like Sarah, Rivkah, Rachel, and Leah.*" However, every one of the *Imahos* (Matriarchs) had a hard life. Sarah didn't have children for a very long time. Rivkah's husband was blind and Esav was one of her sons. Rachel had no children for years, while her sister and maidservant had them with ease. The Torah even tells us that Leah felt hated by her husband (*Bereishis* 29:31). What kind of blessing are we giving our daughters?

Our *Imahos* never asked, "Why me?" despite their challenges. Their unwavering *emunah* in Hashem remained strong and they stayed loyal to their husbands no matter how difficult their circumstances. They are our role models throughout history.

Perhaps this is the underlying message in the blessing we give our daughters Friday night: "May Hashem make you like Sarah, Rivkah, Rachel, and Leah." Whatever happens in life, be like these great women who never wavered. Life is filled with challenges. Do not let life break you. Build it into an edifice of faith.

܀§ *Perfect Fit*

Every morning in the *Birchas Hashachar* (morning blessings), we recite the blessing, בָּרוּךְ אַתָּה ה' ... שֶׁעָשָׂה לִי כָּל צָרְכִּי, *Blessed are You, Hashem ... Who has provided me my every need.* This is conventionally understood to mean that one is grateful for having shoes. Indeed the *Shulchan*

Aruch (*O.C.* 41:1) writes that originally, before the *berachos* were organized to be said in the order we follow today, one recited this blessing when donning his shoes. Why did *Chazal* understand that this blessing refers specifically to shoes? Why are shoes any different from other needs? What makes shoes the quintessential necessity alluded to in the *berachah*?

R' Mendy Lebovits of Brooklyn recently told me the following story, which sheds light on the issue.

Someone once asked the Rebbe Reb Zishe (1718-1800) (the brother of Reb Elimelech of Lizhensk [1717-1787]) how the Rebbe could recite this *berachah*. "You are so poverty-stricken you don't even own a pair of shoes! And besides, what needs does Hashem provide for you? You own hardly anything!"

Reb Zishe replied with great insight. "Imagine that someone offered you a 100-ruble suit for 30 rubles. You would grab the bargain. But what if it was too large? That would not be a problem, for you would have a tailor make the necessary alterations. What if the suit were a bit small? Again it would not be a problem. You would have a tailor let out the seams.

"But if someone offered you a pair of shoes at a great bargain price, but they were too big or too small, there would be no way that you could wear them comfortably. Shoes, unlike suits or other clothing, can't be adjusted.

"And that," said Reb Zishe, "is how we must understand this blessing. In the material world, shoes must be designed to be a perfect fit. Indeed, that is why the blessing refers to shoes — symbolic of the perfect fit. So too, everything that happens to a person is tailored exactly to his needs at the moment, even if he doesn't understand it. Hashem is the ultimate Designer. He fashions everything we need for our spiritual growth."

~§ Compassion Priorities

Rabbi Eliezer Ginsburg is both the Rav of Agudas Yisrael Zichron Shmuel in Flatbush and the Rosh Kollel in the Mirrer Yeshiva of Brooklyn. When he discusses the following incident, he speaks in tones of reverence and awe as though he can hardly believe what he himself is saying. And truthfully, if one had not witnessed it, it really would be hard to believe.

In the early 1980's a chassidishe *bachur*, Lazer Wolf, became a talmid in the Mirrer Beis Midrash in Brooklyn. He was diligent, always intensely learning with his *chavrusas* (study partners), and hardly wasted a moment. There were 200 young men in the Mirrer Beis Midrash at the time, but very few of them were chassidish, so Lazer stood out.

Rabbi Ginsburg noticed that Lazer would attend yeshivah for many days in a row but then would be missing for a day or two. This was a pattern. Lazer would be out for a day or two, and then resume learning at full throttle. Obviously, learning was his first priority, so Rabbi Ginsburg was curious. He therefore introduced himself to Lazer and asked about his schedule. What Rabbi Ginsburg learned startled him.

Lazer Wolf was battling a life-threatening illness that required chemotherapy treatments. Both the illness and the treatments weakened him, so he had moved in with his uncle, Reb Shimon England, who lived on the block of the Mir, so that he would not have to travel to attend yeshivah. Some days he was too weak to walk even that short distance, and that is why he often missed days. But Lazer made the effort to be in the Mir whenever he could.

Rabbi Ginsburg became friendly with Lazer and gave him much attention and encouragement. When he had to be hospitalized, Rabbi Ginsburg and others visited and tried to cheer him up.

Tragically, the illness grew progressively worse, and Lazer was hospitalized for an extended stay. He was becoming weaker by the day and slowly losing the battle for survival. During one visit,

Rabbi Ginsburg immediately saw how pale and frail he had become. Lazer could hardly speak. Rabbi Ginsburg asked if there was anything he could do for him. The answer was astonishing.

"There is an older *bachur* who sits two rows in front of me in the Beis Midrash. He needs a *shidduch*. Perhaps the Rosh Kollel could get involved and help him find his *basherte* (destined marriage partner)?"

Rabbi Ginsburg was stunned. "You are such a *tzaddik*," he said. "You are in such a perilous *matzav* (situation) yourself and all you think is someone else's problem? Hashem should bless you for your *ahavas Yisrael* (love of a fellow Jew)!"

Lazer forced a smile and said, "Recently the Skulener Rebbe [Rabbi Yisroel Avrohom Portugal] visited me and taught me something. *Chazal* teach אֲפִילוּ חֶרֶב חַדָּה מוּנַחַת עַל צַוָּארוֹ שֶׁל אָדָם אַל יִמְנַע עַצְמוֹ מִן הָרַחֲמִים, *Even if a sharp sword rests on a person's neck, he should not refrain from [praying for] mercy* (*Berachos* 10a). The Rebbe said that *Chazal* are teaching that a person in danger should not pray only for himself, he should pray that Hashem should show mercy to others as well. [A Jew's sincere concern for another can be a merit for himself.] That is why," said Lazer, "I have that older *bachur* in mind."

> Great people understand the words of *Chazal* in myriads of ways. May we only merit learning from them.

◈§ Medical Counsel

Dr. Naftali H. Bursztyn, of the Williamsburg section of Brooklyn, New York, was known for his piety, for his selfless dedication to his patients, and for the awe and reverence he had for *Gedolei Yisrael*. Raised in Vienna, he came to the United States in 1939 and practiced medicine in his quiet, humble manner. He was the sort of doctor who would not take a fee if he knew a patient was needy.

When great *talmidei chachamim* in New York needed medical care, Dr. Bursztyn and Dr. Raphael Moeller, in Washington Heights, were among the first doctors they would consult. As a result, Dr. Bursztyn forged a close friendship with many *gedolim*, among them the Satmar Rav, Rabbi Yoel Teitelbaum (1887-1979), who lived diagonally across the street from the doctor's office. When Rabbi Elchonon Wasserman (1874-1941) came to the United States (see p. 68) and was introduced to Dr. Bursztyn. After a warm conversation, Reb Elchonon said, "You have a very great *zechus*. You are involved in *pikkuach nefashos* (saving lives)."

"It's my *parnassah* (livelihood)," replied Dr. Bursztyn humbly, trying to minimize the magnitude of what he did.

"Let me tell you a story about the Chofetz Chaim," said Reb Elchonon, who had learned in the Chofetz Chaim's *Kollel Kodshim*, from 1907 to 1910 in Radin and remained very close to the Chofetz Chaim for the rest of his life.

The Chofetz Chaim was once in an inn overnight and in the morning, as he left, he said to the innkeeper, "You are fortunate to have so many *zechusim* because of your *hachnasas orchim* (tending to guests)."

"Rebbe," the man said, "it is my *parnassah*, so I have no choice. I have to be *machnis orchim*."

"Yes," said the Chofetz Chaim, "but if you were not paid, you would be able to do the mitzvah only once in a while!"

> We all have to "make *parnassah*." Fortunate is the one whose means of making a living constantly involves Torah, mitzvos, and good deeds. That was Reb Elchonon's message to Dr. Bursztyn, and that was the message Dr. Bursztyn transmitted to his wonderful children, who all benefit their respective communities, from Los Angeles to Lakewood, with their distinguished involvement in Torah, mitzvos, and good deeds.

◆§ Clouds on the Horizon

A number of years ago a dear friend of mine, Chaim Leiman,* lost a significant amount of income when a long-time client took his business elsewhere. Not only was Chaim humiliated by the client's decision, he was in line to suffer even greater financial loss when the news spread that this prestigious client had left him.

Chaim is a family man who was supporting his younger children and in the midst of marrying off his older ones. He could hardly afford this loss of income at this time. The future, especially in the midst of the severe financial recession, seemed bleak. He knew that he had to either find a client of equal stature or start a new business venture that would supplement his income.

For weeks he networked and pitched his business acumen to potential clients. His company had a wonderful reputation, but wherever he went people said they were cutting back on expenses and even laying off people. After much thought and consultation with friends, he finally hit on an idea. He created an original, most desirable product that soon became a household word. (Because of its popularity, were I to mention its name, Chaim's true identity would be revealed and at this point, he and his wife wish to remain anonymous.)

On the first anniversary of Chaim's launch of this business venture, he hosted a *seudas hoda'ah* (a party of thanksgiving), to which I was invited. The evening was festive and the mood joyous; the attendees were happy to be able to celebrate this moment with Chaim and his family. Numerous speakers lauded Chaim's tenacity and *emunah* (faith in Hashem) even in difficult times. And then Chaim rose to speak. What he said was remarkable and memorable.

Over the years Chaim had become close to Rabbi Don Segal, the noted *mashgiach* in Jerusalem. He cited a teaching of Rabbi Segal that had given him strength throughout his ordeal. David HaMelech writes, עֱנוּ לַה׳ בְּתוֹדָה ... הַמְכַסֶּה שָׁמַיִם בְּעָבִים הַמֵּכִין לָאָרֶץ מָטָר הַמַּצְמִיחַ הָרִים חָצִיר, *Call out to Hashem with thanks ... Who covers the heavens with clouds, Who prepares rain for the earth, Who makes mountains sprout with grass (Tehillim 147:7, 8).*

"One can read the verse," said Rabbi Segal, "as meaning that before Hashem produces the benevolent rain, He first covers the heavens with clouds from which the rain pours forth. However, these verses can be understood to apply to crises in everyday life. הַמְכַסֶּה שָׁמַיִם בְּעָבִים — at times it is cloudy. Things seem to be dark in someone's life, business is not going well; there is illness in a family — but that is a preparation for the good that is coming. The clouds symbolize darkness, worry, and hard times, but it is only because of such a challenge that a person is forced to devise a solution or an idea that is beneficial not only to him but also to many others. Thus, the result is, הַמֵּכִין לָאָרֶץ מָטָר, *Who prepares rain for the earth* — He sends the benefits that are the outcome of the times of crisis."

"I would never have come up with this idea," said Chaim, "were I not struggling because of my financial losses. That was the impetus for me to think of an idea that has turned out to be the best thing that ever happened to me and my family. And so I am grateful for the 'clouds,' because they led to the 'rain.' "

> How true this is for so many people. Sometimes a person is disappointed that the house he wished to buy in one neighborhood was simply not affordable, so he had to move elsewhere. And only there did he find the rav who is perfectly suitable for him and his family. In the new neighborhood, his wife found the perfect friend, and he found the perfect school for his children. The sadness at not affording the first house turns out to be a great blessing. The *shidduch* that did not work out, the interview that did not go right, the train that was missed, or, as with Chaim, the client who was lost, create new opportunities that are better than those that came before.
>
> The clouds were temporarily dark, but more than anything they contained blessing.

✥ Far Sighted

The Boyaner Rebbe, Rabbi Mordechai Shlomo Friedman (1891-1971), was a saintly, humble, beloved *tzaddik* who was revered by all who came in contact with him. He lived on the Lower East Side of Manhattan and was a close friend of Rabbi Moshe Feinstein (1895-1986), with whom he served on the Moetzes Gedolei Ha-Torah of Agudas Yisrael. Every year on Erev Rosh Hashanah, Reb Moshe, who also lived on the Lower East Side, would come to the Boyaner Rebbe to get his blessing for the new year.

For the first 25 years after World War I, the Rebbe was the primary link to the Ruzhiner dynasty that had begun with his great-grandfather, Rabbi Yisroel Friedman of Ruzhin (1796-1850). The Boyaner Rebbe had been living in Vienna, but after he visited America in 1925, Boyaner chassidim in New York pleaded with him to move to America. He refused, for he feared for the *chinuch* of his children, but in 1926, at the encouragement of his uncle, Rabbi Yisrael Friedman of Chortkov (1854-1934), the Rebbe consented to move to the East Side, where a Boyaner *beis medrash* had been established at 247 East Broadway.

After his arrival, those who came to him for blessing and counsel were almost exclusively Boyaner chassidim, but soon people from many facets of Jewish life sought his guidance. Everyone felt comfortable in his presence. He never judged someone by the size of his yarmulke or whether or not he had a beard. He tried to build people up and encourage them to grow in their spirituality, no matter what their level was. The simple laborer, the unlearned businessman, and the accomplished Torah scholar all left his presence spiritually and emotionally invigorated.

In a wonderful article, R' Avrohom Birnbaum of the *Yated Ne'eman* cites a remarkable insight from the Rebbe. The Mishnah (*Negaim* 2:3) states, "A *Kohen* who is blind in one eye is not permitted to rule on whether a *nega*, a white spot on the skin, renders the person a *metzora*."

The Boyaner would say, "When a person comes to a Rebbe seeking a blessing or encouragement, the Rebbe may not look at him with only 'one eye,' an eye that only sees the *nega*, the terrible stain embedded in his soul. He must look at him with *two* eyes, the second eye must see the future: it should look ahead and see the person's potential to grow. He must look at the pure root of every Jew, a being who was created by Hashem. Only then, when the Rebbe views him with both eyes, will he be able to purify him from the stains on his *neshamah* and set him on the proper path."

What vision! What insight!

However, I wondered, *if a person is looking with only one eye, why did the Rebbe assume that the person would find fault with another? Couldn't that same eye see the good in the other person?*

Undoubtedly the Rebbe understood that the natural inclination of man is to look for the negative in others. The Torah teaches: כִּי יֵצֶר לֵב הָאָדָם רַע מִנְּעֻרָיו, *The inclination of man is [naturally] bad from his youth* (Bereishis 8:21). Indeed, "one eye" is *not* enough. The Rebbe would quote the Noam Elimelech, Rav Elimelech of Lizhensk, whose famous prayer requests, תֵּן בְּלִבֵּנוּ שֶׁנִּרְאֶה ... מַעֲלַת חֲבֵרֵינוּ וְלֹא חֶסְרוֹנָם, *Place in our hearts the capacity to see the virtues of our friends and not their faults.*

May we all be such visionaries.

◆§ *Life Chapters*

A prominent rabbi from Switzerland received a call from a worried father who asked if the rabbi could see his deeply troubled teenage daughter. After hearing the severity of the girl's anxiety, the rabbi agreed to meet her in his office.

When the girl arrived and began to talk, she burst into uncontrollable tears. Finally, she calmed down and explained her dilemma. Over the past two years, she had been stricken with cancer and, after treatments, was now in remission. "When I was ill," she said,

"I davened so intensely, I felt so connected to Hashem and I treasured that closeness. But now that I am in remission, I don't daven with the same intensity and I no longer feel that closeness. How can I regain that connection? It's not that I want to be sick again, but the intensity of my *tefillah* is no longer there."

The rabbi was taken aback. In all his years in the rabbinate, he never heard such a question. He was impressed by the girl's sincerity and sought to give her direction. He spoke about the relevance of *tefillah* in one's life and the importance of feeling a connection to Hashem. He said, "The *Ribono Shel Olam* presents us with different phases in life. Each is a challenge. Throughout every stage of life, Hashem wants to see how we connect with Him. In times of sorrow it is one way, in times of happiness it is another way. A *kallah* connects to Hashem in a different manner than a new mother does. A newly orphaned girl relates to Hashem differently than does a girl longing for her recovery from illness. The intensity of the *tefillah* and the strength of the connection vary with each chapter. We have to search ourselves for the way to remain connected in the way that is appropriate in that phase."

When I heard his approach, I recalled a thought I once heard from Rabbi Yaakov Hopfer of Baltimore regarding an interesting phenomenon in *tefillah*. At a burial, the mourner recites a version of *Kaddish* that is different from the daily mourners' *Kaddish*. Strangely, this same unique *Kaddish* is also recited at a *siyum* when one completes the study of a tractate. What is the connection between a joyous *siyum* and a heartrending burial?

The answer is that just as a *mesechta* has many chapters, life has many chapters. Some Talmudic chapters are hard and others are comparatively easy. Some are longer, others are shorter. It is the same with life. We go through many stages; some are harder (like finding a *shidduch* or job), others are easier (studying for exams), some are shorter (period of engagement), and others are longer (periods of raising children); the sum total is what our life is all about; it is a combination of many different phases.

As the rabbi told the young woman, Hashem seeks our closeness in good times and in bad. It is what David HaMelech meant when he wrote in *Tehillim*, צָרָה וְיָגוֹן אֶמְצָא. וּבְשֵׁם ה' אֶקְרָא, *Trouble and sorrow I would find, Then I would invoke the Name of Hashem* (*Tehillim* 116:3, 4). However, he also wrote, כּוֹס יְשׁוּעוֹת אֶשָּׂא וּבְשֵׁם ה' אֶקְרָא, *I will raise the cup of salvations, and I will invoke the Name of Hashem* (ibid. v. 13). David HaMelech is telling us to find a way to be close to Hashem through troubles and through gladness.

The rabbi bid the young woman farewell and gave her a blessing for good health. May she and the rest of *Klal Yisrael* learn to achieve closeness to Hashem in good times, and that we need not be tested with bad times.

✍ Moving On

Sometimes a pithy reply to a question can speak volumes. This conversation overheard in an elevator in Yerushalayim says so much. It behooves us to pay attention and take heart. I thank Rebbetzin Dinah Fink of Brooklyn, noted lecturer, teacher, and founder of *Lechu V'nelchah*, for sharing it with me.

In the Belz section of Yerushalayim on Rechov Dover Shalom, the Gestetner* family was having their *mirpeset* (porch) extended outward, thus converting it into a room to add space to their apartment. It soon became obvious that the extension would protrude in such a manner that it would block most of the sunlight that currently shone into the dining room of their neighbors, the Greenblatts.*

People in the apartment building were incredulous because the Greenblatts did not protest or speak to the Gestetners about it. One day, one of the apartment dwellers, Mr. Meister,* met Mr. Greenblatt in the elevator and inquired, "Aren't you upset that your neighbors are going to be blocking your sunlight?"

Mr. Greenblatt smiled and said, "I'm moving."

Taken by surprise Mr. Meister asked, "Where to?"

Mr. Greenblatt smiled and with his index finger quietly pointed heavenward.

With the words, "I'm moving," Mr. Greenblatt said worlds. This world is only temporary. Comforts are fleeting and transitory. It's more important to let others have what they feel are necessities than to insist on our having niceties that we can well manage without.

৯§ *Winter Spring Summer Fall*

Rav Yehoshua Hartman of Golders Green, London, is the author of more than 15 volumes on the *Gur Aryeh*, the Maharal's commentary on *Rashi*, among other *sefarim* he has written on the works of the Maharal. He is a close talmid of Rav Moshe Shapiro in Israel, who is one of today's greatest authorities on the Maharal. Rabbi Hartman's enthusiasm and excitement for *limud HaTorah* is contagious.

On Rosh Chodesh Shevat in 2012, I spoke to the *bachurim* of "The Beis," Rabbi Hartman's Beis Medrash program in the Hasmonean School for Boys in Golders Green. Since Rosh Chodesh Shevat is the Rosh Hashanah for trees (according to Beis Shammai, *Rosh Hashanah* 2a), the topic was about renewal and growth. On the verse, כִּי הָאָדָם עֵץ הַשָּׂדֶה, *Is a man like a tree?* (*Devarim* 20:19), *Sifri* writes that the life of man is indeed like a tree. We have roots and our fruits are our children and good deeds.

The *Bnei Yissas'schar* (*Shevat, Maamar* 1) points out that Shevat is a time for new clarity and understanding of Torah, for it was on Rosh Chodesh Shevat that Moshe Rabbeinu began clarifying the Torah (*Devarim* 1:3,5), as he knew he would soon be taking leave of *Klal Yisrael*.

As Rabbi Hartman drove me home after the assembly, he shared with me a unique insight from his rebbi, Rabbi Moshe Shapiro, encapsulating the difference between a Jew and a gentile's view of life and growth.

Reflections, Sense, and Wisdom

Rav Shapiro said that when the Chasam Sofer (1762-1839) and more recently the Steipler Gaon, Rabbi Yaakov Yisroel Kanievsky (1899-1985), wrote a *chiddush* (an original Torah thought) that they composed in their youth, they used the phrase from *Iyov* 29:4, בִּימֵי חָרְפִּי, *in my youthful days*. However, חָרְפִּי can also be related to חוֹרֶף, winter.

It is noteworthy, says Rabbi Shapiro, that when *talmidei chachamim* refer to their youth, they call it their days of winter, yet when gentiles, especially athletes, refer to their early days, they call it the "spring" of their lives. Because they concentrate on the physical prowess of their youth, they see it as "spring and summer," and when their abilities wane, they deem their lives as "autumn and winter."

With Torah scholars it is different; their wisdom and understanding grow with years of study. Their young years are considered winter, the time that they plant the basis of their Torah learning and sow the seeds of Talmudic study; as they mature, they consider their years to be a productive spring and summer, as they reap the harvest of their knowledge. Spring and summer are their later years of life.

In the past few years we have lost great Torah scholars who were close to a hundred years old and beyond, including Rabbi Yosef Sholom Elyashiv (1910-2012), Rav Yitzchak Dov Koppelman (1905-2011), Rabbi Michel Yehuda Lefkowitz (1913-2011), Rabbi Chaim Pinchus Scheinberg (1910-2012) and Rabbi Chaim Stein (1913-2011). They were revered more than ever in their elderly [summer] years as they became more and more sought after.

Talmidei chachamim are known as the *ziknei hador*, literally, the elders of the generation. However, *Chazal* (*Kiddushin* 32b) teach that the word זָקֵן is an acronym for the words זֶה קָנָה חָכְמָה, *This one has acquired wisdom*. Age is the blossoming of summer, youth is the immaturity and naiveté of winter.

It's a matter of perspective and priorities. Hearing these thoughts in Shevat, a month for vegetational growth, clarified a Torah perspective for spiritual growth.

It's Life of Course

During World War I, the city of Brisk was being bombed and people had to run for their lives. Among those who fled was the great *gaon*, Rabbi Chaim Soloveitchik (1853-1918), who made his way to Poland. He settled in Warsaw, where he later passed away. He is buried in the great Jewish cemetery in Warsaw, next to the Netziv, Rabbi Naftoli Tzvi Yehuda Berlin (1817-1893), his wife's grandfather, with whom he shared the title of Rosh Yeshivah of Volozhin, the mother of all yeshivos. Rav Chaim and the Netziv headed the yeshivah for 18 years, so it was appropriate that they should be buried next to each other, in the same *ohel*.

As I stood by Reb Chaim's *kever* during a trip to Poland, I told the people who gathered there an insight of his that can give people *chizuk*, especially in difficult times. It is recorded in the *Shimusho Shel Torah* (page 201), by Rabbi Asher Bergman, grandson of Rabbi Elazar Menachem Mann Shach (1898-2001).

A wealthy man in Brisk was known for his philanthropy to many causes and for his kindness to the poor. Over a period of time, his business turned sour. Soon he became poverty-stricken. It was hard to believe. How could there have been such as tragic transformation? Didn't he deserve to remain wealthy in the merit of all his beneficence and charity?

Someone asked Reb Chaim why the man had been punished. Reb Chaim's answer was striking and illuminating. "The man was not punished," he said. "He is a wonderful person who did the right things with his money. However, one must look at life using the metaphor of a father who sends his son to a university. The boy takes a course with the objective of gaining knowledge and achieving high marks. At the end of the course — even if he receives the highest marks — he must leave and enroll in the next course. And there he starts anew, gaining knowledge and striving to do well.

Reflections, Sense, and Wisdom

"For many years, Hashem enrolled this generous man in the course of wealth. There were challenges and adversity, but he passed with flying colors. He did the right things with his money; he had the right perspectives and attitudes toward Hashem's decision to make him rich. Afterward, Hashem, his Father, enrolled him into the next course, which is poverty. Now he must work in a new manner to maintain his connection to Hashem. Now he is being tested on how he views others who have more than he does, on how he dispenses charity with whatever money he has. He was not penalized for anything he did; he is just taking the next step."

This lesson is vital in how we view ourselves and others. If one is not wealthy or if one is going through hard times, it is not because he is being punished; it is because he is being tested. Every stage of life is a test. If one is in a difficult situation, the challenge is to achieve "high marks," and soon Hashem will graduate him to the next course. Let him pray that he succeeds and that the next "course" will be easier and more rewarding.

✑§ A Light for Generations

Rav Elazar Menachem Mann Shach (1899-2001) once remarked, "A Jew who is not tied to the past has no hope of being connected to the future." The legacies of our history are guideposts for our future. The Ramban expresses this with the phrase, מַעֲשֵׂה אָבוֹת סִימָן לַבָּנִים, *The happenings of fathers are signposts for children* (see *Sotah* 34a and *Medrash Tanchuma, Lech Lecha* 9).

For this reason, in 2003 I agreed to lead a tour arranged by Mr. Eli Slomovits of E&S tours, to Lithuania and Belarus where yeshivos and *Yiddishkeit* once flourished. Being in cities like Vilna, Ponevehz, Telshe, Kelm, Mir, and Radin, and relating the history of the Torah growth that took place there elevated and inspired me in ways I could not have imagined. (See *Traveling with the Maggid*, published by ArtScroll.)

After that remarkable trip I accepted Eli's invitation to lead subsequent trips, arranged by Eli and Mrs. Miriam Schreiber. Over the last few years these trips included Poland, Frankfurt, Prague, Vienna, Morocco, Gibraltar, Spain, and, most recently, in 2010, Italy.

As I prepared for the trip to Italy, I realized that our day in Rome would be the most poignant and dramatic of our journey. Rome is unique. Most cities wish to foster an image of being contemporary and modern. Not so Rome. As one walks through the historic parts of the city, it becomes obvious that Rome's pride and honor are its ancient temples, arenas, arches, and buildings which are mostly dilapidated and crumbling.

The structure that I felt would be the perfect culmination of our trip was the imposing 51-foot-high Arch of Titus. Built in the year 81 (by Titus's brother) to commemorate Titus's conquest of Jerusalem and the destruction of the Second *Beis HaMikdash*, the arch remains almost intact. It is the oldest surviving example of a Roman arch.

High on its inner wall is a sculpted depiction of broken and defeated Jews being led from Jerusalem, carrying a Menorah from the *Beis HaMikdash*. It is depressing to look at, for it depicts one of the saddest moments in Jewish history, the exile of thousands of captive Jews from Jerusalem to Rome. Aside from the countless thousands who were killed in Jerusalem, many Jews died on the way to Rome, and of those who survived many were beaten during their journey and many were sold as slaves once they reached the ancient city.

Throughout the weeks and months of my preparation, I wondered why Hashem allowed this monument of disgrace to Jews to exist for all these years. So much of ancient Rome is in ruins — why did this arch not crumble as well? Could there be a message here?

The tour went off as scheduled and after visiting Venice, Padua, Verona, Florence, and other cities, we came to Rome to close out the trip. As we gathered alongside the arch, I asked everyone to sing together the heartrending song with the searing words, הַבֵּט מִשָּׁמַיִם וּרְאֵה, כִּי הָיִינוּ לַעַג וָקֶלֶס בַּגּוֹיִם, *Look from Heaven and perceive that we have become an object of scorn and derision among the nations* .... Each of us, with arms around the next fellow's shoulders, swayed to the haunting tune. I then recounted the moving *kinnah*, אֵשׁ תּוּקַד בְּקִרְבִּי, *A fire burns within me ...*, that we recite on Tishah B'Av, contrasting the Jews' triumphant Exodus from Egypt to their tragic exit from Jerusalem after the destruction of the Temple (see ArtScroll *Kinnos, Kinnah* 31).

I told the following story that I heard from my dear friend Rav Menachem Gross, a Rosh Mesivta in the Novominsker Yeshivah in Brooklyn.

About 30 years ago, an American journalist was asked to write a report on Hadrian's Wall, the 73-mile-long wall originally built by the Roman emperor, Hadrian, as a military fortification in the northern part of the Roman Empire. Today much of the wall has disappeared, and long sections of it have been used for road building. Part of the wall stands near Newcastle and the River Tyne in northern England. The journalist soon realized that the great wall was not as revered as it once was, and that tourists chip off bits of its rocks and stones as souvenirs. He began interviewing people and making notes of his impressions. In a conversation with one of his interviewees, the journalist mentioned that he was Jewish.

"If you are Jewish, then why don't you visit the thriving Jewish neighborhood not far from here?" he was asked.

"I didn't know there was one," he replied.

He was directed to the Jewish community in Gateshead, known throughout the Orthodox Jewish world as a major Torah center in Europe. It was a mere two miles from where he had been standing. When he arrived in Gateshead, he was taken to the home of the Rosh Yeshivah, Rabbi (Arye Zev) Leib Gurwicz (1906-1982), the son-in-law of Rabbi Eliyahu Lopian (1876-1970). After speaking with him for a little while, Rav Leib asked the journalist to accompany him to the *beis medrash* of the yeshivah. (Rav Mattisyahu Salomon told me he remembers the day of the journalist's visit to the *beis medrash*.)

As he entered with the Rosh Yeshivah, the journalist was awestruck by what he heard and saw. There were close to 200 fellows in the *beis medrash*. Some were concentrating on various texts, some were arguing, some were deliberating. Hands were waving, fingers were pointing, nearly a hundred animated conversations and debates were all going on simultaneously.

"Just what is going on here?" asked the bewildered journalist.

"I wanted you to see this," said the perceptive Rosh Yeshivah, "so that you would understand something. You came to write about a wall that was built by Hadrian [Hebrew: *Adriyanus*]. It was under his rule that Rabbi Akiva was convicted of teaching Torah publicly and eventually martyred. Yet, today few people know of Hadrian. His descendants do not exist, few of his writings exist, and the Roman Empire itself does not exist. However, these boys in this study hall, and in study halls throughout the world, are still debating the writings and the thoughts of Rabbi Akiva! These young men here and young men like them around the world are all the spiritual descendants of Rabbi Akiva! Hadrian thought that by having Rabbi Akiva killed, he would halt the transmission of Torah. In reality, it is just the opposite. Torah and Rabbi Akiva live in the minds and hearts of Jews everywhere."

I told the tour members how in 1953, the Ponevezher Rav, along with his friend Dr. Moshe Rothschild, founder of the Bnei Brak hospital, came to this spot in Rome. Looking up at the daunting arch, the Rav proclaimed, "Titus, Titus, You thought you would destroy the *Beis HaMikdash* and defeat *Am Yisrael*. That you would take the holy implements to Rome and leave us, *Bnei Yisrael*, with nothing. What remains of you, Titus? Not a single remnant. But we are still here! We were victorious. We can be found everywhere, sitting and learning Torah in every corner. Titus, Titus — we defeated you!"

After relating these incidents, I pointed to the carving within the arch and suggested that perhaps the etching symbolizes for us the difficult journey that we are making through the Diaspora. Rabbi Menachem Nissel, my colleague on the trip, pointed out that the first words that Hashem said to Avrohom Avinu were לֶךְ לְךָ, *Go for yourself* (*Bereishis* 12:1). That long journey has taken thousands of years and its final destination lies at the footsteps of Mashiach. When he arrives we will begin the glorious march home.

Shlomo HaMelech writes, כִּי נֵר מִצְוָה וְתוֹרָה אוֹר, *for a commandment is a lamp and [the study of] the Torah is a light* (*Mishlei* 6:23). The Diaspora journey is moving to its inevitable, glorious end. If we are not to be diverted from its goal, we must maintain standards of Torah study and mitzvah observance symbolized by the Menorah. Perhaps this is why the Arch of Titus is still there: to remind Jews in exile that only by continuing to carry the Menorah and all it stands for will we be able to reach the end of our journey.

Many rulers from many countries have sought to stop us with exile, mass murder, and genocide, but to no avail. The glow and radiance of the Jews' commitment to Torah and mitzvos will enlighten our path until the coming of Mashiach. The Menorah held aloft by the downtrodden Jews of Jerusalem sends us a message of survival for all generations.

Index of Personalities

Note: Included in this index are those historical personalities who played a role (or made a comment about) the stories which appear in this book. Excluded are most fictionalized names, minor characters, and narrators of the commentaries cited in the text. Page numbers indicate the first page of the story in which the person appears.

All titles have been omitted from this index to facilitate finding names.

Ackerman, Moshe   197
Alexander Sender of Zholkov   245
Alter, Avrohom Mordechai (see Imrei Emes)
Applebaum, Shaindy   99
Arama, Isaac ben Moshe   245
Assaf, Ruth   189
Attias, Rus   145
Auerbach, Shlomo Zalman   171
Ausband, Avrohom   159
Baal HaTanya   68
Belzer Rebbe   250
Ben-Attar, Chaim (see Ohr Hachaim)   86
Bender, Basya   197
Bender, Dovid   197
Bender, Yaakov   46, 79, 270
Bengis, Zelig Reuvain   248
Bentley, Caryn   67
Bentley, Lizzy   67
Bentley, Richard   67
Berditchiver Rebbe (R' Levi Yitzchok)   226
Berenbaum, Shmuel   52
Berenbaum, Usher   52
Bergman, Asher   285
Berkowitz, Boruch   265
Berlin, Naftali Tzvi Yehuda (see Netziv)
Bernfeld, Esther   161
Bernfeld, Mayer   161
Bernfeld, Yoel   161
Beyda, Jamie   128

Beyda, Lillian   128
Beyda, Meir (Mickey)   128
Beyda, Raymond   128
Birnbaum, Avrohom   279
Bluszhiver Rebbe   49
Bobrowsky, Moshe   267
Boyaner Rebbe   279
Braun, Sheya   132
Brazil, Shmuel   248
Brezlov, R' Nachman   226
Brodt, Abish   248
Bursztyn, Naftali   275
Byron, Moshe Chaim   105
Carlebach, Binyomin   245
Carlebach, Naftoli   245
Chaimovits, Raizey   187
Chaimovits, Shlomo   187
Chasam Sofer   245, 283
Chazon Ish   226
Chernobyler Rebbe   279
Chiddushei HaRim   248
Chodosh, Moshe Mordechai   79
Chofetz Chaim   68, 176, 275
Cohen, Aaron   220
Cohen, Dovid   248
Cohen, Shlomo   147
Cohen, Yitzchok   147
David, Hillel   265
Diskin, Yehoshua Leib   213
Dvoritz, Yitzchok   248
Eisman, Gedalye   245
Ekstein, Basya   93
Ekstein, Benzion   93

Index of Personalities / 293

Ekstein, Kalman Eliezer   93
Ekstein, Pessel   93
Ekstein, Yosef   93
Elimelech of Lezhensk   99, 272, 279
Eliyashiv, Yosef Shalom   47, 283
Emanuel, Batya   39
Emanuel, Chana (Goldschmidt)   39
Englard, Shimon   274
Esther, wife of Ohr HaChaim   86
Ezrachi, Yitzchok   114
Feinstein, Moshe   46, 49, 75, 124, 211, 279, 230
Feldman, Emanuel   199
Fine, Peter   145
Fink, Dinah   282
Finkel, Nosson Tzvi   114, 245
Finkel, Yitzchok   114
Fischer, Yitzchok Aaron   29
Fishoff, Benny   75
Freifeld, Shlomo   267
Freund, Avrohom   124
Friedland, Meir   173
Friedman, Mordechai Shlomo (see Boyaner Rebbe)
Friedman, Moshe Yechiel   142
Friedman, Yehuda   265
Friedman, Yisroel   279
Fuchs, Yitzchok   187
Geldzahler, Baila   99
Geldzahler, Chana Malka   99
Geldzahler, Eliezer   99
Gelernter, Zalman   149
Gertzulin, Rabbi Shlomo   254
Gibber, Dovid   234
Gifter, Mordechai   187, 224
Ginsburg, Eliezer   64, 274
Ginzberg, Aryeh   171
Glenner, Avrohom Dovid   239
Glenner, Chayale   239
Glenner, Daniel   239
Glenner, Freida   239
Glenner, Sidney   239
Glieberman, Binyomin   132
Glieberman, Eli   132
Glieberman, Estie   132
Glieberman, Label   132
Glieberman, Yossi   132
Goffin, Uri   213
Goldberg, Joseph   213
Goldschmidt, Yehoshua   39
Gottesman, Yocheved   61
Greenwald, Eli   261
Greenwald, Shani   261
Greenwald, Shaye   261
Greenwald, Yosef (see Puppa Rav)
Grodzinsky, Chaim Ozer   75
Gross, Menachem   286
Grunburger, Yehuda   131
Gurwicz, Avrohom   103
Gutman, Yehoshua   114, 163
Gutman, Yehuda   114
Gutman, Yitty   163
Gutterman, Chaim Michoel   179
Hager, Chaim Meir (see Viznitzer Rebbe)
Hakohein, Adam   176
Halperin, Yehoshua Ozer   114
Halpern, Shea Ozer   114
Hartman, Yehoshua   283
Heiman, Shlomo   46
Hersch, Aubrey   168
Hersch, Itzak   29
Heschel, Avrohom Yehoshua (see Kopishnitzer Rebbe)
Hillel, Yaakov   236
Hirschprung, Pinchos   49, 159
Hochberg, Ephraim   147
Hollander, Tzvi   189
Hopfer, Yaakov   280
Horowitz, Avrohom   226
Hutner, Yitzchok   267
Imrei Emes   159, 226
Ischakis, Haim   57
Jacobovitch, Avrohom   226
Jakobovits, Amélie   83
Jakobovits, Immanuel   83
Joseph, Yaakov   195

Kagan, Aryeh Leib   176
Kagan, Yisroel Meir (see Chofetz Chaim)
Kahaneman, Yosef (See Ponevezher Rov)
Kamenetzky, Yaakov   155, 230
Kanievsky, Batsheva   47, 145
Kanievsky, Chaim   47, 131, 201
Kanievsky, Yaakov Yisroel (see Steipler Gaon)
Karelitz, Avrohom Yeshaye (see Chazon Ish)
Kleinman, Shaindy   230
Kleinman, Yisroel   230
Kletzky, Leiby   27
Kletzky, Nachman   27
Kohn, Sarah Rifkah   93
Kopishnitzer Rebbe   49
Koppelman, Yitzchok Dov   283
Kotler, Aharon   49
Kotler, Schneur   49
Kotler, Shragy   49
Kramer, Chananya   128
Kreiswerth, Chaim   262
Krieger, Yisroel Avrohom Abba   213
Krigsman, Saadia   270
Krigsman, Sarah   270
Krohn, Avrohom   248
Krohn, Eliezer   201
Krohn, Genendel   83
Krohn, Hindy   23, 173
Krohn, Kolman   269
Krohn, Miriam   105
Krystal, Binyamin Peretz   147
Krystal, Pinchas   147
Kunstadt, Boruch   245
Kupferstein, Dina   49
Landau, Yechezkel   201
Lasker, Ben Zion Raphael   126
Lasker, Moshe   126
Lax, Malka   142
Lax, Shlomo   142
Leibovits, Mendy   272
Lerner, Ivan   37

Levenstein, Yechezkel   226
Levi, Michoel   108
Levine, Aryeh   47
Levine, Boruch   192
Levinson, Tzvi Hirsch   68
Levovitz, Yeruchem   168
Levy, Chanie   211
Levy, Dov   61
Levy, Moshe Dovid   211
Liebowitz, Boruch Ber   139
Lipschutz, Pinchos   114
Livian, Yehoshua   193
Livian, Aviel Michoel   193
Livian, Rivka   193
Lopian, Chaim Shmuel   139
Lopian, Elya   139, 267
Lorencz, Shlomo   79
Mandel, Manis   54
Mandel, Shlomo   54
Mann, Mitchell   173
Mannies, Moshe   224
Meir Simchah of Dvinsk   213
Meisels, Dov Berish   81
Meltzer, Issur Zalman   139
Mendelowitz, Shraga Feivel   211
Mendelson, David   250
Mendelson, Yaakov   250
Merlis, Martin   234
Mertzbach, Yonah   245
Mezeritcher Maggid (R' Dov Ber)   189
Miller, Avigdor   211
Mitzman, Avrohom   29
Mitzman, Tzirel Liba   29
Mitzman, Yeedis   29
Mitzman, Yisroel   29
Moeller, Raphael   275
Moskovitz, Binyomin   46
Muller, Nosson   176
Munk, Chaya   150
Munk, Eliyahu   83
Netziv   29, 285
Neuberger, Ruth   83
Nissel, Menachem   248, 286
Nitsun, Gidon   75

Index of Personalities / 295

Nitsun, Meir Simchah   75
Nitsun, Peninah   75
Novominsker Rebbe   176
Nussbaum, Chaim   267
Oelbaum, Noach Isaac   195
Ohr HaChaim   86
Ohr Someyach   70
Ottensoser, Esther   245
Ottensoser, Lazer   245
Ottensoser, Yehoshua   245
Ozer, Hyman   173
Palatnik, Lori   216
Palatnik, Yaakov   216
Pam, Avrohom   179
Pam, Sarah   126
Patzonia, wife of Ohr HaChaim   86
Perlow, Yaakov (see Novominsker Rebbe)
Perlstein, Ephraim   132
Pfeiffer, Sholom Dovid, 193
Piaseczno Rebbe   189
Pincus, Heshy   168
Pinter, Avrohom   218
Pirutinsky, Moshe Bunim   226
Plutchok, Moshe   207
Plutchok, Yisroel   207
Pollack, Rifka   211
Ponevezher Rov   197
Portugal, Eliezer Zushia (see Skulener Rebbe)
Pressburger, Yosef Eliezer   41
Puppa Rav   226
Raber, Rachel   41
Reifer, Moshe   23
Reifer, Rochel   23
Reisman, Yisroel   199
Ridvaz   195
Rockove, Esther   142
Rockove, Label   142
Rokeach, Sholom R' (See Belzer Rebbe)
Rosen, Dovid   114
Rosenfeld, Dovid   21
Rosenfeld, Yisroel   21
Rovinsky, Avi   67

Rovinsky, Michoel   67, 71
Rovinsky, Selina   67, 71
Salomon, Mattisyahu   263
Samuels, Jack   216
Sar Sholom (See Belzer Rebbe)
Satmar Rebbe   21, 49, 124, 168, 197, 226, 275
Schapiro, Meir   155
Schapiro, Moshe   283
Scheinberg, Chaim Pinchos   283
Schlesinger, Michel   245
Schneuer Zalman of Liadi   68
Schnirer, Sarah   211
Schonbrun, Chaim   176
Schreiber, Miriam   286
Schreiber, Moshe (see Chasam Sofer)
Schwadron, Sholom   254
Segal, Don   277
Segal, Josh   155
Seif, Yussi   168
Serebrowski, Akiva   155
Sfas Emes   248
Shach, Elazar Menachem Mann   285, 286
Shami, Hayyim   57
Shapira, Kalonymus Kalman (see Piaseczno Rebbe)
Shapiro, Meir   159
Sheinfeld, Chaim   226
Sherer, Shimshon   132
Shklover, Hillel   226
Shkop, Shimon   139
Shmulowitz, Aaron   265
Shteinman, R' Aaron Leib   29
Silverfarb, Chedvah   230
Silverfarb, Yankel   230
Skulener Rebbe   187
Slatus, Avigdor   226
Slomovits, Eli   286
Smilow, Mutty   136
Sofer, Chaim   61
Soloveitchik, Chaim   285
Soloveitchik, Velvel   254
Sonnenfeld, Yosef Chaim   99

Sorotzkin, Boruch   124
Sorotzkin, Chasidah   124
Sorotzkin, Michoel   124
Sorotzkin, Shmuli   124
Sorotzkin, Yisroel   124
Sorotzkin, Zalman   124
Spira, Yisroel (see Bluszhiver Rebbe)
Spitzer, Nachi   49
Sputz, Hirshy   149
Steger, Eliyahu   226
Stein, Chaim   283
Steipler Gaon   47, 226, 283
Stern, Moshe   226
Sternbuch, Moshe   193
Sternhartz, Nosson   226
Stoll, Jacob   245
Sullenberger, Chesley   93
Surasky, Aaron   176
Svei, Elya   192
Tchebiner Rov   193
Teitelelbaum, Yoel (see Satmar Rebbe)
Tenenbaum, Betzalel   52
Toscanini, Arturo   207
Troppe, Shoshanna   149
Twerski, Aaron   250
Twerski, Benzion   250
Twerski, Faige   250
Twerski, Michel   250
Vilensky, Yosef   267
Vilna Gaon   201, 226
Vizhnitzer Rebbe   187, 226
Volbe, R' Shlomo   262

Volozhiner, Chaim   111
Volozhiner, Yitzchok   111
Wachtfogel, Elya Ber   176
Wachtfogel, Nosson   168
Wasserman, Aaron   37
Wasserman, Elchonon   68, 275
Wasserman, Faige   79
Wasserman, Moshe   37
Wasserman, Simcha   79, 245
Weichbrod, Aaron Zisel   75
Weidenfeld, Dov Berish (See Tchebiner Rov)
Weinberger, Brocha   179
Weinberger, Moshe (Brooklyn)   173
Weinberger, Moshe (Cedarhurst)   193
Weinfeld, Chaim   147
Weiser, Tova   136
Weiss, Joe   136
Wikler, Meir   64
Wilovsky, Yaakov Dovid (See Ridvaz)
Wolf, Bruchie   61
Wolf, Goldie   61
Wolf, Lazer   274
Wolf, Lazer Yehuda   61
Yelen, Eli   207
Zholkov, Alexander Sender of   245
Zimmerman, Shmuel   111
Zimmerman, Shraga Zev (Philip)   111
Zolty, Shira   226
Zolty, Yosef   226
Zucker, Dovid   147
Zushe, Rebbe Reb   272

Index of Personalities / 297

Index of Topics

Note: Included in this index are topics from all nine Maggid books. **MS** indicates *The Maggid Speaks*; **AMT** indicates *Around the Maggid's Table*; **FM** indicates *In the Footsteps of the Maggid*; **MJ** indicates *Along the Maggid's Journey*; **EM** indicates *Echoes of the Maggid*; **RM** indicates *Reflections of the Maggid*; **SM** indicates *In the Spirit of the Maggid*, and **SPL** indicates *In the Splendor of the Maggid*.

Achdus **FM** 268
Acid, Hydrofluoric **SPL** 136
Affidavit **EM** 115, 177, 210, 213
Agunah **AMT** 34
　MJ 274
　SM 174
Ahavas Yisrael **MS** 57, 61, 63, 81, 83, 92, 96, 151
　AMT 32, 34, 37, 40, 42, 47, 48, 51, 52, 54, 59, 62, 64, 66, 67, 68, 73, 75, 76, 78, 79, 81, 82, 91, 141, 181, 184
　FM 27, 28, 34, 37, 47, 58, 62, 64, 68, 142, 150
　MJ 78, 79, 84, 92, 100, 102, 106, 107
　SM 27, 33, 44, 60, 61, 67, 72, 143, 162, 166, 214, 248
　SPL 269
Air Force **RM** 29
Airport **SM** 61, 171, 234
Aish Hatorah (Discovery)
　RM 2, 10
Alacrity　see Zerizus
Aliyah **MJ** 133
Alphabet, Hebrew **SPL** 13
Al Tirah **SPL** 23
Alzheimer's **RM** 166
Amen **SM** 157
Angels **MS** 217, 238
　SPL 241
Anger **AMT** 76, 120
　MJ 94, 118
　EM 65
Anniversary **RM** 89
Antiques **SPL** 139
Arab-Israeli Conflict **FM** 27
　RM 202

Arachim **RM** 222
Arch of Titus **SPL** 286
Armed Forces **SM** 56
Army **SPL** 111
Army, Israeli **FM** 121, 189, 261
Army Service **MS** 111, 199, 206
　AMT 106, 192, 237
　FM 107
　EM 143, 235
Asara B'Teves **SPL** 226
Aseres Yemei Teshuvah **MJ** 124
　EM 301
Askan **FM** 123
Atheist **RM** 229
Atonement **FM** 172
Aufruf **AMT** 244
　FM 219
Av **FM** 266
Aveilus **FM** 78, 161, 174
　MJ 75, 98, 241, 263
　SM 17, 41, 185
　SPL 23, 187, 124
Avel **AMT** 32, 90
Baal Korei **EM** 42, 79, 255
Baal Tefillah　see Chazzan
Baalei Teshuvah **MS** 106, 114, 133, 178, 191, 197, 203, 206
　AMT 106, 112, 115, 116,
　FM 72, 82
　MJ 24, 234
　EM 91, 112, 127, 281
　RM 229, 44,
　SM 133, 138, 161, 177, 186, 189, 255
　SPL 67, 179, 199, 220
Badchan **EM** 296
Bais Yaakov **SM** 271

Index of Topics / 301

Bar Mitzvah **MS** 140
  AMJ 82, 90, 122, 162, 254
  FM 78, 100, 201
  EM 165, 244, 266, 268
  RM 19, 185, 241
  SM 45, 78, 87, 109, 152,
  SPL 132, 145, 193, 199
Baseball **EM** 46
Bechinah **FM** 135
  MJ 58
Beis Din **MJ** 256
Beis HaMikdash **MJ** 51, 205
  EM 183, 271, 300
  SPL 286
Berachos **MS** 163
  SM 157
  SPL 261
Bikkur Cholim **AMT** 73
  FM 64
  EM 152 Bikur Cholim
  SPL 46, 128, 145, 163, 274
Bingo **SM 212**
Bircas HaMazon **FM** 145
Birchas HaShachar **SPL** 272
Birkas Kohanim **SM** 83
Bitachon **SPL** 270
Blessing Children **SPL** 201
Blessing From Tzaddik **RM** 64, 86, 100, 117, 120, 143,
  SM 50, 65, 255, 259, 303
Blindness **MJ** 75
Blood Transfusion **FM** 145
Boa Constrctor **SM** 161
Boating accident **SPL** 93
Bris Milah **MS** 190, 259
  AMT 106, 138, 141
  FM 31, 72, 109, 156, 159
  MJ 118, 188, 243, 248
  EM 275
  RM 36, 143, 161, 215
  SM 44, 149, 182, 267, 317
  SPL 21, 29, 71, 179, 226, 265
Burial **FM** 154
  EM 145, 194, 240

  SM 218
Business **MS** 66
  FM 52, 148, 189, 211
  EM 102, 119, 156, 158, 283, 293, 19
  RM 166
Camera **SM** 208
Candle Lighting **MS** 197
  SPL 193
Candlesticks **SM** 189
Car Accident **EM** 152, 249
Cemetery **MJ** 128
  RM 82, 159, 177, 198
Challah **MS** 87
Challah Cover **FM** 168
Chanukah **MS** 145,
  AMT 93
  MJ 251
  EM 135, 299
  RM 207
  SM 162
  SPL 13, 114, 176, 213
Character **FM** 250
Charity see Tzedakah
Chassidus **MJ** 49, 249
Chazzan **AMT** 32, 114, 153
  FM 66, 220
  RM 147
Cheder **FM** 193
Chess **EM** 91
Chessed **MS** 39, 48, 57, 61, 66, 81, 89, 95, 96, 99
  AMT 40, 42, 48, 75, 78, 82, 91, 95, 97, 189, 271
  FM 40
  MJ 34, 72, 78, 87, 200
  RM 92, 94, 177, 271
Chevra Kadisha **MS** 78, 122, 128, 180
  AMT 130, 237
  FM 121, 154
  EM 194
  SM 218
Chevron **RM** 202
Child-bearing **RM** 235, 116, 143, 120
Childbirth **FM** 86

MJ 161, 188, 205, 249
EM 39, 95, 129, 140, 204
SM 50, 299
Childlessness **SPL** 52, 250
Children **MS** 74, 81, 106, 111, 113, 117, 120, 123, 190, 191, 209, 215, 243, 265
   AMT 37, 48, 87, 97, 104, 122, 128, 145
   FM 123, 156
   MJ 27, 40, 110, 174
   EM 39, 43, 46, 57, 135, 165, 194, 231, 266, 278
   SM 69, 311
Chillul Hashem **MS** 48
Chinuch **RM** 219, 234, 237
   SM 30, 69, 257, 300
Choir **SPL** 61
Cholent **SM** 89, 189
Chol Hamoed **MS** 154
Cholov Yisrael **FM** 34
Coast Guard **SM** 105
Coffee **SM** 51, 138
Congress (U.S.) **RM** 219
Consistency **RM** 265
Conversion see Giyur
Chutzpah **MS** 178
Confession see Viduy
Creation **EM** 289
Crossroads **SM** 303
Custom see Minhag
Cycling **EM** 105, 127
Daf Yomi **EM** 240
   SM 51
Dancing **SPL** 189
Danube River **SM** 83
Davening **RM** 55, 175
Dayan **FM** 68, 163, 244, 245
Death **MS** 65, 99, 226
   AMT 34, 118, 120, 145, 237, 258
   FM 54, 58, 118, 140, 161, 173, 174, 258, 264
   MJ 61, 68, 78, 84, 128, 142, 251
   EM 145, 148, 161, 168, 289
   RM 47, 70, 78, 82, 92, 100, 104, 131, 137, 155, 177, 198, 202, 231, 265
   SM 45, 305, 317
   SPL 23, 41, 71, 176
Derech Eretz **SPL** 142
Diabetes **SPL** 41
Diligence in Learning see Hasmadah
Din Torah **MS** 99, 149
   AMT 64, 120, 177, 211, 253
   MJ 82
Disability
   see Handicap and Disability
Divine Providence
   see Hashgachah Pratis
Divorce **RM** 265
   SM 178, 230
Dor Yeshorim **SPL** 93
DP Camp **SM** 89, 114
Dreams **MS** 52, 152
   AMT 118, 120
   EM 268
   SM 154, 230
Drought **FM** 43
Drunkard **MS** 128
Dwarf **SPL** 99
Earthquake **RM** 193
Elderly **SPL** 149, 171, 261, 283
Electrician **FM** 28
Eliyahu HaNavi **MS** 114, 162
Elul **RM** 262
   SM 306
Emunas Chachamim **MS** 187, 194
   MJ 72
Endocronologist **FM** 250
Engagement **SM** 143
Entebbe **FM** 138
Enthusiasm **RM** 255
   SPL 189
Esrog see Lulov and Esrog
Ethiopia **SM** 275
Eulogy **MS** 149
   FM 64, 258
Eyes **RM** 103, 113
Eyesight **SPL** 279
Fasting **MS** 52, 57

Index of Topics / 303

Father/son **SPL** 201
Fire **EM** 171
  SM 226
Flood **RM** 274
Flowers **SM** 69
  SPL 124
Foliage **SPL** 263
Forgiveness **MJ** 82
  EM 51, 70
  SM 33
Free Loan see G'mach
Friendship **RM** 75, 78, 80, 94, 100, 110, 116, 117, 120, 122, 137, 226, 271
Fundraising **MJ** 156, 239
Funeral **FM** 64, 174
  RM 166, 177, 191
Gabbai Tzedakah **MS** 78, 85, 147, 200
Gan Eden **MS** 78, 145, 165, 178, 203, 253, 263
  AMT 118, 120, 273
  FM 159, 226, 264
  MJ 250
  EM 135
Gartel **AMT** 122
  FM 180
Gateshead Yeshiva **SPL** 286
Gematria **SPL** 226
German Jews **FM** 148
  MJ 153
Ghetto **SPL** 21
Gifts **FM** 233
Giyur **FM** 107
  SM 189
G'mach **MS** 36, 85, 99
Gravestone **SPL** 211
Greece **SPL** 57
Grocery Store **SM** 166
Hachnasas Orchim **MS** 25, 89, 95, 164
  AMT 48, 52, 54, 152
  FM 123, 193
  MJ 200

EM 135
RM 207
Hadrian's Wall **SPL** 286
Hakafos **FM** 230
Hakaras Hatov **AMT** 271
  FM 31, 40, 58, 206
  MJ 87, 115
  RM 44, 82
  SM 145, 264
  SPL 142
Hallel **SM** 87, 231
Handicap and Disability
  MJ 79, 87, 174, 205
  EM 57
  SPL 149, 218
Hashavas Aveidah **AMT** 134, 223
  FM 22, 60, 88, 98
  MJ 234, 271
  EM 169
  RM 104
Hashgachah Pratis **MS** 34, 89, 224, 233
  AMT 126, 192, 194, 197, 201, 206, 209, 211, 213, 217, 220, 223, 225, 233, 237
  FM 78, 82, 86, 88, 93, 98, 100
  MJ 49, 174, 177, 183, 188, 193, 200
  EM 51, 95, 91, 100, 102, 105, 110, 112, 115, 119
  RM 185, 196
  SM 56, 74, 105, 123, 138, 203, 208, 212, 218, 221, 226, 228, 234, 238, 241, 244, 246
  SPL 108, 207, 211, 226
Hasmadah **MS** 48, 117, 120, 165, 182, 186, 199
  AMT 171, 248 **SPL** 176, 207
Haste **MJ** 118
Hastoras Panim **SM** 311
Hatzalah **RM** 100
  SM 287
  SPL 41, 234
Haughtiness **MS** 96, 158
  RM 36, 246

SM 302
Havdalah   SM 295
Hearing Impaired   SM 27
Heart Transplant   SM 45
Hijack Victim   FM 138
HILF   SPL 108
Holocaust   MS 106, 114
   AMT 164, 247
   FM 98, 100, 128, 161, 164, 178, 255, 262
   MJ 24, 92, 168, 193, 248, 251, 274
   EM 183, 188, 194, 203, 204, 208, 210, 213, 272
   RM 32, 41, 47, 55, 122, 140, 222
   SM 54, 87, 89, 92, 117, 121, 123, 150, 152, 154, 182, 272, 317
   SPL 21, 75, 81, 83, 108, 142, 245, 265
Home Construction   SPL 282
Honesty   MS 66, 133, 154
   AMT 145, 162, 177, 253
   FM 52, 233, 254
   MJ 124, 150, 165
   EM 140, 152, 161
   RM 149, 166
Hospital   SM 244
Humility   MJ 259
   EM 155
   RM 103
   SM 255, 302
Hungarian Jewry   EM 33, 95, 183
ID Booklet   SM 92
Illness   MS 57, 66, 128, 145, 147, 160, 169, 171, 180, 224
   AMT 66, 276
   FM 54, 58, 62, 118, 226
   MJ 75, 131
   SM 45, 74, 143, 157, 161, 226, 287
   EM 42, 57, 65, 77, 81, 100, 102, 140, 246, 262, 307
   RM 44, 59, 62, 70, 117, 165, 166, 172, 231, 244, 263, 271
   SPL 280
Immigrants   SM 56
Indian Reservations   RM 215

Inheritance   FM 245
Interest   RM 92
Intermarriage   MJ 243
   SPL 47
Israeli Army   SM 41, 214
Italy   SPL 286
Jail, Prison   RM 268
   SPL 68, 187
Japan   EM 213
Jerusalem   FM 126, 254
   MJ 122, 133
   EM 60, 19
   RM 143
Jet fighter   RM 29
Judo   SM 177
Juggling   SM 246
Kabbalah   FM 154
Kaddish   MS 34, 114
   AMT 197
   MJ 75
   EM 213
   RM 47, 198
   SM 55, 83, 171
   SPL 197, 280
Kaf Zechus   MS 36, 39, 99, 209, 226
   AMT 164, 244, 269
   MJ 55, 98
   RM 113
Kashrus   MS 111
   RM 177, 222
   SM 135, 238
   SPL 195
Kedushah   FM 220
Kever Rachel   RM 67
Kibbutz   MS 106
   SM 154
Kibud Av V'aim
   see Parent(s)/ Children
Kiddush   RM 55, 152
   SM 295
Kiddush Cup   RM 152
   SPL 21
Kiddush HaChodesh   MJ 153
Kiddush Hashem   RM 51, 155, 133

Index of Topics / 305

Kiruv **FM** 214
  EM 91, 105, 112, 204, 268, 272, 278
  RM 59, 222, 229, 241
Kittel **FM** 257
Kivrei Tzaddikim **FM** 126
  SPL 49, 52, 79
Klaf **SPL** 241
Knessiah Gedolah **MS** 167
Kohen, Kohanim **FM** 64
  MJ 55
  EM 73
  RM 159
  SM 83, 178
  SPL 147, 201, 279
Kollel **MS** 48, 85
  AMT 75, 95, 171, 179
Korban Pesach **SM** 317
Korean War **SPL** 111
Kosel HaMaaravi **MS** 81
  AMT 105, 201
  FM 90, 116, 254
  EM 131
  SM 145
Kovod HaTorah **MS** 63
  AMT 61, 251
  FM 60, 62, 224, 237
  EM 73
Kovod Hatzibur **FM** 39
Krias HaTorah see Torah Reading
Kristallnacht **RM** 32
  SM 117
Lashon Hara see Shemiras HaLashon
Leadership **SM** 285
Left-handers **SPL** 201
Letter of Recommendation **FM** 43
Letters of approbation **SPL** 139
Leukemia **SPL** 128
Life Saved **MS** 42, 74, 147, 169, 213
  AMT 106, 112, 126, 132, 164, 171, 192, 194, 225, 237, 276
  FM 93
LINKS **SPL** 93
Livelihood **MJ** 269
Longevity **MS** 169, 206

  AMT 258
  EM 244
Lost Items see Hashavas Aveidah
Lottery **MS** 147
Lulav and Esrog **MS** 117
  AMT 37
  FM 118
  MJ 159, 239
  EM 148
  SPL 114, 131
Machtzis Hashekel **MS** 39
Machzor **FM** 257
Maftir Yonah **RM** 275
Maggid **MS** 18, 114, 133, 167, 182, 214, 245,
  AMT 24
  FM 189
  EM 19
Marfan **SPL** 236
Marriage **MS** 36, 92, 96, 106, 122, 161, 180
  AMT 62, 79, 93, 95, 101, 187, 217, 244, 248
  FM 43, 78
  MJ 72, 102, 105, 109
  EM 65, 70, 82, 91, 110, 262, 271, 305
  RM 268
  SM 139, 157, 174, 189
  SPL 105, 124, 171, 261
Mashgiach **MJ** 66
Mashiach **MS** 258
  AMT 122
  FM 268
  MJ 159
  EM 94, 253
  SM 305
Medicine **RM** 44, 62
  SM 287
Megillah **AMT** 223
Memory **EM** 246
Menorah **SPL** 286
Mercaz Harav **SM** 275
Mesiras Nefesh **MS** 42
  FM 128, 164, 262

EM 33, 183
Mezuzah **RM** 171
Mikveh **AMT** 267
  MJ 106
  EM 291, 19
Milah see Bris Milah
Milk and Meat **SM** 238
Minhag **FM** 148, 154
Minyan **MS** 34
  AMT 197
  FM 100, 137, 163
  EM 161
  RM 47, 275
  SM 41, 133, 171
  SPL 46, 218
Mir Yeshiva **EM** 213
Mishnah Berurah **FM** 227
  MJ 165
  SPL 173
Mishkan **RM** 13, 260
Mishnayos **SPL** 187
Mitzvos **MS** 229, 243, 247, 249, 250, 253, 260
  AMT 130, 159, 167, 173, 254, 278
  FM 121, 135, 156, 181, 258, 261
  MJ 262
  EM 42, 43, 49, 60, 77, 145, 148, 150, 183, 208, 254, 283
Modeh Ani **SM** 259
Modesty **RM** 32
Mohel **RM** 143, 161
  SPL 29
Monument **EM** 145
  SM 121
  SPL 211
Mourner see Avel
Music **MJ** 147
  EM 73, 75, 87
  SPL 207, 263
Mussar **AMT** 24, 51, 120, 128, 147, 206, 263
  FM 31, 215, 235
  EM 81
Names **SM** 44, 74, 149, 230, 241, 267

Names (Jewish) **SPL** 211, 213, 216, 226, 230, 248
Nature **MS** 223
Nazis **FM** 40, 93
  EM 33, 62, 119, 177, 188
  RM 32, 41, 47, 55, 140, 222
Necklace **SM** 248
Negel Vassar **FM** 34
Neshamah **MS** 243, 257
  RM 13
Netilas Yadayim **AMT** 81
  FM 34, 128
  SPL 179
Nichum Aveilim **RM** 89, 92, 155
  SPL 27, 41
Olam Habah see Gan Eden
Old Age **RM** 47, 247, 246, 265
Olympics **EM** 105
Omens **MJ** 266
Operation Moses **SM** 275
Orchard **MS** 66
Orchestra **SPL** 207
Orphan **MS** 81
  AMT 40
  FM 28
  MJ 75
  EM 19, 148, 188, 298
  SM 78, 157, 257, 259
Overlooking Evil **FM** 43
Painting **SM** 290
Parchment **SM** 65, 92
Parents see Kibud Av V'aim
Parents / Children **MS** 74, 106, 111, 114, 117, 120, 122, 191, 215, 229, 243, 265,
  AMT 68, 86, 87, 90, 104, 116, 122, 132, 169, 173, 184, 256,
  FM 54, 86, 90, 109, 121, 123, 170, 181, 189, 196, 258
  MJ 24, 27, 40, 59, 61, 75, 92, 116, 153, 231, 274
  EM 43, 46, 67, 77, 135, 145, 161, 167, 168, 210, 231, 275, 278, 303
  RM 62, 235, 237, 234, 247

SM 290, 298
SPL 171, 239
Parenting   SPL 239
Parnassah   SPL 55, 131, 267, 275
Passport   SM 92, 221
Pesach   AMT 68, 106, 233, 244
   FM 257
   MJ 168, 183, 268
   EM 19, 49, 208, 254,
   RM 257, 268, 259
   SM 238
   SPL 83, 121
Photography   SM 281
Physical Therapy   RM 165
Pidyon Sh'vuyim   MS 42, 52
   RM 104
Pike Street Shul   SPL 195
Plane crash   SPL 93
Playbill   SPL 267
Police Force   SM 290
Poverty   MS 81, 92, 96, 253
   AMT 40, 42, 248
   FM 62, 116, 133, 208, 254
   EM 60, 62, 79
   RM 122, 179, 244
   SPL 285
Prayer   see Tefillah
Presidential Election   SM 282
Priest   MS 52, 78
Prison   see Jail, Prison
Prophets   FM 220
Psak Halachah   MS 63
Public Life   see Askan
Purim   MS 140, 162
   AMT 106
   FM 182
   MJ 188
   EM 77, 81, 161
   SM 303
Purimopoulo   SPL 57
Rabbinical Counsel   SM 152, 185, 292
Rabbinical Inauguration   SM 303
Rabbinics   MS 65, 156
   AMT 256

FM 214, 224, 258
EM 51, 148
Railroad Tracks   SM 272
Rebbe-Talmid Relationship   RM 59,
   185, 207, 215, 219, 239
   SM 72
   SPL 103, 114, 155, 159, 163, 173, 192, 263
Refugees   FM 150, 208
   EM 33, 62, 95, 115, 119, 177, 183, 194, 213, 272
Relatives   FM 60
   MJ 260
Repentance   see Teshuvah
Reward (for Mitzvos)   MS 34, 89, 133
   AMT 115, 237
   FM 116, 159
Roman Ruins   SPL 286
Rosh Chodesh   FM 268
Rosh Hashanah   MS 183, 240, 250
   AMT 32, 114
   EM 19, 39
   RM 270
   SPL 224
Royalty   RM 171
Ruach HaKodesh   MJ 161
Salt   RM 259
Sandak   RM 239
Satan   SM 292
School   MJ 75
Scorpions   RM 207
Seat Belts   SM 72
Seder   FM 245
   MJ 183
   RM 257, 268
Sefarim   SM 299, 300
Sefer Torah   AMT 152, 167, 265
   FM 180, 206
   MJ 27
   EM 42, 266
   RM 41, 131
   SM 65, 92, 98, 168, 303

SPL 37
Sefiras HaOmer   AMT 258, 265
Self-esteem   MJ 57
  EM 275
Selichos   RM 247
Seminary   SM 248, 272
Seudah HaMafsekes   MS 42, 228
Seudas Mitzvah   FM 78
September 11   RM 51
Shabbos   MS 87, 106, 152, 171, 182, 197, 206, 215, 259,
  AMT 42, 48, 51, 52, 73, 126, 128, 141, 147, 201, 225, 273
  FM 37, 54, 82, 116, 123, 168, 189, 201
  MJ 113, 133, 137
  EM 43, 65, 87, 91, 105, 135, 143, 171, 299
  RM 62, 55, 172, 185, 193
  SM 17, 89, 189
  SPL 111, 124, 199
Shalom Bayis   FM 168
  MJ 102, 105
Shammes   MJ 129   SPL 37
Sharing Mitzvos   MS 52
Shas   MJ 224
  SM 203
Shatnez   MJ 102
Shavuos   AMT 167
  MJ 231
  EM 110
  RM 131
  SM 57
Shema   FM 58, 128
Shemiras HaLashon   MS 48, 59, 165
  FM 169, 237
  MJ 144
  EM 79, 284
  RM 259
  SPL 230
Sheva Brochos   RM 152, 255
  SM 27, 30
  SPL 114
  SPL 47, 132, 171, 241, 261
Shidduchim   SM 139, 168, 208, 241, 244

Shivah   FM 161
  RM 89, 92, 152, 155, 166
Shtreimel   AMT 244
Shoes   SM 83
  SPL 272
Shochet   MS 151, 152
  AMT 159, 220
  FM 140
Shul   MS 34, 42, 120, 129, 133, 187
  AMT 32, 47, 52, 59, 95, 106, 114, 122, 141, 150, 152, 153, 177, 264, 269
  FM 66, 78, 146, 163, 201
  MJ 27, 156, 193
  EM 131
  SM 51, 98, 117, 174, 203
  SPL 37
Shushan Purim   SM 50
Siberia   MS 175
  FM 93, 150
Siddur   FM 262
  MJ 24
  EM 67
  SPL 161
Simchah   FM 266
  EM 19
Simchas Beis Hashoevah   SM 33
Simchas Torah   FM 230
  MJ 223
  EM 266
Siyum   SPL 173
Siyum HaShas   EM 33, 240, 301
  SPL 61, 155, 159, 254
Siyum Mesechtah   SPL 64, 280
Sleep   MJ 164
Schochet   RM 110
Shofar   RM 270
Shmittah   RM 159
Shul   RM 41, 113, 147, 175, 196, 133, 275
Silversmith   RM 276
Slichos   SM 105
Smichah   SM 275
Soccer   RM 219

Sofer   **FM** 118
  SM 168
  SPL 86, 241
Soldiers   **SM** 214
Speeding Ticket   **RM** 243
Storm   **MS** 74
Study Group   **RM** 276
Succah   **RM** 140
  SM 161
  SPL 179
Succos   **AMT** 13, 37, 101, 162
  FM 72, 118, 121, 135
  EM 148, 155, 293
Summer camp   **MJ** 51
  RM 133
  SM 228
Sunrise   **SM** 105
Swimming   **SM** 296
Synagogue   see Shul
Tabernacle   see Mishkan
Tach and Tat   **EM** 251
Talents   **MS** 262
Tallis   **AMT** 81, 118
  FM 148, 154
  RM 265
Taxi   **SM** 60, 133, 285
Talmud, printing of   **FM** 237
Teacher of Torah   **SPL** 126
Teacher/Student   **MS** 61, 180
  AMT 86, -87, 97, 153, 173, 260, 261, 270
  FM 54, 116, 137, 156, 182, 193, 196, 199, 201, 206, 211, 217, 227, 230, 233, 244, 264
  MJ 40, 43, 58, 66, 107, 110, 115, 116, 125, 142, 161, 227, 238, 255, 265
  EM 67, 70, 75, 87, 150, 165, 255, 267, 271, 277
  RM 67, 80, 94, 215, 231, 235
Techum   **MJ** 133
Tefillah   **MS** 158, 175, 217, 226, 262
  AMT 32, 47, 106, 114, 130, 137, 138, 157, 217, 242, 247, 271
  FM 22, 43, 66, 72, 86, 90, 100, 126, 128, 137, 138, 145, 146, 181, 199, 220, 260, 262, 268
  MJ 94, 125, 260
  EM 19, 87, 131, 255, 286, 301,
  RM 67, 147, 175, 171, 196, 219, 274, 237, 244, 247, 275
  SM 89, 117, 133, 145, 208, 259, 282, 287, 306
  SPL 23, 189, 265, 274, 277
Tefillah Zakah   **MS** 92a
Tefillin   **MS** 140, 160, 259
  AMT 51
  FM 34, 164, 182
  MJ 36, 210
  EM 165, 266
  RM 47
  SM 121, 152,186
  SPL 47, 68, 86, 241
Tehillim   **MS** 66, 74
  AMT 201, 247
  FM 31, 72
  EM 131
  RM 265
  SPL 47
Telshe Dynasty   **RM** 145
Terrorist Attacks   **RM** 51
Teshuvah   **MS** 240, 243, 265
  AMT 206, 247, 267
  FM 37, 140, 182, 235
  MJ 94, 231
  RM 13, 215, 262
  SPL 224
Theater   **SPL** 267
Time   **SM** 305
Tish (Rebbe's)   **FM** 47
Tishah B'Av   **MS** 81
  FM 266
Titanic   **RM** 36
Tochachah   **EM** 79
Torah Crown   **SM** 98
Torah Reading   **FM** 230
  EM 42, 79, 255
  SM 78
  SPL 145, 147, 168

Torah Study   **MS** 103, 199, 217
  AMT 67, 128, 150, 171, 187, 248, 259, 260, 261, 273
  FM 27, 123, 140, 170, 173, 178, 181, 188, 189, 196, 208, 211, 217, 219, 223, 226, 227, 230
  MJ 34, 36, 43, 58, 59, 65, 133, 157, 216, 219, 223, 228, 233, 237, 239, 241, 243
  EM 19, 150, 231, 235, 240, 244, 246, 249, 251, 260,
  RM 51, 59, 94, 145, 165, 179, 219, 234, 241, 253, 276
  SM 17, 55, 114, 168,203, 292, 296
  SPL 64, 75, 155, 159, 176, 195, 263, 283
Toys   **SM** 281
Trade Laws   **RM** 219
Transplant (organ) **FM** 145
Truth   **MJ** 122, 150, 256
Tuition   **SPL** 121
Tzaddik, Influence   **FM** 169
Tzaddik, Service to   **FM** 34
Tzaddik's Blessing   **MS** 57, 171, 194
  FM 86, 90, 118
Tzedakah   **MS** 36, 52, 78, 81, 85, 87, 99, 140, 145, 156, 162, 200
  AMT 40, 42, 75, 78, 82, 91, 97, 132, 153, 164, 170, 179, 181, 189, 211, 251, 265, 275, 276
  FM 22, 28, 40, 47, 66, 132, 133, 142, 173, 255
  MJ 102, 128, 164
  EM 33, 51, 55, 60, 62, 119, 131, 142, 150, 249, 255, 305
  RM 59, 82, 94, 137, 145, 166, 191, 198, 226, 263
  SM 150, 162, 166, 168, 229, 257, 259, 269, 272, 295, 298, 300
  SPL 61, 105, 108, 121, 220
Tznius   **RM** 32
Tzitzis   **AMT** 51, 106, 254
  FM 154
  EM 143

SM 138
SPL 27
Twin Towers   **RM** 51
University   **SPL** 285
Vertigo   **RM** 29
Viduy   **MS** 42, 65, 74, 133
  AMT 225
Violin   **SPL** 263
Volcano   **SM** 161
Warsaw   **SPL** 189
Watch   **SM** 30, 154
Wealth   **SPL** 285
Wedding   **MS** 96, 106, 161
  AMT 62, 82, 132, 137, 164, 184
  FM 22, 47, 193
  MJ 100, 147, 167, 241, 233, 266, 271
  EM 150, 156, 204
  RM 123, 75, 78, 104, 89, 64
  SPL 67, 105, 124, 171, 261
Widow   **MS** 59
  AMT 32, 68, 76
  FM 28
  SM 44, 78, 259
Wine   **SPL** 261
World War I   **SM** 203
World War II   **FM** 93, 150, 206
  MJ 193
  EM 143
  RM 55, 94
  SM 105, 109, 114
  SPL 39, 54, 83, 161
Wurzberg Seminary   **SPL** 245
Yahrzeit   **MS** 34, 87, 120, 198
  FM 163
  RM 47
  SPL 61, 75, 147, 197
Yarmulke   **MS** 111
  FM 237
  SM 89
Yeshivah Curriculum   **MJ** 234, 238
Yeshivah Education   **SM** 212
Yetzer Hara   **MS** 96, 226, 238
  AMT 150, 278
  FM 215

Index of Topics / 311

EM 298
RM 29
Yizkor   **EM** 251
Yom Kippur   **MS** 42, 92, 175, 228, 246
   AMT 153
   FM 37, 257, 264
   MJ 131
   EM 28, 131, 156, 188, 291

RM 246, 275
SM 157
Yom Kippur War   **SPL** 262
Yom Tov   **MJ** 116
Zemiros   **FM** 223
   SPL 230
Zerizus   **AMT** 34
   MJ 253
   RM 159, 161, 255

Index of Sources

Scriptural and Talmudic Index for all nine Maggid books.

Note: **MS** indicates *The Maggid Speaks*; **AMT** indicates *Around the Maggid's Table*; **FM** indicates *In the Footsteps of the Maggid*; **MJ** indicates *Along the Maggid's Journey*; **EM** indicates *Echoes of the Maggid*; **PM** indicates *Perspectives of the Maggid*; **RM** indicates *Reflections of the Maggid*; **SM** indicates *In the Spirit of the Maggid*; and **SPL** indicates *In the Splendor of the Maggid*.

Page numbers reflect the page on which stories begin.

Tanach
Bereishis 1:1   **EM** 140
Bereishis 1:2   **EM** 291
Bereishis 1:4 (Baal Haturim)   **SPL** 226
Bereishis 1:4, 10, 12, 18, 21, 25, 31   **EM** 102
Bereishis 1:5   **PM** 205
Bereishis 1:7   **EM** 102
Bereishis 1:11 (Ramban)   **SPL** 192
Bereishis 1:12   **EM** 102
Bereishis 1:16   **SM** 315
Bereishis 1:28   **PM** 129
Bereishis 2:7   **MS** 265
Bereishis 2:8 (Ramban)   **SPL** 192
Bereishis 2:16-17   **MS** 229
Bereishis 2:18   **PM** 147
Bereishis 2:19 Rabbeinu Bechaya   **FM** 143
Bereishis 2:21   **PM** 147, 241
Bereishis 3:9   **MJ** 269
Bereishis 3:19   **PM** 45, 91
Bereishis 4:6-7, 8   **PM** 61
Bereishis 4:7   **PM** 147
Bereishis 5:1   **SM** 300, 301
Bereishis 5:3-32   **RM** 255
Bereishis 4:4   **PM** 61 (see Kli Yakar)   **MS** 140   **MJ** 102
Bereishis 4:13   **RM** 147
Bereishis 6:16   **EM** 213   **RM** 274 (Rashi)
Bereishis 8:21   **SPL** 279
Bereishis 11:32 (Rashi)   **PM** 177

Bereishis 12:1   **PM** 129   **SPL** 286
Bereishis 12:2   **PM** 119   **SPL** 93
Bereishis 12:5   **SM** 301
Bereishis 14:13   **EM** 284
Bereishis 14:20   **RM** 263
Bereishis 17:9   **RM** 161
Bereishis 17:11   **MS** 260   **RM** 161
Bereishis 17:27   **MJ** 245
Bereishis 18:1-8   **MS** 89
Bereishis 18:12   **PM** 147
Bereishis 18:13 and Rashi   **PM** 147
Bereishis 18:19   **MS** 52
Bereishis 18:21 (Rashi)   **SPL** 236
Bereishis 19:27   **FM** 146   **SM** 175
Bereishis 21:1   **EM** 39
Bereishis 21:19   **PM** 129
Bereishis 22:1 (see Rashi, Ramban, Rabeinu Bechaya)   **SM** 123
Bereishis 22:5   **EM** 168
Bereishis 23:3 Ohr HaChaim   **AMT** 131
Bereishis 24:2 (See Kli Yakar)   **EM** 306   **PM** 91
Bereishis 24:65 (see Haamek Davar)   **PM** 147
Bereishis 26:12   **EM** 19   **RM** 263
Bereishis 27:20   **MJ** 117
Bereishis 27:29   **FM** 237
Bereishis 27:33   **FM** 237
Bereishis 28:15   **MJ** 250
Bereishis 28:22   **RM** 263
Bereishis 29:25   **SPL** 105
Bereishis 29:31   **EM** 272   **SPL** 270

Index of Sources / 315

Bereishis 29:35 **PM** 53
  RM 82 (See Sforno)
Bereishis 30:1 (see Ramban) **PM** 147
Bereishis 30:2 **PM** 147
Bereishis 30:25 **MJ** 115 **RM** 247
Bereishis 32:5 **PM** 45
Bereishis 32:24 **EM** 274
Bereishis 32:28-30 **MS** 238
Bereishis 32:35 (see Kli Yakar)
  SM 292
Bereishis 34:7 **AMT** 58
Bereishis 35:22 **MJ** 119
Bereishis 37:2 **EM** 168
Bereishis 37:3 **RM** 257
Bereishis 37:11 **MJ** 40 **PM** 215
  RM 172
Bereishis 37:24 (Rashi) **EM** 285
Bereishis 37:25 **PM** 81 **RM** 257
Bereishis 37:33 **PM** 99
Bereishis 41:9 **FM** 236
Bereishis 42:1 **MJ** 259 **PM** 99
Bereishis 42:24 **SM** 154
Bereishis 44:17 Rabbeinu Bechaya
  MJ 83
Bereishis 44:18 **AMT** 88
Bereishis 44:30 **RM** 231
Bereishis 44:34 **EM** 135
Bereishis 45:5 **MJ** 83
Bereishis 45:24 **EM** 150 **SM** 114
Bereishis 45:28 **PM** 71 **SM** 182
  SPL 230
Bereishis 46:29 Rashi **MS** 25
Bereishis 48:7 (Rashi) **SPL** 49
Bereishis 49:4 **MJ** 118, 119
Bereishis 49:10 **PM** 53 **EM** 95
Bereishis 50:17 Rabbeinu Bachaya
  MJ 83 **PM** 197
Bereishis 50:20-21 **PM** 197
Bereishis 50:21 **MJ** 83

Shemos 1:15, 17 **EM** 208
Shemos 1:20,21 **SM** 265
Shemos 1:22 **EM** 207

Shemos 2:6
  RM Intro (See Baal HaTurim)
Shemos 2:15 **FM** 32 **MJ** 33
Shemos 2:20 **MJ** 33
Shemos 3:2 **PM** 99
Shemos 3:4 **PM** 119
Shemos 3:7 **PM** 167
Shemos 6:9 **MJ** 47
Shemos 7:2 **RM** Intro (Rashi)
Shemos 8:2 **PM** 61
Shemos 10:22 **FM** 171
Shemos 12:19 **EM** 255
Shemos 12:36 **AMT** 35
Shemos 12:42 **RM** 268
Shemos 13:16 **MJ** 213
Shemos 13:18 (Rashi) **EM** 298
Shemos 13:19 **MS** 260
Shemos 15:2 **AMT** 21
Shemos 15:20 **PM** 259
Shemos 16:1 (Rashi) **EM** 298
Shemos 16:31 **FM** 14
Shemos 17:9 **RM** 80 **SM** 32 (Rashi)
Shemos 18:1 (Rashi) **MS** 221
Shemos 19:2 **RM** 257 (and Rashi)
Shemos 19:12 **EM** 308
Shemos 20:6 **RM** 271 (Ohr HaChaim)
  PM 241 (Ohr HaChaim)
Shemos 20:7 **MS** 211
Shemos 20:13, 14 **PM** 91
Shemos 20:15 **PM** 3
Shemos 22:21 (see Rambam and Rashi)
  PM 167
Shemos 22:24 **SM** 151
Shemos 23:2 **MJ** 65
Shemos 23:7 **PM** 53 **EM** 161
Shemos 25:8 **MJ** 205
Shemos 25:8 Malbim **MJ** 205
  PM 225
Shemos 25:23 **FM** 173
Shemos 25:34 **EM** 259
Shemos 30:7-8 **SPL** 241
Shemos 30:12 **RM** 179 (Baal HaTurim)
Shemos 30:34-36 **SPL** 241
Shemos 31:1, 4 **MS** 201

Shemos 31:13, 17   MS 260
Shemos 31:14   RM 172
   PM (Torah Temimah) 215
Shemos 31:16,17   SM 92
Shemos 32:19   FM 239   SM 154
Shemos 33:22   RM 215
Shemos 34:3   PM 71
Shemos 34:7   FM 43
Shemos 34:9   MJ 72
Shemos 35:3   EM 171
Shemos 39:29   PM 61

Vayikra 1:1   EM 55
Vayikra 2:13   RM 259
Vayikra 3:16   MS 140
Vayikra 5:23   AMT 65
Vayikra 7:19   FM 256
Vayikra 9:1   SPL 13
Vayikra 10:3   PM 31   SM 318
Vayikra 16:30   EM 293   PM 215
Vayikra 18:5   MJ 158   EM 209
Vayikra 19:2   AMT 187
Vayikra 19:11,13   PM 91
Vayikra 19:17   MJ 107
Vayikra 19:18   MS 49   SM 250
   MJ 81   PM 71   RM 275
Vayikra 19:22   RM 246
Vayikra 21:1-3   RM 159
Vayikra 21:14   MJ 55
Vayikra 22:32   SPL 67
Vayikra 23:16   AMT 266
Vayikra 23:27   MJ 131   PM 119
Vayikra 23:43   RM 140
Vayikra 26:17   FM 137
Vayikra 26:37   RM 13
Vayikra 19:17   Ituri Torah   MJ 108

Bamidbar 1:2   RM 110
Bamidbar 1:45   RM 86
Bamidbar 6   RM 235
Bamidbar 6:23
   (Torah Temimah note 130)   SPL 201
Bamidbar 8:2   SM 228
Bamidbar 9:23   RM 260

Bamidbar 13:16   MJ 172
Bamidbar 13:22   SPL 49
Bamidbar 13:33   MJ 57
Bamidbar 15:24   EM 249   SPL 54
Bamidbar 15:39   AMT 256
Bamidbar 15:41   RM 265
Bamidbar 20:12 (Rashi)   SPL 49
Bamidbar 20:15 (Rashi)   SPL 49
Bamidbar 23:9   RM 276
Bamidbar 23:10   MJ 264
Bamidbar 23:23   RM 67 (Rashi)
Bamidbar 23:24   RM 262
Bamidbar 25:12   MJ 105
Bamidbar 26:33   SPL 211
Bamidbar 31:2   FM 32
Bamidbar 31:6   FM 32

Devarim 1:3-5   SPL 283
Devarim 2:3   MJ 259
Devarim 3:25   RM 86
Devarim 4:9   MJ 220
Devarim 4:15   MJ 132 PM 119
Devarim 5:6-18   SM 67
Devarim 6:5   MS 247   PM 71
   SM 293   AMT 153   SM 293
   SPL (Ramban) 68
Devarim 6:7   MJ 67, 99   PM 233
Devarim 7:26   MS 159
Devarim 8:8   FM 169
Devarim 8:10   PM 81
Devarim 8:12   PM 99
Devarim 9:17   SM 154
Devarim 10:2   FM 239
Devarim 10:12 see Daas Zekeinim
   PM 129
Devarim 11:12   SPL 168
Devarim 11:15   SPL 236
Devarim 11:26-28   SM 304
Devarim 11:27 see Daas Zekeinim
   SM 303
Devarim 12:23   SPL 78
Devarim 14:22   EM 258   RM 263
Devarim 15:7   PM 99   RM 137
Devarim 16:11   FM 134

Devarim 16:19   **FM** 235
Devarim 17:11   **EM** 258
Devarim 18:15   **FM** 221
Devarim 20:19 and Sifri   **SPL** 283
Devarim 21:1-9   **MJ** 53
Devarim 22:1-4   **MJ** 122
Devarim 22:1   **FM** 61
Devarim 22:3   **FM** 61   **PM** 225
Devarim 22:10   **FM** 142
Devarim 22:11   **AMT** 173
Devarim 24:14   **PM** 91
Devarim 25:3   **AMT** 266
Devarim 25:18   **MJ** 254
Devarim 27:18   **MS** 152
Devarim 27:26 Ramban   **EM** 184
Devarim 28:10   **SPL** 68
Devarim 28:17   **EM** 79
Devarim 28:19   **EM** 79
Devarim 28:21   **EM** 79
Devarim 28:47   **FM** 37 (Me'am Loez)   **PM** 147
Devarim 28:57-61   **SM** 96
Devarim 29:6   **EM** 292
Devarim 29:9   **SM** 97
Devarim 29:28   **MJ** 60
Devarim 30:2   **PM** 215
Devarim: 31:9   **RM** 131
Devarim 31:21   **EM** 267
Devarim 32:2 Torah Temimah   **FM** 266
Devarim: 32:7   **RM** 222
Devarim 32:15   **PM** 81
Devarim 34:5   **FM** 261
Devarim 34:6   **RM** 159
Devarim 34:12   **SM** 153, 170

Yehoshua 1:1 Radak   **FM** 259

Shoftim 3:20   **FM** 159
Shoftim 4:17   **MJ** 33
Shoftim 4:21   **MJ** 33
Shoftim 5:8   **EM** 235
Shoftim: 13:8   **RM** 235
Shoftim: 13:13   **RM** 235
Shoftim: 13:14   **RM** 235

Shmuel I 1:1   **EM** 39
Shmuel I 2:2   **EM** 39
Shmuel I 9:1,2   **SPL** 193
Shmuel I 16:7   **MJ** 100

Shmuel II 19:1, 5   **PM** 241

Melachim I 18:36   **RM** 196

Melachim II 23:25   **EM** 184

Yeshayahu 2:3   **PM** 225
Yeshayahu 8:10   **SPL** 23
Yeshayahu 8:17   **EM** 267
Yeshayahu 25:8   **MJ** 107
Yeshayahu 27:13   **PM** 205
Yeshayahu 29:13   **AMT** 137
Yeshayahu: 30:20   **RM** 67
Yeshayahu 38:16   **SM** 189
Yeshayahu: 40:31   **RM** 271
Yeshayahu 41:6   **EM** 208
Yeshayahu 43:22   **MS** 249
Yeshayahu 46:4   **SPL** 23
Yeshayahu 49:3   **AMT** 28
Yeshayahu 55:6   **MS** 242   **EM** 302
Yeshayahu 58:7   **FM** 61
Yeshayahu 61:10   **SM** 248
Yeshayahu 62:5   **SM** 248

Yirmiyahu 2:13   **MS** 250
Yirmiyahu 9:8   **EM** 161
Yirmiyahu 12:11   **MS** 250
Yirmiyahu 17:13   **AMT** 267
Yirmiyahu 23:29   **MJ** 48
Yirmiyahu 24:6   **RM** 86
Yirmiyahu 31:15   **RM** 67
Yirmiyahu 31:21   **PM** 147
Yirmiyahu 32   **MS** 185

Yechezkel 1:3   **AMT** 252
Yechezkel 11:9   **MJ** 63
Yechezkel 16:6   **AMT** 107   **SM** 317
Yechezkel 36:25   **AMT** 267

Hoshea 10:12   **EM** 62

Amos 2:6   **SM** 85

Ovadiah: 1:18   **PM** 251   **RM** 247
SM 295

Yonah 1:8,9   **EM** 283
Yonah 8:9   **PM** 45

Michah 6:9   **SPL** 248

Habakkuk 2:4   **EM** 165

Tzephaniah 3:6,7   **SM** 310

Chaggai 2:8   **EM** 304

Malachi 2:6   **EM** 19
Malachi 3:3   **RM** 276
Malachi 3:7   **PM** 233
Malachi 3:24   **AMT** 124   **SPL** 179

Tehillim 6:3   **FM** 77
Tehillim 8:5   **RM** 104
Tehillim 12   **FM** 77
Tehillim 15:22   **MS** 66
Tehillim 17:8   **RM** 103
Tehillim 19:8   **MJ** 258   **SM** 116
   SPL 78
Tehillim 19:9   **SM** 296
Tehillim 19:11   **MJ** 94, 228
Tehillim 19:15   **PM** 1
Tehillim 20:2   **AMT** 110
Tehillim 20:8   **RM** 70
Tehillim 20:9   **RM** 70
Tehillim 24:3, 4   **EM** 127
Tehillim 24:4   **MS** 258
Tehillim 27:4   **EM** 295
Tehillim 27:5   **MJ** 198   **RM** 140
Tehillim 27:14   **SM** 307
Tehillim 30:6   **RM** 244
Tehillim 30:7   **AMT** 206

Tehillim 34:13-14   **MJ** 165   **EM** 140
Tehillim 34:15   **MS** 242   **EM** 102
Tehillim 36:8-11   **RM** 265
Tehillim 37:11   **EM** 19
Tehillim 37:23   **MS** 224   **RM** 100
Tehillim 41:2   **AMT** 73
Tehillim 43:1   **SPL** 47
Tehillim 49:17   **FM** 58
Tehillim 49:18   **FM** 58
Tehillim 50:23   **EM** 257
Tehillim 51:14   **MJ** 162
Tehillim 51:17   **SM** 283   **SPL** 13
Tehillim 51:19   **EM** 155
Tehillim 55:15   **MJ** 156
Tehillim 55:23   **AMT** 218
Tehillim 61:7 (and Radak)   **EM** 253
Tehillim 68:7   56
Tehillim 69:13   **AMT** 265
Tehillim 81:2   **RM** 207
Tehillim 84:5   **RM** 244
Tehillim 86:2   **SPL** 248
Tehillim 90:10   **SM** 17
Tehillim 90:12   **PM** 71
Tehillim 91   **MJ** 165
Tehillim 92:6   **FM** 82
Tehillim 92:6-7   **MS** 233
Tehillim 92:7   **AMT** 194
Tehillim 93:4   **EM** 87
Tehillim 94:1-2   **MS** 237
Tehillim 97:11   **SM** 232
Tehillim 100   **MS** 77
Tehillim 100:2   **FM** 266
Tehillim 102:1   **AMT** 25
Tehillim 104:24   **AMT** 233
Tehillim 111:5   **PM** 99
Tehillim 112:4   **SPL** 248
Tehillim 112:5, 6   **EM** 142
Tehillim 116:3   **SPL** 280
Tehillim 116:3,4   **PM** 129   **SM** 148
Tehillim 116:8   **SM** 87
Tehillim 116:13   **PM** 129
   SM 148   **SPL** 280
Tehillim 116:16   **FM** 260   **EM** 119
   RM 19

Index of Sources / 319

Tehillim 118:1   **SM** 48, 233
Tehillim 118:5   **SM** 234
Tehillim 118:17   **EM** 100   **RM** 255
Tehillim 118:19   **SPL** 15
Tehillim 118:25   **FM** 260   **EM** 182
Tehillim 119:54   **SPL** 248
Tehillim 119:60   **PM** 21
Tehillim 119:64   **SM** 13
Tehillim 119:162   **SM** 296
Tehillim 119:176   **MJ** 232
Tehillim 121:1   **PM** 139 (see Midrash)
   PM 205
Tehillim 121:1-2   **AMT** 206
Tehillim 121:5   **PM** 53
Tehillim 121:7   **MJ** 208
Tehillim 121:15   **EM** 304
Tehillim 126:5   **FM** 148
Tehillim 128:5   **SPL** 99
Tehillim 137:1   **PM** 251
Tehillim 137:1,4,5,7   **SM** 85
Tehillim 142   **PM** 233
Tehillim 144:7   **SM** 295   **PM** 251
Tehillim 144:15   **RM** 244
Tehillim 145:9   **RM** 207
Tehillim 145:16   **RM** 244
   SPL 55
Tehillim 145:16,17   **SM** 316
Tehillim 145:18   **EM** 162
Tehillim 145:19   **PM** 251
Tehillim 146:3   **SM** 314
Tehillim 146:8   **RM** 149
Tehillim 146:9   **RM** 149
Tehillim 147:3,4   **SM** 315
Tehillim 147:7-8   **SPL** 277
Tehillim 149:6   **SPL** 265
Tehillim 150:6   **PM** 53   **RM** 82

Mishlei: 1:5   **RM** 110
Mishlei: 1:8   **RM** 32
Mishlei: 1:9   **RM** 253
Mishlei 3:2   **MJ** 208
Mishlei 3:9   **SM** 247
Mishlei 3:15   **EM** 235   **SM** 110
Mishlei: 3:17   **RM** 89   **SPL** 103

Mishlei 3:18   **SM** 311
   SPL 263
Mishlei 3:25   **SPL** 23
Mishlei 4:25   **MS** 155
Mishlei 6:23   **SPL** 195, 286
Mishlei 10:2   **MS** 164   **MJ** 92
   SM 230
Mishlei 10:8   **AMT** 35
Mishlei 11:4   **MJ** 164   **SM** 231
Mishlei 12:18   **AMT** 276
Mishlei 14:1   **SPL** 161
Mishlei 15:1   **AMT** 78   **MJ** 98
   PM 61   **RM** 117
Mishlei 15:27   **AMT** 136
Mishlei 16:5   **MS** 159
Mishlei 18:23   **SM** 269
Mishlei 19:21   **AMT** 220   **SM** 304
Mishlei 20:24   **EM** 51   **PM** 197
Mishlei 20:27   **SM** 267   **SM** 91
Mishlei 21:21   **AMT** 96
Mishlei 22:6   **FM** 196   **EM** 270
Mishlei 22:9   **EM** 246
Mishlei 27:2   **FM** 253
Mishlei 27:21   **EM** 19
Mishlei 28:14   **FM** 226
Mishlei 30:10   **SM** 208
Mishlei 31:10-31   **AMT** 274
Mishlei 31:20   **MJ** 128
Mishlei 31:29   **SPL** 15

Iyov 5:7   **AMT** 260
Iyov 22:28   **AMT** 209
Iyov 23:13   **SM** 157
Iyov 29:4   **SPL** 283
Iyov 29:34   **EM** 19
Iyov 31:32   **AMT** 54
Iyov 38:4   **EM** 291
Iyov 41:3   **AMT** 144   **PM** 241
Ivov 42:10   **PM** 119

Daniel 2:21   **AMT** 253   **RM** 116
Daniel 10:7   **SPL** 224
Daniel 12:3   **MJ** 43

Ezra 10:44 **MJ** 245

Shir HaShirim 1:4 **SM** 296
Shir HaShirim 3:10 **MJ** 66
Shir HaShirim 5:1-7 **MS** 266
Shir HaShirim 7:11 **EM** 260

Eichah 1:3 **EM** 255
Eichah 1:12 **EM** 300
Eichah 3:31, 32 **MJ** 171 **PM** 225
Eichah 5:21 **PM** 233

Koheles 1:2 **MS** 250
Koheles 3:1 **FM** 82 **SPL** 263
Koheles 3:1,4 **SM** 282 **SM** 282
Koheles 4:12 **FM** 13
Koheles 7:2 **FM** 175
Koheles 7:29 **MS** 230
Koheles 9:8 **RM** 259
Koheles 10:19 **EM** 305
Koheles 11:1 **FM** 31 **MJ** 92
Koheles 12:13 **MS** 250

Esther 1:6 **RM** 257
Esther 1:7 **MJ** 254
Esther 2:10 **PM** 259
Esther 2:12 **SPL** 201
Esther 2:15 **SPL** 201
Esther 3:9 **MS** 162
Esther 4:5 **MJ** 254
Esther 4:11 **PM** 259
Esther 4:14 **PM** 259
Esther 4:16 **PM** 259
Esther 5:3 **PM** 259
Esther 6:1 **SPL** 57
Esther 7:8 **FM** 128
Esther 8:16 **MJ** 255
Esther 9:25 **MJ** 125 **PM** 259
  SM 313
Esther 9:27 **SPL** 57

Divrei Hayamim I 8:33 **SPL** 193

Medrashim
Bereishis Rabbah 2:4 **RM** 234
  PM 251
Bereishis Rabbah 4:6 **EM** 102
Bereishes Rabbah 14:9 **PM** 53
  RM 82 **SPL** 15
Bereishes Rabbah 17:5 **PM** 241
Bereishes Rabbah 17:6 **PM** 147
Bereishis Rabbah 20:1 **EM** 285
Bereishis Rabbah 20:12 **EM** 296
Bereishis Rabbah 21:14 **PM** 129
Bereishis Rabbah 22:13 **PM** 215
Bereishis Rabbah 42:8 **EM** 284
  PM 45 **RM** 36
Bereishes Rabbah 44:7 **RM** 36
Bereishis Rabba 48:8 **SPL** 29
Bereishis Rabbah 67:3 **FM** 237
Bereishis Rabbah 68:4 **FM** 79
Bereishis Rabbah 71:7 **PM** 147
Bereishis Rabbah 94:3 **PM** 71
  SM 182

Tanchuma Bereishis 9 **MJ** 102
  PM 61

Tanchuma Lech Lecha 8 **FM** 258
Tanchumah Lech Lecha 9 **SPL** 286

Tanchuma Toldos 5 **MJ** 259

Shemos Rabbah 1:27 **PM** 119
Shemos Rabbah 4:2 **MJ** 33
Shemos Rabbah 14:3 **FM** 171
Shemos Rabbah, 15:12, 17:3, 19:5
  SM 317
Shemos Rabbah 21:6 **MS** 224
Shemos Rabbah 35:6 **AMT** 176

Tanchuma Ki Sisa 31 **PM** 71

Vayikra Rabbah 2:8 **AMT** 252
Vayikra Rabbah 9:3 **MJ** 115
Vayikra Rabbah 9:9 **SM** 163
Vayikra Rabbah 11:8 **PM** 31 **RM** 75

Vayikra Rabbah 15:9 **RM** 234
Vayikra Rabbah 27:2 **PM** 241
Vayikra Rabbah 30:14 **FM** 120
Vayikra Rabbah 32:2 **EM** 87

Tanchuma Tazriah 11 **RM** 234

Bamidbar Rabbah 3:6 **SPL** 161
Bamidbar Rabbah 14:2 **PM** 241
Bamidbar Rabbah 21:2 **PM** 147
Bamidbar Rabbah 22:8 **FM** 173
Bamidbar Rabbah 142 **AMT** 14:2

Tanchuma Bamdibar 22:8 **PM** 99

Tanchuma Matos Chapter 3 **FM** 32

Devarim Rabbah 2:31 **MJ** 40

Tanchuma Nitzavim 1 **PM** 157

Tanchuma Ha'Azinu 7 **SM** 267
  SPL 211

Tanchumah Eikev 6 **SPL** 168

Koheles Rabbah 1:7:5 **AMT** 253
  RM 116
Koheles Rabbah 1:13 **PM** 91

Esther Rabbah 2:11 **MJ** 254
Esther Rabbah 8:5 **MJ** 254
Esther Rabbah 10:11 **MJ** 259

Shir Ha'Shirim Rabbah 1:1:4:3
  SM 296
Shir Hashirim Rabbah 4:2 **EM** 129
Shir Hashirim Rabbah 5:2:2 **RM** 268

Yalkut Shimoni-Bo 187:11 **RM** 207
Yalkut Shimoni Mishlei 31 **FM** 57

Ruth Rabbah 2:9 **FM** 159

Eichah Rabbah 1:28 **EM** 255

Medrash Eileh Ezkarah **MJ** 83

Zohar, Tzav 31b **SM** 233

Mishnah and Talmud
Berachos 3b **AMT** 157
Berachos 4b **SM** 316
Berachos 5a **MJ** 163 **SM** 306
Berachos 5b **FM** 161
Berachos 6b **FM** 146, 163
  RM 196 **SM** 175
Berachos 6b Rabbeinu Yonah and
  Shiltei HaGiborim **FM** 147
Berachos 7b **FM** 16,34
  EM 150 **RM** 67 **SM** 267
Berachos 8b **MS** 228
Berachos 8b Rashi **EM** 87
Berachos 9b **AMT** 47
Berachos 10a **AMT** 214 **SPL** 274
Berachos 10a Rashi **EM** 39
Berachos 12a **MJ** 61
Berachos 13b **EM** 295 **PM** 45
Berachos 16b **MJ** 262
Berachos 17a **MJ** 253 **RM** 110
  SPL 142
Berachos 26a **FM** 128
Berachos 28b **AMT** 90, 130
Berachos 29b **SPL** 111
Berachos 30a **RM** 171
Berachos 30b **MJ** 35
Berachos 32a **EM** 296
Berachos 33a **RM** 13
Berachos 35b **PM** 91
Berachos 47b **RM** 175
Berachos 54a **FM** 97 **MJ** 61
Berachos 55a **MS** 153 **FM** 173
  RM 116
Berachos 60a **FM** 226
Berachos 60b **RM** 185
Berachos, Meiri (Intro.) **SM** 309

Yerushalmi Berachos 5:2 **SM** 295

Yerushalmi Peah 1:1 **AMT** 277

Tosefta Peah 3:13   **AMT** 134

Yerushalmi Sheviis 3:7   **SPL** 193

Bikkurim 3:3   **EM** 150

Shabbos 10a   **MS** 76
Shabbos 21b   **FM** 116
Shabbos 22a   **EM** 285
Shabbos 23b   **AMT** 94   **RM** 145
Shabbos 31a   **AMT** 171   **EM** 298
   FM 170   **PM** 91, 107
Shabbos 31b   **RM** 260
Shabbos 32a   **AMT** 222   **EM** 227
   RM 104   **RM** 177   **SM** 97
Shabbos 35b Rashi **PM** 251
Shabbos 49a Tosafos   **MS** 160
Shabbos 49b   **RM** 260
Shabbos 67a   **EM** 265
Shabbos 87a   **SM** 67
Shabbos 89b see Rashi   **SM** 67
Shabbos 92b   **AMT** 227
Shabbos 104a   **FM** 90   **RM** 268
   SPL 13
Shabbos 118b   **PM** 205
Shabbos 119a   **AMT** 43
Shabbos 127a   **AMT** 227
Shabbos 130a   **FM** 164
   RM 161   **SPL** 71
Shabbos 133b   **MJ** 107   **SPL** 171
Shabbos 146a   **FM** 111
Shabbos 151b   **PM** 99
Shabbos 153a   **SPL** 41
Shabbos 153b   **AMT** 227
Shabbos 156b   **FM** 243

Eruvin 13b   **RM** 67
Eruvin 21b   **FM** 131
Eruvin 22a   **MS** 264
Eruvin 34a   **MJ** 218
Eruvin 41b   **MJ** 140
Eruvin 54a   **PM** 233   **SPL** 78
Eruvin 55a   **FM** 232
Eruvin 65a   **MS** 166

Eruvin 65b   **AMT** 82   **MJ** 200

Pesachim 49a   **SPL** 261
Pesachim 50b   **EM** 260
Pesachim 65b   **RM** 257
Pesachim 88b   **FM** 259
Pesachim 116b   **MJ** 269
Pesachim 118b   **AMT** 271
Pesachim 119b   **PM** 129   **SM** 147

Yoma 4b   **EM** 55
Yoma 9b   **FM** 52   **EM** 272
Yoma 23a   **AMT** 263
Yoma 37a   **RM** 239
Yoma 38b   **SM** 133
Yoma 44a   **EM** 285
Yoma 52a   **EM** 259
Yoma 69b   **EM** 87
Yoma 74b   **EM** 180
Yoma 75a   **FM** 14
Yoma 85b   **MS** 139
Yoma 86a   **EM** 158   **RM** 51

Succah 11b   **FM** 60
Succah 41a   **FM** 171
Succah 56b   **EM** 234

Beitzah 15b   **AMT** 213

Rosh Hashanah 16a   **MS** 184   **PM** 99
Rosh Hashanah 17a   **EM** 70, 287
Rosh Hashanah 17b   **FM** 43
Rosh Hashanah 18a   **EM** 302

Taanis 7a   **AMT** 270   **SM** 297
Taanis 8a   **SPL** 218
Taanis 8b   **PM** 107
Taanis 8b-9a   **RM** 263
Taanis 9a   **FM** 133   **EM** 258
Taanis 10b   **EM** 150
Taanis 21a   **AMT** 238
Taanis 23a   **FM** 271
Taanis 25b   **FM** 43   **EM** 287
   PM 187   **SPL** 105

Index of Sources / 323

Taanis 26b   **FM** 267
Taanis 29a   **FM** 267
Taanis 31a   **MJ** 225

Megillah 3a   **RM** 51   **SPL** 220
Megillah 6b   **FM** 213
Megillah 13b   **FM** 69
Megillah 14a   **MS** 186
Megillah 16b   **MJ** 255
Megillah 17b   **AMT** 130
Megillah 24b   **EM** 296
Megillah 24b Rashi   **EM** 293
Megillah 27b-28a   **RM** 265
Megillah 28a   **PM** 99

Moed Katan 5a   **EM** 257
Moed Katan 8b   **SPL** 132
Moed Katan 9a   **MJ** 116
Moed Katan 27b   **RM** 259

Chagigah 9b   **MJ** 221
Chagigah 12a   **EM** 291
Chagigah 15b   **SPL** 192

Yevamos 62b   **FM** 62   **MJ** 144   **SM** 77
Yevamos 62b, Maharal Chiddushei Aggados   **MJ** 144   **RM** 110
Yevamos 63a   **EM** 162   **RM** 13   **SM** 162, 310
Yevamos 69a   **EM** 60
Yevamos 79a   **AMT** 73
Yevamos 87b   **SM** 231
Yevamos 89a   **SPL** 64
Yevamos 97a   **EM** 260
Yevamos 121b   **MS** 114   **AMT** 86

Kesubos 8b   **MJ** 251   **PM** 45
Kesubos 17a   **RM** 88
Kesubos 21a   **RM** 165
Kesubos 30a   **MS** 175
Kesubos 50a   **MJ** 129
Kesubos 67a   **AMT** 86
Kesubos 77b   **FM** 237
Kesubos 105a   **EM** 19
Kesubos 105b   **FM** 91, 235
Kesubos 107b   **MS** 68

Nedarim 39b   **FM** 66
Nedarim 49b (Meiri)   **PM** 107
Nedarim 64b   **MS** 243
Nedarim 81a   **EM** 43

Sotah 2a   **MS** 39   **RM** 268   **SM** 140
Sotah 7b   **MS** 75
Sotah 8b   **EM** 305   **PM** 241
Sotah 10b   **AMT** 62
Sotah 11b   **SPL** 161
Sotah 12a   **EM** 207
Sotah 13a   **AMT** 34
Sotah 14a   **RM** 159   **RM** 198
Sotah 17a   **MJ** 104
Sotah 21a   **FM** 27
Sotah 34a   **SPL** 286
Sotah 38b   **EM** 246
Sotah 47a   **AMT** 51   **EM** 75   **RM** 239
Sotah 49b   **PM** 139

Yerushalmi Sotah 7:4   **EM** 183

Gittin 7a   **FM** 132   **PM** 107
Gittin 14b   **AMT** 131
Gittin 52a   **RM** 172
Gittin 55b   **FM** 226
Gittin 56a   **AMT** 115
Gittin 62a   **FM** 243
Gittin 90b   **PM** 167

Mishnah Kiddushin 1:9   **RM** 265

Kiddushin 2a   **MS** 180
Kiddushin 2b   **MJ** 273   **SPL** 241
Kiddushin 26a   **MJ** 67
Kiddushin 30b   **MJ** 65   **PM** 167
Kiddushin 31a   **RM** 246
Kiddushin 32b   **RM** 75   **SPL** 283
Kiddushin 33a   **FM** 224   **EM** 150

Kiddushin 38a   **FM** 266
Kiddushin 39b   **RM** 243
Kiddushin 82a   **PM** 91
 (Maharsha)   **PM** 107
Kiddushin 82b (Maharsha)   **PM** 107

Yerushalmi Kiddushin 4:12   **PM** 81

Bava Kamma 17a   **AMT** 270
Bava Kamma 35a   **RM** 166
Bava Kamma 92a   **FM** 99
 PM 107, 119
Bava Kamma 92b   **FM** 32   **PM** 259

Mishnah Bava Metzia 2:11   **FM** 199

Bava Metzia 21b   **EM** 235, 237
Bava Metzia 24a   **MJ** 237   **PM** 225
Bava Metzia 29b   **MS** 68   **PM** 91
Bava Metzia 30a   **FM** 61
Bava Metzia 38a   **MJ** 272
Bava Metzia 58b   **AMT** 60   **FM** 140
Bava Metzia 2:11   **RM** 231
Bava Metzia 107b   **MS** 168   **PM** 119

Bava Basra 8a   **MJ** 43
Bava Basra 8b   **RM** 241
Bava Basra 9a   **AMT** 170   **SM** 269
Bava Basra 10a   **MS** 243
Bava Basra 11a   **RM** 259   **SM** 269
Bava Basra 21a   **MJ** 205
Bava Basra 22a   **FM** 141
Bava Basra 25   **PM** 91
Bava Basra 25a   **PM** 225
Bava Basra 29a   **RM** 80
Bava Basra 29b   **AMT** 261
Bava Basra 74a   **FM** 156
Bava Basra 91a   **RM** 19
Bava Basra 103b, 104b,   **MJ** 220
Bava Basra 119b   **SPL** 211
Bava Basra 205b   **MJ** 220
Bava Basra 121b   **MJ** 225

Mishnah Sanhedrin 10:1
 MS 137, 138, 263

Sanhedrin 19b   **AMT** 100
Sanhedrin 20a   **RM** 226
Sanhedrin 22b   **PM** 31
Sanhedrin 27b   **RM** Intro p.13
Sanhedrin 32b   **FM** 262
Sanhedrin 37a   **AMT** 183
Sanhedrin 38b   **MS** 229   **EM** 241
Sanhedrin 40a   **SPL** 201
Sanhedrin 59b   **PM** 45
Sanhedrin 88b   **MJ** 266
Sanhedrin 89a   **AMT** 115
Sanhedrin 90a   **MS** 137, 138, 263
Sanhedrin 96a   **FM** 159
Sanhedrin 97b   **MS** 67 footnote
Sanhedrin 98b   **MS** 258
Sanhedrin 99a   **EM** 291
 RM 229 (See Rashi)
Sanhedrin 99b   **AMT** 260
Sanhedrin 100b   **EM** 131
Sanhedrin 104b   **EM** 300
Sanhedrin 107a   **SM** 140

Makkos 10b   **MJ** 134   **SPL** 224
Makkos 22b   **AMT** 161, 266   **FM** 180

Shevuos 39a   **AMT** 186   **RM** 13
Shevuos 45a   **RM** 166

Yerushalmi Shevuos 1:5
 MS 77 (footnote)

Avodah Zarah 3a   **PM** 215
Avodah Zarah 10b   **SM** 157   **SPL** 176
Avodah Zarah 17b   **FM** 150
Avodah Zarah 25a   **MJ** 264
Avodah Zarah 39b   **FM** 35
Avodah Zarah 54b   **RM** 159

Kallah Rabbasi Perek 2   **MS** 178

Mishnah Avos 2:15   **PM** 61

Avos 1:1   **RM** 113
Avos 1:4   **MS** 20, 24   **EM** 155

Index of Sources / 325

Avos 1:5   **FM** 126   **PM** 139
Avos 1:6   **AMT** 271
Avos 1:12   **EM** 19
Avos 1:15   **AMT** 55
Avos 2:1   **MS** 253   **RM** 155
Avos 2:4   **MS** 206   **MJ** 113
Avos 2:5   **FM** 229
Avos 2:10   **SM** 303
Avos 2:19   **SPL** 262
Avos 2:21   **MS** 56
Avos 3:1   **AMT** 121   **MJ** 222
Avos 3:10   **MJ** 220
Avos 3:11 Tiferes Yisrael 72   **FM** 140
Avos 3:21   **SPL** 201
Avos 4:1   **MS** 48   **AMT** 128   **RM** 271
Avos 4:2   **FM** 159   **RM** 177
Avos 4:11   **AMT** 249
Avos 4:12   **SM** 32
Avos 4:15   **RM** 80
Avos 4:20   **EM** 102
Avos 4:21   **FM** 265   **MS** 248, 261, 264
Avos 5:20   **MS** 178   **SPL** 168
Avos 5:22   **MJ** 243   **RM** 86
Avos 5:23   **PM** 21
Avos 5:26   **FM** 25
Avos 5:30 Bartenura   **SM** 123
Avos 6:2   **SPL** 263
Avos 6:6   **FM** 62   **EM** 67

Avos D'Rav Nosson 1:4   **RM** 113

Horayos 12a   **MJ** 268
Horayos 14a   **FM** 220

Zevachim 13b   **EM** 235, 237

Menachos 13b   **EM** 235, 237
Menachos 20b Tosafos   **EM** 299
Menachos 29b   **PM** 233
Menachos 35b   **SPL** 68
Menachos 43b   **MS** 165   **PM** 129
   SM 13
Menachos 44a   **SM** 189
Menachos 99a   **FM** 238

Chulin 92a   **MS** 67 footnote

Bechoros 58b   **AMT** 275

Arachin 16a   **EM** 285

Kereisos 6a   **SPL** 241
Kereisos 14a   **MJ** 244

Tamid 32a   **FM** 245   **MJ** 34

Mishnah Keilim 2:1   **EM** 155

Mishnah Negaim 2:3   **SPL** 279

Niddah 45b   **FM** 42   **PM** 241
Niddah 70b   **PM** 91   107

Rambam
Rambam Hilchos Chometz U'Matzah 8:2
   RM 260
Hilchos Megillah 2:17   **PM** 259
Rambam Hilchos Sefer Torah 7:1
   RM 131
Rambam Hilchos Shmittah V'yovel 5:13
   RM 159   **PM** 21
Rambam Hilchos Talmud Torah 1:8
   FM 94
Rambam Hilchos Teshuvah 2:1
   SM 40
Rambam Hilchos Teshuvah 2:9
   FM 185   **EM** 70   **MJ** 146
Rambam Hilchos Teshuvah 2:11
   MS 139
Rambam Hilchos Teshuvah 3:4
   MS 241
Rambam Hilchos Teshuvah 7:3
   PM 241
Rambam Hilchos Teshuvah 7:4
   EM 291
Rambam Huchos Lulav 8:15   **FM** 38
Rambam Hilchos Geirushin 2:20
   AMT 28
Rambam Hilchos Issurei Mizbei'ach 7:11
   MS 140

Rambam Hilchos Melachim 11:3 **FM** 241
Rambam Pirush Hamishnayos Maakos 3:16 **RM** 265

Shulchan Aruch
Orach Chaim 6:2 Darchei Moshe **MJ** 205, 209
Orach Chaim 8:2 **FM** 148
Orach Chaim 8:2 Mishnah Berurah 4 **FM** 150
Orach Chaim 28 Mishnah Berurah Note 9 **FM** 165
Orach Chaim 44:1 **MS** 160
Orach Chaim 46:3 **MS** 165
Orach Chaim 51:7 Mishnah Berurah note 19 **EM** 150
Orach Chaim 51:7 **SM** 316
Orach Chaim 51 B'eer Hativ note 7 **EM** 150
Orach Chaim 61:3 **SM** 158
Orach Chaim 90 **FM** 157
Orach Chaim 90:19 **SM** 175
Orach Chaim 92:2 **AMT** 124 **FM** 180
Orach Chaim 115 (Tur) **PM** 233
Orach Chaim 123 Mishnah Berurah Note 2 **FM** 159
Orach Chaim 124:7 **RM** 147
Orach Chaim 124:7 Mishnah Berurah note 26 **RM** 147
Orach Chaim 125:1 **FM** 222
Orach Chaim 128:6 **EM** 73
Orach Chaim 128:45 **EM** 73
Orach Chaim 128 Mishnah Berurah note 172 **EM** 73
Orach Chaim 135 Mishnah Berurah 28 **FM** 231
Orach Chaim 142:6 Mishnah Berurah **EM** 256
Orach Chaim 167:5 **RM** 259
Orach Chaim 218:6 **FM** 200
Orach Chaim 223 Mishnah Berurah Note 2 **MJ** 62

Orach Chaim 230:4 **SM** 290
Orach Chaim 230:5 **RM** 185
Orach Chaim 233:1 **FM** 127
Orach Chaim 248:3 Mishnah Berurah Note 20 **MJ** 136
Orach Chaim 257:8 and Mishnah Berurah note 49 **SM** 195
Orach Chaim 262:5 **RM** 172
Orach Chaim 271:4 **RM** 55
Orach Chaim 271 Mishnah Berurah Note 41 **FM** 169
Orach Chaim 272:9 **RM** 55
Orach Chaim 316:10 **RM** 207
Orach Chaim 405 **MJ** 140
Orach Chaim 425:2 Mishnah Berurah note 10 **SM** 248
Orach Chaim 426:2 **MJ** 154
Orach Chaim 428:6 Mishnah Berurah note 17 **EM** 79
Orach Chaim 428:8 **SM** 248
Orach Chaim 490:9 **MS** 265
Orach Chaim 494:3, Shaarei Teshuva note 7 **RM** 131
Orach Chaim 547:1 **EM** 289
Orach Chaim 554:1 **SM** 296
Orach Chaim 581:1 Mishnah Berurah 7 **AMT** 34
Orach Chaim 581:4 **RM** 198
Orach Chaim 581:4 Mishnah Berurah note 27 **RM** 198
Orach Chaim 583:1 **MJ** 268
Orach Chaim 602:4 **MJ** 154
Orach Chaim 606:1 Mishnah Berurah note 11 **PM** 197
Orach Chaim 626 **RM** 140
Orach Chaim 633:2 **RM** 140
Orach Chaim 638 Mishnah Berurah Note 24 **FM** 136
Orach Chaim 639:1 **EM** 155
Orach Chaim 649:5 **MJ** 160
Orach Chaim 651:5 **FM** 120
Orach Chaim 678:1 **AMT** 95
Orach Chaim 694:3 **MS** 162

Index of Sources / 327

Choshen Mishpat 259   **RM** 156
   PM (259:3) 225

Even HaEzer 61:1   **MJ** 167

Yoreh Deah 53:2   **FM** 68
Yoreh Deah 115:1   **FM** 35
Yoreh Deah 179   **MJ** 268
Yoreh Deah 240:2   **PM** 139
Yoreh Deah 242:16   **MJ** 116
Yoreh Deah 244:8   **RM** 268
Yoreh Deah 249:1   **MJ** 129
Yoreh Deah 249-251   **MS** 52
Yoreh Deah 263:1   **RM** 161
Yoreh Deah 268:2   **FM** 111   **SM** 197
Yoreh Deah, Tur 286; Darchei Moshe
   EM 19
Yoreh Deah 336   **EM** 266
Yoreh Deah 336 (Birkei Yosef)
   SM 290
Yoreh Deah 342   **MJ** 242
Yoreh Deah 351:2   **FM** 155
Yoreh Deah 362:2   **AMT** 131

Chayei Adam 155:4   **SM** 207

Tefillos

Aleinu prayer   **SM** 238
Al HaNissim   **SPL** 114
Al Tirah   **SPL** 23
Ashamnu prayer   **SM** 286
Ashrei   **PM** 107
Bareich Aleinu   **PM** 45, 107
Baruch She'amar   **PM** 31
Birchas HaMazon   **PM** 81, 107, 129, 139, 233, 259
Birchas Hashachar   **SM** 210
Birkas Hatorah prayer   **SM** 114, 297
Birkas Rosh Chodesh prayer   **SM** 108
Borei Nefashos prayer   **SM** 50
Friday night blessing   **SPL** 270
Kinnos Tishah B'Av   **SPL** 286
Kol Nidrei prayer   **PM** 119
Kriyas Shema   **PM** 61, 71, 107, 187
Lechah Dodi   **PM** 215
Maariv Friday night   **SPL** 230
Modeh Ani   **PM** 53
Modim   **SPL** 250
Mussaf Shabbos   **SPL** 121, 168
Mussaf Shabbos (Sefard)   **SPL** 61
Ne'ilah   **PM** 99   **SPL** 262
Ribon Kol Haolamim prayer   **SM** 90
Shacharis   **SPL** 272
Shalom Aleichem prayer   **SM** 90
Selichos Aseres Yemei Teshuvah
   SPL 81
Selichos prayers   **PM** 233
Shema Koleinu prayer   **PM** 61, 107
Shemoneh Esrei prayer
   PM 31, 45, 61, 99, 107, 119, 233, 259
   SM 288, 295, 312, 315
Shemoneh Esrei prayer of Mussaf of
   Yom Kippur   **PM** 205
Shemonah Esrei (Rabbi Avrohom
   Chaim Feuer) p. 134   **SPL** 78
Sheva Brochos prayer   **SM** 160
Shimusha Shel Torah 228   **SM** 300
Tachanun   **SPL** 248, 286
Tefillah Kodem Tefillah, Reb
   Elimelech   **SPL** 99, 248, 279
U'Nesaneh Tokef prayer   **SM** 14, 46
Vayivarech David prayer   **PM** 107
Yizkor   **PM** 251
Zemiros Friday night   **SPL** 230

Other Sources

Ahavas Chessed 2:4   **FM** 150
Alei Shur Vol. 2, Ch. 12, Vaad 5
   PM 21
ArtScroll Bris Milah 35, 39   **MS** 238
ArtScroll Bris Milah 77, 97   **RM** 239
ArtScroll Bris Milah 84   **MS** 260
Atarah Lamelech p. 120   **RM** 271
B'derech Eitz HaChaim p. 53
   MJ 72
Birchas Cheretz, Parashas Va'eira
   PM 61

Bnei Yissachar, Av, Maamar 4 **PM** 259
Bnei Yissaschar (Shevat Maamar 1) **SPL** 283
Chayei Adam 57:2 **SPL** 261
Chayei Adam 155:4 **SM** 207
Daas Torah, Bereishis-p.11 **SM** 170
Divrei Eliyahu (Bava Basra 11a) **SM** 269
Divrei Eliyahu p. 96 **SM** 176
Drashos HaRan 8 **SPL** 49
Eliyahu Rabbah 25 **MJ** 262 **PM** 233
Emes L'Yaakov, Bereishis 3:14 **PM** 21
Gesher HaChaim 14:20 **FM** 175
Guardian of Jerusalem p. 210-211 **RM** 143
Ha'amek Davar (Bamidbar 15:41) **SPL** 29
Iggeres HaRamban **MS** 206 **SM** 298 **SPL** 55
Igros Moshe (Orach Chaim) Vol. 4 :66 **SPL** 211
Igros Moshe Y.D. 2:122 Bris Milah (ArtScroll) p.45 **SM** 231
Igros Moshe 2:122 **SPL** 230
Igros Moshe YD Volume 2:122, OC Volume 4:66 **SM** 267
Igros U'Michtavim, Letter 94 (Rabbi Y. Hutner) **PM** 45
Inspiration and Insight Volume 2 p. 91 **RM** 13
Kad Hakemach, Emunah **EM** 162
Kovetz He'Aros 6:6 **SM** 292
Kovetz Maamarim V'Agados Volume 1, 252 **SM** 293
Kuntros Ish Itair (note 43) **SPL** 201
Leket Kemach Hachodosh Vol. III Intro **EM** 95
Leket Kemach HaChadash, Hakdamah **PM** 53
Lev Eliyahu, Vol. 3, pp. 337-339, 276) **PM** 139
Maaseh Avos Siman L'Bonim Volume 3, p. 105 **RM** 172

Maaseh Rav no. 248 **EM** 162
Maayan Bais Hashoevah Shemos 5:22 **RM** 244
Maayan Bais Hashoevah Haftarah Naso p. 310 **RM** 235
Meir Einei Yisrael Volume 4 p. 503 **RM** 94
Meishiv Davar No. 48 **FM** 231
Meshech Chochmah (Bereishis 2:16) **PM** 81
Mesillas Yesharim Chapter 1 **FM** 216
Mesillas Yesharim Chapter 13 **PM** 81
Mesillas Yesharim Chapter 19 **SPL** 105
Michtav Me'Eliyahu p.187 **MJ** 269
Michtav Me'Eliyahu Volume 1, p. 140 **RM** 92
Michtav Me'Eliyahu Volume 4, p. 246 **RM** 110
Mishnas Rav Aharon Volume 1 p. 84, 92 **RM** 274
Mishnas Rav Aharon Volume 1, p. 88 **PM** 129
Mishnas Rav Aharon Vol. 3, p.15 **FM** 62
Mishnas Rav Aharon Vol. 3, p. 54 **MJ** 205 **PM** 225
Mishnas Rav Aharon Vol 3, p. 176 **EM** 148
Moreshes Avos, Devarim p. 140 **MJ** 72
Nefesh HaChaim Intro **EM** 49 **PM** 119 **SPL** 111
Ner Mitzvah p. 12 n. 60 **PM** 187
Nesivas Sholom Vol. 2, p. 125 **MJ** 51
Nesivos Olam (Nesiv Ha'Avodah Chapter 7) **SM** 33
Ohr Tzaddikim 29 **SPL** 201
Ohr Yechezkel, p. 327 **PM** 81
Ohr Yechezkel Vol. 3 p. 288 **FM** 171
Ohr Yechezkel Vol. 4, p. 101 **PM** 119
Olelos Ephraim Tehillim 24:3 **EM** 127
Orach Chaim 1:1 **SPL** 211

Index of Sources / 329

Orach Chaim 39:10 **SPL** 241
Orach Chaim 51:7 and Mishnah Berurah Note 14 **SPL** 55
Orach Chaim 61:3 (Mishnah Berurah note 6) **SPL** 78
Orach Chaim 132 (Biur Halachah) **SPL** 147
Orach Chaim 132 (Tur) **SPL** 241
Orach Chaim (Ba'er Heiteiv) 581:17 **SPL** 49
Orchos Rabbeinu Vol. 1: 249-250
Orchos Tzaddikim, Shaar 15 Hazrizus **PM** 21
Otzros Hatorah, Elul Chapter 8:251 **SM** 306
Pachad Yitzchok, Purim Chapter 18 **SM** 32
Pesikta Rabbasi 9:2 **MJ** 259
Pesikta Rabbasi 41 **SPL** 82
Pirkei D'Rav Eliezer 29 **AMT** 139
Rabbenu Bechaya, Shulchan Shel Arbah **PM** 81
Rabbi Schwab on Prayer 179,180 **SM** 316
Sefer HaBris p. 303 **SPL** 226
Sefer HaIkarim 4:33 **MJ** 222
Sefer Chassidim 210 **RM** 265
Sefer Chassidim 254 **RM** 94
Sefer Chassidim 323 **PM** 99
Sefer Chassidim 324 **PM** 99
Sefer Chassidim 454 **PM** 99
Sefer HaGilgulim Chapter 59 **SPL** 211
Selichos Kodem Rosh Hashanah (Motza'ei Shabbos) **MS** 77
Shaarei Teshuvah 2:3 **SPL** 155
Shaarei Teshuvah Shaar 3:71 **RM** 100
She'elos Uteshuvos Maharatz Chayes #26 **RM** 198

Shemiras Halashon Shaar Hazechiran Ch. 10 **EM** 288
Sefer HaChinuch Mitzvah 33 **PM** 139, 177
Sefer HaChinuch Mitzvah 430 **PM** 107 **SM** 313
Shehasimchah B'me'ono p. 76 **SM** 140
Sichos Levi p. 34 **MJ** 115
Sichos Mussar Maamer #7 (5731) **RM** 226
Sichos Mussar Maamer #8 (5731) **RM** 92
Shimusho Shel Torah p. 201 **SPL** 285
Taamei HaMinhagim 90 **SPL** 248
Tammei Haminhagim p. 397 (Kuntros HaAcharon note 929) **SPL** 211
Taamei HaMinhagim No. 1034 **FM** 175
Table for Two **PM** 147
Tanna D'vei Eliyahu 10:8 **EM** 235
Tanya Chapter 18 **RM** 51
Tehillim Treasury p. 149 **RM** 265
Terumas Hadeshen 2:57 **EM** 262
Toras Hamilachos Intro **EM** 119
Tuvcha Yabiu Volume 1, p. 311 **RM** 172
Tuvcha Yabiu Volume 2, p. 247 **RM** 145
Tzidkas HaTaddik **PM** 21, 187
Wisdom in the Hebrew Alphabet **PM** 147
Yoreh Deah 335:3 **SPL** 46
Yoreh Deah 335:4 **SPL** 46
Zeriyah U'Binyan B'Chinuch p. 35 **RM** 237
Zohar (Hashmatos 1:61) **SPL** 192

Glossary

aliyah – call to the Torah at the public reading
Amoraim – rabbis of the Talmud
Aron Kodesh – Holy Ark
Aseres HaDibros – Ten Commandments
avinu – our father

baal korei – the reader of the Torah
baal tefillah – leader of the prayer service
baal teshuvah – one who returns to Jewish life, observance and study
bachur – unmarried young man
baruch Hashem – thank G-d
Beis HaMikdash – the Holy Temple
beis medrash – study hall
berachah – blessing
blatt – folio pages
bris – circumcision

challos – braided Sabbath loaves
chassan – bridegroom
chassid – a pious individual; follower of a chassidic Rebbe
chavrusa – study partner
chazzan – leader of the prayer service
chessed – benevolence; kindness
chessed shel emes – kindness without expectation of reward
Chevrah Kaddisha – Burial Society
chiddush – innovative Torah thought
chillul Hashem – desecration of G-d's Name
chillul Shabbos – desecration of the Sabbath
chinuch – education

Chumash – the Five Books of Moses

Daf Yomi – worldwide Talmud study project in which all Jews study the same folio – page of the Talmud every day
daven – to pray
dayan – rabbinical judge
divrei Torah – Torah thoughts

emunah – faith; belief in G-d
Eretz Yisrael – the Land of Israel

gadol hador – leading Torah sage of a generation
Gemara – Talmud
gabbai – synagogue sexton; attendant of a Chassidic Rebbe; person responsible for the proper functioning of a synagogue or other communal body

hakaras hatov – gratitude
halachah – Jewish law
hamelech – the king
hanavi – the prophet
Hashgachah Pratis – Divine Providence
hashkafah – Jewish perspective
hatzlachah – success
hesped – eulogy

Kabbalas Shabbos – the Friday evening service
Kaddish – prayer sanctifying G-d's Name
kallah – bride
kashrus – laws of keeping kosher

kesubah – the marriage contract
Kiddush – sanctification of the Sabbath and festivals, usually recited over wine
kiddush Hashem – sanctification of G-d's Name
Klal Yisrael – the entire Jewish community
Kol Nidrei – prayer recited at the beginning of Yom Kippur
kollel – post-graduate yeshivah, usually for married students
korban – offering

l'chaim – traditional toast, "To life!"
levayah – funeral

Maariv – the evening prayer service
maggid shiur – Talmudic lecturer
mara d'asra – the leader of the community
mashgiach – spiritual guide
Mashiach – the Messiah
masmid – diligent student
mechitzah – divider between men's and women's sections in a synagogue
menachem avel – consoling the mourner
mesader kiddushin – performer of the marriage ceremony
mesechta – tractate
mezuzah – small parchment scroll affixed to doorpost
Midrash – the Sages' homiletical teachings on the Torah
milah – circumcision
Minchah – the afternoon prayer service
minyan – a quorum of ten men

Mishkan – the Tabernacle
mitzvah – Torah commandment; good deed
mohel – one who performs circumcision
Motza'ei Shabbos – the evening after the Sabbath
Mussaf – an additional prayer service recited on the Sabbath and holidays
mussar – ethical teachings

neshamah – soul
niftar – a person who has passed away

pasuk – a verse of Scripture
payos – sidelocks
posek – halachic authority
psak – religious ruling

rabbeinu – our teacher
rachmanus – mercy
rebbi – teacher
refuah sheleimah – complete recovery
Ribono Shel Olam – Master of the world; G-d
rosh yeshivah – head of a yeshivah

safrus – the writing of sacred parchments such as Torah scrolls
sandak – the person holding the infant during the *bris*
Sanhedrin – the supreme ruling body in the times of the Talmud
Seder – festive meal on the first two nights of Passover
sedrah – Torah portion of the week

sefarim – holy books
Sefer Torah – the Torah scroll
Selichos – prayers of supplication
seudah – (Sabbath or festive) meal
Shabbaton – a weekend seminar
Shacharis – the morning prayer service
shaliach – messenger
shaliach tzibbur – leader of the prayer service
shalom bayis – harmony in the home
shammas – sexton
Shas – the Six Orders of the Talmud
she'eilah – halachic question
Shechinah – Divine Presence
shechitah – ritual slaughter
Shemoneh Esrei – the prayer containing eighteen blessings which is recited three times a day
Sheva Berachos – a festive meal tendered during the first week of marriage, at which seven blessings are recited in honor of the newlyweds
shidduch – marriage match
shiur – lecture on Torah topics
shivah – the seven-day period of mourning
shmuessen – lecture on ethical topics
shochet – ritual slaughterer
Shomer Shabbos – one who observes the Sabbath
shtiebel – small synagogue
shul – synagogue
siddur – prayer book
simchah – joy; a joyous occasion

siyum – finishing a portion of learning and the celebration thereof
sofer – one who writes sacred parchments such as Torah scrolls
succah — temporary dwelling used during the festival of Succos

tallis – prayer shawl
talmid chacham – Torah scholar
Tanach – the Written Torah, the Bible
tatteh — father
tefachim — handbreadths
tefilah — (pl. tefillos) - prayer
tefillin — phylacteries
teshuvah — repentance; rediscovery of Torah Judaism; an answer to a halachic query, responsum
Tehillim — Psalms
Tishah B'Av – the ninth day of the month of Av, a day of mourning
treif – not kosher
tzaddik – a pious individual
tzedakah – charity
tzitzis – four-cornered garment with fringes, worn by Jewish men and boys

Yamim Noraim – the High Holy Days
yamim tovim – festival days
yarmulke – skullcap
yerios – sheets of parchment
yetzer hara – evil inclination
Yid – a Jew
yiras Shamayim – fear of Heaven

z"l – acronym for "zichrono livrachah", appended to the name of a deceased righteous person

z'man – time
zaide – grandfather
zechus – benefit

This volume is part of
THE ARTSCROLL SERIES®
an ongoing project of
translations, commentaries and expositions on
Scripture, Mishnah, Talmud, Midrash, Halachah,
liturgy, history, the classic Rabbinic writings,
biographies and thought.

For a brochure of current publications
visit your local Hebrew bookseller
or contact the publisher:

Mesorah Publications, ltd

4401 Second Avenue
Brooklyn, New York 11232
(718) 921-9000
www.artscroll.com